# Complete Russian

## Daphne West

For UK order enquiries: please contact
Bookpoint Ltd, 130 Milton Park, Abingdon, Oxon OX14 4SB.
*Telephone:* +44 (0) 1235 827720. *Fax:* +44 (0) 1235 400454.
Lines are open 09.00–17.00, Monday to Saturday, with a 24-hour message
answering service. Details about our titles and how to order are available at
www.teachyourself.com

For USA order enquiries: please contact
McGraw-Hill Customer Services,
PO Box 545, Blacklick, OH 43004-0545, USA.
*Telephone:* 1-800-722-4726. *Fax:* 1-614-755-5645.

For Canada order enquiries: please contact
McGraw-Hill Ryerson Ltd, 300 Water St, Whitby,
Ontario L1N 9B6, Canada.
*Telephone:* 905 430 5000. *Fax:* 905 430 5020.

Long renowned as the authoritative source for self-guided learning – with more
than 50 million copies sold worldwide – the *Teach Yourself* series includes over
500 titles in the fields of languages, crafts, hobbies, business, computing and
education.

*British Library Cataloguing in Publication Data:* a catalogue record for this title is
available from the British Library.

*Library of Congress Catalog Card Number:* on file.

First published in UK 1991 as Teach Yourself Russian by Hodder Education,
part of Hachette UK, 338 Euston Road, London NW1 3BH.

First published in US 1992 by The McGraw-Hill Companies, Inc.

This edition published 2010.

The *Teach Yourself* name is a registered trade mark of Hodder Headline.

Typeset by MPS Limited, A Macmillan company

Printed in Great Britain for Hodder Education, an Hachette UK Company, 338
Euston Road, London NW1 3BH, by CPI Cox & Wyman, Reading, Berkshire
RG1 8EX.

The publisher has used its best endeavours to ensure that the URLs for external
websites referred to in this book are correct and active at the time of going to
press. However, the publisher and the author have no responsibility for the websites and can make no guarantee that a site will remain live or that the content will
remain relevant, decent or appropriate.

Hachette UK's policy is to use papers that are natural, renewable and recyclable
products and made from wood grown in sustainable forests. The logging and
manufacturing processes are expected to conform to the environmental regulations
of the country of origin.

Impression number 10 9 8 7 6 5 4 3 2 1

Year 2014 2013 2012 2011 2010

# Contents

Acknowledgements                                    vi
Meet the author                                     vii
Only got a minute?                                  viii
Only got five minutes?                              x
Only got ten minutes?                               xii
Introduction                                        xvii
How to use this course                              xviii
Using the course with the recording                 xix
The alphabet                                        xix
Pronunciation                                       xx

1   **Ваш паспорт, пожалуйста!** *Your passport, please!*   1
    • Responding to requests for personal information
      and identification
    • Using some forms of courtesy
2   **Меня зовут Ира** *I'm called Ira*              17
    • Giving further information about yourself
    • Requesting such information from others
3   **Где здесь телефон?** *Where's the telephone?*  33
    • Asking for and giving directions
    • Using some more forms of courtesy
4   **Здесь можно фотографировать?** *May one take
    photographs here?*                              51
    • Asking/stating whether something is permitted or not
    • Asking/stating whether something is possible,
      impossible or necessary
5   **Сколько стоит?** *How much is it?*             68
    • Asking for and giving simple information about
      cost and availability
    • Using further ways of describing where things are
6   **Я предпочитаю плавать** *I prefer to swim*     85
    • Talking about likes and dislikes
    • Asking people about their preferences

**7**  **На почте** *At the post office*  100
- Requesting information about cost, availability and necessity
- Giving information about cost, availability and necessity

**8**  **Это место свободно?** *Is this place free?*  117
- Obtaining information about availability, variety and cost
- Placing an order
- Indicating that a mistake has been made
- Apologizing for a mistake

**9**  **Во сколько отходит поезд?** *When does the train leave?*  137
- Asking and telling the time
- Asking and answering questions about particular times
- Requesting and giving information about travel

**10**  **По средам я обычно** … *On Wednesdays I usually …*  156
- Talking about daily and weekly routine
- Asking for and giving information about age
- Talking about days of the week
- Expressing approximation with regard to time

**11**  **Это зависит от погоды** *It depends on the weather*  173
- Talking about future actions and intentions
- Giving and seeking information about the weather

**12**  **Ира дома?** *Is Ira at home?*  192
- Holding a conversation on the telephone (how to identify yourself, ask for the person you want to speak to and how to deal with wrong numbers)
- Talking about past events and actions

**13**  **Мне нужно к врачу?** *Must I go to the doctor's?*  208
- Saying how you feel
- Asking others how they feel
- Seeking and giving advice
- Talking about necessity

**14**  **Свитер тебе очень идёт** *The sweater really suits you*  226
- Talking about clothes and appearance
- Asking for advice about size and colour
- Expressing simple comparisons and negatives

iv

**15** **С днём рождения!** *Happy birthday!*                     246
- Talking about dates
- Saying when and where you were born and stating your age
- Asking other people about their age, place and date of birth
- Greeting people on special occasions

**16** **Было бы лучше ...** *It would be better ...*               265
- Expressing your opinion about arrangements and events
- Indicating preference in arrangements
- Expressing hopes and intentions about arrangements
- Making hypothetical statements
- Expressing statements contrary to fact

**17** **Давай заглянем в бюро путешествий** *Let's pop into the travel agent's*               286
- Talking about holidays and holiday accommodation
- Talking about what is best and most comfortable
- Giving more information in the negative

**18** **Что случилось?** *What happened?*                     303
- Asking what has happened
- Reporting on what has happened and what has been said
- Asking what is wrong
- Expressing concern and purpose

**19** **Спасибо за письмо** *Thank you for the letter*            321
- Presenting formal and informal letters in Russian
- Reporting what people have asked
- Further expressing feelings and opinions

**20** **Приезжайте к нам опять!** *Come and see us again!*       342
- Using further expressions involving possession and self
- Using numerals in a more detailed way
- Using other ways of expressing appreciation and thanks

*Appendix 1: Grammar*                                           359
*Appendix 2: Pronunciation*                                     375
*Key to the exercises*                                          380
*Russian–English vocabulary*                                    399
*English–Russian vocabulary*                                    412
*Index to grammar points*                                       420

# Acknowledgements

The author and publishers would like to thank Irina Vorobyova, Elena Selyanina, Tanya Shlyakhtenko-Deck, Frank Beardow, Tatyana Izmailova and Michael Ransome for their invaluable advice, criticism and suggestions. They would also like to thank VAAP for permission to reproduce material from: *Literaturnaia gazeta, Pravda, Zdorov'e, Sovetskii soyuz, Sputnik.*

# Meet the author

My passion for Russian began when it was offered at my school as an alternative to O-level Physics. At the University of Durham I gained a first-class honours degree in Russian with distinction in spoken Russian, and a PhD on the poet Mandelstam.
I have taught in schools and further education colleges; I was Head of Modern Languages at Sherborne School for Girls and Sevenoaks School, and Headmistress of the Maynard School in Exeter.
I have been Chief Examiner for GCSE and A-level Russian and my publications include three *Teach Yourself* titles, as well as A-level textbooks (*Poshli dal'she, Tranzit, Kompas*). In 1993 I was awarded the Pushkin Medal by the Pushkin Institute, Moscow, for contributions to the teaching of Russian. In the early 1990s I established an exchange which has flourished for nearly twenty years with School No. 7 in Perm (a city in the Urals closed to foreigners in Soviet times). Now I am a freelance teacher and writer; my former Russian students include teachers of Russian in schools and universities, as well those who have made their careers in Russia working for businesses and charitable organizations. In January 2010 I became the editor of *Rusistika*, the Russian journal of the Association of Language Learning.

*Daphne West*

# Only got a minute?

**Russian is one of the most commonly spoken languages in the world: approximately 270 million speak it worldwide, with just over 140 million living in the Russian Federation.**

Russian is a Slavonic language which belongs to the same Indo-European family as English. Its vocabulary has been influenced by a range of languages, including Old Church Slavonic, English, French, German, Latin and Greek. Since the collapse of the Soviet Union, the influence of Western European languages has increased, and many Russian words sound reassuringly familiar:

| English word | Russian equivalent sounds like |
|---|---|
| marketing | *markyeteeng* |
| office | *ofeess* |
| printer | *preentyer* |

The first part of this course will help you get to grips with the Russian (Cyrillic) alphabet, so that you will be able to feel confident about what Russian words look and sound like. Some letters look familiar: к, о and т, for example (кот = *cat*). Others look the same, but sound different: н is the Russian character for *n* and с sounds like *s* (нос = *nose*). Some Russian letters look much less familiar: ж (*zh*) and я (*ya*), for example. Although the alphabet is different, pronunciation is quite straightforward: just pronounce the sound of each letter, and you get the sound of the whole word!

Russian grammar has quite a few rules – about the way the endings of words change according to their meaning, for example. Luckily, these rules are reassuringly reliable and there are relatively few irregularities in Russian.

There is much more to the study of language than the study of vocabulary and grammar, however, and this course aims to equip you with the skills needed to communicate in practical and social situations, and to give you some background information about Russian society and culture.

# 5 Only got five minutes?

Whether your interest in learning Russian has been sparked by the prospects of travel, business or culture, you will find that knowledge of the language will enhance your experience. Although in Russia's major cities English is spoken by many involved with tourism, business and education, it is certainly not spoken everywhere. Russians understand that their language is not known by many non-Russians, and the effort made by visitors to communicate in Russian is usually met with much appreciation.

Russian is one of the six most widely spoken languages in the world, with approximately 270 million speakers; it is one of the official languages of the United Nations and UNESCO. Just over 25% of the world's scientific literature is in Russian and it is becoming increasingly important in the sphere of business. Russia is the largest country in the world, spreading over two continents, eleven time zones and embracing a wide variety of climatic and geographic conditions, as well as a vast wealth of natural resources. Although the Russian Federation covers an area of over 10 million square kilometres, there is a surprising degree of uniformity in the Russian spoken in St Petersburg in the far west and Vladivostok on the eastern Pacific coast. Russian continues to be the main language in much of eastern Europe and northern Asia; it is still widely spoken in countries which used to be part of the Soviet Union and which still have large Russian communities (Estonia, Kazakhstan and Ukraine, for example).

The first striking difference between English and Russian is that Russian uses the Cyrillic alphabet (named after the ninth-century monk, St Cyril, its reputed author). The first aim of this course is to introduce you to the alphabet, so that you can gain confidence in what Russian looks like and sounds like. Knowledge of the alphabet is the essential first building block in your study of

Russian (and gives you immediate independence when in Russia – you can read the street signs!).

Pronunciation in Russian is straightforward: if you pronounce each letter individually, you will produce the whole word, i.e. the spelling represents the sound, which is not always the case in English (think of *draft* and *draught*, for example). 'Stress' is an important feature in Russian pronunciation – however many syllables there are in a word, only one of them can be emphasized. This course aims to help you develop authentic pronunciation both with the recorded material, and also by showing where the stress falls in each word (indicated by an acute accent ´ over the vowel to be emphasized).

Is Russian grammar complicated? As in many languages, there are genders (masculine, feminine and neuter), but there are no articles (*the*, *a*). Russian has a case system, according to which the endings of words change, depending on their meaning; thanks to the case system, Russian word order is very flexible, as the meaning is made clear by the endings of words. This course aims to help you feel confident about recognizing the patterns involved in the case system, through listening as well as reading. The good news is that with verbs, as well as nouns and adjectives, there are reassuringly few irregularities in Russian.

As well as equipping you with language skills, this course aims to give you some insights into Russian society and culture. Russia's history is studded with dramatic, tumultuous characters and events since the founding of Kievan Rus' in the tenth century (the time of the first examples of written Russian). Russian culture is vast and varied, and includes some of the world's greatest writers (e.g. Chekhov, Dostoevsky, Gogol, Mandelshtam, Pushkin, Tolstoy, Turgenev) and composers (e.g. Prokofiev, Shostakovich, Stravinsky, Tchaikovsky) as well as some of the finest exponents of ballet, chess, film, opera, painting, film, sport – all linked by what Turgenev called the 'great, powerful, true and free Russian language!'

# 10 Only got ten minutes?

According to the great 18th-century Russian scientist and writer Mikhail Lomonosov, the Russian language has 'the greatness of Spanish, the liveliness of French, the force of German, the tenderness of Italian, and, in addition, the richness and strong terse descriptiveness of Greek and Latin.' Quite a recommendation!

The study of the Russian language can indeed be an enriching experience in itself, and a knowledge of the language opens doors to the infinite variety of Russian culture and society.

One of the official languages of the United Nations and UNESCO, Russian is spoken by approximately 270 million people world wide, with about 140 million living in the Russian Federation; it is the most widespread of the Slavic languages and continues to be the main language in much of eastern Europe and northern Asia. Russian is still widely spoken in countries which used to be part of the Soviet Union and which still have large Russian communities (Estonia, Kazakhstan and Ukraine, for example); more than 25% of the world's scientific literature is in Russian.

The Russian Federation straddles Europe and Asia, but Russian, like English, belongs to the Indo-European family of languages and it developed from Eastern Slavic, a language spoken by Slavs who migrated eastwards after the seventh century BC.

Although the roots of the Russian language lie in Old East Slavonic and Old Church Slavonic, it has also been influenced by Greek and Latin, Dutch, English, French and German. Russian's closest relatives, in the spoken language at least, are Belorussian and Ukrainian.

How important is it to learn Russian for the purposes of business, travel and tourism? And what about literature, music, theatre and sport? Whilst it is true that in most major Russian cities there are excellent speakers of English in all these spheres, it is certainly not the case that English is spoken widely everywhere. Russians understand that their language is often viewed as 'difficult', so that the effort by visitors to speak Russian is greatly appreciated; an ability to understand and communicate, even at a basic level, can enhance a tourist's enjoyment and understanding of their visit, and enable more effective relations in the business context, for example.

So how difficult a language is Russian? For the English speaker, it is less straightforward initially (particularly from the point of view of vocabulary) than Western European languages such as French, German, Italian and Spanish. However, Russian shares a significant amount of vocabulary and grammatical structures with modern Western European languages, as well as with Greek and Latin, so that students encounter lots of reassuringly familiar items as their study progresses.

The first important task when beginning the study of Russian is to learn the Cyrillic alphabet, named after the ninth-century monk, St Cyril, its reputed author. This alphabet was influenced primarily by Greek, with extra letters created to represent Slavic sounds. The first examples of written Russian date from the tenth century, after which the alphabet developed various cursive forms, until the reign of Peter the Great in the eighteenth century, when the alphabet was regularized. After the Revolution in 1917, the alphabet was further 'tidied up' and unnecessary characters deleted, leaving the alphabet as we have it today. Learning the Cyrillic alphabet is not a daunting task, because it has so much in common with the Latin alphabet (as used in English), whilst some letters may be familiar already (via Greek and mathematics), and those letters created to represent Slavic sounds are so intriguing that it is difficult *not* to remember them!

- So, for example, the following letters look and sound like their English counterparts: the letters **к, т** and **о** give **кто** (the Russian word for *who*). The Cyrillic letters **т, а** and **м** give **там** (the Russian word for *there*). Some letters look familiar but sound different: e.g. **н** sounds like the English letter *n* and **с** sounds like the English letter *s* – so the Russian for *nose* is **нос.**

- Students of Greek or Mathematics will recognize the Cyrillic **п** as *Pi* (π) and **ф** as *Phi* (φ). So, **пакт** is a *pact* and **факс** is a *fax*.

- Amongst the intriguingly different characters is the beautiful letter **ж** (pronounced *zh*), as in the word **нож** (meaning *knife*), and the letter **ц** gives the *ts* sound which starts the Russian word for *tsar* (**царь**).

Pronunciation in Russian is achieved simply by pronouncing each letter individually – i.e. words sound as they are spelt; this makes Russian pronunciation a good deal easier than English, where very often a word is not pronounced as it is written (e.g. *cough*) or may mean different things when pronounced differently ('Have you *read* this book? It's a good *read*.')

A characteristic feature of the 'sound' of Russian is due to its system of 'hard' and 'soft' vowels. So, for example. Russian has both the 'hard' sounding vowel A (which sounds like the English *a* in *far*) and **Я** which is pronounced like the letters *ya* in *yak*. 'Soft' vowels 'soften' (or 'palatalize') the consonants which precede them. This may sound complicated, but it is not unlike English: try saying these two words and listen to the difference caused by the hard *oo* sound and the soft *u*:

Hard:    moon                          Soft:    music

And in Russian:

Hard:    **на** (which means *on/onto*)    Soft:    **няня** (which means *nanny*).

Another very important feature of Russian pronunciation is stress: however many syllables there are in a Russian word, only one of them can be emphasized. To achieve authentic pronunciation it is very important to get the stress right – just think how strange it would sound in English if you emphasized the second syllable of the word *purchase* instead of the first. This course aims to help you develop authentic pronunciation both with the recorded material, and also by showing where the stress falls in each word (indicated by an acute accent ´ over the vowel to be emphasized). So, for example, the word **НЯ́НЯ** given above is stressed on the first syllable.

As in many languages, there are genders of nouns (masculine, feminine and neuter), but there are no articles (*the*, *a*). Russian has a case system, according to which the endings of words change, depending on their meaning. Thanks to the case system, Russian word order is very flexible, as the meaning is made clear by the endings of words. There are six cases: nominative, accusative, genitive, dative, instrumental and prepositional, and the cases apply to nouns, adjectives and pronouns. This course aims to help you feel confident about recognizing the patterns involved in the case system, through listening as well as reading. The good news is that compared with some other languages, there are reassuringly few irregularities in Russian. This applies to verbs as well as to nouns. There is just one form of the present tense verb in Russian, which gives the equivalent of 'I read, I am reading, I do read.' Perhaps the most interesting feature about Russian verbs is the concept of 'imperfective and perfective aspects': so, for example, in the past tense, the first decision to make is whether the action being described was habitual/general/unspecific or specific/completed. In the former case, the past tense is made from the 'imperfective infinitive' and in the latter, from the 'perfective infinitive'. This is very different from English, which has lots of different ways of expressing the past tense ('I was reading', 'I used to read', 'I read', 'I have read', 'I had read', 'I had been reading'). Once the decision about aspect has been made, the formation of the past tense is easy and involves only four possible endings for non-reflexive verbs, and four for reflexives, depending on whether the subject of the verb is masculine singular, feminine singular, neuter singular or plural.

Since the collapse of the Soviet Union in 1991, Russian vocabulary has been increasingly influenced by Western European culture. The influence of English words is particularly strong in the spheres of business, the media and entertainment, sport, the internet and computer technology. For example, the words for goal keeper (**голки́пер** – pronounced *golkeepyer*) and half time (**хавта́йм** – pronounced *khaftayim*) are clearly straight from English. Russia is the largest country in the world, spreading over two continents, eleven time zones and embracing a wide variety of climatic and geographic conditions, as well as a vast wealth of natural resources. Although the Russian Federation covers an area of over 10 million square kilometres, there is a surprising degree of uniformity in the Russian spoken in St Petersburg in the far west and Vladivostok on the eastern Pacific coast.

As well as equipping you with language skills, this course aims to give you some insights into Russian society and culture, with some glimpses at the history, geography, literature, painting and music of Russia. Russia is not only the largest country in the world (with the longest continuous railway on earth – the Trans-Siberian), but it has an astonishingly rich history and culture. Its history has been studded with dramatic, tumultuous characters and events ever since the founding of Kievan Rus' in the tenth century, with some characters being particularly well known: Ivan the Terrible, Peter the Great, Catherine the Great, Rasputin, Lenin, Trotsky, Stalin – to name but a few. Its literature is vast and varied, and includes some of the world's greatest writers (e.g. Chekhov, Dostoevsky, Gogol, Mandelshtam, Pushkin, Tolstoy, Turgenev) and composers (e.g. Borodin, Glinka, Prokofiev, Rimsky-Korsakov, Shostakovich, Stravinsky, Tchaikovsky) as well as some of the finest exponents of ballet (Pavlova, Nureyev, Nijinsky, Diaghilev), chess (Karpov, Kasparov), film (Eisenstein, Sokurov, Tarkovsky), painting (Goncharova, Larionov, Levitan, Rublyov, Repin), mathematics and science (Bugaev, Kovalevskaya, Mendeleyev, Pavlov, Sakharov, Zhukovsky), sport (from figure skating to football, ice hockey to gymnastics) and theatre (Stanislavsky, Meyerhold). No wonder the nineteenth-century poet Tyutchev said that Russia could not be 'measured with a standard yardstick'!

# Introduction

A holiday, a business trip, an interest in world affairs or in the riches of Russian culture and history – there are many reasons for learning Russian, a language spoken by approximately 270 million people worldwide, of whom over 140 million live in the Russian Federation – a country which covers more than an eighth of the world's surface and has eleven time zones.

The aim of this course is to equip the complete beginner with the skills needed to communicate in practical, everyday situations and to give some background information about Russia and the nature of Russian society. The units of the course are designed to teach specific uses of language; these are related to situations that visitors to Russia may encounter. For example, you will learn how to give and seek information about people and places, how to make requests, complaints, apologies, arrangements, how to express opinions and explain what has happened and what will happen. You will meet topics such as shopping, health, accommodation and entertainment, and learn how to cope with them in related settings – in a shop, with the doctor, in a hotel, at the theatre. A clear indication is given, at the beginning of each unit, of the language uses covered and of the setting of the dialogue which forms the basis of the unit.

Many dramatic changes have taken place in Russian society since the collapse of the Soviet Union in 1991. Change is still very much the order of the day, so that, for example, the names of streets and the prices used in this book may not always tally with the current situation. Nevertheless, the language you are learning through this course is the language used in Russia today.

## How to use this course

First, work carefully through the sections on the alphabet and
pronunciation before you attempt Unit 1. If you feel you need
more practice in mastering the Cyrillic alphabet, there are lots of
exercises which would help you in *Read and Write Russian Script*.
For more practice on specific grammatical points, you will find a lot
of material in *Essential Russian Grammar*. Each unit of *Complete
Russian* follows the same pattern, starting with a dialogue; study this
carefully, noting all the new language forms and vocabulary. The
vocabulary list at the end of the dialogue contains key words and
expressions which are necessary to understand it. Other words are
given in the Russian–English vocabulary at the end of the book. Any
important cultural points are explained in the section which follows.
Next, the section *How do you say it?* points out the purpose of some
of the sentences used in the dialogue, and the main grammatical
structures are explained and illustrated in sentences in the *Grammar*
section.

Once you have grasped the meaning of the dialogue, read it through
again until you are satisfied that it is clear. Then turn to the questions
and test your understanding of the dialogue (you can check your
answers in the Key to the exercises, which begins after Appendix 2).

The exercises are designed to help you practise the written and spoken
language and they will involve a range of activities: reading, asking,
answering, looking (at pictures, maps, charts, forms) and writing. The
answers to all the exercises can be found in the Key to the exercises.

The penultimate section is divided into three parts: conversation,
reading and key phrases. In each unit, the conversation is based
on the topic and language points of the dialogue and it is followed
by a set of questions. Study the conversation carefully until you
understand it clearly, then answer the questions (checking your
answers in the Key to the exercises). The texts in the reading section
give information about the geography, history, culture and society
of Russia. You will meet new vocabulary here – you will not need to
understand every word or every grammatical form in order to answer

the questions and the important vocabulary will be given for you at the end of the text; try to work out what you think the new words mean before you look at the vocabulary at the end of the text (or at the end of the book) and use the questions which precede the text to help you follow the passage more easily and concentrate on the main points. The reading section is designed to improve your ability to understand written Russian and the questions (and your answers) will always be in English. You will probably find that you need to spend rather more time on the later units, which contain more material than the earlier ones. The key phrases provide useful revision of essential material in the unit. In the course of each unit you will find *Insight* boxes with tips to help you understand and remember essential or tricky points, and the final part of each unit will give you opportunities to test yourself on your overall understanding of the unit, with tips and questions to help you.

## Using the course with the recording

All items with the sign ◀ are recorded. As well as the alphabet and words in the Introduction, the dialogue, some exercises, the conversation and key phrases for each unit are recorded. You will find it very helpful for your comprehension and pronunciation of Russian to listen to the recording as you work through the course. The more times you listen, the better; try to concentrate on the pronunciation and intonation of the speakers. The conversations can be used as listening comprehension exercises; listen to the conversation to get the general gist (don't worry about understanding every single word), look at the questions that follow, then listen again before you try to answer them.

## The alphabet

Is Russian difficult? It is certainly very different from English; this is part of its fascination. An obvious difference is the Cyrillic alphabet – named after the ninth-century monk, St Cyril, its reputed author.

Using the Cyrillic alphabet to write Russian is actually a great deal easier than transliterating it – i.e. writing Russian in the English (Latin) alphabet – because two or more English letters are often needed to render a single letter in Russian. In the following example only two Russian letters are needed to provide the word meaning *cabbage soup*, while five are needed in English:

| Cyrillic | English |
|---|---|
| щи | shchi (pronounced 'shchee') |

Learning the alphabet is the first step to learning Russian.

---

## Pronunciation

◀◈ CD 1, TR 1, 00:46

The alphabet can be divided into three different groups of letters: those which look and sound very much like English letters; those which look like English letters but have different sounds; those which neither look nor sound like English letters. If you are familiar with Greek or Hebrew letters, you will recognize that some Russian letters have been developed from these sources.

Five letters fall into the first group (those which are equivalent to their English counterparts):

| | | | | |
|---|---|---|---|---|
| **a** | sounds slightly shorter than | *a* | in | father |
| **к** | sounds like | *k* | in | kit |
| **м** | sounds like | *m* | in | motor |
| **о** | sounds like | *aw/law* | in | bore |
| **т**[1] | sounds like | *t* | in | tired |

There are seven letters in the second group (those which look like English letters but which sound different):

| в | sounds like | *v* | in | *v*isit |
|---|---|---|---|---|
| е | sounds like | *ye* | in | *ye*t |
| н[1] | sounds like | *n* | in | *n*ovel |
| р[2] | sounds like | *r* | in | *r*at |
| с | sounds like | *s* | in | *s*ip |
| у | sounds like | *oo* | in | sh*oo*t |
| х | sounds like | *ch* | in | lo*ch* (Scots) |

The letters in the third group do not look like any English letters:

| б | sounds like | *b* | in | *b*ox |
|---|---|---|---|---|
| г | sounds like | *g* | in | *g*oat |
| д[1] | sounds like | *d* | in | *d*aughter |
| ё | sounds like | *yo* | in | *yo*nder |
| ж[3] | sounds like | *s* | in | plea*s*ure |
| з | sounds like | *z* | in | *z*oo |
| и | sounds like | *ee* | in | f*ee*t |
| й[4] | sounds like | *y* | in | bo*y* |
| л[5] | sounds like | *l* | in | bott*l*e |
| п | sounds like | *p* | in | *p*each |
| ф | sounds like | *f* | in | *f*ather |
| ц | sounds like | *ts* | in | qui*ts* |
| ч | sounds like | *ch* | in | *ch*ick |
| ш[3] | sounds like | *sh* | in | *sh*ift |
| щ | sounds like | *shch* | in | po*sh ch*ina |
| ъ[7] | hard sign – see note | | | |
| ы[6] | sounds like | *i* | in | *i*ll |
| ь[7] | soft sign – see note | | | |
| э | sounds like | *e* | in | l*e*t |
| ю | sounds like | *yu* | in | *yu*le |
| я | sounds like | *ya* | in | *ya*k |

Notes 1–7: These refer to Appendix 2.

The English equivalents given are only approximate and the best way to master Russian pronunciation is to listen to native speakers and try to imitate them – the recording will help you do this.

## Handwritten Russian

| Printed capital | Handwritten capital | Printed small | Handwritten small |
|---|---|---|---|
| А | *А* | а | *а* |
| Б | *Б* | б | *б* |
| В | *В* | в | *в* |
| Г | *Г* | г | *г* |
| Д | *Д* | д | *д, ∂* |
| Є | *Є* | є | *е* |
| Ё | *Ё* | ё | *ё* |
| Ж | *Ж* | ж | *ж* |
| Э | *З* | э | *з* |
| И | *И* | и | *и* |
| Й | *Й* | й | *й* |
| К | *К* | к | *к* |
| Л | *Л* | л | *л* |
| М | *М* | м | *м* |
| Н | *Н* | н | *н* |
| О | *О* | о | *о* |
| П | *П* | п | *п* |
| Р | *Р* | р | *р* |
| С | *С* | с | *с* |
| Т | *Т* | т | *т, ⊤* |
| У | *У* | у | *у* |
| Ф | *Ф* | ф | *ф* |
| Х | *Х* | х | *х* |

| Printed capital | Handwritten capital | Printed small | Handwritten small |
|---|---|---|---|
| Ц | *Ц* | ц | *ц* |
| Ч | *Ч* | ч | *ч* |
| Ш | *Ш* | ш | *ш* |
| Щ | *Щ* | щ | *щ* |
|  |  | ъ | *ъ* |
|  |  | ы | *ы* |
|  |  | ь | *ь* |
| Э | *Э* | э | *э* |
| Ю | *Ю* | ю | *ю* |
| Я | *Я* | я | *я* |

Some letters in the handwritten alphabet look a little different from those in the printed alphabet – the full alphabet, typed and handwritten, is given above. Compare each version of the letters, and practise saying them out loud.

◀) **CD 1, TR 1, 04:45**

Here are some words given in both the printed and the handwritten form—note that the letters **л, м** and **я** must always begin with a little hook, wherever they occur in the word; **т** and **ш** are often written with a line above and a line below, for the sake of clarity; while most letters in a word are joined together, it is not possible to join **о** to certain letters which follow it (e.g. **л, м** and **я**), otherwise it will look like an **а**. Practise saying these words aloud and try copying them out. Pay special attention to the relative height of the letters:

| | | | |
|---|---|---|---|
| 1 Бага́ж | бага́ж | (luggage) | *багаж* |
| 2 Во́дка | во́дка | (vodka) | *водка* |
| 3 Го́род | го́род | (town) | *город* |
| 4 Да | да | (yes) | *да* |
| 5 Друг | друг | (friend) | *друг* |
| 6 Дя́дя | дя́дя | (uncle) | *дядя* |
| 7 Е́сли | е́сли | (if) | *если* |
| 8 Лы́жи | лы́жи | (skis) | *лыжи* |
| 9 Мать | мать | (mother) | *мать* |
| 10 Сад | сад | (garden) | *сад* |
| 11 Тётя | тётя | (aunt) | *тётя* |
| 12 Футбо́л | футбо́л | (football) | *футбол* |
| 13 Хлеб | хлеб | (bread) | *хлеб* |
| 14 Цирк | цирк | (circus) | *цирк* |
| 15 Ча́сто | ча́сто | (often) | *часто* |

## Practice

**1** Now that you are acquainted with the alphabet, try to decipher these place names (answers in the Key to exercises).

| | | | |
|---|---|---|---|
| **a** | Лондон | **f** | Абердин |
| **b** | Ланкастер | **g** | Хантингдон |
| **c** | Мадрид | **h** | Бирмингам |
| **d** | Корнуолл | **i** | Эпсом |
| **e** | Амстердам | **j** | Мельбурн |

**2** Given below is the room allocation list for a group of tourists. Look at the second list in English and work out who is in which room (answers in the Key to exercises).

| | | | |
|---|---|---|---|
| Джон Смит | 201 | Хью Райли | 206 |
| Джейн Кларк | 202 | Ричард Харрисон | 207 |
| Вероника Томсон | 203 | Стефани Браун | 208 |
| Лилиан Уэст | 204 | Маргарет Дэйвиз | 209 |
| Саймон Макензи | 205 | Николас Тэйлор | 210 |

| | | | |
|---|---|---|---|
| **a** | Stephanie Brown | **f** | Hugh Riley |
| **b** | Jane Clark | **g** | John Smith |
| **c** | Margaret Davies | **h** | Nicholas Taylor |
| **d** | Richard Harrison | **i** | Veronica Thomson |
| **e** | Simon Mackenzie | **j** | Lilian West |

## The appendices and vocabulary

Appendix 1 includes summaries and notes on nouns, pronouns, adjectives, prepositions and verbs. Common irregularities are noted in Appendix 1. Appendix 2 contains more on pronunciation. Other irregularities are noted in the Russian–English vocabulary.

## Stress

Stress (indicated by an acute accent ´ over the vowel to be emphasized) is very important – however many syllables there are in a word, only one of them can be stressed. Every time you learn a new word, make sure you learn which syllable is stressed. If you get the stress wrong then your Russian will sound rather strange – just as your English would sound strange if you emphasized the wrong syllable (e.g. hótel, visít). In Russian the stressed vowel is 'given its full value' (it is pronounced quite distinctly) whereas the unstressed vowel is passed over quickly, almost 'thrown away'. This is heard most clearly with 'o'. If an 'o' comes immediately before the stressed syllable of the word, it is 'reduced' to a sound rather like the 'a' in the English word 'matter': e.g. **Москва́** (*Moscow*). In any other position in the word, an unstressed 'o' is pronounced like the second syllable of 'matter': **го́род**. (See Appendix 2 for further details on how stress affects vowels – note 8.) Note that the letter **ё** always carries the stress. In texts where the stress is not indicated (which includes most Russian publications), the two dots are not normally marked above this letter.

Note that stress is marked in all words in the dialogues, role-play exercises, conversations, reading texts, commentaries, key phrases, *Insight* boxes, end-of-unit self-tests and tips on things to remember, grammars and vocabularies.

# 1

# Ваш паспорт, пожалуйста!
## Your passport, please!

In this unit you will learn
- *How to respond to requests for personal information and identification*
- *Some forms of courtesy*

## Dialogue

Anna Prince, a tourist from England, has just arrived at Sheremetevo airport in Moscow and is passing through passport control and customs. A young man at passport control checks her passport; she then moves on to customs, where a young woman checks her luggage and currency declaration.

| | |
|---|---|
| **Молодо́й челове́к** | Здра́вствуйте! Ваш па́спорт, пожа́луйста. |
| **А́нна** | Здра́вствуйте! Вот мой па́спорт. |
| **Молодо́й челове́к** | Вы тури́стка? |
| **А́нна** | Да, я тури́стка. |
| **Молодо́й челове́к** | Вы англича́нка, да? |
| **А́нна** | Да, я англича́нка. |
| **Молодо́й челове́к** | Как ва́ша фами́лия? |
| **А́нна** | Моя́ фами́лия – Принс. |
| **Молодо́й челове́к** | Хорошо́. Вот ваш па́спорт. |

◉ CD 1, TR 2, 00:06

| | |
|---|---|
| **Áнна** | Спасибо. |
| **Молодóй человéк** | Пожáлуйста. |
| **Дéвушка** | Где ваш багáж? |
| **Áнна** | Вот он. |
| **Дéвушка** | Пожáлуйста, где вáша деклара́ция? |
| **Áнна** | Вот онá. |
| **Дéвушка** | Хорошó. Вот вáша деклара́ция. |
| **Áнна** | Спасибо. |
| **Дéвушка** | Пожáлуйста. До свидáния. |
| **Áнна** | До свидáния. |

| | |
|---|---|
| **молодóй человéк** | *young man* |
| **здрáвствуйте** | *hello; how do you do* |
| **ваш пáспорт** | *your passport* |
| **пожáлуйста** | *please* |
| **вот** | *here/there is/are* |
| **вы** | *you* |
| **да** | *yes* |
| **я** | *I* |
| **англичáнка** | *English(woman)* |
| **Как вáша фами́лия?** | *What's your surname?* |
| **хорошó** | *good, fine* |
| **спаси́бо** | *thank you* |
| **дéвушка** | *girl* |
| **где** | *where* |
| **ваш багáж** | *your luggage* |
| **он** | *he, it* |
| **вáша деклара́ция** | *your currency declaration* |
| **онá** | *she, it* |
| **до свидáния** | *goodbye* |

## Пáспорт *Passport*

Visitors to Russia must be in possession of a passport (**пáспорт**) and a visa (**ви́за**). Russian border guards are renowned for taking their time over scrutinizing these documents! On entering Russia visitors must give details of money, traveller's cheques and other valuables they have with them on their currency declaration form (**деклара́ция**) and this is checked again when they leave Russia.

## Фами́лия *Surname*

Anna supplies her surname (**фами́лия**) and her first name (**и́мя**). Russians would also give their patronymic (**о́тчество**) – a middle name derived from their father's first name and usually ending in -**овна** or -**евна** (for a woman) and -**ович** or -**евич** (for a man). Women's surnames usually end in -**a** (which is why Tolstoy's novel is so called: Anna is married to a man called Karenin):

| First name | Surname | Father's name | Full name |
|---|---|---|---|
| Гали́на | Петро́ва | Влади́мир | Гали́на Влади́мировна Петро́ва |
| Бори́с | Петро́в | Серге́й | Бори́с Серге́евич Петро́в |
| Ири́на | Его́рова | Никола́й | Ири́на Никола́евна Его́рова |
| Алексе́й | Его́ров | Па́вел | Алексе́й Па́влович Его́ров |

There is no Russian equivalent for the English 'titles' *Mr, Mrs, Ms, Miss*; members of the family, close friends, children and young people address each other by the first name (or a 'diminutive' – affectionate – version of the first name, e.g. the diminutive of **Светла́на** is **Све́та**); in more formal situations the first name and patronymic are used. So, **Гали́на Влади́мировна Петро́ва** would be known as **Гали́на** (or diminutive **Га́ля**) to her close friends and formally as **Гали́на Влади́мировна**. **Това́рищ** (*comrade*), which used to be used with the surname as an official form of address (or to address someone whose name you didn't know), is no longer used and **господи́н** *Mr* (feminine **госпожа́** *Mrs*) has come back into usage as an official form of address.

## Вы *You*

In Russian there are two ways of saying *you*; **вы** is used to indicate both singular (i.e. one person) and plural (more than one) – in the former case, it is the polite form of address used when talking to someone you don't know, or don't know very well (like the French word *vous*). If you are speaking to a member of your family, a close friend or a child, you would use the word **ты** (like the French word *tu*).

## Insight

As well as being the plural form of *you*, **вы** is the polite, respectful way to address someone you are meeting for the first time, or a person not well known to you. You can switch from **вы** to **ты** when you get to know someone better, but it's usually best to wait for that person to invite you (they'll probably say **давай на ты** – *let's call each other* **ты**).

### Здра́вствуйте! *Hello!*

This literally means *be healthy* and is used to greet a group of people or one person you would call **вы**. Note that the first **в** is not pronounced. If you were addressing one person whom you call **ты** you would say **Здра́вствуй!**

### Пожа́луйста *Please; you're welcome*

This means *please*, but is also used to mean *don't mention it, you're welcome* when someone has said **спаси́бо** to you (like the German word *bitte*).

---

## Questions

### 1 *True or false?*

**a** А́нна – америка́нка.
**b** Её (*her*) фами́лия – Петро́ва.
**c** А́нна – тури́стка.

## 2 Answer the questions!

**a** Áнна англичáнка?
**b** Как её фами́лия?

---

## How do you say it?

How to:
**1** *Greet people*
Здрáвствуйте!

**2** *Say please and thank you*
пожáлуйста
спаси́бо

**3** *Ask someone's surname and say your own*
Как вáша фами́лия?
Моя́ фами́лия Принс.

**4** *Ask people their nationality and state yours*
Вы англичáнка?
Да, я англичáнка.

**5** *Respond to requests for items, say here it is, etc.*
Где ваш пáспорт?
Вот мой пáспорт.

## Insight

Remember that the polite thing to do when someone thanks you (**спаси́бо** – *thank you*) is to reply **пожáлуйста** – *don't mention it* (literally *please*).

## Grammar

### 1 'The' and 'a'

There are no words in Russian for *the* (the definite article) or *a* (the indefinite article), so **паспорт** means *the passport* or *a passport*.

### 2 'To be'

The verb *to be* is not used in Russian in the present tense (*I am*, *you are* and so on). So **Вы турист** (which means literally *you tourist*) is the way of saying *you are a tourist*. If both words separated by the 'missing' verb *to be* are nouns, a dash may be used: **Моя фамилия – Петрова**.

### 3 Statements and questions

The only difference between a statement and a question in written Russian is that a question ends with a question mark ... and a statement does not!

There is no change in word order:

**Áнна турúстка.**     *Anna is a tourist.*
**Áнна турúстка?**     *Is Anna a tourist?*

In spoken statements, the voice usually falls on the last stressed syllable of the last word:

**Áнна турúстка.**

In a spoken question, the voice is raised on the last stressed syllable of the last word:

Áнна турúстка?

If the question begins with a question word (an interrogative), the voice is raised on that word:

Где ваш багáж?

If a question implies a contrast, a dip occurs:

А э́то?

---

## Insight

Three pieces of good news!

- There is no word for *the* or *a* in Russian
- There is no present tense of the verb *to be* in Russian
- The difference between making a statement and asking a question is very straightforward in Russian: just do it with your voice – down at the end for a statement, and up at the end for a question.

---

### 4 Groups of nouns

Nouns (words which name someone or something) are randomly divided into different groups – in Russian there are three groups (also known as 'genders'): masculine, feminine and neuter. The important thing to remember is that it is usually possible to work out which group a Russian word belongs to by looking at its ending. The most common endings are:

| | | | |
|---|---|---|---|
| Masculine words | end in | consonant | (**стол** table) |
| Feminine words | end in | **-a** | (**кни́га** book) |
| Neuter words | end in | **-o** | (**письмо́** letter) |

Sometimes a word has two forms to distinguish between males and females, e.g.

**Бори́с тури́ст.**        *Boris is a tourist.*
**А́нна тури́стка.**      *Anna is a tourist.*

You will soon become familiar with these endings as they are also present in certain pronouns, adjectives and past tense verbs. Other groups' endings are:

| | |
|---|---|
| Masculine words end in | a diphthong (e.g. **-ой**, **-ай**, **-ей**) (**май** *May*) |
| | a soft sign (**ь**) (**автомоби́ль** *car*) |
| Feminine words end in | **-я** (**неде́ля** *week*) |
| | **-ия** (**А́нглия** *England*) |
| | a soft sign (**ь**) (**тетра́дь** *exercise book*) |
| Neuter words end in | **-е** (**по́ле** *field*) |
| | **-ие** (**зда́ние** *building*) |

So, the only ending 'shared' by more than one group is **ь** (the soft sign) and this is the only time you will need to learn the gender of a word. Very occasionally you will meet exceptions to these patterns – the most common are **вре́мя** (*time*) and **и́мя** (*first name*), which are both neuter.

## Insight

Remember that there are three groups of nouns in Russian: masculine, feminine and neuter – the grammatical word for these groups is *genders*. Usually the ending of a noun will tell you whether it is masculine, feminine or neuter.

### 5 *How to say 'I, you, he, she, it, we, you' and 'they'*

The grammatical name for these words is the personal or subject pronoun and the table below gives a full list of them:

| **я** | *I* |
| **ты** | *you* (singular, informal) |
| **он** | *he* (person), *it* (when referring to a masculine noun) |
| **она́** | *she* (person), *it* (when referring to a feminine noun) |
| **оно́** | *it* (can only refer to a neuter noun) |
| **мы** | *we* |
| **вы** | *you* (singular, formal; plural) |
| **они́** | *they* |

## 6 'My, our, your'

These are known as possessive adjectives because they denote possession. They change their endings depending on the gender of the noun they are describing:

| **мой** (for masculine words): | **мой па́спорт** | *my passport* |
| **моя́** (for feminine words): | **моя́ деклара́ция** | *my declaration* |
| **моё** (for neuter words): | **моё и́мя** | *my (first) name* |

The word **твой** (*your*, i.e. belonging to **ты**) works in just the same way.

| **ваш** (for masculine words): | **ваш бага́ж** | *your luggage* |
| | | (i.e. belonging to **вы**) |
| **ва́ша** (for feminine words): | **ва́ша фами́лия** | *your surname* |
| **ва́ше** (for neuter words): | **ва́ше письмо́** | *your letter* |

The word **наш** (*our*, i.e. belonging to **мы**) works in just the same way.

### 'His, her, its'

The following words never change form:

> **его́**\*     *his, its* (when referring to a masculine or a neuter noun)

\*Note the pronunciation of this word, which is not what you would expect: **yevó**.

| **её** | *her, its* (when referring to a feminine noun) |
| **их** | *their* |
| **Где его деклара́ция?** | *Where is his declaration?* |
| **Вот её бага́ж.** | *Here is her luggage.* |
| **Как их фами́лия?** | *What is their surname?* |

### 7 Как? *How?*

This word means *how* and is frequently used in questions:

| **Как вы?** | *How are you?* |
| **Как дела́?** | *How are things?* |
| **Как ваш брат?** | *How's your brother?* |

Remember to raise your voice on question words.

### 8 *Nationalities*

Russian uses two nouns (one masculine, one feminine) to describe nationality:

| **Он англича́нин.** | *He is English.* |
| **Он америка́нец.** | *He is American.* |
| **Он испа́нец.** | *He is Spanish.* |
| **Она́ англича́нка.** | *She is English.* |
| **Она́ америка́нка.** | *She is American.* |
| **Она́ испа́нка.** | *She is Spanish.* |

A general rule would be that the feminine nouns end in -**a**.

*He is Russian, she is Russian*, etc. look rather different:

**Он ру́сский.**          **Она́ ру́сская.**

(This is because they are adjectives – see Unit 4).

---

## Practice

The exercises in this unit give you practice in recognizing the alphabet and in using some of the vocabulary and grammatical items covered in the unit.

### 1.1 *Read and answer!*

Look carefully at the form below and then answer the questions that follow it.

```
                                          №210
Национальность    Русская

Фамилия           Воробьёва

Имя, отчество     Галина , Сергеевна

Профессия            пианист
```

**a** What nationality is indicated on this form?
**b** What is the person's surname?
**c** What is her occupation?

### 1.2 *Write!*

Make up sentences similar to the following for the people listed below, indicating their name and occupation. Practise saying the sentences aloud.

Гали́на Серге́евна Воробьёва ру́сская. Она́ пиани́ст.

| | | | |
|---|---|---|---|
| **a** | Джим | америка́нец | журнали́ст |
| **b** | Мари́я | италья́нка | актри́са (*actress*) |
| **c** | Бори́с | ру́сский | инжене́р |
| **d** | Па́трик | ирла́ндец | студе́нт |

### 1.3 *Look and answer!*

Which city features on the hotel emblem below?

| | |
|---|---|
| **гости́ница** | *hotel* |

### 1.4 *Read and answer!*

Match the question with the answer.

**1** Как ва́ша фами́лия?        **a** Нет, она́ англича́нка.
**2** Где ва́ша деклара́ция?    **b** Да, мой.

**3** Она́ ру́сская?

**4** Э́то ваш бага́ж?

**c** Вот она́.

**d** Воробьёв.

> **нет** *no*    **э́то** *it is/this is/these are*

### 1.5 Read and write!

Где ваш паспорт? *Вот мой паспорт*

Make up similar answers to the following:

**a** Где ва́ша деклара́ция? _____

**b** Где ва́ше письмо́? _____

**c** Где ваш бага́ж? _____

**d** Где ваш журна́л? _____

**e** Где ва́ша ви́за? _____

> **журна́л** *magazine*    **письмо́** *letter*

## Insight

The key is to remember that for *my*, *your* and *our* you need to be sure to use **мой, наш, ваш** with masculine nouns, **моя́, на́ша, ва́ша** with feminine and **моё, на́ша, ва́ша** with neuter.

🔊 **CD 1, TR 2, 01:25**

### 1.6 Read, write and listen!

Practise writing answers about yourself to the following questions, then listen to the exchange on the recording which gives you sample answers.

**a** Как ва́ша фами́лия?

**b** Вы англича́нин/англича́нка?

**c** Вы студе́нт/студе́нтка?

## Comprehension

### 1 Conversation

**Read, listen and answer!**

A Russian tourist has just boarded a plane at Sheremetevo for a holiday in Yalta. He is talking to the stewardess.

CD 1, TR 2, 01:55

| | |
|---|---|
| **Стюардéсса** | Здрáвствуйте. |
| **Турúст** | Здрáвствуйте. |
| **Стюардéсса** | Как вáша фамúлия? |
| **Турúст** | Цвéтов. Борúс Владúмирович Цвéтов. |
| **Стюардéсса** | Где ваш билéт? |
| **Турúст** | Вот он. |
| **Стюардéсса** | Спасúбо. Вáше мéсто пять Б. |
| **Турúст** | Спасúбо. |
| **Стюардéсса** | Пожáлуйста. |

**мéсто** *place, seat*     **пять** *five*

**True or false?**

Read the statements about the tourist and state whether they are true or false.

a Егó фамúлия – Петрóв.
b Егó úмя – Борúс.
c Он турúст.

### 2 Reading

Read the text and answer the questions in English.

**a** Where is Viktor from?
**b** What is his job?
**c** Which famous places are mentioned?

Ви́ктор москви́ч.
Ви́ктор ру́сский. Он журнали́ст. Он москви́ч.
Москва́ – столи́ца Росси́и. Э́то центр поли́тики и культу́ры.
Там Большо́й теа́тр, Моско́вский университе́т и Кремль.

| | | | |
|---|---|---|---|
| **Москва́** | *Moscow* | **Росси́и** | *of Russia* |
| **москви́ч** | *Muscovite* | **там** | *there* |
| **столи́ца** | *capital* | **Кремль** | *Kremlin* |

---

## Key phrases

◀)) **CD 1, TR 2, 02:32**

Can you remember how to say the following in Russian? Listen to the recording and practise saying each phrase.

**a** Your passport, please.
**b** What is your surname?
**c** Goodbye.
**d** Hello.
**e** Thank you.

---

## Test yourself

**1** How can you tell if a noun is neuter?

**2** How do you say *the* in Russian?

**3** What would you need to do to make the following statement into a question? **Ви́ктор журнали́ст.**

**4** Why would you say **мой па́спорт/ваш па́спорт** but **моя́ ви́за/ва́ша ви́за?**

**5** What is a 'patronymic'?

**6** What should you say in reply if someone says **Спаси́бо** to you?

**7** If you wanted to ask the question 'where? would you use a) **как?** or b) **где?**

**8** What is the word for 'good-bye'?

**9** Can you give your nationality in Russian?

**10** If you were being introduced to someone for the first time, would you call them **вы** or **ты?**

# 2

# Меня зовут Ира
## I'm called Ira

In this unit you will learn
- *How to give further information about yourself*
- *How to request such information from others*

## Dialogue

Anna is travelling with a group of tourists from England who are all interested in painting and architecture. The travel company has arranged a social evening at which they are to meet a group of Russian artists and teachers of art.

| | | |
|---|---|---|
| **Ира** | Давáйте познакóмимся! Меня́ зовýт Ира. | CD 1, TR 3, 00:08 |
| **Áнна** | Óчень прия́тно. | |
| **Ира** | Как вас зовýт? | |
| **Áнна** | Меня́ зовýт Áнна. | |
| **Ира** | Óчень прия́тно, Áнна ... Вы ужé хорошó говори́те по-рýсски! | |
| **Áнна** | Спаси́бо. Я изучáю рýсский язы́к ужé три гóда. Ира, вы москви́чка? | |
| **Ира** | Да, я живý в Москвé. А где вы живёте? В Лóндоне? | |
| **Áнна** | Нет, я живý в Бри́столе. Я рабóтаю там в шкóле, преподаю́ англи́йский язы́к. А где вы рабóтаете? | |

| Йра | Здесь в Москве́, в университе́те. Я – худо́жница, преподаю́ жи́вопись. |
|---|---|
| Áнна | Ой, как интере́сно! |

**QUICK VOCAB**

| | |
|---|---|
| дава́йте познако́мимся | *let's introduce ourselves* |
| меня́ зову́т | *I'm called* (lit. 'they call me') |
| о́чень прия́тно | *pleased to meet you* |
| как вас зову́т? | *what are you called?* (lit. *how do they call you?*) |
| вы уже́ хорошо́ говори́те по-ру́сски | *you already speak Russian well* |
| я изуча́ю | *I'm learning (I have been learning)* |
| ру́сский язы́к | *Russian (language)* |
| три го́да | *(for) three years* |
| москви́чка | *a Muscovite (female)* |
| я живу́ | *I live* |
| в Москве́ | *in Moscow* |
| а | *and; but* |
| вы живёте | *you live* |
| в Ло́ндоне | *in London* |
| я рабо́таю | *I work* |
| там | *there* |
| в шко́ле | *in (a/the) school* |
| я преподаю́ | *I teach* |
| англи́йский язы́к | *English (language)* |
| здесь | *here* |
| в университе́те | *at the university* |
| худо́жница | *(female) artist* |
| жи́вопись (f.) | *drawing, painting* |

### Дава́йте познако́мимся! *Let's get to know each other*

This literally means *let's get to know each other* and is used when you're introducing yourself (or a group of which you are a member). If you were introducing two people to each other you would say **познако́мьтесь!** (lit. *get to know each other!*).

### Меня́ зову́т Йра *I'm called Ira*

This literally means *me they call Ira*. Russians will often introduce themselves at the sort of function described here by just giving their first name (in this case, Ira is the diminutive of Irina).

### Insight

The question to listen out for is **Как вас зову́т? –** *What are you called?* (literally *How do they call you?*). Practise the reply by saying **Меня́ зову́т** then adding your own name.

### Óчень прия́тно *Pleased to meet you*

The literal meaning of this is *very pleasant*. There is another common way of saying *pleased to meet you*: you could say **о́чень рад** (if you're a man) or **о́чень ра́да** (if you're a woman).

### В университе́те *At the university*

### Insight

Russia's higher education system includes universities, academies, conservatories, colleges and technical institutions. Since the end of 1990 education has been compulsory between the ages of six and seventeen. Crèches (**я́сли**) are for children under three, and for three- to six-year-olds there is the kindergarten (**де́тский сад**). In Soviet times education was free; however, there are now fee-paying private secondary schools (and terms such as **лице́й** and **гимна́зия** have reappeared). Higher education is no longer free for all students, and students' studies are sometimes linked to work for commercial concerns.

## Questions

**1** *True or false?*

**a** Йра англичáнка.
**b** Áнна говорúт по-рýсски.
**c** Йра – инженéр.

**2** *Answer the questions!*

**a** Как Áнна говорúт по-рýсски?
**b** Где Áнна живёт?
**c** Что (*what*) Йра преподаёт?

## How do you say it?

How to:
**1** *Introduce yourself*

Давáйте познакóмимся!

**2** *Say your name and ask someone else's name*

Меня зовýт …
Как вас зовýт?

**3** *Say 'pleased to meet you'*

Óчень приятно!
Óчень рад! Óчень рáда!

**4** *Ask people where they live, and say where you live*

Где вы живёте?
Я живý в …

**5** *Ask people where they work, and say where you work*

Где вы рабо́таете?
Я рабо́таю в …

## Grammar

### 1 *Verbs*

#### a Forming the present tense

We saw in Unit 1 that the verb *to be* is not used in the present tense in Russian, but this is an exception. Other verbs in Russian *do* have a present tense and it is important to know how this is formed (just as we need to know how present tense endings change in English – *I play, she plays* etc.).

There are two main groups (or conjugations) of verbs in Russian:

**i** Most verbs whose infinitive (the *to do* part of the verb) ends in -**ать** will work like the verb **рабо́тать** (*to work*) in the present tense:

| | | | |
|---|---|---|---|
| **я рабо́таю** | *I work* | **мы рабо́таем** | *we work* |
| **ты рабо́таешь** | *you work* | **вы рабо́таете** | *you work* |
| **он/она́/оно́ рабо́тает** | *he/she/it works* | **они́ рабо́тают** | *they work* |

i.e. remove the **ть** and add: -**ю, -ешь, -ет, -ем, -ете, ют**.

### Insight

It really is worth taking some time to learn the present tense of **рабо́тать**, because then you will have a model to use for almost all verbs in Russian which end in -**ать**. Try reading and repeating out loud each part of the present tense as it is set out above.

**ii** Most verbs whose infinitive ends in **-ить** will work like **говори́ть** (*to speak*) in the present tense:

| | | | |
|---|---|---|---|
| **я говорю́** | *I speak* | **мы говори́м** | *we speak* |
| **ты говори́шь** | *you speak* | **вы говори́те** | *you speak* |
| **он/она́/оно́ говори́т** | *he/she/it speaks* | **они́ говоря́т** | *they speak* |

i.e. remove the **ить** and add: **-ю, -ишь, -ит, -им, -ите, -ят**.

And if you spend some time learning the present tense of **говори́ть**, then you will be in a good position to cope with the majority of Russian verbs which end in **-ить**.

## b Irregular verbs

Like other languages, Russian has verbs which do not conform to the usual patterns (*irregular verbs*). In Russian, however, even irregular verbs are fairly consistent, and in order to be able to use them, the important thing is to know their stem and the **я, ты, они́** endings (and these are always given for irregular verbs in the vocabulary at the end of the book), e.g.:

> **жить** (*to live*) has the stem **жив-** and the following endings:
> я живу́, ты живёшь, он живёт, мы живём, вы живёте, они́ живу́т

In other words, the **он, мы** and **вы** forms will follow the pattern set by **ты**, but the **я** and **они́** forms will be different.

## c Verbs ending in -авать

**Преподава́ть** (*to teach*) like all verbs ending in **-авать** loses its middle (**ав**) and is conjugated as follows:

| | | | |
|---|---|---|---|
| **я преподаю́** | *I teach* | **мы преподаём** | *we teach* |
| **ты преподаёшь** | *you teach* | **вы преподаёте** | *you teach* |
| **он преподаёт** | *he teaches* | **они́ преподаю́т** | *they teach* |

It is important to know this, because there are some very common verbs that work this way: e.g. **дава́ть** (*to give*), **продава́ть** (*to sell*).

## Insight

So, the extra good news about Russian verbs is that even the irregular ones usually conform to a standard pattern. The key to learning irregular verbs in Russian is: make sure you know the stem, and the **я, ты** and **они́** forms.

### 2 Endings

These change according to the function of the words (nouns, adjectives, pronouns) in a given sentence; the different endings are called cases. So far you have the met the nominative case – this is used to talk about the person or thing doing an action (i.e. for the *subject* of the sentence):

The nominative is also used for the complement of the verb *to be* (i.e. the word(s) which complete(s) our knowledge of the subject):

| Subject | Complement | Meaning |
|---|---|---|
| **Москва́** | **столи́ца Росси́и** | *Moscow is the capital of Russia* |
| **А́нна Принс** | **тури́стка** | *Anna Prince is a tourist* |

There are six cases in Russian, including the nominative. (Nouns, adjectives and personal pronouns always appear in dictionaries and vocabularies in the nominative.)

### 3 Describing place or position

To describe the place or position of something or someone after the following prepositions:

**в**      *in* (*inside*), *at*          **на**          *in, on, at*

the prepositional (or locative) case is used.

The prepositional is usually formed by adding the letter **e** to the end of the nominative form of a noun.

| | | Remove | Add |
|---|---|---|---|
| *Masculine* | | | |
| **университе́т** | | – | **e** |
| **в университе́те**[1] | *in/at the university* | | |
| **автомоби́ль** | | **ь** | **e** |
| **в автомоби́ле** | *in the car* | | |
| **трамва́й** | | **й** | **e** |
| **на трамва́е** | *on the/by tram* | | |
| | | | |
| *Feminine* | | | |
| **Москва́** | | **а** | **e** |
| **в Москве́** | *in Moscow* | | |
| **ку́хня** | | **я** | **e** |
| **на ку́хне** | *in the kitchen* | | |
| | | | |
| *Neuter* | | | |
| **письмо́** | | **о** | **e** |
| **в письме́** | *in the letter* | | |
| **мо́ре** | | **e** | **e** |
| **в мо́ре**[2] | *in the sea* | | |

[1]Note that the preposition **в** is elided with the word which follows i.e.: **в университе́те** is pronounced as if it were one word.

[2]i.e. neuter nouns ending in -**e** stay the same.

The only exceptions to the usual ending are:

**a** Feminine soft sign nouns, feminine nouns which end in -**ия** and neuter nouns which end in -**ие**:

| | | Remove | Add |
|---|---|---|---|
| **тетра́дь** | | **ь** | **и** |
| **в тетра́ди** | *in the exercise book* | | |
| **А́нглия** | | **я** | **и** |
| **в А́нглии** | *in England* | | |

| зда́ние | | **е** | **и** |
|---|---|---|---|
| **в зда́нии** | *in the building* | | |

**b** A group of masculine nouns which all take the stressed ending **у** (instead of -**e**). A full list of these is given in Appendix 1, but here are some common examples:

| | | Remove | Add |
|---|---|---|---|
| **аэропо́рт** | | – | **ý** |
| **в аэропортý** | *at the airport* | | |
| **Крым** | | – | **ý** |
| **в Крымý** | *in the Crimea* | | |
| **пол** | | – | **ý** |
| **на полý** | *on the floor* | | |
| **сад** | | – | **ý** |
| **в садý** | *in the garden* | | |
| **ýгол** | | – | **ý** |
| **в углý**\* | *in the corner* | | |
| **шкаф** | | – | **ý** |
| **в шкафý** | *in the cupboard* | | |

\*Note that **ýгол** has what is known as a 'fleeting vowel' – i.e. a vowel which is omitted in every case except the nominative (words which have fleeting vowels are indicated in the vocabulary at the end of this book).

**c** A small group of words (known as *indeclinable*) never change their form in any case – these tend to be words imported from other languages. Common examples are:

| **бюро́** | **в бюро́** | *in/at the office* |
|---|---|---|
| **кафе́** | **в кафе́** | *in/at the café* |
| **такси́** | **в такси́** | *in the taxi* |

......................................................................

## Insight

Case endings help to make the meaning of a sentence clear.
A singular noun in the prepositional usually ends in -**е** or -**и**.

- **-e** for nouns ending in a consonant, **-a, -e, -o** or **-я** and for masculine nouns ending in **-ь**
- **-и** for nouns ending **ие** or **-ия** and for feminine nouns ending in **-ь**
- **NB!!** A small group of masculine nouns take the ending **-у**
- the word ends in **ь, я** or **е**, in which case the ending is **и**
- the word is part of the small group of masculine nouns which take **ý**
- the word is indeclinable (its endings never change).

## 4 По-ру́сски *In Russian*

This word describes the way in which something is done, is formed from **ру́сский** and means *in Russian*. Such words are called adverbs. Note the following similar adverbs:

| | |
|---|---|
| **Пьер говори́т по-францу́зски.** | *Pierre speaks French.* |
| **Пи́тер говори́т по-англи́йски.** | *Peter speaks English.* |
| **Мари́я говори́т по-итальянски.** | *Maria speaks Italian.* |

## Practice

### 2.1  *Read and answer!*

Which is the correct alternative?

**a** мы рабо́таю/рабо́таем/ рабо́тают

**b** она́ преподаёт/преподаёшь/ преподаёте

**c** вы живу́/живёте/живёшь

**d** они́ зна́ете/зна́ю/ зна́ют

**e** я говорю́/говори́те/ говори́т

| | |
|---|---|
| **знать** | *to know* |

## 2.2 Read, listen and answer

**CD1, TR 3, 01:24**

Read the questions then match them up with the answers that you will hear on your recording:

**a** Вы рабо́таете в Москве́?
**b** Как вас зову́т?
**c** Вы живёте в Ки́еве?
**d** Где вино́?

> **вино́** *wine*

## 2.3 Look and answer!

The information below is taken from a theatre ticket.

```
                Серия БТ
          9 ноября  000307
       ПАРТЕР   ряд 16   место 6
  Большой театр России   Театральная пл., дом 1
            Телефон 292-00-50
```

**a** What is the name of the theatre?
**b** What is the theatre's telephone number?

## 2.4 Read and write!

**Кто где рабо́тает?** *Who works where?*

| | | | |
|---|---|---|---|
| **a** | Ви́ктор | рабо́тать | университе́т |
| **b** | Са́ша | рабо́тать | сад |
| **c** | Ты | рабо́тать | шко́ла |
| **d** | Гали́на | рабо́тать | лаборато́рия |
| **e** | Вы | рабо́тать | бюро́ |

| **f** | Я | рабóтать | гостúница |
|---|---|---|---|
| **g** | Борúс | рабóтать | Москвá |

*Вuкmoр рабоmаеm в учuверсumеm*

**a** _____

Write similar sentences about the others listed above; use either the handwritten alphabet, or print the letters.

**Insight**

Once you have checked your answers with the Key, practise saying each sentence out loud. If your ears, as well as your eyes, get used to the prepositional endings it will be easier for you to remember them.

**2.5  Read and answer!**

Can you work out which composers are featured in the concert programme below?

**1 отделéние**

**a** И. С. Бах –    Токкáта, адáжио и фýга до мажóр
               Трúо-сонáта – 5

**2 отделéние**

**b** Мóцарт – Фантáзия фа минóр
**c** Шýман – Канóн си минóр

**2.6  Read and write!**

| **a** | Áнна | Брúстоль | по-англúйски |
|---|---|---|---|
| **b** | Я | Бúрмингам | по-англúйски |
| **c** | Пьер | Парúж | по-францýзски |
| **d** | Хосé | Испáния | по-испáнски |
| **e** | Вы | Москвá | по-рýсски |

**a**

$$\text{\textit{Анна живёт в Бристоле.}}$$
$$\text{\textit{Она говорит по-английски.}}$$

Write similar sentences about the others listed above.

## Comprehension

### 1 *Conversation*

**Read, listen and answer!**

Michael Jones, a journalist, is met at St Petersburg airport by his guide.

| | |
|---|---|
| **Гид** | Извините, пожалуйста, вы Майкл Джонс? |
| **Майкл** | Да, это я. |
| **Гид** | Здравствуйте! Я ваш гид. Меня зовут Володя. |
| **Майкл** | Очень приятно, Володя. |
| **Гид** | Вот наш автобус, номер пять, Майкл. |
| **Майкл** | Спасибо. |
| **Гид** | Скажите, Майкл, вы англичанин? |
| **Майкл** | Да, англичанин. |
| **Гид** | Вы живёте в Лондоне? |
| **Майкл** | Нет, нет, я живу в Оксфорде. |
| **Гид** | Как интересно. Вы работаете в университете? |
| **Майкл** | Нет, я журналист. |
| **Гид** | Вы очень хорошо говорите по-русски. |
| **Майкл** | Спасибо. Я работаю в Оксфорде, но иногда в России тоже. |
| **Гид** | А, понятно … вот почему вы говорите по-русски. |

CD1, TR 3, 01:54

| Майкл | А где вы живёте, Воло́дя? |
|---|---|
| Гид | Я живу́ и рабо́таю здесь в Санкт-Петербу́рге. |
| Майкл | В це́нтре? |
| Гид | Да, да, в це́нтре … Ну, вот и* ва́ша гости́ница. |

*Note that **и** means *and*, but it is also used to give emphasis: ***Here is your** hotel.*

| | | | |
|---|---|---|---|
| **вот почему́** | *that's why* | **здесь** | *here* |
| **извини́те** | *excuse me* | **иногда́** | *sometimes* |
| **поня́тно** | *I see* (lit. *it is understood*) | **пять** | *five* |
| **то́же** | *also* | | |

## True or false?

**a** Майкл Джонс живёт в Ло́ндоне.
**b** Майкл Джонс журнали́ст.
**c** Майкл Джонс хорошо́ говори́т по-ру́сски.
**d** Майкл Джонс рабо́тает то́лько в О́ксфорде.
**e** Воло́дя живёт в Москве́.

| | |
|---|---|
| **то́лько** | *only* |

## 2 Reading

Read the text and answer the questions in English.

**a** What sort of city is St Petersburg?
**b** What do we learn about the population?
**c** Where exactly does Elena live?
**d** What does she say about the architecture?
**e** Where does she work?

Еле́на Петро́вна Его́рова живёт в Санкт-Петербу́рге. Санкт-Петербу́рг о́чень большо́й го́род, культу́рный и администрати́вный центр. В Санкт-Петербу́рге живёт пять миллио́нов челове́к. Ле́на живёт в кварти́ре в це́нтре. Жить в це́нтре о́чень прия́тно! Там архитекту́ра о́чень краси́вая. Наприме́р, в це́нтре нахо́дятся Зи́мний дворе́ц и Эрмита́ж. И, коне́чно, в Санкт-Петербу́рге о́чень краси́вая река́ – Нева́. В це́нтре та́кже нахо́дится о́чень большо́й, ста́рый университе́т, где Еле́на рабо́тает. Еле́на – гео́лог.

| | |
|---|---|
| **большо́й** | *big* |
| **гео́лог** | *geologist* |
| **Зи́мний дворе́ц** | *Winter Palace* |
| **кварти́ра** | *flat* |
| **коне́чно** | *of course* |
| **краси́вая архитекту́ра** | *beautiful architecture* |
| **наприме́р** | *for example* |
| **находи́ться** | *to be situated* |
| **пять миллио́нов** | *5 million* |
| **река́** | *river* |
| **ста́рый** | *old* |
| **та́кже** | *also* |
| **челове́к** | *person* |

QUICK VOCAB

---

## Key phrases

🔊 **CD1, TR 3, 03:07**

Can you remember how to say the following in Russian? Listen to the recording and practise saying each phrase.

   **a** What are you called?
   **b** I am called Anna.
   **c** Pleased to meet you.
   **e** I work in Moscow.
   **e** I live in London.

## Test yourself

**1** You will probably find you need to use the **я** and **вы** forms of the present tense most often. So, do you know how to say *I work, I speak, you work, you speak*?

**2** Irregular verbs have reassuring patterns in Russian! What do you need to know in order to form the present tense?

**3** How would you reply if someone said the following to you: **Как вас зову́т?**

**4** Can you remember how to say: *at the university, in the school, in the letter*?

**5** As well as stating your nationality, you can now say which languages you speak... how would you ask someone if they speak Russian?

**6** There are some short words in this unit which come in very useful in all sorts of situations. Can you remember what the following mean: **здесь, там, о́чень, а, да, нет**?

**7** When would you use the phrase **о́чень прия́тно**?

**8** When would you use the phrase **извини́те, пожа́луйста**?

**9** Now you have covered the verbs *to live* and *to work*, and the prepositional case, you can explain in Russian where you live and work. Try it!

**10** In Unit 1 you learnt how to say *my, your, our*. Can you remember how to say *my passport, your visa, our hotel*?

# 3

..................................................................

# Где здесь телефон?
Where's the telephone?

In this unit you will learn
- *How to ask for and give directions*
- *Some more forms of courtesy*

_____

## Dialogue

Ira, who lives near the hotel Салют, has invited Anna to her flat. Anna has some trouble in finding the flat and asks passers-by for help.

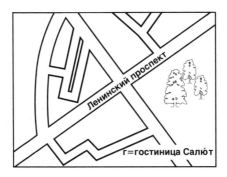

| | |
|---|---|
| **А́нна** | Извини́те, пожа́луйста, вы не зна́ете, где гости́ница Салю́т? |
| **Прохо́жий 1** | Извини́те, не зна́ю. |
| **А́нна** | Извини́те, пожа́луйста, вы не зна́ете, как пройти́ в гости́ницу Салю́т? |
| **Прохо́жий 2** | Куда́? |
| **А́нна** | В гости́ницу Салю́т. |
| **Прохо́жий 2** | Зна́ю. У вас есть план? |
| **А́нна** | Да, у меня́ есть план. Вот он. |
| **Прохо́жий 2** | Ну, хорошо́. (*Points to map.*) Мы вот здесь. Поня́тно? |
| **А́нна** | Да, поня́тно. |
| **Прохо́жий 2** | Хорошо́. Ви́дите рестора́н вон там? |
| **А́нна** | Да, ви́жу. |
| **Прохо́жий 2** | Хорошо́. Отту́да иди́те напра́во, пото́м нале́во, пото́м опя́ть нале́во. |
| **А́нна** | Хорошо́, я понима́ю: напра́во, нале́во, пото́м опя́ть нале́во. Спаси́бо большо́е. |
| **Прохо́жий 2** | Пожа́луйста. |
| **А́нна** | (*Follows instructions and arrives at Салю́т.*) Вот гости́ница Салю́т. А где живёт И́ра? (*Looks in her bag for the address.*) Вот её а́дрес: Ле́нинский проспе́кт, дом 120, ко́рпус 3, кварти́ра 5. Ой, как сло́жно! … Скажи́те, пожа́луйста, как пройти́ в дом 120? Э́то далеко́? |
| **Прохо́жий 3** | Нет, не о́чень. Ви́дите апте́ку, да? Отту́да иди́те пря́мо, пото́м нале́во. |
| **А́нна** | Спаси́бо большо́е. |
| **Прохо́жий 3** | Не́ за что. |
| **А́нна** | Ну, хорошо́, вот дом 120. А где ко́рпус 3? … Вот ко́рпус 1 … Уже́ по́здно! (*Anna sighs and decides to give in and ring Ira.*) … Скажи́те, пожалуйста, где здесь телефо́н? |
| **Прохо́жий 4** | Телефо́н-автома́т вон там, напра́во. |
| **А́нна** | Спаси́бо большо́е. |
| **Прохо́жий 4** | Пожа́луйста. |

| | |
|---|---|
| здесь | *here* |
| не | *not* |
| прохо́жий | *passer-by* |
| как пройти́ в? | *how do I/does one get to?* |
| куда́? | *where to?* |
| у вас есть? | *have you got?* |
| у меня́ есть | *I have* |
| план | *plan, map* |
| ви́дите, ви́жу (ви́деть) | *you see, I see (to see)* |
| вон там | *over there* |
| отту́да | *from there* |
| иди́те! (идти́) | *go! (to go on foot, to walk)* |
| напра́во | *on/to the right* |
| пото́м | *then* |
| нале́во | *on/to the left* |
| опя́ть | *again* |
| я понима́ю (понима́ть) | *I understand (to understand)* |
| спаси́бо большо́е | *thank you very much* |
| её | *her* |
| а́дрес | *address* |
| Ле́нинский проспе́кт | *Lenin Prospect (Avenue)* |
| дом | *house; block of flats* |
| 120 – сто два́дцать | *120* |
| ко́рпус | *block* |
| сло́жно | *complicated* |
| далеко́ | *a long way* |
| апте́ка | *chemist's shop* |
| пря́мо | *straight on* |
| не́ за что | *don't mention it* |
| по́здно | *(it is) late* |
| телефо́н-автома́т | *telephone box* |

## Вы не зна́ете? *You don't know by any chance?*

Verbs are made negative by the use of **не** (*not*) – e.g.: **я не понима́ю** (*I don't understand*). **Вы не зна́ете?** is the polite formula to use when requesting information (roughly equivalent to *You don't know by any chance …?*).

## Спаси́бо большо́е *Thank you very much*

This literally means *a big thank you*. As we saw in Unit 1, this usually attracts the response **пожа́луйста**; an alternative form of courteous response is **не́ за что**, *don't mention it*.

### Russian urban addresses

Ле́нинский проспе́кт, дом 120, ко́рпус 3, кварти́ра 5

Russian urban addresses tend to look like this, giving the number of the block of flats (**дом**), the individual building (**ко́рпус**) number – if the block of flats is made up of several sections – and finally the flat number itself (**кварти́ра**).

It is not surprising that Anna feels daunted by the task of finding Ira's flat – the blocks and wings, which all look very similar, are built in large groups and in a typical **микрорайо́н** (*microregion*) such complexes of flats will have their own shops, school, health centre and so on.

Accommodation remains something of a problem in Russian cities; finding a flat can be a long and expensive affair. Typically, Russian flats are not large – a small family might expect to have a kitchen, bathroom, sitting room and one bedroom (it is usual for rooms to have more than one use – e.g. sitting room doubles up as second bedroom).

### Скажи́те, пожа́луйста *Tell (me), please*

This literally means *say/tell*, *please* and, like **извини́те, пожа́луйста** (*excuse, please*), it is a good way of attracting someone's attention.

## Телефо́н-автома́т *Telephone box*

## Questions

**1** *True or false?*

**a** А́нна зна́ет, где гости́ница Сало́т.
**b** А́нна зна́ет, где ко́рпус три.
**c** Сло́жно пройти́ в дом **120.**

**2** *Answer the questions!*

**a** Пе́рвый (*first*) прохо́жий зна́ет, где гости́ница Салю́т?
**b** Где живёт Йра? _____ **120,** _____ **3,** _____ **5.**
**c** Где телефо́н? Напра́во или нале́во?

## How do you say it?

How to:

**1** *Request information: Do you happen to know …?*

Вы не зна́ете …?

**2** *Ask the way*

Как пройти́ в …?

**3** *Ask if someone has, and say that you have*

У вас есть …?
У меня́ есть …

**4** *Give directions*

вон там
напра́во
нале́во
отту́да
пря́мо

**5** *Ask and say if a place is far or not*

Э́то далеко́?
Нет, не о́чень далеко́.

**6** *Attract someone's attention*

Скажи́те, пожа́луйста.
Извини́те, пожа́луйста.

## Insight

Practise saying the two phrases **скажи́те, пожа́луйста** and **извини́те, пожа́луйста** many times – they are extremely useful! Remember that **извини́те** can mean *sorry* as well as *excuse me*.

**7** *Respond to thanks, saying 'Don't mention it'*

Пожáлуйста.
Нé за что.

---

## Grammar

### 1 Кудá? *Where to?*

This means *where to?* (like the English word *whither*) – i.e.
it must be used when you are asking a question about direction
(as opposed to **где**, used when you are asking about position):

| | |
|---|---|
| **Кудá он идёт?** | *Where (lit. where to) is he going?* |
| **Где он рабóтает?** | *Where does he work?* |

> **Insight**
> **Кудá** or **где?** The key is to remember that **кудá** seeks
> information about a destination: **Кудá он идёт? – В теáтр**
> (*Where is he going? – To the theatre*), whilst **где?** seeks
> information about a place, a position: **Где вы живёте? – В
> Лóндоне.** (*Where do you live? – In London*).

### 2 *Negative*

To make the negative of a verb, simply use **не** in front of the verb:

| | |
|---|---|
| **Я не говорю́ по-испáнски.** | *I don't speak Spanish.* |
| **Я не понимáю, что он говори́т.** | *I don't understand what he says.* |

**не** is pronounced as part of the verb: **не говорю́** as *nigavaryú*.

**Идти́** means *to go on foot*, *to walk*; this is another irregular verb. Remember that what you need to know here is:

| Stem | Я form | Ты form | Они́ form |
|------|--------|---------|-----------|
| ид- | иду́ | идёшь | иду́т |

If you compare this with **жить** (in Unit 2), you will see that the pattern is the same.

**Ви́деть** (*to see*), like most verbs whose infinitive ends in **-еть**, is a second conjugation verb and so it works like **говори́ть** – but care is needed with second conjugation verbs with a **д** in their stem. Whenever you meet a verb like this, remember that in the present tense, **я** form only, the **д** changes to a **ж**:

**я ви́жу, ты ви́дишь, он ви́дит, мы ви́дим, вы ви́дите, они́ ви́дят**

Another very common second conjugation verb which works in this way is **сиде́ть** (*to sit*, *be seated*): **я сижу́, ты сиди́шь** etc.

Note that the personal pronoun (with the exception of **он, она́, они́**) can be omitted in direct speech: **Ви́дите апте́ку** (*you see the chemist's?*).

## Insight

When learning new words, sometimes it can be helpful to think whether they resemble English words. Notice, for example, that the verb **ви́деть** sounds a little like the English word *video* – this might help you to remember that it means *to see*.

### 4 Иди́те! *Go!*

This is the command (or *imperative*) form of the verb. You have already met several of these (**здра́вствуйте, извини́те, скажи́те**). They are very straightforward to form. Take the **ты** form of the present tense and remove the last three letters – if you're left with a vowel add **йте** (if you're commanding **вы**; just **й** if you're commanding **ты**), and if you're left with a consonant add **ите** (or just **и** if you're commanding **ты**):

работаешь → работа- → + й/йте → рабо́тай/рабо́тайте!
идёшь → ид- → + и/ите → иди́/иди́те!

Note that commands are usually followed by an exclamation mark in Russian.

### 5 *Accusative case*

In Unit 2 we learnt about the nominative and prepositional cases. Now we meet the accusative case, which is used in the following ways.

### a For the 'object' of the sentence

In Russian the person or thing to whom/which an action is being done (known as the *object*) in a sentence must be put into the accusative case:

| Subject | Verb | Object | Meaning |
|---------|------|--------|---------|
| А́нна | ви́дит | зда́ние | *Anna sees the building* |
| А́нна | ви́дит | рестора́н | *Anna sees the restaurant* |
| А́нна | ви́дит | апте́ку | *Anna sees the chemist's* |

The good news is that for neuter nouns the accusative is exactly the same as the nominative. For masculine nouns the accusative and the nominative are the same if you're dealing with *inanimate* nouns (i.e. nouns which don't refer to people or animals). The accusative of masculine animate nouns will be dealt with in Unit 5. *All* feminine nouns except those ending in a soft sign change their nominative endings to form the accusative:

| | Remove | Add |
|---|---|---|
| Москва́ | а | у |
| Он хорошо́ зна́ет Москву́ *He knows Moscow well* | | |
| фами́лия | я | ю |
| Он зна́ет её фами́лию *He knows her surname* | | |
| дверь | — | — |
| Он открыва́ет дверь *He's opening the door* | | |

(i.e. а → у; я → ю; ь stays the same).

## b Describing motion or direction

In Unit 2 we learnt that **в/на** + prepositional case is used to describe the *position* of something/someone:

> **Ива́н рабо́тает в рестора́не.** *Ivan is working in the restaurant.*

But if you're describing motion towards (i.e. if you're answering the question *where to?*), when you're describing *direction*, **в/на** and the accusative must be used:

> **Ива́н идёт в рестора́н.** *Ivan is going into/to the restaurant.*

> ## Insight
> So, if you ask a question with **куда́? (where to?)**, you will receive an answer using the accusative case: **Куда́ вы идёте? – В сад.** (*Where are you going? – Into the garden*).

## 6 У вас есть ...? *Have you got ...?*

If you want to say *have you got*, the phrase you use literally means *by you is there?* Take away the question mark and, of course, you have the statement *you have*.

**NB**

**a** This is *not* a verb, but a phrase used instead of a verb.

**b** It is not essential to include the word **есть** (which means *there is/are*): **У меня́ план** and **У меня́ есть план** both mean *I have a plan*. **Есть** lends greater emphasis: *I do have a plan*.

**c** Note these forms:

| | | |
|---|---|---|
| **ты** | **у тебя́** | *you have* |
| **он/оно́** | **у него́** | *he/it has* |
| **она́** | **у неё** | *she has* |
| **мы** | **у нас** | *we have* |
| **вы** | **у вас** | *you have* |
| **они́** | **у них** | *they have* |

**Insight**

When shopping, you can find out if the shop has the item you are looking for by saying **У вас есть...?** For example, if you want to buy a magazine, you will say: **У вас есть журна́л?** Remember that your voice will need to rise on the word **есть**.

Practice

### *3.1 Read and answer!*

**i** Which is the correct alternative (motion or position)?

**a** Куда́/где вы идёте?
**b** Она́ живёт в Омск/в Óмске.
**c** Мы рабо́таем в университе́т/в университе́те.
**d** Cáша идёт в апте́ку/в апте́ке.
**e** Воло́дя сиди́т в рестора́н/в рестора́не.

**ii** Which is the correct alternative (subject or object)?

  **f** Вы зна́ете Я́лта/Я́лту?
  **g** Вот его́ деклара́ция/деклара́цию.
  **h** Он ви́дит О́льга/О́льгу.

### 3.2 Look and answer!

Look at the following extract from a theatre programme:

  **a** Will the audience be watching an opera or a ballet?
  **b** What is the title of the performance?

---

# ДОН КИХОТ

## Балет в 3 де́йствиях
## Либретто М. Петипа по роману
## М. Сервантеса

---

### 3.3 Read and write!

**Кто где живёт?** *Who lives where?*

  **a** О́льга/Самарка́нд → О́льга живёт в Самарка́нде
  **b** Ви́ктор/Ки́ев            **c** Я/А́нглия
  **d** Ты/Оде́сса              **e** Мари́я и Анто́нио/Ита́лия

🔊 **CD 1, TR 4, 02:23**

### 3.4 Read, answer and listen!

You are asking a passer-by how to get to the chemist's. Complete your part of the conversation, then listen to the complete conversation on the recording.

| **Вы** | a Ask how to get to the chemist's. |
|---|---|
| **Прохо́жий** | Иди́те пря́мо, пото́м нале́во. |
| **Вы** | b Ask if it is far. |
| **Прохо́жий** | Нет, не о́чень. |
| **Вы** | c Say thank you very much. |
| **Прохо́жий** | Не́ за что. |

### 3.5 Read and answer!

Work out what question was asked for each of these answers:

**a** Меня́ зову́т А́нна.
**b** Я живу́ в А́нглии.
**c** Я рабо́таю в Бри́столе.
**d** Я иду́ в гости́ницу.
**e** У меня́ есть план.

---

## Comprehension

### 1 Conversation

**Read, listen and answer!**

A tourist stops a passer-by to ask for directions to the Cosmos cinema.

| **Тури́ст** | Извини́те, пожа́луйста. |
|---|---|
| **Прохо́жий** | Да? |
| **Тури́ст** | Вы не зна́ете, где нахо́дится кинотеа́тр Ко́смос? |
| **Прохо́жий** | Кинотеа́тр Ко́смос? … ну, да … на проспе́кте Ми́ра. |
| **Тури́ст** | Спаси́бо. А как пройти́ туда́, пожа́луйста? |
| **Прохо́жий** | Вы не зна́ете, где проспе́кт Ми́ра? |
| **Тури́ст** | Нет, не зна́ю. Я не о́чень хорошо́ зна́ю Москву́. |
| **Прохо́жий** | Ничего́. Кинотеа́тр Ко́смос не о́чень далеко́. |
| **Тури́ст** | Хорошо́! |

CD 1, TR 4, 02:45

| Прохо́жий | Вы ви́дите ста́нцию метро́ вон там? |
|---|---|
| Тури́ст | Да, ви́жу. |
| Прохо́жий | Хорошо́. Отту́да иди́те напра́во. Это проспе́кт Ми́ра. Нале́во гости́ница Ко́смос. |
| Тури́ст | А кинотеа́тр то́же там? |
| Прохо́жий | Нет. Иди́те пря́мо. Напра́во нахо́дится музе́й космона́втики. |
| Тури́ст | Хорошо́, я понима́ю – гости́ница нале́во, музе́й напра́во. |
| Прохо́жий | Да. Иди́те пря́мо. Кинотеа́тр на углу́. Поня́тно? |
| Тури́ст | Да, спаси́бо большо́е. |
| Прохо́жий | Не́ за что. |

**QUICK VOCAB**

| | |
|---|---|
| **кинотеа́тр** | *cinema* |
| **туда́** | *to there* |
| **ничего́** (pronounced niche**v**o) | *never mind* |
| **ста́нция метро́** | *metro station* |
| **музе́й космона́втики** | *space museum* |

① станция метро
② гостинице
③ музей
④ кинотеатр

**1** Кинотеа́тр Ко́смос нахо́дится

 **a** в гости́нице Ко́смос

 **b** в музе́е космона́втики

 **c** на проспе́кте Ми́ра

**2** Кинотеа́тр Ко́смос нахо́дится

    **a** о́чень далеко́
    **b** не о́чень далеко́
    **c** в метро́

**3** Вот ста́нция метро́. Отту́да

    **a** тури́ст идёт напра́во
    **b** тури́ст идёт нале́во
    **c** тури́ст идёт в гости́ницу

**4** Вот у́гол. Там нахо́дится

    **a** кинотеа́тр
    **b** гости́ница
    **c** музе́й

### 2 *Reading*

**Read the text and answer the questions in English.**

    **a** What is Anatoly's surname?
    **b** Where does his wife work?
    **c** How long has Marina worked at the cinema?
    **d** Where exactly do they live?
    **e** What is a typical Russian flat like?
    **f** What amenities are there in the area where Anatoly and his family live?

Анато́лий Фёдорович Маша́тин – инжене́р. Он живёт в Москве́ не в це́нтре, а на окра́ине. У него́ жена́, Валенти́на Никола́евна; дочь, Мари́на; и соба́ка, Ша́рик. Валенти́на рабо́тает в апте́ке, а Мари́на уже́ три го́да рабо́тает в кинотеа́тре; она́ касси́рша. Ша́рик, коне́чно, не рабо́тает. Они́ живу́т в кварти́ре, на окра́ине. Это типи́чная кварти́ра: ку́хня, ва́нная, спа́льня и гости́ная. Зна́чит, э́то не о́чень больша́я кварти́ра. На окра́ине, где они́ живу́т, есть супермáркет, аптéка, кинотеáтр, шкóла и стáнция метрó. Итáк, Валентúна и Марúна рабóтают на окрáине, а Анатóлий рабóтает в цéнтре, то есть óчень далекó.

QUICK VOCAB

| вáнная | bathroom |
|---|---|
| гостúная | sitting room |
| дочь (f) | daughter |
| женá | wife |
| знáчит | that means, so |
| итáк | and so |
| кассúрша | cashier |
| конéчно | of course |
| кýхня | kitchen |
| на окрáине | on the outskirts |
| собáка | dog |
| спáльня | bedroom |
| супермáркет | supermarket |
| типúчная квартúра | typical flat |
| то есть | that is (i.e.). |

---

## Key phrases

🔊 **CD 1, TR 4, 04:13**

Can you remember how to say the following in Russian? Listen to the recording and practise saying each phrase.

**a** Thank you very much.
**b** Have you got a map?
**c** Tell me, please …
**d** How do I get to the theatre?
**e** Is it far?

## Ten things to remember

1  Russian has different words for *where to?* (**куда?**) and
   *where at?* (**где?**) Notice that there are also different words
   for *to there* (**туда**) and *there* when it describes position (**там**).

2  You can now ask various questions with the word **как**
   (*how*): **как дела?** (*how are things?*); **как вас зовут** (*what
   are you called?*); **как пройти в** (*how do I get to?*).

3  Making a verb negative (i.e. saying *not*) is simple in
   Russian – just place the word **не** in front of the verb: e.g.
   **Извините, я не знаю.** (*Sorry, I don't know*).

   Remember to pronounce **не** and the verb which follows
   it as if they were one word: **не знаю** – *niznáyu*.

4  Some of the most useful everyday phrases in this unit are:
   **извините, пожалуйста** (*excuse me, please*); **скажите,
   пожалуйста** (*tell me, please*) and **спасибо большое**.

5  To help you seek and give information about where things
   are, remember the words **направо** (*on the right*), **налево**
   (*on the left*), **прямо** (*straight on*), **далеко** (*it is far*).

6  Verbs tells us what action is being performed (e.g. *to see, to
   hear, to work*); the 'subject' of a sentence is the person or
   thing performing an action and the 'object' is the person or
   the thing that has an action done to it: *I* (subject) *see* (verb)
   *the restaurant* (object): **Я вижу ресторан**.

7  In Russian, the object must be put into the accusative case
   (have another look at point 5 of the grammar section of
   Unit 3 to remind yourself how straightforward this is!).

8  In this unit, we have learnt what happens to 'inanimate'
   masculine nouns in the accusative; we will learn what to

do with 'animate nouns' in Unit 5. Remember that an 'animate noun' refers to people or animals. So **журналист** (*a journalist*) is an animate noun, but **журнал** (*a magazine*) is inanimate.

**9** As well as being used for the object of the verb, the accusative is used in order to say *to/into* – in other words, to answer the question *where to?* **Я иду́ в теа́тр** – *I am going to the theatre.*

**10** Remember that if you want to say '*Have you got?*' you need the phrase **У вас есть? У вас есть соба́ка?** (*Have you got a dog?*) **Да, у меня́ есть соба́ка.** (*Yes, I do have a dog.*)

# 4

# Здесь можно фотографировать?

## May one take photographs here?

In this unit you will learn
- *How to ask/state whether something is permitted or not*
- *How to ask/state whether something is possible, impossible or necessary*

## Dialogue

Ira has taken Anna to see Kolomenskoye, a former royal estate on the banks of the Moskva river.

CD 1, TR 5, 00:08

| | |
|---|---|
| **Áнна** | Какóе красúвое мéсто! |
| **Úра** | Да, здесь здáния óчень красúвые. |
| **Áнна** | А какóе э́то здáние, вон там, налéво? |
| **Úра** | Э́то óчень стáрая цéрковь. Красúвая, да? |
| **Áнна** | Да, óчень. Я хочý посетúть музéй. Мóжно? |
| **Úра** | Да, конéчно. |
| **Áнна** | Хорошó. Я óчень люблю́ музéи. |
| **Úра** | Хорошó ... Нáдо купúть билéты в кáссе. |
| **Áнна** | Лáдно ... Скажú, Úра, в кáссе мóжно купúть открытки? |
| **Úра** | Не знáю ... (*Asks at ticket office.*) ... Нет, нельзя́. Здесь мóжно купúть тóлько билéты. |

| | |
|---|---|
| **А́нна** | Ничего́. |
| **И́ра** | Ну, вот вход в музе́й … Смотри́, А́нна, вон там напра́во, о́чень ста́рая ка́рта. |
| **А́нна** | Да, э́то действи́тельно интере́сная ка́рта. А э́то что? |
| **И́ра** | Э́то о́чень ста́рый деревя́нный стул. |
| **А́нна** | Скажи́, И́ра, здесь мо́жно фотографи́ровать? |
| **И́ра** | (*Asks the museum attendant*.) … Нет, А́нна, к сожале́нию в музе́е нельзя́ фотографи́ровать. |
| **А́нна** | (*Sighs*.) … Ну, ничего́ … |

| | |
|---|---|
| **како́е краси́вое ме́сто** | *what a beautiful place* |
| **зда́ния** | *buildings* |
| **це́рковь** (f.; fleeting **о**) | *church* |
| **я хочу́, ты хо́чешь (хоте́ть)** | *I want, you want (to want)* |
| **посети́ть** | *to visit* |
| **я люблю́ (люби́ть)** | *I like (to like)* |
| **на́до** | *it is necessary* |
| **купи́ть** | *to buy* |
| **биле́ты** | *tickets* |
| **в ка́ссе** | *at the ticket office* |
| **ла́дно** | *OK* |
| **мо́жно** | *it is possible, one may* |
| **откры́тки** | *postcards* |
| **вход** | *entrance* |
| **смотре́ть** | *to look, watch* |
| **ка́рта** | *map* |
| **действи́тельно** | *really* |
| **деревя́нный** | *wooden* |
| **стул** | *chair* |
| **фотографи́ровать** | *to photograph* |
| **к сожале́нию** | *unfortunately* |
| **нельзя́** | *it is not possible, one may not* |

## Музе́й *The museum*

Moscow is full of museums; the only pressure on the tourist is how to fit in all the interesting sights!

**Коло́менское** is a **музе́й-заповéдник** – a museum and conservation area.

It is usual for an attendant to be on duty in each room of a museum (often an elderly person) and in all but the smallest museums visitors are expected to leave their hats and coats in the **гардеро́б** (*cloakroom*) – indeed it is considered **некульту́рно** (*uncivilized*) to wear one's outdoor clothing in public places (e.g. theatres, restaurants).

## Скажи́, Йра *Tell me, Ira*

Anna and Ira have clearly become friends and now address each other as **ты**; this can be seen because Anna uses **Скажи́**, rather than **Скажи́те** (see Unit 3, part 4 of the Grammar section). Remember that **вы** is the polite form of address and on the whole it is better to use this unless a Russian invites you to change to **ты** (e.g. by saying **дава́й на ты**).

---

## Questions

### 1 *True or false?*

**a** А́нна ду́мает, что це́рковь краси́вая.
**b** В ка́ссе нельзя́ купи́ть откры́тки.
**c** В музе́е мо́жно фотографи́ровать.

> **ду́мать**     *to think*

## 2 Answer the questions!

**a** Где надо купить билеты?
**b** Что они видят в музее?
**c** Что нельзя делать в музее?

> **делать**  *to do*

---

## How do you say it?

How to:

**1** *Ask/state whether something is possible or if one may do something*

Здесь можно фотографировать?
Здесь можно купить билеты.

### Insight

**Можно** has to be at the top of the list as potentially the most useful word in this unit! It is usually followed by an infinitive, but if, for example, you wanted to ask if a seat on the bus/metro/tram or in a restaurant/theatre were free, just indicate it with your hand, and say **Можно**?

**2** *Ask/state whether something is impossible or if one may not do something*

В кассе нельзя купить открытки?
В музее нельзя фотографировать.

**3** *Ask/state whether it is necessary to do something*

Надо идти в кассу?
Надо купить билеты.

**4** *Express regret*
К сожалению …

## Grammar

### 1 *Plural nouns*

The nominative plural of masculine or feminine nouns usually ends in **ы** if the noun is 'hard' (i.e. if it ends in a consonant or **a**), or **и** if it is 'soft' (i.e. if it ends in **ь, й,** or **я**):

| Nom. sing. | Remove | Add | Nom. pl. | Meaning |
|---|---|---|---|---|
| *Masculine* | | | | |
| университе́т | – | ы | университе́ты | *universities* |
| автомоби́ль | ь | и | автомоби́ли | *cars* |
| трамва́й | й | и | трамва́и | *trams* |
| *Feminine* | | | | |
| газе́та | а | ы | газе́ты | *newspapers* |
| дверь | ь | и | две́ри | *doors* |
| ста́нция | я | и | ста́нции | *stations* |

There is an essential rule of spelling in Russian which it is important to learn now. There are certain letters which can **never** be followed by **ы, ю, я**.

They are:

| | |
|---|---|
| **г, к, х** | (gutturals) |
| **ж, ч, ш, щ** | (sibilants) |

After these letters:

| instead of | **ы** | use | **и** |
|---|---|---|---|
| instead of | **ю** | use | **у** |
| instead of | **я** | use | **а** |

### Insight

This spelling rule came about because it is quite difficult to pronounce the 'prohibited' vowels (**ы, ю, я**) after **г, к, х, ж, ч, ш, щ** and easier to say the alternatives (**и, у, а**). Try repeating the sounds **г, к, х, ж, ч, ш, щ** out loud to memorize them.

This rule often affects different forms of nouns and verbs, and you will see that it affects what we have just learnt about making the nominative plural of masculine and feminine nouns, e.g.:

| Nom. sing. | Remove | Add | Nom. pl. | Meaning |
|---|---|---|---|---|
| москвич | – | и | москвичи | *Muscovites* |
| дéвушка | а | и | дéвушки | *girls* |

The nominative plural of neuter nouns is **а** for 'hard' nouns (i.e. those ending in **о**) and **я** for soft nouns (i.e. those ending in **е**):

| Nom. sing. | Remove | Add | Nom. pl. | Meaning |
|---|---|---|---|---|
| письмó | о | а | пúсьма | *letters* |
| здáние | е | я | здáния | *buildings* |

Notice that the stress moves in the nominative plural of **письмó** – in many Russian nouns the stress is constant throughout the singular and plural, but there are some where it is not. On the whole it is better to try to learn instances of where stress moves as you meet them (but see also the note on stress patterns in Appendix 1).

## Insight

So, the most common nominative plural endings for nouns are: -**ы** or -**и** for masculine and feminine nouns, and -**а** or -**я** for neuter nouns. Remember to apply the spelling rule, though: never try to put -**ы** or -**я** after **г, к, х, ж, ч, ш, щ**.

Some very common nouns have irregular nominative plurals. The following are the most common (a fuller list is given in Appendix 1): notice how (apart from the words for *people* and *children*) there are recognizable patterns to these irregulars:

| Meaning | Singular | Plural | Meaning | Singular | Plural |
|---|---|---|---|---|---|
| *address* | áдрес | адресá | *child* | ребёнок | дéти |
| *bank, shore* | бéрег | берегá | *person* | человéк | лю́ди |

| eye | глаз | глаза́ | | | |
|-----|------|--------|---|---|---|
| town | го́род | города́ | daughter | дочь | до́чери |
| house | дом | дома́ | mother | мать | ма́тери |
| train | по́езд | поезда́ | | | |
| brother | брат | бра́тья | time | вре́мя | времена́ |
| friend | друг | друзья́ | name | и́мя | имена́ |

......................................................................

### Insight

Some of the most irregular nominative plural forms are
for nouns which are very common indeed. Make sure you
take a special look at these plurals: children (**де́ти**), friends
(**друзья́**), people (**лю́ди**).

......................................................................

The good news is that the accusative plural is exactly the same as
the nominative plural for all inanimate nouns (for animate nouns
see Unit 7), e.g.:

Nominative plural                    Accusative plural

Тури́сты            смо́трят            фи́льмы
*The tourists*      *are watching*     *films*

### 2 Adjectives

We have already met the possessive adjective (Unit 1) – i.e. the
word which describes to whom something belongs. All adjectives
*describe*. We have already met the following phrases which
include adjectives:

**краси́вая архитекту́ра**        *beautiful architecture*
**типи́чная кварти́ра**          *a typical flat*

The famous **Большо́й теа́тр** includes an adjective – **большо́й**
simply means big (see Unit 2). The most important thing to
remember about adjectives is that they must agree with the

noun they describe in *number* (i.e. singular or plural), *gender* (masculine, feminine, neuter) and *case* (i.e. nominative, accusative, etc.). The most usual endings for adjectives in the nominative singular and plural are:

| Masc. sing. | Fem. sing. | Neut. sing. | Plural |
|---|---|---|---|
| -ый | -ая | -ое | -ые |
| типи́чный | типи́чная | типи́чное | типи́чные |
| университе́т | кварти́ра | зда́ние | тури́сты |

Note that the plural ending is the same for all genders. The spelling rule we met in (1) above is important when dealing with the masculine singular and the plural of adjectives – if an adjective's stem (i.e. the last letter before the ending) ends in **г, к, х, ж, ч, ш, щ** then the masculine singular ending will be **-ий** and the plural will be **-ие**:

| ма́ленький университе́т | *a small university* |
|---|---|
| хоро́шие журна́лы | *good magazines* |

A small group of adjectives, called 'stressed adjectives', have the masculine ending **-ой** (not **-ый**), e.g.:

| большо́й дом | *a big house* |
|---|---|
| молодо́й актёр | *a young actor* |

In dictionaries and vocabularies adjectives are always given in the nominative masculine singular.

---

**Insight**

Remember that feminine nouns usually end in **-а** or **-я**, so it is pleasingly logical that the most common feminine adjective ending is **-ая: ста́рая кварти́ра** (*an old flat*). Similarly, neuter nouns usually end in **-о** or **-е**, so this will help you to remember that most neuter adjectives end in **-ое**.

---

### 3 Какóй *Which?*

This is a stressed adjective and means either *which?/what sort of?* or *what a!*:

| | |
|---|---|
| Какóй фильм ты хóчешь смотрéть? | *Which film do you want to see?* |
| Какáя красúвая цéрковь! | *What a beautiful church!* |

### 4 *Possibility/impossibility/necessity*

**Мóжно, нельзя́** and **нáдо** are extremely common and very useful words. They are all used with an infinitive (*to do*), e.g.:

В теáтре нельзя́ курúть!    *No smoking in the theatre!*

### 5 *Verbs*

#### a Хотеть *to want*

**Хотéть** (*to want*) doesn't conform to the pattern of irregular verbs we have met so far and is one of a very small number for which it is not sufficient just to know **я, ты, онú** forms:

| | |
|---|---|
| я хочу́ | мы хотúм |
| ты хóчешь | вы хотúте |
| он хóчет | онú хотя́т |

#### b Любúть *to like, to love*

**Любúть** is a second conjugation verb (like **говорúть**), but notice that it has an extra **л** in the **я** form *only*: **я люблю́, ты лю́бишь, он лю́бит**, etc. This applies to all second conjugation verbs whose stems (i.e. what's left when you remove **-ить**) end in **б, в, м, п, ф**, e.g.:

готóвить  *to prepare*
я готóвлю, ты готóвишь, он готóвит, мы готóвим, вы готóвите, они готóвят

## Insight

Luckily, verb irregularities often sound so strange that they are easy to remember: **я хочý** (*I want*) sounds rather like a sneeze and the sound of **я люблю́** (*I like*) might remind you of the character in *Andy Pandy* Looby Lou.

## Practice

### 4.1  *Read and answer!*

Match the questions with the answers:

**1** Где мóжно смотрéть фи́льмы?   **a** в универсáме (*super-market*)

**2** Где мóжно купи́ть винó?   **b** в кáссе

**3** Где мóжно смотрéть балéт?   **c** в кинотеáтре

**4** Где мóжно купи́ть билéты?   **d** в теáтре

### 4.2  *Read and answer!*

You are trying to find your way round Kolomenskoye. Complete your part of the conversation:

| Вы | a 'Say excuse me, please'. |
|---|---|
| Прохóжий | Да? |
| Вы | b Ask how to get to the church. |
| Прохóжий | Цéрковь вон там, налéво. |
| Вы | c Say 'thank you' and ask where the museum is. |
| Прохóжий | Пря́мо, потóм напрáво. |

| | |
|---|---|
| **Вы** | **d** Ask where you can buy tickets. |
| **Прохо́жий** | В ка́ссе, коне́чно. |
| **Вы** | **e** Say 'thank you' and 'goodbye'. |
| **Прохо́жий** | Пожа́луйста, до свида́ния. |

### 4.3  Look and answer!

These items are from a leaflet in a hotel room.
What instructions are being given?

**a**  В ли́фте нельзя́ кури́ть!
**b**  В посте́ли не кури́ть!

(a)

(b)

**c**  If **фа́брика** means *factory*, what sort of factory is being advertised below?

---

**Россия**
**шоколадная фабрика**

# СКАЗКИ ЛЕСА
## КОНФЕТЫ

---

### 4.4 Read, answer and listen!

Here are some answers. What were the questions? The first one is done for you. When you have worked through the exercise, listen to the complete dialogue on the recording.

| | |
|---|---|
| **a** Какой это город? | Это большой город |
| **b** ..................... | Это старая церковь |
| **c** ..................... | Это интересный музей |
| **d** ..................... | Это маленькое здание |
| **e** ..................... | Это новая книга |
| **f** ..................... | Это большой дом |

## Insight

Apart from helping you to learn the word **какой**, exercise 4.4 is also designed to help you remember the different endings for masculine, feminine and neuter adjectives. If you were at all unsure about any of the endings, just check again with parts 2 and 3 of the Grammar section.

### 4.5 Look and answer!

Viktor is standing outside the school. Give the six instructions (indicated by the arrows) which will enable him to get to the **театр**.

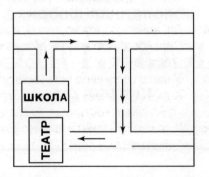

Иди́те _____ , пото́м _____ , пото́м _____ , пото́м _____ , пото́м _____ , пото́м _____ .

### 4.6 Read and write!

Answer these questions about yourself:

**a** Как вас зову́т?
**b** Где вы живёте?
**c** Где вы рабо́таете?
**d** Вы живёте в до́ме и́ли (*or*) в кварти́ре?
**e** Како́й у вас дом?/Кака́я у вас кварти́ра?

## Comprehension

### 1 *Conversation*

**Read, listen and answer!**

Ю́лия has just arrived in St Petersburg for a holiday and is chatting to the **го́рничная** (*maid*) on her floor in the hotel.

| | |
|---|---|
| **Ю́лия** | (*Indicating the armchair next to the maid's desk.*) Мо́жно? |
| **Го́рничная** | Да, пожа́луйста. |
| **Ю́лия** | Скажи́те, пожа́луйста, в гости́нице мо́жно купи́ть откры́тки и ма́рки? |
| **Го́рничная** | Да, коне́чно, мо́жно, внизу́, в кио́ске. |
| **Ю́лия** | Спаси́бо. А что мо́жно де́лать ве́чером в гости́нице? |
| **Го́рничная** | У нас в гости́нице есть кинотеа́тр. |
| **Ю́лия** | Хорошо́. Я о́чень люблю́ смотре́ть фи́льмы. В гости́нице и теа́тр есть? |
| **Го́рничная** | К сожале́нию, нет. Но у нас есть дискоте́ка. |

CD 1, TR 5, 02:30

| | |
|---|---|
| **Ю́лия** | Да, интере́сно … но я не о́чень люблю́ поп-му́зыку. |
| **Го́рничная** | И, коне́чно, в гости́нице есть о́чень хоро́ший рестора́н. |
| **Ю́лия** | Ага́. А ве́чером что мо́жно де́лать в го́роде? |
| **Го́рничная** | В го́роде? Ну, в го́роде есть коне́чно теа́тры, кинотеа́тры, рестора́ны, дискоте́ки. |
| **Ю́лия** | Хорошо́. (*Pointing to television near maid's desk.*) Скажи́те, пожа́луйста, здесь мо́жно смотре́ть телеви́зор? |
| **Го́рничная** | Да, коне́чно мо́жно. |
| **Ю́лия** | Хорошо́ … (*Moves to sit by television and takes out a cigarette.*) |
| **Го́рничная** | Извини́те, здесь нельзя́ кури́ть! |

QUICK VOCAB

| | |
|---|---|
| **ве́чером** | *in the evening* |
| **внизу́** | *downstairs* |
| **дискоте́ка** | *disco* |
| **кио́ск** | *kiosk* |
| **ма́рка** | *stamp* |
| **поп-му́зыка** | *pop music* |
| **телеви́зор** | *television* |

**True or false?**

**a** Ю́лия рабо́тает в Санкт-Петербу́рге.
**b** В гости́нице мо́жно купи́ть ма́рки.
**c** Ю́лия лю́бит дискоте́ки.
**d** В го́роде нельзя́ смотре́ть фи́льмы.
**e** В гости́нице мо́жно смотре́ть телеви́зор.
**f** На́до кури́ть, когда́ вы смо́трите телеви́зор.

| | |
|---|---|
| **когда́** | *when* |

64

## 2 Reading

Read the text and answer the questions in English.

**МОСКВА – ВЛАДИМИР**

127 км

**ВЛАДИМИР – СУЗДАЛВ**

38 км

**a** What expression is used to describe the cities of Moscow–Vladimir–Suzdal?
**b** What sort of cities are Vladimir and Suzdal?
**c** What sort of buildings are to be found there?
**d** What is produced in the factories in Vladimir?
**e** Why is Suzdal called a 'museum town'?
**f** What else is Suzdal famous for?

Поéздка в Москву́, Влади́мир и Су́здаль? Кака́я хоро́шая иде́я! Почему́? Потому́ что Москва́ – Влади́мир – Су́здаль – э́то «золото́е кольцо́» – зна́чит там и ру́сская исто́рия и ру́сская культу́ра и ру́сская красота́. Мы уже́ зна́ем, что Москва́ – столи́ца Росси́и, но э́то та́кже, коне́чно, о́чень ста́рый ру́сский го́род. Влади́мир и Су́здаль то́же о́чень ста́рые ру́сские города́, краси́вые и истори́ческие. В Су́здале и Влади́мире есть краси́вые, ста́рые музе́и, це́ркви, собо́ры и па́мятники. Хотя́ Влади́мир о́чень ста́рый го́род, там та́кже нахо́дятся заво́ды, где произво́дят тра́кторыи, компью́теры и де́лают краси́вый хруста́ль. Су́здаль – э́то музе́й-го́род – зна́чит там интере́сные музе́и, па́мятники, о́чень ста́рая, краси́вая архитекту́ра. В Су́здале есть краси́вые сады́ и огоро́ды, где выра́щивают огурцы́ и помидо́ры.

| | |
|---|---|
| **выра́щивать** | *to grow* |
| **заво́д** | *factory* |
| **золото́й** | *golden* |
| **и ... и** | *both ... and* |
| **исто́рия** | *history* |
| **кольцо́** | *ring* |

| | |
|---|---|
| **красота́** | *beauty* |
| **огуре́ц** (fleeting **e**) | *cucumber* |
| **огоро́д** | *kitchen garden* |
| **па́мятник** | *monument* |
| **пое́здка** | *journey* |
| **помидо́р** | *tomato* |
| **потому́ что** | *because* |
| **производи́ть** | *to produce* |
| **собо́р** | *cathedral* |
| **хотя́** | *although* |
| **хруста́ль** (*m.*) | *crystal* |

---

## Key phrases

🔊 **CD1, TR 5, 04:07**

Can you remember how to say the following in Russian? Listen to the recording and practise saying each phrase.

**a** Where is it possible to buy postcards?
**b** It is necessary to buy a ticket.
**c** What sort of museum is it?
**d** It's not possible (one may not) smoke here.
**e** OK.

**краси́вая ру́сская це́рковь**
*a beautiful Russian church*

## Test yourself

**1** Which word would you use if you wanted to ask if something were possible?

**2** What is the important thing to remember about the **я** form of the verb **любить**?

**3** What are the most common nominative plural endings for masculine and feminine nouns?

**4** Adjectives must 'agree' with the nouns they describe. So, if a noun is neuter, will the adjective describing it end in **-ый, -ая** or **-ое**?

**5** If someone said to you **Нельзя!** what would you understand by this?

**6** In English we say 'I like watching television' or 'I like to watch television'. What would you say in Russian?

**7** **Город** (*town, city*) is a very common word, but it has an irregular plural. Can you remember what it is?

**8** It is important to be able understand the question **Вы хотите ...?** Can you remember what it means?

**9** If you wanted to explain that you need to/must do something, would you use: **можно, надо** or **нельзя**?

**10** After which letters would you not use **ы, ю,** or **я**?

# 5

## Сколько стоит?

# How much is it?

In this unit you will learn

- *How to ask for and give simple information about cost and availability*
- *Further ways of describing where things are*

## Dialogue

Anna is trying to get two tickets for the theatre and tries first at the hotel service bureau (**бюро́ обслу́живания**), then at a kiosk.

CD1, TR 6, 00:06

| Áнна | Скажи́те, пожа́луйста, здесь мо́жно заказа́ть биле́ты в теа́тр? |
| --- | --- |
| Де́вушка 1 | Мо́жно. |
| Áнна | Хорошо́. У вас есть биле́ты на сего́дня на ве́чер? |
| Де́вушка 1 | Нет. Но на сего́дня на ве́чер у нас ещё есть биле́ты в цирк. Хоти́те? |
| Áнна | Спаси́бо, нет, в цирк я не хочу́. |
| Де́вушка 1 | У нас есть биле́ты в теа́тр, но то́лько на за́втра. Хоти́те? |
| Áнна | Спаси́бо, нет. Я хочу́ биле́ты на сего́дня на ве́чер. |
| Де́вушка 1 | Зна́ете, иногда́ мо́жно купи́ть биле́ты в ка́ссе и́ли в кио́ске. |

| | |
|---|---|
| **А́нна** | В кио́ске? |
| **Де́вушка 1** | Да, кио́ск нахо́дится на у́лице, нале́во от апте́ки, недалеко́ от ста́нции метро́. |
| **А́нна** | Спаси́бо. До свида́ния. |
| **Де́вушка 1** | Пожа́луйста. |
| **А́нна** | (At the kiosk.) Скажи́те, пожа́луйста, у вас есть биле́ты на сего́дня? |
| **Де́вушка 2** | На како́й спекта́кль? |
| **А́нна** | На бале́т «Жизе́ль». |
| **Де́вушка 2** | Нет. У нас оди́н биле́т на о́перу «Карме́н» и четы́ре биле́та на пье́су «Три сестры́» Че́хова. |
| **А́нна** | Ой, как хорошо́. Я Че́хова о́чень люблю́. Ско́лько сто́ит биле́т на пье́су? |
| **Де́вушка 2** | Во́семьдесят рубле́й. |
| **А́нна** | Да́йте, пожа́луйста, два биле́та на пье́су. |
| **Де́вушка 2** | Пожа́луйста … С вас сто шестьдеся́т рубле́й. (Anna hands over a 200-rouble note.) У вас нет ме́лочи? |
| **А́нна** | Извини́те, нет. (Receives change and tickets.) Спаси́бо большо́е. |
| **Де́вушка 2** | Пожа́луйста. |

| | |
|---|---|
| **заказа́ть** | to book, reserve |
| **биле́ты на сего́дня на ве́чер** | tickets for this evening |
| **ещё** | still |
| **сего́дня** (pronounced sivodnya) | today |
| **за́втра** | tomorrow |
| **иногда́** | sometimes |
| **у́лица** | street |
| **нале́во от** | to the left of |
| **недалеко́ от** | not far from |
| **на како́й спекта́кль?** | for which show? |
| **на пье́су «Три сестры́»** | for the play 'The Three Sisters' |
| **ско́лько сто́ит биле́т?** | how much does a ticket cost? |
| **во́семьдесят рубле́й** | eighty roubles |
| **да́йте** | give (command form) |

QUICK VOCAB

| два биле́та | two tickets |
| с вас сто шестьдеся́т рубле́й | that comes to 160 roubles (lit. *from you 160 roubles*) |
| у вас нет ме́лочи? | haven't you got any change? |

### Бюро́ обслу́живания *Service bureau*

Most large hotels have a 'service bureau', where guests can book tickets for excursions and the theatre, and plane and train tickets, arrange car hire and obtain information about what is available in the hotel itself, from business facilities to beauty treatments. Hotels throughout Russia now have their own **официа́льный сайт** and it is usually possible to book **онла́йн**.

### Кио́ск *Kiosk*

Kiosks are a frequent feature on the streets of big cities in Russia and are a convenient way of buying such things as flowers, postcards, maps and newspapers. They usually bear a sign indicating what is on sale (e.g. look out for **цветы́** for flowers, **театра́льный** if you want to buy theatre tickets).

### У вас нет ме́лочи? *Haven't you got any change?*

Note that **ме́лочь** (f). is *small change*; the Russian word for money given to the buyer as change is **сда́ча**.

---

## Questions

### 1 *True or false?*

**a** А́нна хо́чет купи́ть биле́т в цирк.
**b** Нельзя́ купи́ть биле́т в кио́ске.
**c** А́нна хо́чет купи́ть два биле́та.

## 2 Answer the questions!

**a** Какие билеты можно купить в бюро обслуживания на сегодня на вечер?

**b** Где находится киоск?

**c** Сколько стоит билет на пьесу?

---

## How do you say it?

How to:
**1** *Enquire about availability*

У вас есть билеты?

**2** *Ask for tickets to places and events*

У вас есть билеты в театр?
У вас есть билеты на оперу?

**3** *Ask how much something costs*

Сколько стоит билет?

**4** *Express the amount due*

С вас десять рублей.

**5** *Express location and distance from*

Налево от театра.
Недалеко от станции метро.

## Grammar

### 1 В *and* на + *accusative:* 'to'

We already know that these two prepositions are used with the accusative case in order to express motion and direction towards: **Он идёт в гости́ницу**, *He is going into the hotel.* In this unit we see a further very useful role for **в/на** + accusative:

| | |
|---|---|
| **биле́т в теа́тр** | *a ticket to the theatre* |
| **биле́т на о́перу** | *a ticket to the opera* |

Notice that when a *place* is specified **в** + accusative is used, but when the performance or day/date is specified, **на** + accusative is used. This use of **на** + accusative involves the idea of planned for/intended for and is very common in such phrases as:

| | |
|---|---|
| **Я хочу́ купи́ть молоко́ на у́жин.** | *I want to buy some milk for supper.* |
| **Я не зна́ю, что купи́ть на сва́дьбу.** | *I don't know what to buy for the wedding.* |

In the case of **цирк** (*circus*) **в** + accusative is usually used, as in Russian it is the (permanent) circus building that is implied, rather than the event.

| | |
|---|---|
| **молоко́** | *milk* |
| **у́жин** | *supper* |
| **сва́дьба** | *wedding* |

### Insight

It is useful to know that **на** + accusative can mean for *the purpose of*, *intended for*. Notice how to say *a ticket for today*, **биле́т на сего́дня**, and *a ticket for tomorrow* – **биле́т на за́втра**. The words for *today* and *tomorrow* are indeclinable (i.e. their endings never change).

## 2  На + *prepositional: 'in' or 'at'*

There is a group of words with which the preposition **в** is not used when expressing the position *in* or *at*; with these words you must use **на**. Here are the most common (a fuller list is given in Appendix 1):

| | | |
|---|---|---|
| вокза́л | на вокза́ле | at the (railway) station (terminus, main line) |
| ста́нция | на ста́нции | at the (bus/underground/ small railway) station |
| по́чта | на по́чте | at the post office |
| стадио́н | на стадио́не | at the stadium |
| пло́щадь (f.) | на пло́щади | in/on the square |
| у́лица | на у́лице | in/on the street |
| конце́рт | на конце́рте | at the concert |
| рабо́та | на рабо́те | at work |
| восто́к | на восто́ке | in the east |
| за́пад | на за́паде | in the west |
| се́вер | на се́вере | in the north |
| юг | на ю́ге | in the south |

## Insight

These words (and the fuller list in Appendix 1) are mainly about events (e.g. a concert) or about places that are not just one enclosed space (railway station, south).  The best way to remember which words must be used with **на** is to learn the whole phrase: e.g. **на у́лице** (*in the street*).

## 3  *The genitive case*

Once you know this case, all sorts of possibilities are opened up! The principal meaning of this case is *of*. For example, if you want to say *This is Viktor's book*, in Russian you must say *This is the book of Viktor* – the way you do this is to put the word *Viktor* into the genitive case. The genitive case is also used:

**a** after quantity words: e.g. **мно́го**, *a lot*; **ско́лько**, *how many* and *how much*; **буты́лка**, *a bottle*

**b** after certain prepositions: e.g. **без**, *without*; **для**, *for*; **до**, *until, before, as far as*; **из**, *from (out of)*; **от**, *(away) from*; **по́сле**, *after*; **с** *(down) from, since*; **у**, *by, near, at the house of*

**c** after numerals: after 2, 3, 4 the genitive singular is used; for numbers 5 and above, see point 5, later in this section, Unit 7 (Grammar section, point 3) and Unit 20 (Grammar section, point 4).

**d** in negative phrases: e.g. *I haven't got ...*

| Use | Example | Meaning |
|---|---|---|
| of | Э́то кни́га Ви́ктора | *This is Viktor's book* |
| quantity | У вас мно́го багажа́! | *You've a lot of luggage!* |
| prepositions | Недалеко́ от теа́тра | *Not far from the theatre* |
| numerals | Два биле́та | *Two tickets* |
| negatives | У меня́ нет биле́та | *I haven't got a ticket* |

The genitive singular of nouns is formed from the nominative in the following way:

| | | Remove | Add |
|---|---|---|---|
| *Masculine* | | | |
| университе́т | | – | а |
| недалеко́ от университе́та | *not far from the university* | | |
| автомоби́ль | | ь | я |
| у меня́ нет автомоби́ля | *I haven't got a car* | | |
| трамва́й | | й | я |
| два трамва́я | *two trams* | | |

*Feminine*

| | | а | ы |
|---|---|---|---|
| гости́ница | | | |
| напра́во от гости́ницы | *to the right of the hotel* | | |
| неде́ля | | я | и |
| три неде́ли | *three weeks* | | |
| ста́нция | | я | и |
| недалеко́ от ста́нции | *not far from the station* | | |
| тетра́дь | | ь | и |
| у него́ нет тетра́ди | *he hasn't got an exercise book* | | |

*Neuter*

| | | о | а |
|---|---|---|---|
| письмо́ | | | |
| у меня́ нет письма́ | *I haven't got the letter* | | |
| мо́ре | | е | я |
| недалеко́ от мо́ря | *not far from the sea* | | |
| зда́ние | | е | я |
| напра́во от зда́ния | *to the right of the building* | | |

Notice that there is a pattern here and that each gender of noun has two options: masculine and neuter nouns in the genitive singular have the same endings (**a** or **я**), while feminine nouns end in **ы** or **и**; straightforward nouns (i.e. masculine nouns ending in a consonant, neuter nouns endings in -**o**, feminine nouns ending in -**a**) take the first option, and all the others take the second option.

·········································································

## Insight

Remember the spelling rule in Unit 4! When you remove the **a** from the end of a feminine noun, if you are left with **г, к, х, ж, ч, ш,** or **щ**, you must add **и**, not **ы** (*three books* = **три кни́ги**).

·········································································

The genitive case of the personal pronouns is shown in bold below:

| я | **меня́** | он, оно́ | **его́** | мы | **нас** | они́ | **их** |
|---|---|---|---|---|---|---|---|
| ты | **тебя́** | она́ | **её** | вы | **вас** | | |

Note that whenever **его́, её** or **их** is used after a preposition, then the letter **н** must be added; **у него́** (*he has*) – a phrase we met in Unit 3. **У него́** literally means *by him there is*; **у** is the preposition meaning *by* or *at the house of*, and it is always followed by the genitive case – so if you want to say, for example, *Boris has a passport*, all you need to do is use **у** with the genitive of Boris:
**У Бори́са есть па́спорт.**

### 4 Animate accusative

As we saw in Unit 3, masculine animate nouns (i.e. people and animals) have their own accusative ending; the good news is that this ending is exactly the same as the genitive singular ending:

| Subject (nom.) | Verb | Object (acc.) | Meaning |
|---|---|---|---|
| Вы | зна́ете | Бори́са? | *Do you know Boris?* |
| Я | зна́ю | Ви́ктора | *I know Viktor* |

**NB** Similarly, the genitive form of the personal pronouns is also their accusative form: **Óля уже́ зна́ет тебя́?** *Does Olya already know you?*

### 5 Numerals

We have now met several of the numerals 1–20. Here is the full list:

| | | | |
|---|---|---|---|
| **1** оди́н | **6** шесть | **11** оди́ннадцать | **16** шестна́дцать |
| **2** два | **7** семь | **12** двена́дцать | **17** семна́дцать |
| **3** три | **8** во́семь | **13** трина́дцать | **18** восемна́дцать |
| **4** четы́ре | **9** де́вять | **14** четы́рнадцать | **19** девятна́дцать |
| **5** пять | **10** де́сять | **15** пятна́дцать | **20** два́дцать |

Note that if you are counting aloud from, say, 1 to 10, you start with the word **раз** (literally *one time*), not **оди́н**.

**Оди́н** functions like an adjective – i.e. it has masculine, feminine and neuter forms and must agree with the word it describes:

| оди́н биле́т | одна́ неде́ля | одно́ письмо́ |
|---|---|---|
| *one ticket* | *one week* | *one letter* |

**Два** has two forms – **два** is used with masculine and neuter nouns, but it must change to **две** before feminine nouns (and, like 3 and 4, 2 is always followed by the genitive singular):

| два биле́та | две неде́ли | два письма́ |
|---|---|---|
| *two tickets* | *two weeks* | *two letters* |

......................................................................
**Insight**

Apart from **три** and **де́сять** (linked to the English word *decimal*), Russian numerals do not bear much resemblance to their English counterparts. With the teens of numbers, it might help you to think, e.g., that the idea behind **трина́дцать** (13) is 'three on ten'.
......................................................................

One of the most frequent uses of numerals is when you're dealing with money, so it's important to know the genitive singular of the word *rouble*, Russia's main unit of currency:

**оди́н рубль** *one rouble*          **два рубля́** *two roubles*

Numbers above 4 are followed by the genitive plural (see Unit 7), but as the genitive plural form of *rouble* is so frequently used, it is worth noting it now:

**пять рубле́й** *five roubles*

There are 100 copecks to the rouble and it is important to know how the copeck (**копе́йка**) forms its genitive singular and genitive plural:

**три копе́йки** *three copecks*    **пять копе́ек** *five copecks*

### 6 Ско́лько сто́ит? *How much does it cost?*

The verb *to cost, to be worth* – **сто́ить** – is a regular second conjugation verb, like **говори́ть**; remember to use the 3rd person plural (*they*) form of the verb if you're asking the price of more than one item:

Ско́лько сто́ит биле́т?        *How much is a ticket?*
Ско́лько сто́ят биле́ты?      *How much are the tickets?*

### 7 Word order

Note how flexible word order is – it's quite acceptable to vary the position of, say, subjects and objects in a sentence:

Я о́чень люблю́ Че́хова.⎫
Я Че́хова о́чень люблю́.⎭   *I really like Chekhov.*

У вас нет ме́лочи?⎫
Ме́лочи у вас нет?⎭   *Haven't you got any change?*

---

## Practice

### 5.1 Read and answer!

How many times is the genitive singular used in this sentence?

У А́нны два биле́та на пье́су Че́хова «Три сестры́».

## 5.2 Read, answer and listen!

🔊 **CD1, TR 6, 02:20**

Work out what question was asked for each of these answers, then check your answers by listening to the recording.

**a** У меня́ нет па́спорта.
**b** Кио́ск нахо́дится недалеко́ от ста́нции метро́.
**c** План го́рода сто́ит де́сять рубле́й.
**d** Он рабо́тает на заво́де.
**e** Да, я о́чень люблю́ Че́хова.

## 5.3 Read and answer!

You like listening to music. Look at the kiosk signs below and decide which one you would be most likely to visit.

**a** ТАБАК

**b** КОМПАКТ-ДИСКИ

**c** ЛОТО

## 5.4 Look and write!

Look at the list below, then write sentences explaining what each person has (✓) or hasn't (✗) got. The first one is done for you:

| Кто? | Соба́ка | Автомоби́ль | Телефо́н |
|------|---------|-------------|----------|
| **a** Óльга | ✓ | ✗ | ✓ |
| **b** Вади́м | ✗ | ✓ | ✓ |

| c | Нина | ✓ | ✓ | ✗ |
| d | Алексей | ✗ | ✓ | ✓ |

**a** У Ольги есть собака и телефон, но у неё нет автомобиля.

### 5.5 Read and answer!

Which is the correct alternative?

**a** Вы видите Виктор/Виктора?
**b** Это пьеса/пьесу Чехова.
**c** Она очень любит опера/оперу.
**d** Я хочу купить билет на пьеса/пьесу.
**e** Вот Владимир/Владимира.

---

## Comprehension

### 1 Conversation

**Read, listen and answer!**

Hungry and thirsty after a day's sightseeing, Igor visits the **буфет** (*snack bar*) in his hotel.

CD1, TR 6, 02:45

| Игорь | Скажите, пожалуйста, у вас есть минеральная вода? |
| Девушка | Есть. |
| Игорь | Сколько стоит одна бутылка? |
| Девушка | Десять рублей. |
| Игорь | Дайте, пожалуйста, две бутылки. |
| Девушка | Пожалуйста. А ещё что? |
| Игорь | Дайте, пожалуйста, три булочки и кусочек сыра. |
| Девушка | Масло хотите? |

| | |
|---|---|
| **Игорь** | Да, дайте, пожалуйста, три порции масла. |
| **Девушка** | Пожалуйста. Это всё? |
| **Игорь** | Гм … минуточку … У вас есть шоколад? |
| **Девушка** | Нет, у нас сегодня нет шоколада. |
| **Игорь** | Гм … Дайте, пожалуйста, одно пирожное. |
| **Девушка** | Пожалуйста. Это всё? |
| **Игорь** | Да, спасибо, это всё. Сколько с меня? |
| **Девушка** | С вас семьдесят рублей. |
| **Игорь** | Вот … сто. |
| **Девушка** | Мелочи у вас нет? |
| **Игорь** | Минуточку … да … есть. (*Gives her 70 exactly.*) |
| **Девушка** | Спасибо большое. |
| **Игорь** | Пожалуйста. |

| | |
|---|---|
| **минеральная вода** | *mineral water* |
| **бутылка** | *bottle* |
| **ещё что?** | *anything else?* |
| **булочка** | *roll* |
| **кусочек сыра** | *a piece of cheese* |
| **масло** | *butter* |
| **порция** | *portion* |
| **минуточку** | *just a moment* |
| **пирожное** | *cake, bun* |

**1** Игорь хочет купить

  **a** вино    **b** водку    **c** воду

**2** Одна бутылка стоит

  **a** 100 рублей    **b** 1000 рублей    **c** 10 рублей

**3** В буфете сегодня нет

  **a** масла    **b** шоколада    **c** сыра

**4** У Игоря

  **a** есть мелочь    **b** нет мелочи    **c** только два рубля

## Insight

Did you notice the phrase **две буты́лки** in the conversation? **Буты́лка** is a feminine noun, so we need to use the feminine form **две**, not **два** (which is only to be used with masculine and neuter nouns).

## 2 Reading

**Read the text and answer the questions in English.**

**a** Of which country is Kiev the capital?
**b** Why is Kiev known as the mother of Russian cities?
**c** How many people live there?
**d** Why do tourists like it?
**e** What do Kiev's factories produce?

Ки́ев – столи́ца Украи́ны. Э́то о́чень ста́рый го́род, «мать ру́сских городо́в». В Ки́еве живёт два миллио́на челове́к. Ки́ев о́чень краси́вый го́род. Он стои́т на берегу́ Днепра́. Тури́сты о́чень лю́бят отдыха́ть в Ки́еве. Здесь есть па́рки, леса́ и сады́, ке́мпинги, гости́ницы, дома́ о́тдыха, истори́ческие и архитекту́рные па́мятники.

Одна́ко, Ки́ев – не то́лько туристи́ческий центр, но та́кже администрати́вный, экономи́ческий и культу́рный центр Украи́ны. В Ки́еве нахо́дятся больши́е заво́ды, где де́лают самолёты, телеви́зоры, мотоци́клы.

| | |
|---|---|
| **Днепр** | *Dniepr (river)* |
| **дом о́тдыха** | *holiday centre* (lit. *house of rest*) |
| **ке́мпинг** | *campsite* |
| **«мать ру́сских городо́в»** | *the mother of Russian cities* |
| **мотоци́кл** | *motorbike* |
| **но и** | *but also* |
| **одна́ко** | *however* |
| **отдыха́ть** | *to rest, have a holiday* |
| **па́мятник** | *monument* |
| **самолёт** | *aeroplane* |
| **стоя́ть (сто́ю, стои́шь)** | *to stand* |
| **Украи́на** | *Ukraine* |

QUICK VOCAB

## Key phrases

🔊 **CD1, TR 6, 04:20**

Can you remember how to say the following in Russian? Listen to the recording and practise saying each phrase.

**a** Have you got any tickets?
**b** How much does a ticket cost?
**c** How much do I owe you?
**d** Not far from the theatre.
**e** To the left of the school.

## Ten things to remember

**1** Three vital phrases in the shopping process: **У вас есть?** (*Have you got?*) **Ско́лько сто́ит?** (*How much does it cost?*) **Ско́лько с меня́?** (*How much do I owe you?*).

**2** The Russian unit of currency is the rouble (**рубль**) and it is divided into 100 copecks (**сто копе́ек**).

**3** *One* has three forms in Russian, depending on the gender of the noun, so: **оди́н биле́т** (*one ticket*), **одна́ о́пера** (*one opera*), **одно́ ме́сто** (*one place, seat*).

**4** The numbers *two, three* and *four* are followed by nouns in the genitive singular: **два музе́я** (*two museums*), **три гости́ницы** (*three hotels*), **четы́ре зда́ния** (*four buildings*).

**5** If you need to explain what belongs to whom, then you need the genitive case: *Nina's ticket* = *the ticket of Nina* = **биле́т Ни́ны**.

**6** If you need to use the following prepositions, then you need the genitive case: **без, для, до, из, от, по́сле, с, у.** Check back to the

Grammar section of the unit to make sure you know what each of these words mean.

**7** If you need to talk about quantities, you need the genitive case: **мно́го багажа́** (*a lot of luggage*); **полкило́ са́хара** (*half a kilo of sugar*); **буты́лка вина́** (*a bottle of wine*); **нет молока́** (*there isn't any milk*).

**8** Thanks to the genitive case, you can now give and understand more precise directions, because you know how to say *not far from/to the left/to the right of*: **недалеко́/нале́во/напра́во от кио́ска**.

**9** If you have a masculine animate noun which is the object of a sentence, remember that the masculine animate accusative endings are just the same as the genitive: **Она́ лю́бит Никола́я** (*She loves Nikolai*).

**10** If you want to buy a ticket for a particular event, then remember you'll need to use **на** + accusative: **биле́т на о́перу на за́втра** (*a ticket for the opera tomorrow*).

# 6

# Я предпочитаю плавать
## I prefer to swim

In this unit you will learn
- *How to talk about likes and dislikes*
- *How to ask people about their preferences*

## Dialogue

Anna has spent the morning at the museum with Ira and Ira's friend, Volodya.

◀) CD 1, TR 7, 00:09

| | |
|---|---|
| **Йра** | Что ты предпочитáешь, Áнна, пейзáжи йли портрéты? |
| **Áнна** | Бóльше всегó я люблю́ пейзáжи, но мне óчень нрáвится э́тот портрéт, вон там. |
| **Йра** | Ах, да, портрéт Рéпина, замечáтельная картúна ... Я óчень хочу́ показáть её Волóде, а где он? |
| **Волóдя** | (*Sitting in the corner, yawning.*) Ой, как ску́чно! |
| **Йра** | Ну, что ты, Волóдя! Здесь всё так интерéсно! И картúны такúе интерéсные! Я тебя́ не понимáю! |
| **Волóдя** | Ну, Йра, всё óчень прóсто. Ты худóжник – знáчит в свобóдное врéмя ты лю́бишь смотрéть картúны. А я предпочитáю игрáть в хоккéй ... А ты, Áнна, лю́бишь хоккéй? |

| | |
|---|---|
| **А́нна** | (*Embarrassed.*) Нет, не о́чень … Я предпочита́ю пла́вать … И́ра, здесь о́чень интере́сно и карти́ны о́чень краси́вые. Но мы здесь уже́ три часа́ … |
| **Воло́дя** | Пра́вда! Мы уже́ три часа́ смо́трим карти́ны. Тепе́рь мне хо́чется пить … Нам пора́ идти́, И́ра. |
| **И́ра** | Но я хочу́ показа́ть А́нне ещё … (*Volodya groans.*) … Ну ла́дно, пойдёмте в гардеро́б … А́нна, да́й мне тво́й номеро́к, пожа́луйста. |
| **А́нна** | Вот он, И́ра … и спаси́бо большо́е за о́чень интере́сное у́тро. |
| **И́ра** | Зна́чит, тебе́ нра́вится э́тот музе́й? |
| **А́нна** | Да, о́чень. |
| **Воло́дя** | А сейча́с пойдём в буфе́т! Мне фрукто́вый сок. А тебе́ что, А́нна? |
| **А́нна** | Мне чай, пожа́луйста. |
| **Воло́дя** | А тебе́, И́ра? |
| **И́ра** | Мне то́же чай, пожа́луйста. |

| | |
|---|---|
| **ты предпочита́ешь (предпочита́ть)** | *you prefer (to prefer)* |
| **пейза́ж** | *landscape* |
| **портре́т** | *portrait* |
| **бо́льше всего́** (pronounced fsyevo) | *most of all* |
| **мне о́чень нра́вится** | *I really like* |
| **замеча́тельная (замеча́тельный)** | *splendid* |
| **карти́на** | *picture* |
| **показа́ть** | *to show* |
| **ску́чно** | *boring* |
| **пойдём** | *let's go* |
| **что ты!** | *what next!* |
| **таки́е интере́сные** | *so interesting* |
| **про́сто** | *simple* |
| **худо́жник** | *artist* |
| **игра́ть в хокке́й** | *to play hockey* |

| | |
|---|---|
| три часá | *for three hours* |
| мне хóчетя пить | *I'm thirsty* |
| нам порá идти́ | *it's time for us to go* |
| пойдёмте | *let's go* |
| номерóк | *tag, metal disc* |
| спаси́бо большóе за | *thank you very much for* |
| у́тро | *morning* |
| фрукто́вый сок | *fruit juice* |
| что тебé? | *what would you like?* (lit. *what for you?*) |

## Insight

The verb **предпочита́ть** (*to prefer*) is quite a mouthful! Try pronouncing it syllable by syllable to start with: **пред-по-чи-та́ть**. It might help you to remember it by noticing that the last part of the word is the verb for *to read* (**чита́ть**).

### Хоккéй *Hockey*

Football and other games played on grass are only really practical in summer in Russia, but the climate there does favour the playing of ice hockey; when Russians refer to hockey, it is usually this form of the game they have in mind.

### Что ты! *Come on now!*

Literally meaning *that you*, this is a useful way of expressing surprise, indignation or objection in response to what someone has said. **Что вы!** would, of course, be required if addressing more than one person or using the polite form.

### Номерóк *Token*

This is the small disc/token bearing a number, given in exchange for your coat at the **гардеро́б** (see Unit 4).

## Я люблю́/мне нра́вится: *Expressing liking*

Both these phrases express liking, but **я люблю́** is more intense (*I love*) and tends to apply in general (e.g. **Я люблю́ му́зыку** – *I love/like music*), whereas **мне нра́вится** is less intense (*I like*) and tends to apply to a particular occasion or instance (**Мне нра́вится э́тот портре́т** – *I like this portrait*).

---

## Questions

**1** *True or false?*

**a** Бо́льше всего́ А́нна лю́бит пейза́жи.
**b** И́ра не понима́ет, почему́ Воло́дя говори́т «как ску́чно!»
**c** И́ра – касси́рша.
**d** Они́ в музе́е уже́ четы́ре часа́.
**e** И́ра ду́мает, что им пора́ идти́.

| **ду́мать** | *to think* |
|---|---|

**2** *Answer the questions!*

**a** Воло́дя лю́бит музе́й?
**b** Что есть в музе́е?
**c** Почему́ И́ра лю́бит карти́ны?
**d** Что А́нна хо́чет пить?

| **пить** (irregular: **пью, пьёшь … пьют**) | *to drink* |
|---|---|

---

## How do you say it?

How to:
**1** *Enquire about preference*

Что ты предпочита́ешь?
Что вы предпочита́ете?

**2** *State preference*

Я предпочита́ю игра́ть в хокке́й.
Бо́льше всего́ я люблю́ пейза́жи.

**3** *Ask about likes and dislikes*

Ты лю́бишь спорт?                    Вы лю́бите спорт?
Тебе́ нра́вится э́тот музе́й?         Вам нра́вится э́тот музе́й?

**4** *State likes and dislikes*

Я (о́чень) люблю́ …
Я не (о́чень) люблю́ …
Мне (о́чень) нра́вится …
Мне не (о́чень) нра́вится …

## Grammar

### 1 В + *accusative in 'to play (at)'*

A further use of **в** + accusative is found in the construction **'игра́ть в'** – *to play (at)*; note that this is used for games and sports:

**игра́ть в футбо́л**          *to play football*
**игра́ть в ша́хматы**         *to play chess*

**NB** If you want to talk about a musical instrument, **в** + accusative is *not* used; **на** + prepositional is required:

**игра́ть на фле́йте**         *to play the flute*
**игра́ть на гита́ре**         *to play the guitar*

....................................................................................

## Insight

You play *on* (**на** + prepositional) a musical instrument, but *at* a game (**в** + accusative), e.g.: **Я люблю́ игра́ть на кларне́те, но я не люблю́ игра́ть в футбо́л** (*I like playing the clarinet, but I don't like playing football*).

....................................................................................

## 2 'Has/have been ...'

In order to say *we have been looking for three hours* (i.e. an action which is still going on at the moment of speaking), Russian simply uses the present tense and no word for *for*:

Мы уже́ три часа́ смо́трим ...

## 3 Спаси́бо за + accusative *Thank you for ...*

This is the way to say 'thank you' *for* something:

**Спаси́бо за журна́л.**    *Thank you for the magazine.*
**Спаси́бо за кни́гу.**    *Thank you for the book.*

> ## Insight
> Another use of the accusative! You might find it helpful to learn three things to say *thank you* for, one for each gender, e.g. **спаси́бо за биле́т** (*thank you for the ticket*); **спаси́бо за карти́ну** (*thank you for the picture*); **спасибо за письмо́** (*thank you for the letter*).

## 4 Dative case

The principal meaning of this case is *to* or *for*. For example, if you want to say *Olya gives the tickets to Viktor*, then the way to do this is to put *Viktor* into the dative case:

| Subject (nom). | Verb | Object (acc). | Indirect object (dat). |
|---|---|---|---|
| *Olya* | *gives* | *the tickets* | *to Viktor* |
| О́ля | даёт | биле́ты | Ви́ктору |

(Note that in English the indirect object is often hidden, because we do not always include the word *to*: *Olya gives Viktor the tickets*).

The dative case is also used:

- with the prepositions **к** and **по** in the following ways:

| | |
|---|---|
| **к нам** | *towards us/to our house* |
| **к Ире** | *to Ira's (to Ira's house)* |
| **по улице** | *along/down/up the street* |
| **по городу** | *around/throughout the town* |
| **по телевизору** | *on the television* |

- with **можно** (*it is possible, one may*), **нельзя** (*it is impossible, one may not*), **надо** (*it is necessary*) and **пора** (*it is time to*):

| Dative of person | (e.g.) **пора** | infinitive |
|---|---|---|
| **Володе** | **пора** | **идти** |

*It's time for Volodya to go*

- idiomatically in phrases with **нравится** (to express *liking*) and **хочется** (to express *wanting, feeling like*):

| Dative of person | (e.g.) **нравится** | noun |
|---|---|---|
| **Анне** | **нравится** | **этот музей** |

*Anna likes this museum*

| Use | Expression | Meaning |
|---|---|---|
| *to* | Оля даёт билеты Виктору | *Olya gives the tickets to Viktor* |
| *for* | Мне кофе, пожалуйста | *Coffee for me, please* |
| **к** | Я иду к Виктору | *I'm going to Viktor's* |
| **по** | Она говорит по телефону | *She's talking on the telephone* |
| **надо** etc. | Мне надо работать | *I've got to work* |
| | Тебе нельзя курить | *You mustn't smoke* |
| **нравится** | Мне очень нравится эта пьеса | *I really like this play* |
| **хочется** | Володе хочется отдыхать | *Volodya wants to rest* |

The dative singular of nouns is formed from the nominative in the following way:

|  | | Remove | Add |
|---|---|---|---|
| *Masculine* | | | |
| брат | | – | **у** |
| Её бра́ту хо́чется отдыха́ть | *Her brother wants to rest* | | |
| учи́тель | | **ь** | **ю** |
| «Да,» говори́т он учи́телю | *'Yes,' he says to the teacher* | | |
| Алексе́й | | **й** | **ю** |
| О́ля даёт кни́гу Алексе́ю | *Olya gives the book to Aleksei* | | |
| *Feminine* | | | |
| соба́ка | | **а** | **е** |
| Соба́ке хо́чется игра́ть | *The dog wants to play* | | |
| О́ля | | **я** | **е** |
| Куда́ он идёт? – К О́ле | *Where's he going? – To Olya's* | | |
| Мари́я | | **я** | **и** |
| Мари́и пора́ идти́ | *It's time for Mariya to go* | | |
| дверь | | **ь** | **и** |
| Он идёт к две́ри | *He's walking towards the door* | | |
| *Neuter* | | | |
| окно́ | | **о** | **у** |
| Он идёт к окну́ | *He's walking towards the window* | | |
| мо́ре | | **е** | **ю** |
| к мо́рю | *towards the sea* | | |
| зда́ние | | **е** | **ю** |
| Он идёт к зда́нию | *He's walking towards the building* | | |

Note the dative form of the personal pronouns:

| | | | |
|---|---|---|---|
| я | **мне** | мы | **нам** |
| ты | **тебе́** | вы | **вам** |
| он, оно́ | **ему́** | они | **им** |
| она́ | **ей** | | |

### 5 Э́тот *This*

Э́тот is a demonstrative pronoun and means *this*. It has three forms in the nominative singular (masculine, feminine and neuter) and one in the nominative plural, and it must agree with the word it describes (a list of case endings of э́тот is given in Appendix 1):

| | |
|---|---|
| **э́тот университе́т** | *this university* |
| **э́та гости́ница** | *this hotel* |
| **э́то зда́ние** | *this building* |
| **э́ти теа́тры** | *these theatres* |

Note that the neuter form э́то is identical to the word for *it is/ this is/these are.*

## Practice

### 6.1 Read and answer!

Choose a word/words from the list below to complete each
sentence or to answer the question. (**NB** Not all the words in the
list are needed!)

**a** Извини́те, пожа́луйста, вы не _____, где метро́?
**b** У вас есть па́спорт? _____
**c** У меня́ в но́мере телефо́н не _____
**d** Здесь мо́жно фотографи́ровать? _____
**e** У вас мно́го _____?
**f** _____ нельзя́ кури́ть.

| | | | |
|---|---|---|---|
| багажа́ | Да, вот он | Да, мо́жно | зна́ете |
| рабо́таете | Бори́су | Да, вот она́ | рабо́тает |

### 6.2 Read, answer and listen!

You are asking the service bureau in your hotel about museums in
the city. Complete your part of the conversation; then listen to the
complete conversation on the recording.

CD 1, TR 7, 02:25

| **Вы** | **(a)** Ask if there are any museums in the city. |
|---|---|
| **Де́вушка** | Коне́чно! У нас мно́го. |
| **Вы** | **(b)** Ask if these museums are near the hotel. |
| **Де́вушка** | Да, недалеко́ отсю́да (*from here*) есть большо́й музе́й. |
| **Вы** | **(c)** Ask what there is in the museum. |
| **Де́вушка** | В музе́е краси́вые карти́ны и ста́рая ме́бель (*furniture*). |
| **Вы** | **(d)** Ask how much a ticket to the museum costs. |
| **Де́вушка** | Два́дцать рубле́й. |
| **Вы** | **(e)** Say 'thank you very much. Goodbye'. |
| **Де́вушка** | Не́ за что. До свида́ния. |

### 6.3 Read and answer!

Put the words in brackets in the correct form:

**a** Я предпочитáю кóфе без _____ (молокó).

**b** Сегóдня вéчером мы идём к _____ (Борúс).

**c** Знáете, Вéра, _____ (мы) ужé порá идтú.

**d** Нет, музéй не óчень далекó от _____ (гостúница).

**e** (Я) _____ óчень хóчется отдыхáть.

---

## Insight

In an exercise like 6.3, it is helpful first of all to work out what the sentence will mean when you complete it, and therefore what case the bracketed word requires. In 6.3 you needed to use your knowledge of the genitive (a, d) and the dative (b, c, e).

---

### 6.4 Look and write!

Look at the pictures and write a sentence about the preferences of each person:

**a** Борúс предпочитáет игрáть в тéннис.

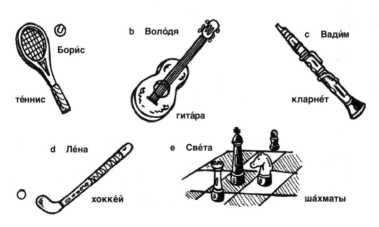

b Волóдя

c Вадúм

d Лéна

e Свéта

Борúс

тéннис

гитáра

кларнéт

хоккéй

шáхматы

## Comprehension

### 1 *Conversation*

**Read, listen and answer!**

A journalist from the newspaper «Спорт» is visiting a university and he interviews Lena Ermakova, a student there.

CD 1, TR 7, 03:10

| | |
|---|---|
| **Журнали́ст** | Здра́вствуйте, Ле́на. Меня́ зову́т Ви́ктор. Я из газе́ты «Спорт». |
| **Ле́на** | Здра́вствуйте. |
| **Журнали́ст** | Скажи́те мне, Ле́на, вы изуча́ете матема́тику, да? |
| **Ле́на** | Да, матема́тику. |
| **Журнали́ст** | Вам нра́вится курс? |
| **Ле́на** | Да, курс о́чень интере́сный. |
| **Журнали́ст** | А что вы де́лаете в свобо́дное вре́мя? |
| **Ле́на** | Ну, я смотрю́ телеви́зор, чита́ю мно́го, и о́чень люблю́ пла́вать. |
| **Журнали́ст** | Вы ча́сто пла́ваете? |
| **Ле́на** | Нет, не ча́сто, потому́ что бассе́йн нахо́дится далеко́ от до́ма. |
| **Журнали́ст** | А здесь, в университе́те, есть спортза́л? |
| **Ле́на** | Да, есть. Э́то небольшо́й спортза́л, где мо́жно игра́ть в волейбо́л и баскетбо́л. |

QV

| | |
|---|---|
| **матема́тика** | *mathematics* |
| **бассе́йн** | *swimming pool* |
| **спортза́л** | *sports hall* |

**1** Ле́на изуча́ет

  **a** ру́сский язы́к

  **b** матема́тику

  **c** му́зыку

  **d** англи́йский язы́к

**2** Она́ ду́мает, что

  **a** курс о́чень ску́чный

  **b** курс не о́чень интере́сный

  **c** курс не о́чень хоро́ший

  **d** курс о́чень интере́сный

**3** Лёна пла́вает не о́чень ча́сто потому́, что

- **a** у неё мно́го рабо́ты
- **b** она́ не о́чень лю́бит пла́вать
- **c** она́ предпочита́ет игра́ть в волейбо́л
- **d** бассе́йн далеко́ от её до́ма

## 2 *Reading*

**Read the text and answer the questions in English.**

- **a** What sort of building is the Tretyakov Art Gallery housed in?
- **b** Exactly where is it situated?
- **c** Who was the founder of the gallery?
- **d** Why are Repin, Surikov and Ivanov popular?

В Москве́ нахо́дится изве́стная Третьяко́вская галере́я. Э́то о́чень краси́вое и типи́чно ру́сское зда́ние. Оно́ нахо́дится в це́нтре го́рода, недалеко́ от ста́нции метро́ «Третьяко́вская». Основа́тель галере́и – Серге́й Миха́йлович Третьяко́в (XIX ве́ка) – бога́тый моско́вский купе́ц. В галере́е уника́льная колле́кция ру́сской жи́вописи. Там наприме́р мо́жно ви́деть изве́стные карти́ны Ре́пина, Су́рикова и Ива́нова (Ре́пин, Су́риков, Ива́нов – худо́жники XIX ве́ка). Там есть портре́ты и пейза́жи, о́чень изве́стные и популя́рные, потому́ что они́ изобража́ют жизнь и пробле́мы Росси́и XIX ве́ка.

| | |
|---|---|
| **изве́стный** | *famous* |
| **Третьяко́вская галере́я** | *Tretyakov Gallery* |
| **основа́тель** (m.) | *founder* |
| **век** | *century* |
| **бога́тый** | *rich* |
| **купе́ц** | *merchant* |
| **уника́льный** | *unique* |
| **колле́кция** | *collection* |
| **жи́вопись** (f.) | *painting* |
| **изобража́ть** | *to depict* |
| **жизнь** (f.) | *life* |
| **пробле́ма** | *problem* |

QUICK VOCAB

## Key phrases

◄)) CD 1, TR 7, 04:15

Can you remember how to say the following in Russian? Listen to the recording and practise saying each phrase.

**a** What do you prefer?
**b** Most of all I like football.
**c** I prefer to play the guitar.
**d** Do you like this picture?
**e** Do you like sport?

## Test yourself

We have now covered the nominative, accusative, genitive, dative and prepositional endings for singular nouns, so it's time to review their uses. Look at the following ten questions and check that you understand the answers:

**1** If you want to ask whether Boris preferred opera or ballet, which case ending will you use for *opera* and *ballet*?

**2** If you want to tell someone you work in an office, what case ending will you use for *office*?

**3** If you want to say that your house is a long way from the railway station, what case ending will you need for *railway station*?

**4** If you want to explain that the book belongs to Olga, which case will you need for *Olga*?

**5** If you want to ask whether someone is going to the hotel, which case ending will you need for *hotel*?

**6** If you want to explain that it is necessary for Vladimir to work today, which case ending would you need for *Vladimir*?

**7** These prepositions have something in common – the case with which they must be used. Can you remember which case it is for **без** (*without*), **для** (*for*), **у** (*by, near*)?

**8** If you want to say thank you for something, which case will follow **Спаси́бо за**?

**9** If you want to explain that you like playing tennis, which case ending will you need after **игра́ть в**?

**10** If you want to ask someone if they're going to Anna's this evening, which case ending will you need for *Anna*?

# 7

## На почте
## At the post office

In this unit you will learn

- *How to request information about cost, availability and necessity*
- *How to give information about cost, availability and necessity*

## Dialogue

Anna has asked Ira to go with her to the post office to help her buy envelopes, stamps and postcards.

CD 1, TR 8, 00:05

| Ира | Скажи, Анна, что тебе нужно? |
|---|---|
| Анна | Я хочу купить конверты, марки и открытки. |
| Ира | Сколько открыток хочешь? |
| Анна | Шесть красивых открыток и шесть марок. |
| Ира | Куда ты хочешь послать эти открытки? В Англию? |
| Анна | Да, в Англию. |
| Ира | Значит, шесть открыток и шесть марок по девять рублей. Сколько конвертов хочешь? |
| Анна | Пять. А где можно купить всё это? |

| | |
|---|---|
| **Йра** | Вон там … вйдишь окóшко? … «Продáжа мáрок, конвéртов, откры́ток». Идй скажй дéвушке: Дáйте, пожáлуйста, шесть мáрок, шесть откры́ток и пять конвéртов. |
| **Áнна** | Поня́тно. |
| **Йра** | А ещё что тебé нýжно, крóме откры́ток, мáрок и конвéртов? |
| **Áнна** | Мне нáдо послáть имéйл домóй. |
| **Йра** | Агá. Это конéчно мóжно в гостйнице, йли у меня́ дóма. |
| **Áнна** | А тебé чтó-нибудь нýжно? |
| **Йра** | Да, мáрки для моегó сосéда. |

| | |
|---|---|
| **что тебé нýжно?** | *what do you need?* |
| **конвéрт** | *envelope* |
| **по дéвять рублéй** | *at nine roubles* |
| **окóшко** | *counter, position* (in a post office or bank) |
| **продáжа** | *sale* |
| **идй скажй дéвушке** | *go and say to the girl* (go and tell the girl) |
| **крóме** | *apart from* |
| **послáть имéйл** | *to send an e-mail* |
| **домóй** | *home* (lit. 'to home', 'homewards') |
| **у меня́ дóма** | *at my house* (lit. 'by me at home') |
| **тебé чтó-нибудь нýжно?** | *do you need anything?* |
| **для моегó сосéда** | *for my neighbour* |

## Insight

Did you notice the word **крóме** (*apart from*) in the
Dialogue? This is another preposition which must be
followed by the genitive case. In Appendix 1 you will find
a useful list of prepositions and the cases which must
follow them.

## На по́чте *At the post office*

At the post office it is possible to buy traditional items such as stamps, postcards, envelopes and writing paper, and nowadays post offices in larger cities offer all sorts of additional services: tickets for the theatre, trains and planes can be obtained, and some post offices offer internet facilities. In major cities the number of wifi hotspots is increasing, and internet access is available either via dial-up (e.g. from hotels) or through internet cafes (**интеренéт-кафé**).

## Скажи́ де́вушке … *Tell the girl …*

Note that the word **де́вушка** (*girl*) is a very useful one! Here it is being used to denote the post office employee; as there are no Russian equivalents for *Miss, Madam,* etc. it is also the way of attracting the attention of a shop assistant, waitress or female (between the ages of about 15 and 50!) whom you don't know. **Молодо́й челове́к** (*young man*) is the masculine equivalent.

---

## Questions

### 1 *True or false?*

**a** А́нна хо́чет купи́ть то́лько откры́тки.
**b** А́нна хо́чет посла́ть откры́тки в А́нглию.
**c** На по́чте нельзя́ купи́ть конве́рты.

### 2 *Answer the questions!*

**a** Каки́е откры́тки А́нна хо́чет купи́ть?
**b** Ско́лько конве́ртов она́ хо́чет?
**c** И́ра хо́чет посла́ть име́йл домо́й?

## How do you say it?

How to:
**1** *Ask what is needed*

Что тебе́/вам ну́жно?
Тебе́/вам ну́жно что́-нибудь?

**2** *Express cost per item*

Шесть ма́рок по де́вять рубле́й.

**3** *Request instructions*

Что на́до де́лать?

**4** *Give instructions*

Иди́ скажи́/Иди́те скажи́те!

## Grammar

### 1 Что тебе́ ну́жно? *What do you need?*

Note that in this phrase the person who needs something is in the dative case and that its literal meaning is *What to you is necessary?*

### 2 Домо́й *(To) home*

The word **дом** (*house*, *home*) is unusual in that it has forms not found in other words when it means *home*, namely:

**до́ма**  *at home*  **домо́й**  *to home*

Note that **в до́ме** means *in the house* and **в дом** means *into the house*.

## 3 Numerals

In Unit 5 we met all the numerals up to 20. Compounds of numerals are formed quite simply (note that there are no hyphens).

| | | | |
|---|---|---|---|
| два́дцать | 20 | сто де́сять | 110 |
| два́дцать три | 23 | две́сти | 200 |
| три́дцать | 30 | три́ста | 300 |
| три́дцать пять | 35 | четы́реста | 400 |
| со́рок | 40 | пятьсо́т | 500 |
| пятьдеся́т | 50 | шестьсо́т | 600 |
| шестьдеся́т | 60 | семьсо́т | 700 |
| се́мьдесят | 70 | восемьсо́т | 800 |
| во́семьдесят | 80 | девятьсо́т | 900 |
| девяно́сто | 90 | ты́сяча | 1000 |
| сто | 100 | | |

### Insight

Notice that 50, 60, 70, 80 all have a soft sign in the middle, not at the end, and are easy to remember by saying the first digit and adding on 10; 40 and 90 are the most unusual, so take a really careful look at them!

In Unit 5 we saw that numerals 2, 3, 4 are always followed by the genitive singular case. Note that this also applies to compounds of 2, 3, 4:

| | |
|---|---|
| три́дцать два биле́та | 32 tickets |
| два́дцать три кни́ги | 23 books |

### Insight

Try pronouncing out loud the words for 12 and 20 syllable by syllable... they are very easy to confuse, so your ears need to get used to the sound of each one: 12 = **двена́дцать** (2 on 10); 20 = **два́дцать** (2 × 10).

Note too that when you are dealing with compounds of 1, the noun that follows stays in the nominative singular – i.e. it agrees with 1:

**три́дцать оди́н биле́т**   *31 tickets*
**два́дцать одна́ кни́га**   *21 books*

See Appendix 1 for more information about numerals.

## 4 По де́вять рубле́й *Nine roubles each*

The preposition **по**, followed by the accusative case of the number, is used to express *price per item*, e.g.:

Э́ти кни́ги по 100 рубле́й.   *These books are 100 roubles each.*

## 5 *Adjectives – genitive singular and plural*

We have seen that adjectives must agree with the nouns they describe in number (singular or plural) and gender (masculine, feminine or neuter) – they must also agree with the noun they describe in case (nominative, accusative, genitive, etc.).

### Adjectives – genitive singular

In the dialogue we saw the phrase **для моего́ сосе́да** (*for my neighbour*). The preposition **для** must be followed by the genitive case, so both the noun (**сосе́д**) and the adjective (**мой**) have been put into the genitive singular. Learning the adjective endings is not too complicated if you remember the pattern: masculine and neuter endings are the same and, as for nouns, there are always two endings to choose from.

For ordinary adjectives, i.e. those like **ста́рый** (*old*) which end in **-ый** (masculine), **-ая** (feminine) and **-ое** (neuter), the genitive singular endings are as follows:

|       | Nom.     | Remove | Add   | Gen. sing. adjective |
|-------|----------|--------|-------|----------------------|
| Masc. | ста́рый  | -ый    | -ого  | ста́рого             |
| Fem.  | ста́рая  | -ая    | -ой   | ста́рой              |
| Neut. | ста́рое  | -ое    | -ого  | ста́рого             |

(Note that the pronunciation of the ending oro is **ovo**).

An exception to this pattern occurs when you are dealing with adjectives whose stem (i.e. what's left when you've removed the last two letters) ends in: **ж, ч, ц, ш, щ**.

This is another important spelling rule: these letters can never be followed by an unstressed **o**. So, for example, in the adjective **хоро́ший**, we cannot use the endings given above for the genitive singular – the following must be used instead (note that the pronunciation of **его́** is *yivó*):

|       | Nom.     | Remove | Add   | Gen. sing. adjective |
|-------|----------|--------|-------|----------------------|
| Masc. | хоро́ший | -ий    | -его  | хоро́шего            |
| Fem.  | хоро́шая | -ая    | -ей   | хоро́шей             |
| Neut. | хоро́шее | -ее    | -его  | хоро́шего            |

Note how this spelling rule also affects the neuter form of the nominative singular – **хоро́шее**.

........................................................................

## Insight

The letters involved in this new spelling rule are not the same as for the first rule (Unit 4). In summary: it is fine to have a stressed **o** after **ж, ц, ч, ш** and **щ** (e.g. **большо́й**), but never try to put an unstressed **o** after these letters. Very occasionally you may see **o** after these letters in words of foreign origin e.g. **шоссе́**, highway; **шотлаидия**.

........................................................................

The possessive adjectives **мой, твой, наш, ваш** all take this second kind of ending:

Это пода́рок для моего́ бра́та.   *This is a present for my brother.*

**Adjectives – genitive plural**

The genitive plural of adjectives is rather more straightforward –
here, whatever the gender of the noun you are describing, there
are only two possible endings: **-ых** and **-их**; always use the first
(**-ых**) unless you are dealing with an adjective whose stem ends
in one of the letters which may never be followed by **-ы** (**г, к, х,
ж, ч, ш, щ**):

| Nom. | Remove | Add | Gen. pl. adjective |
|------|--------|-----|--------------------|
| ста́рый | -ый | -ых | ста́рых |
| ма́ленький (*small*) | -ий | -их | ма́леньких |

## 6 *Nouns – genitive plural*

In the Dialogue we met several examples of the genitive plural (e.g.
**шесть краси́вых откры́ток, ско́лько конве́ртов**). We have just
seen that the genitive plural of adjectives is quite straightforward
(either **-ых** or **-их**); the genitive plural of nouns is rather more
complicated, because here the ending depends on the gender of the
noun (and, unusually, there are more than two endings to choose
from). The table overleaf shows how to form the genitive plural
from the nominative.

Feminine nouns ending in **a** and neuter nouns ending in **o** simply
lose the last letter of the nominative; when the result is a cluster
of consonants at the end of the word this sometimes leads to the
insertion of an **o** or an **e**. Here are some common examples:

| | | |
|---|---|---|
| ма́рка | шесть ма́рок | *six stamps* |
| окно́ | шесть о́кон | *six windows* |
| де́вушка | шесть де́вушек | *six girls* (i.e. **e** after **ш**) |
| де́ньги | мно́го де́нег | *a lot of money* (i.e. **e** replaces soft sign) |

Very occasionally, a **ё** is used, and the most common example of this is in the word **сестра́** (*sister*): **пять сестёр** (*five sisters*).

Note that not all clusters need this treatment! Some common words (such as **ме́сто**, *place*) manage without it.

| | | | |
|---|---|---|---|
| **ме́сто пять мест** | *five places* | | |

| | | **Remove** | **Add** |
|---|---|---|---|
| *Masculine* | | | |
| **биле́т** | | – | **ов** |
| **мно́го биле́тов** | *a lot of tickets* | | |
| **автомоби́ль** | | **ь** | **ей** |
| **здесь нет автомоби́лей** | *there aren't any cars here* | | |
| **трамва́й** | | **й** | **ев** |
| **пять трамва́ев** | *five trams* | | |
| | | | |
| *Feminine* | | | |
| **соба́ка** | | **а** | **–** |
| **ско́лько соба́к?** | *how many dogs?* | | |
| **неде́ля** | | **я** | **ь** |
| **шесть неде́ль** | *six weeks* | | |
| **ста́нция** | | **я** | **й** |
| **семь ста́нций** | *seven stations* | | |
| **тетра́дь** | | **ь** | **ей** |
| **здесь нет тетра́дей** | *there are no exercise books here* | | |
| | | | |
| *Neuter* | | | |
| **ме́сто** | | **о** | **–** |
| **мест нет!** | *no vacancies!* | | |
| **по́ле** | | **е** | **ей** |
| **мно́го поле́й** | *many fields* | | |
| **зда́ние** | | **е** | **й** |
| **мно́го зда́ний** | *many buildings* | | |

Some nouns which have an irregular nominative plural also have an irregular genitive plural. Here are the most common (a full list of irregulars is given in Appendix 1):

| Meaning | Nom. sing. | Nom. pl. | Gen. pl. |
|---------|-----------|----------|----------|
| *child* | ребёнок | де́ти | дете́й |
| *friend* | друг | друзья́ | друзе́й |
| *person* | челове́к | лю́ди | люде́й |

## Insight

Don't worry, the other plural cases of nouns are really straightforward in comparison to the genitive plural! Try learning the following sentence to help you remember the genitive plural of adjectives and nouns:

**Вот пода́рки для мои́х ру́сских друзе́й** (*Here are the presents for my Russian friends*).

### 7 Accusative plural

Now that you have met the genitive plural, you will be able to deal with *all* nouns and adjectives in the accusative plural as well: all *inanimate* (i.e. not alive) nouns and their adjectives in the plural look exactly the same as they do in the nominative, while all *animate* plural nouns and their adjectives look exactly the same as they do in the genitive:

| | |
|---|---|
| **Я о́чень люблю́ чита́ть ру́сские газе́ты.** | *I really like reading Russian newspapers.* |
| **Я о́чень люблю смотре́ть ру́сских ьалери́н.** | *I really like watching Russian ballerinas.* |

## Insight

So, although the genitive plural of nouns is a bit complicated, at least there is more than one use for the endings! Notice in particular that in the plural you need to use the animate accusative for all animate objects (i.e. not just for masculine, as in the singular).

## Practice

### 7.1 Read and answer!

You're on a shopping trip, but aren't having much luck. Every item you ask for has been sold out! (Remember that *not any* is **нет** + genitive).

**a** интере́сные откры́тки
  – У вас есть интере́сные откры́тки?
  – Извини́те, сего́дня у нас нет интере́сных откры́ток.

Now make up similar sentences for the items below:

**b** театра́льные биле́ты
**c** интере́сные кни́ги
**d** ру́сские газе́ты
**e** свобо́дные (*free, vacant*) места́
**f** англи́йские журна́лы

### 7.2 Read, answer and listen!

You are in a post office. Complete your part of the conversation, then listen to the complete conversation on the recording.

CD 1, TR 8, 01:48

| Вы | **a** Say 'excuse me, please'. |
|---|---|
| Де́вушка | Да? |
| Вы | **b** Ask how much it costs to send a postcard to England. |
| Де́вушка | 15 рубле́й. |
| Вы | **c** Ask for five stamps at 15 roubles. |
| Де́вушка | Вот, пожа́луйста. Э́то всё? |
| Вы | **d** Say 'yes, thank you, that is all'. |
| Де́вушка | Пожа́луйста. До свида́ния. |

### 7.3 Look and answer!

Look at the advertisement for a fax machine. What does the advertisement say the fax machine is for?

ФАКСЫ ДЛЯ
ПРОФЕССИОНАЛЬНОГО
БИЗНЕСА

### 7.4 Read and write!

The following people want to send postcards. What kind of stamps do they need to buy? Look at the example, then write similar sentences for the others:

| | Кто | Куда? | Сколько открыток? | Какие марки? |
|---|---|---|---|---|
| **a** | Джейн | Áнглия | 5 | 15р |
| **b** | Пáтрик | Амéрика | 6 | 16р |
| **c** | Ты | Йндия | 3 | 16р 50к |
| **d** | Мы | Фрáнция | 7 | 15р |
| **e** | Саша | Петербýрг | 2 | 12р |
| **f** | Я | Канáда | 10 | 16р 50к |

**a** Джейн хóчет послáть пять открыток в Áнглию. Знáчит ей нáдо купúть пять мáрок по пятнáдцать рублéй.

### 7.5 Read and answer!

Who likes doing what? Match the following information and statements.

1  Ли́дия о́чень лю́бит кни́ги.
2  Бори́с о́чень лю́бит во́дку.
3  Ле́на не лю́бит рабо́тать.

4  Вади́м о́чень лю́бит фи́льмы.

5  А́лла о́чень лю́бит спорт.

a  Зна́чит, он лю́бит пить.
b  Зна́чит, она́ лю́бит отдыха́ть.
c  Зна́чит, она́ лю́бит чита́ть (to read).
d  Зна́чит, она́ лю́бит игра́ть в те́ннис.
e  Зна́чит, он лю́бит смотре́ть телеви́зор.

### 7.6 Read and answer!

Complete the questions below using the appropriate question word:

a  _____вас зову́т?
b  _____биле́тов вы хоти́те?
c  _____вы идёте?

d  Вы не зна́ете, _____метро́?
e  _____ва́ша фами́лия?
f  _____фи́льмы ты лю́бишь смотре́ть?

## Comprehension

### 1 Conversation

**Read, listen and answer!**

On her way to the post office, Natasha meets her friend Olya.

| О́ля | Ната́ша, приве́т! Как дела́? |
|------|------------------------------|
| Ната́ша | Непло́хо. А ты куда́ идёшь, О́ля? |
| О́ля | Я иду́ на по́чту. |
| Ната́ша | И я то́же! Что тебе́ там ну́жно? |

| Оля | Мне? То́лько конве́рты. А тебе́ что ну́жно? |
|---|---|
| Ната́ша | Мне на́до посла́ть э́тот пода́рок бра́ту на его́ день рожде́ния. |
| Оля | А где живёт твой брат? |
| Ната́ша | В Ку́рске. Зна́чит, мне на́до посла́ть ему́ пода́рок по по́чте. |
| Оля | Поня́тно. Но кака́я больша́я посы́лка! |
| Ната́ша | Да, пра́вда, больша́я. |
| Оля | Интере́сно, како́й э́то пода́рок? |
| Ната́ша | Сви́тер. |
| Оля | Кака́я ты хоро́шая сестра́, Ната́ша! |
| Ната́ша | (*Laughs.*) Да, пра́вда, хоро́шая! |

| приве́т | *hello* (informal) |
|---|---|
| непло́хо | *not bad* |
| пода́рок | *present* |
| день рожде́ния | *birthday* |
| по по́чте | *by post* |
| посы́лка | *parcel* |
| сви́тер | *sweater* |
| сестра́ | *sister* |

**1** Оля идёт

   **a** на вокза́л
   **b** в шко́лу
   **c** на по́чту
   **d** на стадио́н

**2** Оля хо́чет купи́ть

   **a** конве́рты и ма́рки
   **b** то́лько откры́тки
   **c** то́лько конве́рты
   **d** откры́тки и ма́рки

**3** Ната́ша хо́чет посла́ть

   **a** име́йл домо́й
   **b** пода́рок бра́ту
   **c** откры́тку сестре́
   **d** письмо́ бра́ту

## 2 Reading

Read the text and answer the questions in English.

**a** What is Novgorod's nickname, according to the old Russian proverb?
**b** From which century does the city date?
**c** On which main road is it situated?
**d** Why do tourists particularly like this city?
**e** What is an icon?
**f** What sort of work is being carried out by the restorers in the 14th-century church?
**g** How long have they already been at work?

Вот одна́ ста́рая ру́сская посло́вица: «Ки́ев – мать ру́сских городо́в, Москва́ – се́рдце, Но́вгород – оте́ц». А почему́ ру́сские говоря́т, что Но́вгород «оте́ц ру́сских городо́в»? – Потому́, что э́то ста́рый го́род IX ве́ка. Но́вгород нахо́дится на реке́ Во́лхов, на автомагистра́ли Москва́ – Санкт-Петербу́рг. Сего́дня э́то кру́пный промы́шленный го́род и изве́стный туристи́ческий центр. Тури́сты лю́бят э́тот го́род, потому́ что там о́чень мно́го краси́вых и ста́рых церкве́й, а та́кже мно́го интере́сных па́мятников. В Но́вгороде есть о́чень изве́стный музе́й. Музе́й изве́стный потому́, что там есть о́чень мно́го ста́рых и интере́сных ру́сских ико́н из новгоро́дских церкве́й. Что тако́е ико́на? Ико́на – э́то религио́зная карти́на, портре́т свято́го и́ли святы́х; э́то па́мятник ру́сской культу́ры и ру́сской исто́рии. Но есть ико́ны не то́лько в музе́е. Есть одна́ це́рковь XIV ве́ка в Но́вгороде, где реставра́торы рабо́тают уже́ мно́го лет. Там не то́лько краси́вые ико́ны, но и краси́вые фре́ски. Кака́я рабо́та у э́тих худо́жников-реставра́торов? Им на́до реставри́ровать фре́ски XIV ве́ка.

| QUICK VOCAB | | |
|---|---|---|
| автомагистра́ль (f.) | | *highway* |
| кру́пный | | *major, large* |
| оте́ц | | *father* |
| посло́вица | | *proverb* |

114

| реставри́ровать | *to restore* |
| свято́й | *a saint* |
| се́рдце | *heart* |
| фре́ска | *fresco* |

## Key phrases

🔊 **CD1, TR 8, 03:30**

Can you remember how to say the following in Russian? Listen to the recording and practise saying each phrase.

  **a** What do you need?
  **b** At my house.
  **c** Do you need anything?
  **d** I need to send an e-mail.
  **e** Is that all?

## Ten things to remember

**1** **На по́чте**: remember that **по́чта** is one of the words you must use with **на**, never with **в** (see Unit 5).

**2** If someone tells you the price per item, you will hear the word **по** and then the price: Э́ти откры́тки по **20рубле́й** (*These postcards are 20 roubles each*).

**3** **Электро́нная по́чта** (*electronic post*) is usually referred to as **име́йл** (*e-mail*).

**4** **Дом** (*house, home*) has two special forms: **до́ма** (*at home*) and **домо́й** (*homewards, 'to home'*). Try learning these phrases to help you remember which is which: **Я сижу́ до́ма** (*I am staying [literally 'sitting'] at home*) and **Я иду́ домо́й** (*I am going home*).

**5** In the Reading passage the words for *why?* (**почему?**) and *because* (**потому́ что**) were used: they both start with **п**, so try to remember which is which by noticing that *because* is a longer word than *why* and similarly **потому́ что** is longer than **почему́**.

**6** The question **Ско́лько сто́ит?** can be used with a noun: **Ско́лько сто́ит откры́тка?** (*How much does the postcard cost?*), or a verb in the infinitive: **Ско́лько сто́ит посла́ть откры́тку в А́нглию?** (*How much does it cost to send a postcard to England?*)

**7** For nouns in the plural, all animate nouns (masculine, feminine and neuter) and their adjectives must be put into the animate accusative if they are the object of the sentence. The plural animate accusative case is exactly the same as the genitive plural: **Я зна́ю но́вых ма́льчиков и де́вушек** (*I know the new boys and girls*).

**8** The endings for genitive plural adjectives are really straightforward: just **-ых** or **-их** for all genders.

**9** The endings for genitive plural nouns are a bit tricky, because they are different for different genders, and there are some irregulars. Try to learn the most common irregulars with this short advert for a gift shop: **Пода́рки для друзе́й, для дете́й, для дороги́х люде́й!** (*Presents for friends, for children, for special [literally 'dear'] people!*)

**10** The second spelling rule: never try to put an unstressed **о** after **ж, ц, ч, ш, щ**!

# 8

**Это место свободно?**
Is this place free?

In this unit you will learn
- *How to obtain information about availability, variety and cost*
- *How to place an order*
- *How to indicate that a mistake has been made*
- *How to apologize for a mistake*

## Dialogue

Anna and Sasha decide to have a meal together in a restaurant.

| | | |
|---|---|---|
| **Áнна** | Ой, как жаль. Ресторáн, кáжется, закрыт. | ◈ CD 1, TR 9, 00:08 |
| **Сáша** | Нет, нет, Áнна, что ты! Дверь закрыта, а ресторáн, по-мóему, открыт. (*Go into restaurant.*) | |
| **Áнна** | Здесь мнóго нарóду! Кáжется, свобóдных мест нет. | |
| **Сáша** | Какáя ты сегóдня пессимúстка! У вхóда все местá зáняты, а по-мóему вон там ... в углý есть свобóдные местá ... (*Approaches table where one young man is seated.*) ... Извинúте, пожáлуйста, здесь свобóдно? | |
| **Молодóй человéк** | Да, свобóдно. Пожáлуйста, садúтесь. | |

| | |
|---|---|
| **Са́ша** | Спаси́бо. А где меню́? |
| **А́нна** | Вот оно́ … (*Waitress approaches.*) А вот официа́нтка, мы мо́жем заказа́ть. |
| **Официа́нтка** | Слу́шаю вас. |
| **Са́ша** | Скажи́те, пожа́луйста, каки́е у вас заку́ски сего́дня? |
| **Официа́нтка** | У нас сего́дня огурцы́ со смета́ной, э́то о́чень вку́сно … и грибы́ есть … А суп хоти́те? |
| **Са́ша** | Спаси́бо, нет. Мы не о́чень го́лодны. А что есть на второ́е? Шашлы́к есть? Я о́чень люблю́ шашлы́к! |
| **Официа́нтка** | К сожале́нию, сего́дня у нас нет шашлыка́. У нас сего́дня то́лько котле́ты с ри́сом. |
| **Са́ша** | А ско́лько сто́ят котле́ты с ри́сом? |
| **Официа́нтка** | 55 рубле́й. |
| **Са́ша** | Хорошо́. Да́йте нам, пожа́луйста, огурцы́ со смета́ной, котле́ты с ри́сом, а на сла́дкое … моро́женое … да, А́нна? |
| **А́нна** | Да … и чай с лимо́ном, пожа́луйста. |
| **Официа́нтка** | Так … вам огурцы́ – две по́рции, котле́ты … то́же две по́рции, моро́женое и чай с са́харом, да? |
| **А́нна** | Нет, э́то непра́вильно … мне чай с лимо́ном, пожалу́йста, не с са́харом. |
| **Официа́нтка** | Ах, да! Извини́те за оши́бку! Прия́тного аппети́та! |

118

| | |
|---|---|
| **сади́тесь, пожа́луйста** | sit down, please, do sit down |
| **меню́** | menu |
| **официа́нтка** | waitress |
| **заказа́ть** | to order |
| **заку́ски** | starters |
| **огурцы́ со смета́ной** | cucumbers in sour cream |
| **вку́сно** | delicious, tasty, nice |
| **Гриб** | mushroom |
| **мы не о́чень го́лодны** | we're not very hungry |
| **на второ́е** | for the second course |
| **шашлы́к** | kebab |
| **котле́ты с ри́сом** | rissoles with rice |
| **на сла́дкое** | for dessert |
| **моро́женое** | ice cream |
| **по́рция** | portion |
| **чай с лимо́ном** | tea with lemon |
| **чай с са́харом** | tea with sugar |
| **непра́вильно** | not right, not correct |
| **извини́те за оши́бку** | sorry about the mistake/excuse the mistake |
| **прия́тного аппети́та** | 'bon appétit', enjoy your meal |

### Рестора́н Restaurant

At busy times you may have to stand in a queue (**о́чередь**) for a table and you will want to attract the attention of the **официа́нт** (*waiter* – use «**молодо́й челове́к!**») or **официа́нтка** (*waitress* – use «**де́вушка!**»). When the waiter/waitress comes to take your order he/she will usually say **слу́шаю вас** (lit. *I'm listening to you*), and when they have taken your order they will often say **сейча́с** (*now, immediately* – not a comment always to be taken literally!).

The menu is usually divided into various sections:

| | |
|---|---|
| **заку́ски** | starters |
| **пе́рвое (блю́до)** | first course [soup] |
| **второ́е (блю́до)** | second course |
| **сла́дкое** | dessert |
| **напи́тки** | drinks |

Although many items may be listed in a menu, usually only those with a price written next to them are actually available. Bread (**хлеб**) is usually on the table as a matter of course. At the end of the meal you will need to ask for the bill (**счёт**).

## Questions

**1** *True or false?*

**a** Рестора́н откры́т.
**b** Есть свобо́дные места́ у вхо́да.
**c** Са́ша хо́чет суп.
**d** Са́ша лю́бит шашлы́к.
**e** А́нна хо́чет чай с лимо́ном.

**2** *Answer the questions!*

**a** Где свобо́дные места́?
**b** Кто (*who*) уже́ сиди́т за столо́м (*at the table*) в углу́?
**c** А́нна и Са́ша голодны́ сего́дня?
**d** Что они́ хотя́т на сла́дкое?
**e** Что А́нна хо́чет пить?

## How do you say it?

How to:
**1** *Enquire about availability*

У вас есть шашлы́к?

**2** *Enquire about variety*

Каки́е заку́ски у вас есть?

**3** *Place an order*

Мо́жно заказа́ть?
Да́йте нам, пожа́луйста, моро́женое.

**4** *Ask about cost*

Ско́лько сто́ит?
Ско́лько с меня́?
Да́йте, пожа́луйста, счёт.

**5** *Indicate that a mistake has been made*

Э́то непра́вильно.

**6** *Apologize for a mistake*

Извини́те за оши́бку.

---

## Grammar

### 1 *Reflexive verbs*

We have already come across the reflexive verb **находи́ться** (*to be situated*) – literally, this verb means *to find itself*; a reflexive verb in Russian corresponds to the sort of verb which in English is followed by *self* or where *self* can be understood: for example, *to get washed* (*to wash oneself*), *to dress* (*to dress oneself*). The ending -**ся** on the infinitive (the *to do* part of the verb) is what identifies a reflexive verb and the only possible reflexive endings are -**ся** (after a consonant) and -**сь** (after a vowel). So, this is what happens to the present tense of **сади́ться** – a second conjugation verb meaning *to sit [oneself] down*:

| | |
|---|---|
| я сажу́сь | мы сади́мся |
| ты сади́шься | вы сади́тесь |
| он сади́тся | они́ садя́тся |

## Insight

So, there are three things to remember about reflexive verbs:

**1** the infinitive of a reflexive verb will end in **-ся**
**2** the **я** and **вы** forms will end in **-сь**
**3** all the other forms (**ты, он, она́, мы, они́**) will end in **-ся**.

### 2 *Short adjectives*

In Unit 4 we learnt how to form adjectives in Russian: e.g.
**свобо́дное вре́мя** (*spare/free time*) – these are called long
adjectives. In this unit we have seen a rather different
ending. This is a short adjective.

**Э́то ме́сто свобо́дно?**  *Is this seat free?*

Here is a typical set of short endings:

**но́вый**: Masculine: **нов**     Neuter: **но́во**
Feminine: **нова́**     Plural: **но́вы**

The short form exists only in the nominative (when you are
talking about the *subject* of a sentence) and is usually found
when the adjective comes last in a phrase or sentence – i.e.
when you're saying *My book is new* (rather than *This is a new
book*): **Моя́ кни́га нова́**. Not all Russian adjectives have a short
form, for example adjectives of colour (e.g. **кра́сный**, *red*) and
nationality (e.g. **ру́сский**, *Russian*) have no short form. In modern
conversational Russian, the long form is almost always used and
the short form hardly at all. However, there are some occasions
when you *should* use the short form when you are using the
adjective at the end of a phrase; the most common are as follows
(note that **рад**, *glad*, *happy* is the only common Russian adjective
which does not have a long form):

| Long form | Short form | | | |
|---|---|---|---|---|
| | **Masculine** | **Feminine** | **Neuter** | **Plural** |
| закры́тый (closed) | закры́т | закры́та | закры́то | закры́ты |
| за́нятый (occupied) | за́нят | занята́ | за́нято | за́няты |
| откры́тый (open) | откры́т | откры́та | откры́то | откры́ты |
| (happy/glad) | рад | ра́да | | ра́ды |
| вку́сный (delicious) | вку́сен | вкусна́ | вку́сно | вку́сны |
| дово́льный (content) | дово́лен | дово́льна | дово́льно | дово́льны |
| свобо́дный (free, vacant) | свобо́ден | свобо́дна | свобо́дно | свобо́дны |
| согла́сный (in agreement) | согла́сен | согла́сна | согла́сно | согла́сны |

Note what has happened in the masculine form of the last four examples: when the stem of a masculine adjective ends in two consonants (e.g. **вку́сный**, stem **вкусн-**) an **e** is inserted: – Э́тот суп о́чень вку́сен! (*This soup is very tasty!*).

Note that the short form neuter adjective is also the adverb (i.e. a word which describes a verb – e.g. **бы́стрый** means *quick*, **бы́стро** means *quickly*).

....................................................................................
## Insight

The endings of short form adjectives never change, but you can only use them when you are making a statement with the following structure: X (a noun) is B (an adjective): – *the restaurant is closed* (**рестора́н закры́т**); *this seat is occupied* (**э́то ме́сто за́нято**); *the door is open* (**дверь откры́та**).
....................................................................................

## 3 Instrumental case

The instrumental case is used to describe the instrument by which an action is performed – so, for example, if you want to say *I eat ice cream with/by means of a spoon*, the word *spoon* must be put into the instrumental case. The instrumental case is also used to describe one's job – if you want to say *I work as a waiter*, the word *waiter* must be put into the instrumental case. The instrumental case is also used after certain prepositions, the most common of which is **c**, which means *with/accompanied by*. Note also **пе́ред** (*in front of*), **за** (*behind*), **ме́жду** (*between*), **над** (*over*) and **под** (*under*), **ря́дом с** (*next to*).

........................................................

### Insight

Notice that **c** + instrumental means *accompanied by*, whereas the instrumental without **c** means *by means of*. In the sentence *I am going to London by train with my sister*, you are going by means of the train (instrumental), in the company of your sister (**c** + instrumental): **Я е́ду в Ло́ндон по́ездом с сестро́й**. (See unit 9 for the verb **е́хать**, to go, travel.)

........................................................

### a Singular nouns

The endings are formed in the following way from the nominative:

|  | | Remove | Add |
|---|---|---|---|
| *Masculine* | | | |
| официа́нт | | – | ом |
| Я рабо́таю официа́нтом | *I work as a waiter* | | |
| учи́тель | | ь | ем |
| Он рабо́тает учи́телем | *He works as a teacher* | | |
| Алексе́й | | й | ем |
| Я иду́ на о́перу с Алексе́ем | *I'm going to the opera with Aleksei* | | |

*Feminine*

| | | | а | ой |
|---|---|---|---|---|
| ло́жка | | | | |

Я ем моро́женое ло́жкой — *I eat ice cream with a spoon*

| | | | я | ей |
|---|---|---|---|---|
| То́ня | | | | |

Я иду́ на бале́т с То́ней — *I'm going to the ballet with Tonya*

| | | | я | ей |
|---|---|---|---|---|
| ста́нция | | | | |

Кино́ нахо́дится за ста́нцией — *The cinema is behind the station*

| | | | ь | ью |
|---|---|---|---|---|
| дверь | | | | |

Стул за две́рью — *The chair is behind the door*

*Neuter*

| | | | о | ом |
|---|---|---|---|---|
| окно́ | | | | |

Стол пе́ред окно́м — *The table is in front of the window*

| | | | е | ем |
|---|---|---|---|---|
| по́ле | | | | |

Дом нахо́дится ря́дом с по́лем — *The house is next to the field*

| | | | е | ем |
|---|---|---|---|---|
| зда́ние | | | | |

Кио́ск за зда́нием — *The kiosk is behind the building*

---

| | |
|---|---|
| **есть (ем, ешь, ест, еди́м, еди́те, едя́т)** | *to eat* |
| **ло́жка** | *spoon* |

---

Remember the spelling rule we met in Unit 7 – you can never write an unstressed **о** after **ж, ц, ч, ш, щ**: so, if you are trying to make the instrumental of a masculine noun ending in one of these letters, or a feminine or neuter noun which ends in one of these letters when you have removed the final **a** or **o**, don't add unstressed ом or ой, add ем or ей:

муж (*husband*)
> я иду́ в кино́ с му́жем (*I'm going to the cinema with my husband*)

у́лица (*street*)
> ря́дом с у́лицей (*next to the street*)

## Insight

The instrumental is the sixth Russian case you have met… and it is the last one! Take note of the pattern for singular nouns: masculine and neuter will end in **-ом** or **-ем** and feminine in **-ой, -ей** or **-ью**.

### b Plural nouns

The instrumental plural of nouns is very straightforward: irrespective of gender, the endings are either **-ами** (for nouns ending in a consonant, **-a** or **-o**), and **-ями** for all others:

гриб (*mushroom*)
> суп с гриба́ми (*mushroom soup*)

гость (*guest*)
> официа́нт стои́т пе́ред гостя́ми
> (*the waiter is standing in front of the guests*)

Note that nouns with irregular nominative plurals form their instrumental plural from the nominative plural, e.g.:

Nom. singular: **друг** (*friend*), nom. plural: **друзья́**, instr. plural: **друзья́ми**.

Note also the highly irregular **лю́ди** (*people*) – **с людьми́** (*with people*); **де́ти** – **с детьми́** (*with children*).

**Insight**

> The pattern for instrumental plural nouns is very
> straightforward: **-ами** or **-ями**. It is a very good idea to
> learn some phrases to help you remember the instrumental
> plural of irregular nouns, e.g. **Я иду́ в кино́ с друзья́ми**
> (*I'm going to the cinema with friends*).

## c Adjectives

The instrumental singular and plural of adjectives are also very
straightforward.

In the singular masculine and neuter adjectives add -ым, unless the
stem ends in г, к, х, ж, ч, ш, щ, in which case add -им. Feminine
adjectives add -ой, unless the rule about the unstressed **o** applies,
in which case add -ей (so their endings are exactly the same as the
feminine noun endings!), e.g.:

**вку́сный со́ус**　　　　　**мя́со со\* вку́сным со́усом**
(*delicious sauce*)　　　　　(*meat with delicious sauce*)

**жа́реная карто́шка** (*fried potato(es), chips*)
**ры́ба с жа́реной карто́шкой** (*fish and chips*)

In the plural, irrespective of gender, add -ыми, unless the stem ends
in г, к, х, ж, ч, ш, щ, in which case add -ими, e.g.:

**но́вые студе́нты** (*new students*)
**Я иду́ на о́перу с но́выми студе́нтами** (*I'm going to the
opera with the new students*)

**ру́сские студе́нты** (*Russian students*)
**Я иду́ на о́перу с ру́сскими студе́нтами** (*I'm going to the
opera with the Russian students*)

\*Note that **co**, not **c**, often needs to be used before words
starting with two consonants to ease pronunciation; compare
**во** in **во Фра́нции** (*in France*).

The first spelling rule is important when you're forming the instrumental plural of adjectives (**ы** cannot follow **г, к, х, ж, ч, ш, щ**). The second spelling rule is important when you're forming the instrumental singular of nouns and adjectives (an unstressed **о** cannot follow **ж, ц, ч, ш, щ**).

Note the instrumental case of the personal pronouns:

| | | | |
|---|---|---|---|
| я | **мной** | мы | **на́ми** |
| ты | **тобо́й** | вы | **ва́ми** |
| он, оно́ | **им** | они́ | **и́ми** |
| она́ | **ей** | | |

### 4 Кто? *who?* and что? *what?*

These two very useful words decline (i.e. have different case endings) as follows:

| | | |
|---|---|---|
| Nom. | Кто э́то? (*Who is it?*) | Что э́то? (*What is it?*) |
| Acc. | Кого́ вы зна́ете? (*Whom do you know?*) | Что вы зна́ете? (*What do you know?*) |
| Gen. | Для кого́? (*For whom?*) | Для чего́? (*For what?*) |
| Dat. | Кому́ нра́вится кни́га? (*Who likes the book?*) | Чему́ э́то помога́ет? (*What does this help?*) |
| Instr. | С кем он идёт туда́? (*Whom is he going there with?*) | С чем чай хо́чешь? С лимо́ном? (*What do you want your tea with? With lemon?*) |
| Prep. | О ком он говори́т? (*Whom is he talking about?*) | О чём он говори́т? (*What is he talking about?*) |

## Insight

This set of questions from a wary receptionist might help you remember some of the cases of **кто** and **что**:

**Вы кто?** *Who are you?*
**Кого́ вы хоти́те ви́деть?** *Whom do you want to see?*
**О чём вы хоти́те говори́ть?** What do you want to talk about?

---

## Practice

### 8.1 *Read, answer and listen!*

You are in a restaurant, ordering a meal. Complete your part of the dialogue with the waiter by choosing items from the menu on the right. You can listen to the complete conversation on the recording.

| | | |
|---|---|---|
| **Официа́нт** | Слу́шаю вас. | |
| **Вы** | **(a)** Order a starter. | |
| **Официа́нт** | Вы хоти́те суп? | |
| **Вы** | **(b)** Say 'no thanks', you're not very hungry. | |
| **Официа́нт** | Что вы хоти́те на второ́е? | |
| **Вы** | **(c)** Ask how much the beef stroganoff costs. | |
| **Официа́нт** | 68 рубле́й. | |
| **Вы** | **(d)** Order the beef stroganoff. | |
| **Официа́нт** | А что вы хоти́те на сла́дкое? | |
| **Вы** | **(e)** Order ice cream. | |
| **Официа́нт** | Что вы хоти́те пить? | |
| **Вы** | **(f)** Order fruit juice and tea with lemon. | |
| **Официа́нт** | Сейча́с. | |

CD 1, TR 9, 02:32

# МЕНЮ

### *Закуски*
огурцы со сметаной ✪ салат с помидорами

### *Первое*
суп с грибами ✪ щи

### *Второе*
котлеты с рисом ✪ бефстроганов

### *Сладкое*
мороженое ✪ фрукты

### *Напитки*
сок ✪ вино ✪ чай ✪ кофе

QUICK VOCAB

| сала́т | salad |
| щи | cabbage soup |
| бефстро́ганов | beef stroganoff |
| суп с гриба́ми | mushroom soup |

### 8.2 Read, look and answer!

Look at the table below showing Sasha's preferences and explain what he prefers. The first one is done for you as an example; make up similar dialogues about each of the others:

| | | | | | | |
|---|---|---|---|---|---|---|
| **a** | чай | + молоко́ | ✓ | + | лимо́н | ✗ |
| **b** | суп | + помидо́ры | ✗ | + | грибы́ | ✓ |
| **c** | котле́ты | + рис | ✓ | + | картошка | ✗ |
| **d** | ры́ба | + гарни́р | ✗ | + | жа́реная карто́шка | ✓ |
| **e** | бифштекс | + рис | ✗ | + | гарнир | ✓ |

**A** Са́ша предпочита́ет чай с молоко́м или с лимоно́м?
**B** Он предпочита́ет чай с молоко́м.

QV

| ры́ба | fish |
| гарни́р | garnish; vegetables |

| жа́реная карто́шка | chips |
| бифште́кс | steak(burger) |
| карто́шка | potato(es) |

### 8.3 Read and answer!

Match the questions with the answers:

**1** А́нна хо́чет чай с молоко́м?

**2** Здесь свобо́дно?

**3** Да́йте, пожа́луйста, счёт.

**4** Са́ша лю́бит ры́бу?

**5** Ско́лько сто́ит сала́т с помидо́рами?

**6** Что вы хоти́те пить?

**a** Да, сади́тесь, пожа́луйста.

**b** Нет, он предпочита́ет мя́со (*meat*).

**c** Нет, с лимо́ном.

**d** Да́йте, пожа́луйста, буты́лку (*bottle*) вина́.

**e** Пожа́луйста, вот он.

**f** 20 рубле́й.

### 8.4 Read and answer!

Complete the following sentences by choosing the appropriate words from the list below. (**NB** Choose carefully – you don't need all of them).

вку́сно, вку́сны, дово́льна, дово́льны, закры́т, за́нят, за́няты, откры́т, рад, ра́ды, свобо́дно, согла́сен, согла́сна

**a** Ой, как жаль, рестора́н уже́ _____.

**b** Скажи́те, пожа́луйста, э́то ме́сто _____?

**c** Са́ша о́чень _____, потому́ что сего́дня есть огурцы́ со смета́ной!

**d** А́нна ду́мает, что все места́ в рестора́не уже́ _____.

**e** Да, спаси́бо, мы о́чень _____. Котле́ты о́чень _____.

**f** Я ду́маю, что на́до заказа́ть вино́. Ты _____, А́нна?

## 8.5 Read, look and answer!

**Вы́берите блю́да для Га́ли!** *Choose a menu for Galya!*

Га́ля не о́чень лю́бит мя́со, но она́ о́чень лю́бит о́вощи и фру́кты.
Она́ не о́чень лю́бит пить вино́, но она́ о́чень лю́бит сок и чай
с лимо́ном. Вот меню́ в рестора́не «Кали́нка».

---

**о́вощи**   *vegetables*

---

**Заку́ски**
сала́т с помидо́рами
сала́т мясно́й

**Пе́рвое**
суп с гриба́ми
суп с мя́сом

**Второ́е**
омле́т с сы́ром
котле́ты с ри́сом
шашлы́к

**Сла́дкое**
моро́женое
фру́кты

**Напи́тки:** Вино́, шампа́нское, сок, минера́льная вода́, чай,
ко́фе

---

**a** Каки́е заку́ски?
**b** Что на пе́рвое?
**c** Что на второ́е?
**d** Что на сла́дкое?
**e** Каки́е напи́тки?

---

## Comprehension

### 1 Conversation

**Read, listen and answer!**

Vadim sits down at a table in a snack bar and Viktor prepares to
go to the counter to get something to eat and drink.

| **Ви́ктор** | Сади́сь, Вади́м! Там у вхо́да есть свобо́дные места́. |
| **Вади́м** | Ла́дно. |
| **Ви́ктор** | Что ты хо́чешь пить, Вади́м? |
| **Вади́м** | А что здесь есть? |
| **Ви́ктор** | Ну, есть чай, ко́фе, минера́льная вода́… и сок. |
| **Вади́м** | А пи́ва здесь нет? |
| **Ви́ктор** | Ну что ты, Вади́м! Коне́чно нет. |
| **Вади́м** | Тогда́ мне ко́фе, пожа́луйста. |
| **Ви́ктор** | А что ты хо́чешь есть? |
| **Вади́м** | Каки́е у них бутербро́ды? |
| **Ви́ктор** | С ветчино́й и с сы́ром. |
| **Вади́м** | Оди́н бутербро́д с сы́ром, пожа́луйста. |
| **Ви́ктор** | Э́то всё? |
| **Вади́м** | Да … а шокола́д и́ли фру́кты есть? |
| **Ви́ктор** | Шокола́да, ка́жется, нет, … а апельси́ны есть. |
| **Вади́м** | Тогда́ мне, пожа́луйста, ко́фе, бутербро́д с сы́ром и апельси́н. |
| **Ви́ктор** | Всё поня́тно. Мину́точку … *(Viktor returns with the tray of sandwiches, coffee, etc.)* |
| **Вади́м** | Ну что ты, Ви́ктор! … Ведь э́то бутербро́д с ветчино́й! |
| **Ви́ктор** | Извини́ за оши́бку, Вади́м! |

| | |
|---|---|
| **пи́во** | *beer* |
| **тогда́** | *then, in that case* |
| **бутербро́д** | *sandwich* |
| **ветчина́** | *ham* |
| **апельси́н** | *orange* |
| **мину́точку** | *just a moment* |
| **ведь** | *you know/realize* |

**QUICK VOCAB**

**1** Есть свобо́дные места́

   **a** у вхо́да
   **b** в углу́
   **c** на у́лице
   **d** в теа́тре

**2** Вади́м хо́чет пить

   **a** вино́
   **b** во́дку
   **c** сок
   **d** пи́во

**3** Вади́м хо́чет бутербро́д

   **a** с помидо́рами
   **b** с ветчино́й
   **c** с сы́ром
   **d** с икро́й (*caviare*)

**4** Вади́м хо́чет есть

   **a** моро́женое
   **b** котле́ты с ри́сом
   **c** щи
   **d** апельси́н

## 2 Reading

**Read the text and answer the questions in English.**

   **a** What different kinds of soup feature prominently in Russian cooking?
   **b** What is the main ingredient of **щи**?
   **c** What are the popular ways of serving mushrooms?
   **d** What particular kind of pie is recommended here?
   **e** What ingredients are needed for the pastry?

Ру́сская ку́хня – всеми́рно изве́стная. Наприме́р, есть таки́е изве́стные национа́льные блю́да, как щи, блины́, пироги́. Ка́ша, грибы́ и супы́ то́же занима́ют большо́е ме́сто в ру́сском национа́льном меню́. В ру́сской национа́льной ку́хне есть мно́го супо́в: наприме́р есть и холо́дные и горя́чие супы́, ры́бные супы́, супы́ с мя́сом и с овоща́ми. Щи – горя́чий суп; основно́й компоне́нт – капу́ста. Ру́сские о́чень лю́бят грибы́, осо́бенно грибы́ со смета́ной и с чесноко́м. Пироги́ то́же о́чень популя́рны. Пиро́г и пирожки́ с ры́бой о́чень вку́сны; основны́е компоне́нты – ры́ба (наприме́р, филе́ ка́мбалы) и те́сто (основны́е компоне́нты – мука́, ма́сло, яйцо́, соль).

| | |
|---|---|
| блины́ | *pancakes* |
| всеми́рно изве́стный | *world famous* |
| горя́чий | *hot (to touch, taste)* |
| занима́ть | *to occupy* |
| капу́ста | *cabbage* |
| ка́ша | *porridge; buckwheat* |
| компоне́нт | *component* |
| ку́хня | *cuisine; kitchen* |
| мука́ | *flour* |
| о́вощи | *vegetables* |
| основно́й | *basic* |
| осо́бенно | *especially* |
| пиро́г | *pie* |
| пирожки́ | *pasties, small pies* |
| соль (f.) | *salt* |
| те́сто | *pastry, dough* |
| филе́ ка́мбалы | *fillet of plaice* |
| холо́дный | *cold* |
| чесно́к | *garlic* |
| яйцо́ | *egg* |

## Key phrases

🔊 **CD 1, TR 9, 04:45**

Can you remember how to say the following in Russian? Listen to the recording and practise saying each phrase.

  **a** Is this place/seat free?
  **b** Could I have the bill, please? (lit. *Give, please, bill*)
  **c** Could I order, please? (lit. *Is it possible to order?*)
  **d** What would you like to drink? (lit. *What do you want to drink?*)
  **e** Sorry about the mistake.

## Test yourself

**1** If you want to apologize for something you use **извините за** and the accusative case. How would you apologize for a problem? (*problem* = **проблéма**).

**2** Saying *thank you* for something also uses **за** and the accusative case. How would you thank someone for lunch (*lunch* = **обéд**)?

**3** At what stage of a meal would you say to the waiter/waitress: **Дáйте, пожáлуйста, счёт**?

**4** At what stage of a meal would you be eating **закýски**?

**5** Which preposition do you need to use with the instrumental case if you want to order a cheese sandwich, or mushroom soup (or anything which is a filling or main ingredient?)

**6** What case will the waiter need to use for *fish* if he wants to explain that there isn't any today?

**7** Your friend is a vegetarian – will she prefer **мясó** or **óвощи**?

**8** How would you ask the waiter what sort of sandwiches are available?

**9** Oh, dear! The restaurant is closed. What sign are you likely to see on the door?

**10** You want to say *I prefer the new restaurant*. Can you use a short adjective?

# 9

## Во сколько отходит поезд?
When does the train leave?

In this unit you will learn
- *How to ask and tell the time*
- *How to ask and answer questions about particular times*
- *How to request and give information about travel*

## Dialogue

Anna is at the railway station waiting with her fellow tourists for the train to St Petersburg. Ira has come to see her off.

◈ CD 1, TR 10, 00:08

| | |
|---|---|
| **Йра** | (*Arriving in a hurry.*) Áнна, вот ты где! Вся твоя́ гру́ппа здесь? |
| **Áнна** | Да, мы все е́дем в Санкт-Петербу́рг. |
| **Йра** | Ско́лько сейча́с вре́мени? |
| **Áнна** | Два́дцать мину́т двена́дцатого. |
| **Йра** | А во ско́лько отхо́дит по́езд? |
| **Áнна** | В по́лночь. Зна́чит, че́рез со́рок мину́т. |
| **Йра** | Ага́, поня́тно. Зна́чит, за́втра у́тром ты уже́ бу́дешь в Санкт-Петербу́рге. |
| **Áнна** | Да, в семь часо́в. |
| **Йра** | Ско́лько дней ты там бу́дешь? |
| **Áнна** | Всего́ три дня. |

| | |
|---|---|
| **Йра** | Тебе́ везёт, А́нна! Санкт-Петербу́рг тако́й краси́вый го́род. И всегда́ удо́бно, коне́чно, е́здить по́ездом. |
| **А́нна** | Почему́? |
| **Йра** | Потому́ что в по́езде тепло́, прия́тно. Мо́жно спать, пить чай. Я о́чень люблю́ е́здить по́ездом. А у тебя́ како́й биле́т на по́езд? В оди́н коне́ц, да? |
| **А́нна** | Нет, и обра́тный биле́т … вот он. |
| **Йра** | Ага́ … шесто́й ваго́н, четвёртое купе́, два́дцать четвёртое ме́сто. От како́й платфо́рмы отхо́дит по́езд? |
| **А́нна** | От пя́той платфо́рмы. |
| **Го́лос** | Объявля́ется поса́дка на по́езд Москва́ – Санкт-Петербу́рг. |
| **Йра** | Зна́чит, тебе́ уже́ пора́, А́нна. Счастли́вого пути́! |

| | |
|---|---|
| вся гру́ппа | the whole group |
| мы все е́дем | we're all going |
| ско́лько сейча́с вре́мени? | what time is it now? |
| два́дцать мину́т двена́дцатого | twenty past eleven |
| во ско́лько? | at what time? |
| отхо́дит (отходи́ть) | leaves (to leave) |
| в по́лночь | at midnight |
| че́рез со́рок мину́т | in forty minutes' time |
| за́втра у́тром | tomorrow morning |
| ты бу́дешь | you will be |
| в семь часо́в | at seven o'clock |
| день (m.; fleeting **e**) | day |
| всего́ | in all, only |
| тебе́ везёт | you're lucky |
| тако́й | such a, so |
| всегда́ | always |
| удо́бно (удо́бный) | convenient, comfortable |
| е́здить | to travel |
| тепло́ | it is warm |
| спать | to sleep |

| | |
|---|---|
| в оди́н коне́ц | *one way* |
| обра́тный биле́т | *a return ticket* |
| шесто́й ваго́н | *sixth carriage* |
| четвёртое купе́ | *fourth compartment* |
| платфо́рма | *platform* |
| го́лос | *voice* |
| объявля́ться | *to be announced* |
| поса́дка | *boarding* |
| счастли́вого пути́! | *bon voyage!* |
| | *have a good journey!* |

---

Действителен в течение 30 дней с момента первого прохода

| 04.01.09 | 60 | 150 | 003359192 |
|---|---|---|---|
| НАЧАТЬ ИСПОЛЬЗОВАТЬ ДО | НЕ БОЛЕЕ ПОЕЗДОК | СТОИМОСТЬ РУБЛЕЙ | № БИЛЕТА |

← ● Билет для проезда в Московском Метрополитене Ⓜ

Просьба сохранить билет до конца поездки.
Подделка проездных документов преследуется по закону.

---

## По́езд *The train*

**Ско́рый по́езд** is an express train, while **электри́чка** is a local electric train and a **пассажи́рский по́езд** is a slow train. **Фи́рменный по́езд** is a long-distance train run by a private company: these trains are fast, clean and comfortable and usually have names – **Росси́я** and **Океа́н** are two of the trains which take passengers from Moscow to Vladivostok, whilst **Ка́ма** is run from the city of Perm in the Ural mountains. **Кама́** has first- and second-class compartments which offer air conditioning, and TV sets, and one compartment per carriage offers internet access and a computer.

On long-distance trains each carriage is looked after by a train attendant (**проводни́к** or **проводни́ца**), who checks passengers' tickets, makes sure that each compartment has the correct supply of bedding and supplies tea to the passengers (although refreshments may also be available in a **ваго́н-рестора́н**).

Public transport within towns (**городско́й тра́нспорт**) includes buses (**авто́бусы**), trams (**трамва́и**), trolleybuses (**тролле́йбусы**) and, in some cities, an underground (**метро́**). Bus/tram/trolleybus tickets can be bought from the kiosks and from the driver, and each ticket must be punched when it is used (**компости́ровать**, *to punch*); access to the Moscow metro is by tickets purchased at the **ка́сса**. It is also possible to buy a **еди́ный биле́т** – an all-in-one ticket which covers transport by bus, tram, trolleybus and underground.

---

## Questions

### 1 *True or false?*

**a** Уже́ семь часо́в.
**b** За́втра у́тром А́нна бу́дет (*Anna will be*) в Санкт-Петербу́рге.
**c** А́нна бу́дет в Санкт-Петербу́рге четы́ре дня.
**d** У А́нны нет обра́тного биле́та.
**e** По́езд отхо́дит от пя́той платфо́рмы.

### 2 *Answer the questions!*

**a** Во ско́лько отхо́дит по́езд?
**b** Во ско́лько А́нна бу́дет в Санкт-Петербу́рге?
**c** Что И́ра говори́т о Санкт-Петербу́рге?
**d** Почему́ И́ра ду́мает, что всегда́ удо́бно е́здить по́ездом?
**e** Каки́е биле́ты у А́нны?

---

## How do you say it?

How to:
**1** *Ask the time*

Ско́лько сейча́с вре́мени?

**2** *Ask at what time the train leaves*

Во ско́лько отхо́дит по́езд?

**3** *Tell the time*

Семь часо́в.

**4** *Say at what time*

В семь часо́в.

**5** *Request and give information about tickets*

У вас есть обра́тный биле́т?
Биле́т в оди́н коне́ц.
Биле́т на по́езд в Санкт-Петербу́рг.

**6** *Ask directions in the station*

От како́й платфо́рмы отхо́дит по́езд?

---

## Grammar

### 1 Вся гру́ппа *The whole group*

*All/the whole group* – in Russian the word for *all* (a determinative pronoun) behaves rather like an adjective; in the nominative it looks like this:

| Masculine: | весь день | *(the whole day)* |
| Feminine: | вся гру́ппа | *(the whole group)* |
| Neuter: | всё письмо́ | *(the whole letter)* |
| Plural: | все тури́сты | *(all the tourists)* |

The full declension (i.e. all the case endings) of **весь** is given in Appendix 1.

When making a purchase in a shop, or an order in a restaurant, you will often hear the question: Это всё? (*Is that all?*) If you don't want anything else, then you will reply: Да, спасибо, это всё (*Yes, thank you, that's everything*).

## 2 Instrumental case

In Unit 8 we learnt that this case is used to describe the instrument by which an action is performed, so it is commonly used when describing means of transport: поездом (*by train*), автобусом (*by bus*), самолётом (*by plane*). It is also used in time phrases, of which the following are very common:

| | |
|---|---|
| у́тром | *in the morning* |
| днём | *during the day* |
| ве́чером | *in the evening* |
| но́чью | *at night* |
| зимо́й | *in winter* |
| весно́й | *in spring* |
| ле́том | *in summer* |
| о́сенью | *in autumn* |

## Insight

It is important to remember that, unlike English, Russian does not use a preposition for these eight time phrases (i.e. when saying *in the morning, in the afternoon, in the evening, at night, in spring, in summer, in autumn, in winter*): just use the instrumental case!

## 3 Ты бу́дешь *You will be*

Although there is no present tense of the verb *to be* (быть) in Russian, there is a future tense (*I will be, you will be*, etc.), which is as follows:

| я бу́ду | мы бу́дем |
|---------|----------|
| ты бу́дешь | вы бу́дете |
| он бу́дет | они́ бу́дут |

## Insight

Even though this is a different tense, you will notice that the endings are reassuringly familiar. Just learn the stem for the future of *to be* (**буд-**) and you should find it easy to learn this new tense.

### 4 Time

In order to tell the time in Russian we need to know two sets of numbers, cardinal (the ones we have already met – 1, 2, 3, etc.). and ordinal (the ones which tell us the order – 1st, 2nd, 3rd, etc.). The lists below show that the two sets of numerals have a lot in common, but note that the ordinals are actually adjectives:

| Cardinal | | Ordinal | |
|----------|----|---------|------|
| оди́н | 1 | пе́рвый | 1st |
| два | 2 | второ́й | 2nd |
| три | 3 | тре́тий | 3rd |
| четы́ре | 4 | четвёртый | 4th |
| пять | 5 | пя́тый | 5th |
| шесть | 6 | шесто́й | 6th |
| семь | 7 | седьмо́й | 7th |
| во́семь | 8 | восьмо́й | 8th |
| де́вять | 9 | девя́тый | 9th |
| де́сять | 10 | деся́тый | 10th |
| оди́ннадцать | 11 | оди́ннадцатый | 11th |
| двена́дцать | 12 | двена́дцатый | 12th |

## Insight

Three useful things to remember about ordinal numbers:

**1** They tell you the order of things (first, second etc).
**2** They look reassuringly like cardinal numbers.
**3** They are adjectives, so must agree with the nouns they describe.

Telling the time 'on the hour' is quite straightforward: simply state the appropriate cardinal numeral and follow it by the word **час** (*hour*) – in the nominative singular after 1, genitive singular after 2, 3, 4 and the genitive plural after five and above:

| | | |
|---|---|---|
| Ско́лько сейча́с вре́мени? | Час. | *One o'clock.* |
| Ско́лько сейча́с вре́мени? | Три часа́. | *Three o'clock.* |
| Ско́лько сейча́с вре́мени? | Де́вять часо́в. | *Nine o'clock.* |

(You will also hear **Кото́рый час?** as a way of asking *What time is it?*)

To tell the time on the left-hand side of the clock (i.e. minutes to the hour), use the word **без** (*without*), which is always followed by the genitive case*; so, if you want to say *ten to five* what you are literally saying in Russian is *without ten five*:

| | |
|---|---|
| Без десяти́ пять. | *Ten minutes to five.* |
| Без че́тверти три | *A quarter to three.* |
| (**че́тверть** (f.) *quarter.*) | |

To deal with the *half hour*, you need the prefix **пол-** (*half*) and you attach this to the appropriate ordinal numeral; if you want to say *half past five* in Russian, what you literally say is *half of the sixth hour*, which is why the ordinal numeral needs to be in the genitive case:

| | | | |
|---|---|---|---|
| Полшесто́го | *or* | Полови́на шесто́го. | *Half past five.* |
| Полдеся́того | *or* | Полови́на деся́того. | *Half past nine.* |

You must think ahead in this way whenever you are dealing with the right-hand side of the clock (i.e. minutes past the hour):

| | |
|---|---|
| Че́тверть седьмо́го. | *A quarter past six.* |
| Де́сять мину́т тре́тьего. | *Ten minutes past two.* |

*See Appendix 1 for the declension of cardinal and ordinal numbers.

To say *a.m.* use **ночи** for the very early hours and **утра** (literally *of the morning*); for *p.m.* use **дня** (*of the day*) and **вечера** (*of the evening*):

Десять часов утра (*10 a.m.*); четыре часа дня (*4 p.m.*); семь часов вечера (*7 p.m.*); два часа ночи (*2 a.m.*).

Note also **полдень** (*midday*) and **полночь** (*midnight*).

To answer the question *At what time?* the preposition **в** is used, except in the case of minutes to the hour:

| | |
|---|---|
| Во сколько отходит поезд? | |
| В три часа. | *At three o'clock.* |
| В двадцать минут второго. | *At twenty past one.* |
| В половине шестого (*or* полшестого). | *At half past five.* |
| Без четверти три. | *At quarter to three.* |

Note that official timetables (e.g. train timetables) often use the twenty-four-hour clock, e.g. **восемнадцать тридцать** – *18.30*.

(You will also hear **в котором часу**… as a way of asking *at what time*…?)

## Insight

Try learning a few specific times to help you remember the different ways of dealing with:

- Hours: **три часа** (3.00); **пять часов** (5.00)
- Half hours: **полчетвёртого** (3.30)
- Left-hand side of the clock: **без пяти три** (2.45)
- Right-hand side of the clock: **четверть пятого** (4.15)

### 5 Через *Across*

**Через** literally means *across* and it is always followed by the accusative case. When used with time expressions it means *after time has elapsed*, e.g.:

| Поезд в Санкт-Петербург | The St Petersburg train leaves |
| отхо́дит че́рез со́рок мину́т. | in forty minutes. |

**Че́рез** is also useful when giving information about the number of stops to be travelled:

| Когда́ мне выходи́ть? | When should I get off? |
| Че́рез три остано́вки. | After three stops. |

### 6 'To go'

The verbs meaning *to go* have two forms of the present tense in Russian. The verb which means *to go on foot*, *to walk* makes its present tense from either **ходи́ть** or **идти́**, while **е́здить** or **е́хать** must be used if you want to say *to go by transport*, *to travel*. Consider the following:

#### On foot

| *Habitual, repeated* | *One occasion, one direction* |
| ходи́ть (я хожу́, ты хо́дишь, они́ хо́дят) | идти́ (я иду́, ты идёшь, они́ иду́т) |
| Она́ всегда́ хо́дит в го́род | Сейча́с она́ идёт в го́род |
| *She always walks into town* | *She is walking into town now* |

#### By transport

| *Habitual, repeated* | *One occasion, one direction* |
| е́здить (я е́зжу, ты е́здишь, они́ е́здят) | е́хать (я е́ду, ты е́дешь, они́ е́дут) |
| Я обы́чно е́зжу на рабо́ту авто́бусом | Сего́дня А́нна е́дет в Санкт-Петербу́рг |
| *I usually go to work by bus* | *Anna is going to St Petersburg today* |

Note that the rules of habit or one occasion/one direction apply to the use of the infinitives too, e.g.:

| Я предпочита́ю е́здить по́ездом | *I prefer to travel by train (in general).* |

| Мне порá идтú на рабóту | *It's time for me to walk to work (now).* |
|---|---|

Note that while people travel (**éздить/éхать**) on vehicles, the movement of certain vehicles is described by **ходúть/идтú** – thus trains and trams, for example, *walk*:

| Поездá хóдят бы́стро и чáсто. | *The trains run quickly and frequently.* |
|---|---|

The other common verbs of motion – *to carry, to fly, to lead, to run, to swim, to transport* – are all governed by the same principles. They all have two infinitives from which you can make the present tense and you must always decide: habit? or one occasion/one direction? (Note that some of these have an irregular present tense. This is indicated below in brackets, but remember that the first person singular of **водúть, возúть** and **носúть** will have a consonant change (see Appendix 1, page 390).

| бéгать/бежáть (бегý, бежúшь, бежúт, бежúм, бежúте, бегýт) | *to run* |
|---|---|
| водúть/вестú (ведý, ведёшь, ведёт, ведём, ведёте, ведýт) | *to lead* |
| возúть/везтú (везý, везёшь, везёт, везём, везёте, везýт) | *to transport* |
| летáть/летéть (лечý, летúшь, летúт, летúм, летúте, летя́т) | *to fly* |
| носúть/нестú (несý, несёшь, несёт, несём, несёте, несýт) | *to carry* |
| плáвать/плыть (плывý, плывёшь, плывёт, плывём, плывёте, плывýт) | *to swim, sail* |

## Insight

Key tips about verbs of motion:

**1** is the journey habitual, a generalization? – then use the first infinitive.

**2** one occasion and one direction? – then use the second infinitive.

Example: to fly – **летáть/летéть**

**Птúцы летáют** (*Birds fly*) – a generalization, so the first infinitive should be used to form the present tense.
**Сегóдня он летúт в Москвý** (*Today he is flying to Moscow*) – this is just one occasion, so the second infinitive should be used.

### 7 Счастлúвого путú! *Have a good journey!*

Wishes of this kind are expressed in the genitive case; this is because the verb **желáть** (*to wish*) must be followed by the genitive case – even if the verb itself is not stated, it is always understood:

| | |
|---|---|
| (Я желáю вам) прия́тного аппетúта! | *Bon appétit/Enjoy your meal!* |
| (Я желáю вам) всегó хорóшего! | *All the best!* |

## Practice

### 9.1 Read, look and answer!

**A** Извинúте, пожáлуйста, скóлько сейчáс врéмени?
**B** Два часá.
**A** Спасúбо.
**B** Пожáлуйста.

Четы́ре часá
*It's four o'clock*

Чéтверть восьмóго
*It's quarter past seven*

Полчетвёртого
*It's half past three*

Бéз десятú пять
*It's ten to five*

Now look at the time and answer:
Ско́лько сейча́с вре́мени?

## 9.2 Read, look and answer!

Во ско́лько отхо́дит по́езд?

| Куда́? | Когда́? | | |
|---|---|---|---|
| **В** Москву́ | 11 a.m. | **a** | В оди́ннадцать часо́в утра́. |
| **В** О́бнинск | 6 p.m. | **b** | |
| **В** Я́лту | 8.30 a.m. | **c** | |
| **В** Ки́ев | 11.30 p.m. | **d** | |

## 9.3 Read, answer and listen!

You are buying a train ticket. Complete your part of the conversation, then listen to the complete conversation on the recording.

| Вы | **(a)** Ask how much a ticket to Yalta costs. |
| Дéвушка | 150 рублéй. |
| Вы | **(b)** Ask for two tickets to Yalta. |
| Дéвушка | Пожáлуйста. С вас 300 рублéй. |
| Вы | **(c)** Say 'here is 500 roubles'. |
| Дéвушка | У вас нет мéлочи? |
| Вы | **(d)** Apologize that you have no change. |
| Дéвушка | Ничегó. |
| Вы | **(e)** Ask what time the train leaves. |
| Дéвушка | Чéрез час. |
| Вы | **(f)** Ask what platform the train leaves from. |
| Дéвушка | От четвёртой платфóрмы. |

## Insight

Did you remember to put *Yalta* into the accusative case when you did sections (a) and (b) in exercise 9.3? Remember that the accusative is needed with **в** for direction/motion towards (see Unit 3), so you should say **билéт в Я́лту**; if you say **в Я́лте**, it means you are there already!

### 9.4 Read and answer!

Look at the advertisement overleaf, for railway travel and answer the questions. (**NB** You don't need to understand all the words in the advert to be able to answer them.)

**a** What different types of journey can the railways cater for?
**b** What sort of carriages are especially designed for long journeys?
**c** Which continents do the railways connect?
**d** What wish is expressed at the end of the advert?

| делова́я поéздка | *business trip* |
| дли́тельный | *long, lengthy* |
| желéзная доро́га | *railway* |
| путешéствие | *travel* |
| СНГ | *CIS (Commonwealth of Independent States)* |

---

## ЖЕЛЕЗНЫЕ ДОРОГИ
## ЖЕЛЕЗНЫЕ ДОРОГИ ПРЕДЛАГАЮТ:

- для деловой поездки
- для туристского путешествия
- для транзита через СНГ

*Поезда и беспересадочные спальные вагоны*
Спальные вагоны прекрасно
приспособлены для длительных
путешествий

*Прямое сообщение с 24 странами Европы и Азии*

# ЖЕЛАЕМ ПРИЯТНОЙ
# ПОЕЗДКИ!

---

## Comprehension

### 1 *Conversation*

**Read, listen and answer!**

Alla is talking to her new neighbour, Boris, about how best to get
to work in the morning.

| | |
|---|---|
| **Борис** | Как вы обы́чно е́здите на рабо́ту, А́лла? |
| **А́лла** | Зна́ете, э́то немно́жко сло́жно … |
| **Борис** | Почему́? |
| **А́лла** | Потому́, что ближа́йшая ста́нция метро́ далеко́ отсю́да. |
| **Борис** | Зна́чит, на́до сади́ться на трамва́й? |
| **А́лла** | Нет. На́до сади́ться на сто два́дцать второ́й авто́бус. |
| **Борис** | А когда́ на́до выходи́ть? |
| **А́лла** | Че́рез шесть остано́вок. |
| **Борис** | Ста́нция метро́ далеко́ от остано́вки авто́буса? |
| **А́лла** | Нет. Отту́да ста́нция метро́ «Беля́ево» недалеко́. |
| **Борис** | А отту́да мо́жно прое́хать в центр? |
| **А́лла** | Да, мо́жно. |
| **Борис** | Без переса́док? |
| **А́лла** | Да, без переса́док. |
| **Борис** | Зна́чит, снача́ла авто́бусом до метро́, а пото́м в метро́, без переса́док. Ну, пото́м что? |
| **А́лла** | Пото́м де́сять мину́т ходьбы́ до институ́та. |
| **Борис** | Да … сло́жно. Пое́здка на рабо́ту занима́ет мно́го вре́мени? |
| **А́лла** | Ну, пятьдеся́т мину́т, час. |

**QUICK VOCAB**

| | |
|---|---|
| сло́жный | *complicated* |
| ближа́йший | *nearest* |
| сади́ться на авто́бус | *to catch a bus* |
| выходи́ть | *to get out* |
| остано́вка | *stop* |
| прое́хать | *to get to* |
| переса́дка | *change* |
| снача́ла | *at first* |
| ходьба́ | *walk* |
| пое́здка | *journey* |
| занима́ть | *to occupy* |

**1** Áлла живёт

  **a** Недалеко́ от ста́нции метро́
  **b** Нале́во от ста́нции метро́
  **c** Далеко́ от ста́нции метро́
  **d** Напра́во от ста́нции метро́

**2** Áлла обы́чно е́здит на ста́нцию метро́

  **a** велосипе́дом
  **b** автомоби́лем
  **c** авто́бусом
  **d** трамва́ем

**3** Ста́нция метро́

  **a** Далеко́ от остано́вки авто́буса
  **b** Недалеко́ от остано́вки авто́буса
  **c** За остано́вкой авто́буса
  **d** Ря́дом с до́мом Áллы

**4** От ста́нции метро́

  **a** Áлла е́здит на рабо́ту трамва́ем
  **b** Áлла хо́дит на рабо́ту
  **c** Áлла е́здит на рабо́ту автомоби́лем
  **d** Áлла е́здит на рабо́ту тролле́йбусом

## 2 *Reading*

**Read the text and answer the questions in English.**

  **a** What sign indicates the presence of a metro station?
  **b** Why do Muscovites prefer to travel by metro?
  **c** How long might you have to wait for a train?

Éсли вы идёте по у́лице и ви́дите большу́ю кра́сную бу́кву «М» – зна́чит э́то ста́нция метро́. Метро́ – о́чень бы́стрый, удо́бный и популя́рный вид городско́го тра́нспорта. Моско́вский метрополите́н всеми́рно изве́стен и москвичи́, как пра́вило, предпочита́ют е́здить на метро́. А почему́? Они́ счита́ют, что моско́вское метро́ хорошо́ организо́вано, поезда́ хо́дят и быстро и ча́сто. Сре́дний интерва́л ме́жду поезда́ми – 2,5 мину́ты. Минима́льный интерва́л в «часы́ пик» – 90 секу́нд. Максима́льный интерва́л мо́жет достига́ть 10 мину́т.

| бу́ква | *letter* (of the alphabet) |
| достига́ть | *to reach* |
| как пра́вило | *as a rule* |
| кра́сный | *red* |
| сре́дний | *average* |
| счита́ть | *to consider* |
| час пик | *rush hour* |

## Key phrases

🔊 **CD 1, TR 10, 04:08**

Can you remember how to say the following in Russian? Listen to the recording and practise saying each phrase.

   **a** What time is it?
   **b** What time does the train leave?
   **c** What platform does the train leave from?
   **d** The train leaves in ten minutes.
   **e** How many days will you be there for?

## Test yourself

**1** Which case do you need to remember to use when you want to wish someone all the best?

**2** To make the future of the verb *to be* (*I will, you will* etc). you need to know its stem. Can you remember the stem, and how to say *I will* and *you* (**ты**) *will*?

**3** Two key words when you are travelling on public transport: **остановка** and **пересадка**. Can you remember what they mean?

**4** **Дайте, пожалуйста, билет в Новосибирск**. Which case has been used here for the word **Новосибирск** and why?

**5** **Девять часов** (it is 9.00). What would you need to add to make this mean 9.00 a.m.?

**6** The words **сначала** and **потом** are often used when you're giving directions or explaining your route to work, for example. Can you remember what they mean?

**7** What would you be wanting to find out if you asked the question **Сколько сейчас времени?** or **Который час?**

**8** The verb **бегать/бежать** (*to run*), like many verbs of motion, has two forms of the present tense. Can you explain why *She often runs* will be **Она часто бегает** and not **бежит**?

**9** Lots of useful time phrases in Unit 9! If you were invited to a concert **завтра вечером**, when would you expect to go?

**10** If someone asked you a question beginning **Почему?**, how would your reply be likely to start?

# 10

## По средам я обычно ...
## On Wednesdays I usually ...

In this unit you will learn
* *How to talk about daily and weekly routine*
* *How to ask for and give information about age*
* *How to talk about days of the week*
* *How to express approximation with regard to time*

## Dialogue

Ira has introduced Anna to her friend Anatoly, who works at a film studio in Moscow.

CD 1, TR 11, 00:07

| Анато́лий | О́чень прия́тно, А́нна. Вы рабо́таете учи́тельницей, да? |
| **А́нна** | Пра́вда. А кем вы рабо́таете? |
| **Анато́лий** | Я сценари́ст ... э́то зна́чит, что я пишу́ сцена́рии для кинофи́льмов. |
| **А́нна** | Ой, как интере́сно! Зна́чит, вы ка́ждый день рабо́таете в киносту́дии? |
| **Анато́лий** | Нет, не ка́ждый день. Обы́чно по понеде́льникам я рабо́таю в киносту́дии, то есть я занима́юсь администрати́вной рабо́той – ча́сто мне на́до отвеча́ть на пи́сьма, сове́товаться с колле́гами. |

| | |
|---|---|
| **Áнна** | Понятно. |
| **Анатóлий** | А по срéдам, напримéр, я обычно работаю дóма, пишý сценáрии. Дóма тихо, я могý спокóйно работáть ... то есть э́то тогдá, когдá моегó сы́на нет дóма! |
| **Áнна** | А скóлько емý лет? |
| **Анатóлий** | Емý шесть лет. |
| **Áнна** | Всё понятно! ... Скажи́те, а киностýдия далекó от дóма? |
| **Анатóлий** | К сожалéнию, да. Я всегдá éзжу тудá на маши́не. |
| **Áнна** | Во скóлько вы обычно начинáете работáть? |
| **Анатóлий** | По понедéльникам, когдá я работáю в киностýдии, я встаю́ полседьмóго, зáвтракаю и начинáю работáть часóв в дéвять. |
| **Áнна** | А éсли вы работáете дóма, когдá вы начинáете? |
| **Анатóлий** | Тогдá я начинáю работáть часóв в семь ... я предпочитáю писáть сценáрии рáно ýтром. |
| **Áнна** | Скóлько часóв вы работаете кáждый день? |
| **Анатóлий** | Понимáете, э́то зави́сит от рабóты. Обы́чно я рабóтаю часóв семь в день. |
| **Áнна** | А по вечерáм вы отдыхáете, да? |
| **Анатóлий** | Да, ... и не тóлько по вечерáм! В киностýдии я обычно обéдаю с друзья́ми, часá в три, потóм мы гуля́ем в пáрке. |
| **Áнна** | А что вы дéлаете пóсле ýжина? |
| **Анатóлий** | Обы́чно я сижý дóма. Иногдá слýшаю рáдио, смотрю́ телеви́зор и́ли читáю интерéсную кни́гу. |

| | |
|---|---|
| учи́тельница | (female) teacher |
| кем вы рабо́таете? | what is your job? (lit. as whom do you work?) |
| сценари́ст | scriptwriter |
| я пишу́ | I write |
| ка́ждый | every |
| киносту́дия | film studio |
| обы́чно | usually |
| по понеде́льникам | on Mondays |
| то есть | that is (i.e.) |
| занима́юсь администрати́вной рабо́той | I do (lit. busy myself with) administrative work |
| отвеча́ть на пи́сьма | to reply to letters |
| сове́товаться с (+ instr.) | to consult, get advice from |
| колле́га | colleague |
| по сре́дам | on Wednesdays |
| ти́хо (ти́хий) | quiet |
| я могу́ | I can |
| споко́йно (споко́йный) | peaceful, calm |
| тогда́ | then, in that case |
| ско́лько ему́ лет? | how old is he? |
| всегда́ | always |
| я встаю́ (встава́ть) | I get up |
| за́втракаю (за́втракать) | I have breakfast (to have breakfast) |
| начина́ть | to begin |
| часо́в в де́вять | at about nine o'clock |
| ра́но у́тром | early in the morning |
| зави́сит от (зави́сеть от + gen.) | it depends on |
| обе́даю (обе́дать) | I have lunch (to have lunch) |
| гуля́ть (гуля́ю, гуля́ешь) | to stroll |
| по́сле у́жина | after supper |

'Who wrote the script for this film?'

## Insight

Anatoly and Anna use the instrumental case to talk/
ask about jobs (**учи́тельницей** – *as a teacher*) and
the instrumental of **кто** (*who*) in the phrase **кем вы
рабо́таете?** NB: you can either say *I am a journalist*
(**я журнали́ст**), or *I work as a journalist* (**я рабо́таю
журнали́стом**).

### *Russian meals:* за́втрак, обе́д, у́жин

За́втрак (*breakfast*) typically consists of ка́ша (*porridge, cooked
cereal*), meat, fish or eggs of some kind – e.g. яи́чница (*fried eggs*),
perhaps a glass of кефи́р (a sort of liquid, sour yoghurt), sweet
buns, tea, coffee and bread (хлеб), which accompanies every meal.
If the main meal of the day is to be late, then in the late morning
there is a second breakfast, which typically consists of a savoury
dish, bread and perhaps a sweet fruit or cottage cheese dish –
e.g. кисе́ль (*sweet fruit jelly*).

The main meal of the day, обе́д, is a moveable feast – it may be at
midday, in the afternoon or in the evening; it may start off with
заку́ски, usually includes a rich soup such as щи, followed by a
meat dish such as котле́ты. У́жин is a lighter meal – a typical dish
would be блины́ (*pancakes*) served with sour cream (смета́на).

## Questions

**1** *True or false?*

**a** Анато́лий – актёр.
**b** А́нна – учи́тельница.
**c** По понеде́льникам Анато́лий рабо́тает до́ма.
**d** Анато́лий живёт недалеко́ от киносту́дии.
**e** Анато́лий встаёт полседьмо́го.

**2** *Answer the questions!*

**a** Кем рабо́тает Анато́лий?
**b** Что он де́лает по сре́дам?
**c** Как он е́здит на рабо́ту?
**d** Когда́ Анато́лий предпочита́ет писа́ть сцена́рии?
**e** Как он отдыха́ет по вечера́м?

## How do you say it?

How to:
**1** *Ask for and give information about daily routine*

Во ско́лько вы начина́ете рабо́тать?
Я обы́чно встаю́ полседьмо́го.
Я обы́чно обе́даю часа́ в три.

**2** *Ask for and give information about weekly routine*

По сре́дам я обы́чно рабо́таю до́ма.
Что вы обы́чно де́лаете по понеде́льникам?

**3** *Say how often you do something*

Я обы́чно рабо́таю в киносту́дии.
Ча́сто мне на́до отвеча́ть на пи́сьма.

Я всегда́ е́зжу туда́ на метро́.
Иногда́ слу́шаю ра́дио.

## Insight

Notice that there are lots of adverbs (words which answer questions such as 'where', 'when', 'how') used in these sentences: **всегда́** (*always*), **иногда́** (*sometimes*), **обы́чно** (*usually*), **ча́сто** (*often*). Notice also that they are usually placed at the beginning of the sentences, or just before the verb.

**4** *Ask and give information about age*

Ско́лько ему́ лет?
Ему́ шесть лет.

**5** *Say someone is not at home*

Моего́ сы́на нет до́ма. (lit. *There is not of my son at home*).

## Grammar

### 1 *Verbs*

Note that two of the verbs met in the Dialogue are common irregular verbs – **писа́ть** (*to write*) and **мочь** (*to be able*):

**писа́ть:** пишу́, пи́шешь, пи́шет, пи́шем, пи́шете, пи́шут
**мочь:** могу́, мо́жешь, мо́жет, мо́жем, мо́жете, мо́гут

## Insight

Remember all you need to learn for the present tense of verbs like these two is: the **я** and **ты** forms (because the **я** form shows you what the **они́** form will be, and the **ты** form shows you what the **он, она́, оно́, мы** and **вы** forms will be).

## 2 Dative case

In Unit 6 we met some of the uses of the dative case and learnt how to form the dative singular of nouns. The dative plural of nouns is as follows: irrespective of gender, the endings are -ам (for nouns ending in a consonant, -а, or -о) and -ям for all others (which, as for other cases, will need final -ь, -й, -е removed first):

| тури́ст (tourist) | Тури́стам нра́вится э́тот музе́й. | The tourists like this museum. |
| учи́тель (teacher) | Учителя́м хо́чется отдыха́ть. | The teachers feel like a rest/want to rest. |

Note that nouns that have an irregular nominative plural form their dative plural from the irregular nominative plural, e.g.:

Nom. singular: **брат** (*brother*), Nom. plural: **бра́тья**, Dative plural: **бра́тьям**

The dative singular and plural of adjectives are also very straight forward. In the singular masculine and neuter adjectives add -ому, unless the rule about the unstressed **о** applies, in which case add -ему. Feminine singular adjectives add -ой, unless the rule about the unstressed **о** applies, in which case add -ей:

| к интере́сному музе́ю | towards the interesting museum |
| по ста́рой у́лице | along the old street |
| к хоро́шему зда́нию | towards the nice building |

### Insight

Expressions *in my opinion, in your opinion* demonstrate the masculine/neuter dative endings (**-ому, -ему**), as they are based on the neuter noun **мне́ние** (*opinion*):

**по-ва́шему мне́нию**   *in your opinion*

It is quite usual, though, to omit the word *opinion* and just say:

**по-мо́ему**   *in my opinion*
**по-ва́шему**   *in your opinion*

In the plural, irrespective of gender, add -ым, unless the stem ends in г, к, х, ж, ч, ш, щ, in which case add -им:

| | |
|---|---|
| **но́вые студе́нты: Но́вым студе́нтам нра́вится ру́сский язы́к.** | *The new students like Russian.* |
| **ру́сские тури́сты: Ру́сским тури́стам нра́вится ста́рый го́род.** | *The Russian tourists like the old town.* |

Note that the dative case is used when asking and giving information about one's age:

| | |
|---|---|
| **Ско́лько ему́\* лет?** | *How old is he?* (lit. *How many years to him?*) |
| **Ива́ну два́дцать оди́н год.** | *Ivan is 21.* |
| **О́льге со́рок два го́да.** | *Olga is 42.* |
| **Ему́ шесть лет.** | *He is six.* |

**Оди́н** is always followed by **год** (*year*); **два, три** and **четы́ре** are followed by **го́да** (i.e. genitive singular of **год**), but note that **ско́лько** and numbers 5 and above (but not compounds of 1, 2, 3, 4) are followed by **лет** (which is actually the genitive plural of **ле́то**, summer).

··········································································

## Insight

In summary:

- **год** whenever the final digit is 1: **Мне два́дцать оди́н год** (*I am 21*)
- **го́да** whenever the final digit is 2, 3, 4: **Ему́ со́рок два го́да** (*He is 42*)
- **лет** for everything else: **Тебе́ шестна́дцать лет**? (*Are you 16?*)

··········································································

\*See page 93 for the dative of **я, ты, он, она́, оно́, мы, вы, они́.**

## 3 Accusative case

The only form of the accusative we have not yet met is for feminine
singular adjectives – in other words, if you want to say *I am
reading an interesting book*:

интере́сная кни́га: Я чита́ю интере́сную кни́гу.

As you see, it is simply a question of changing **-ая** to **-ую**.


## 4 Time phrases

The dative and accusative cases are very useful when dealing with
time phrases that involve days of the week.

Note that days of the week are written with a small letter in
Russian, unless at the beginning of a sentence.

| Day | Accusative | Dative |
|---|---|---|
| понеде́льник | в понеде́льник<br>(*on Monday*) | по понеде́льникам<br>(*on Mondays*) |
| вто́рник | во вто́рник<br>(*on Tuesday*) | по вто́рникам<br>(*on Tuesdays*) |
| среда́ | в сре́ду<br>(*on Wednesday*) | по сре́дам<br>(*on Wednesdays*) |
| четве́рг | в четве́рг<br>(*on Thursday*) | по четверга́м<br>(*on Thursdays*) |
| пя́тница | в пя́тницу<br>(*on Friday*) | по пя́тницам<br>(*on Fridays*) |
| суббо́та | в суббо́ту<br>(*on Saturday*) | по суббо́там<br>(*on Saturdays*) |
| воскресе́нье | в воскресе́нье<br>(*on Sunday*) | по воскресе́ньям<br>(*on Sundays*) |

The accusative is also useful in the phrase *per day*, *per week*, etc.:

| | |
|---|---|
| **семь часо́в в день** | *7 hours a day* |
| **со́рок часо́в в неде́лю** | *40 hours a week* |

If you want to give an approximate time, simply invert the numeral and the number of hours:

| | |
|---|---|
| **часо́в семь в день** | *about 7 hours a day* |
| **Во ско́лько вы за́втракаете?** | *At what time do you have breakfast?* |
| **Часо́в в семь.** | *At about seven o'clock.* |

## Insight

So, if you're talking about a specific Saturday, you will use the accusative singular:

| | |
|---|---|
| **В суббо́ту я бу́ду в Ло́ндоне** | *On Saturday I will be in London* |

But for Saturdays in general, use the dative plural:

| | |
|---|---|
| **По суббо́там я ча́сто де́лаю поку́пки** | *On Saturdays I often do the shopping* |

## Practice

### 10.1 Read and answer!

Look at the shopping list on the right. Make up sentences asking the assistant to show you each item.

**a** кра́сная ру́чка *(pen)*
**b** чёрная ю́бка *(skirt)*
**c** деревя́нный стул
**d** интере́сная кни́га
**e** ру́сский журна́л
**f** но́вая ка́рта

**a** Покажи́те мне *(show me)*, пожа́луйста, кра́сную ру́чку.

## 10.2 Look and answer!

Look at these advertisements for jobs and answer the questions which follow:

### ЕЛАБУЖСКИЙ ЗАВОД АВТОМОБИЛЕЙ ПРИГЛАШАЕТ

преподавателей итальянского языка для обучения специалистов по месту работы.
Телефоны для справок: 2-11-00, 7-19-29

### МОРДОВСКИЙ ПЕДАГОГИЧЕСКИЙ ИНСТИТУТ ОБЪЯВЛЯЕТ КОНКУРС

по вакантным должностям:

● преподавателей русского языка

● преподавателей математики

● преподавателей английского языка

телефоны для справок: 4-40-30, 4-60-39

| QUICK VOCAB | |
|---|---|
| приглаша́ть | to invite |
| преподава́тель (m.) | teacher |
| для спра́вок | for information |
| ко́нкурс | (here) vacancy |
| до́лжность (f.) | job, position |

**a** What sort of teachers are needed at the car factory?
**b** What sort of teachers are needed at the pedagogical institute?

### 10.3 Read and answer!

Complete this paragraph with the correct form of the verb in brackets:

Игорь _____ (жить) в Москве́. Он _____ (рабо́тать) перево́дчиком и о́чень хорошо́ _____ (говори́ть) по-италья́нски. Он ча́сто _____ (ходи́ть) в теа́тр с гру́ппами тури́стов, вот почему́ по вечера́м он ча́сто не _____ (мочь) отдыха́ть до́ма. В свобо́дное вре́мя он о́чень _____ (люби́ть) смотре́ть телеви́зор и он ча́сто _____ (игра́ть) в ша́хматы с друзья́ми. Иногда́ он _____ (писа́ть) пи́сьма и по воскресе́ньям он обы́чно _____ (пла́вать) в бассе́йне и́ли _____ (гуля́ть) в па́рке.

### 10.4 Read, listen and answer

You are explaining your daily routine to a friend. Complete your part of the conversation, then listen to the complete conversation on the recording.

| Друг | Во ско́лько вы встаёте? |
|------|------------------------|
| Вы | (a) Say you get up at 7 a.m. |
| Друг | Как вы е́здите на рабо́ту? |
| Вы | (b) Say 'by tram'. |
| Друг | Во ско́лько вы начина́ете рабо́тать? |
| Вы | (c) Say you start work at 9 a.m. |
| Друг | Ско́лько часо́в вы рабо́таете ка́ждый день? |
| Вы | (d) Say about nine hours. |

🎧 CD 1, TR 11, 02:21

### 10.5 Read and answer!

Answer these questions about yourself:

**a** Где вы живёте?
**b** Вы живёте в до́ме и́ли в кварти́ре?

**c** Кем вы рабóтаете?

**d** Скóлько вам лет?

**e** Во скóлько вы обы́чно встаёте по утрáм?

**f** Как вы éздите на рабóту?

**g** Во скóлько вы начинáете рабóтать?

**h** Во скóлько вы обéдаете?

**i** Что вы обы́чно дéлаете по вечерáм?

**j** Что вы обы́чно дéлаете по суббóтам и по воскресéньям?

---

## Comprehension

**1** *Conversation*

**Read, listen and answer!**

A journalist interviews a waiter from the restaurant 'Kalinka'.

| | |
|---|---|
| **Журналист** | Здрáвствуйте. Как вас зовýт? |
| **Официáнт** | Меня́ зовýт Вади́м. |
| **Журналист** | Вади́м, скóлько вам лет? |
| **Официáнт** | Мне двáдцать вóсемь лет. |
| **Журналист** | И скóлько лет вы рабóтаете официáнтом? |
| **Официáнт** | Ужé шесть лет. |
| **Журналист** | И э́то интерéсная рабóта? |
| **Официáнт** | И да, и нет! Иногдá óчень скýчная, а иногдá интерéсная. Вот примéр, когдá у нас в ресторáне англи́йские тури́сты. |
| **Журналист** | Почемý? |
| **Официáнт** | Потомý, что я немнóжко говорю́ по-англи́йски. |
| **Журналист** | Скóлько часóв в день вы рабóтаете? |
| **Официáнт** | Часóв дéвять. Начинáю в два часá дня, рабóтаю иногдá до оди́ннадцати, а иногдá и до полýночи. |
| **Журналист** | Вы далекó живёте от ресторáна? |

Left margin: 🎧 CD 1, TR 11, 02:54

| | |
|---|---|
| **Официа́нт** | Не о́чень далеко́. |
| **Журнали́ст** | Как вы е́здите на рабо́ту? |
| **Официа́нт** | На трамва́е. |
| **Журнали́ст** | Что вы де́лаете по́сле рабо́ты? |
| **Официа́нт** | Ложу́сь спать! ... Ведь рабо́та конча́ется о́чень по́здно! |

| | |
|---|---|
| **официа́нт** | *waiter* |
| **до полу́ночи** | *until midnight* |
| **ложи́ться спать** | *to go to bed* |
| **ведь** | *you realize/know, after all* |
| **конча́ться** | *to finish* |

**1** Вади́му

**a** два́дцать шесть лет
**b** три́дцать пять лет
**c** два́дцать во́семь лет
**d** три́дцать во́семь лет

**2** Рабо́та Вади́ма

**a** всегда́ интере́сная
**b** всегда́ ску́чная
**c** ча́сто интере́сная
**d** иногда́ интере́сная

**3** Вади́м лю́бит, когда́ в ресторане

**a** нет тури́стов
**b** англи́йские тури́сты
**c** италья́нские тури́сты
**d** журнали́сты

**4** По́сле рабо́ты Вади́м

**a** игра́ет в ша́хматы
**b** пла́вает в бассе́йне
**c** гуля́ет в па́рке
**d** ложи́тся спать

## 2 *Reading*

Read the text and answer the questions in English.

**a** What sort of activities make up 'cultural leisure'?
**b** What choice of newspapers and magazines do Russians have?
**c** How do newspapers and magazines cater for leisure?
**d** Where do Russians play chess?
**e** In which countries is chess taught in schools?

Как прохо́дит ваш обы́чный день? Ско́лько часо́в у вас ухо́дит
на а) рабо́ту? б) дома́шнюю рабо́ту? в) заня́тия с детьми́
г) культу́рный досу́г? (то есть ра́дио и телепереда́чи, кино́, теа́тр,
чте́ние, спорт, тури́зм …) К сожале́нию, о́чень ма́ло вре́мени
ухо́дит на культу́рный досу́г! Но когда́ вре́мя есть, ру́сские
о́чень лю́бят чита́ть – у них мно́жество ра́зных газе́т и журна́лов.
Интере́сно, что о́чень ча́сто в газе́тах и журна́лах есть таки́е
разде́лы как, наприме́р, «кроссво́рды, ю́мор, ша́хматы» – то
есть разде́лы, рассчи́танные на «досу́г». Ру́сские, коне́чно, о́чень
лю́бят ша́хматы … они́ игра́ют в ша́хматы везде́ – и до́ма, и
в па́рке, да́же в шко́ле … в на́ши дни ша́хматы преподаю́тся
в шко́лах СНГ, Герма́нии, Кана́ды, Ме́ксики, Фра́нции и США.
Ру́сские шахмати́сты всеми́рно изве́стны, наприме́р все зна́ют
и́мя и фами́лию Анато́лия Ка́рпова, экс-чемпио́на ми́ра.

| | |
|---|---|
| **везде́** | *everywhere* |
| **в на́ши дни** | *nowadays* |
| **да́же** | *even* |
| **дома́шняя рабо́та** | *housework* |
| **досу́г** | *leisure* |
| **заня́тие** | *activity, occupation* |
| **кроссво́рд** | *crossword* |
| **ма́ло** (+ gen.) | *little* |
| **ме́жду** (+ instr.) | *between* |
| **мир** | *world* |
| **мно́жество** | *multitude* |
| **обы́чный** | *usual* |
| **проходи́ть** | *to pass* |
| **разде́л** | *section* |
| **ра́зный** | *different, various* |
| **рассчи́танный на** | *intended for* |
| **США** | *USA* |
| **телепереда́ча** | *television programme* |
| **уходи́ть** | (here) *to be spent* |

QUICK VOCAB

## Key phrases

CD 1, TR 11, 04:12

Can you remember how to say the following in Russian? Listen to the recording and practise saying each phrase.

  **a** I get up at eight o'clock.
  **b** I usually have lunch at one.
  **c** I always travel by metro.
  **d** How old is he?
  **e** What time do you start work?

## Ten things to remember

**1** If you want to give an approximate time, all you need to do is say the word for *hour/s* first and leave the numeral till later: **часа́ в три** (*at about* 3 *o'clock*).

**2** There are three ways of saying *year/s* when you're asking or talking about age: **год** is the word to use when the last numeral is 1, **го́да** when the last numeral is 2, 3 or 4, **лет** for everything else.

**3** To say *per* in time phrases, use **в** + *the accusative case*: **он смо́трит телеви́зор три часа́ в день** (*he watches television three hours per day*).

**4** If you want to explain that someone is not at home, you need to use the genitive case for the person who is absent: **Ви́ктора нет до́ма**.

**5** To find out someone's age ask **Ско́лько вам (тебе́) лет?**

**6** The dative plural is very useful when generalizing about times of the day or days of the week: **по вечера́м** (*in the evenings*), **по пя́тницам** (*on Fridays*).

**7** You will often need the verbs *to begin/start* and *to finish/end* when you are talking about your typical day. Notice that they are both followed either by a verb in the infinitive, or by a noun: **Я начина́ю рабо́тать в 9 часо́в** (*I start to work at 9 o'clock*); **Я заканчива́ю у́жин в 7 семь часо́в** (*I finish supper at 7 o'clock*).

**8** Remember that verbs ending in -**авать**, such as the verb **встава́ть** (*to get up*), lose the middle syllable (**ав**): **я встаю́, ты встаёшь** (see the Grammar section 1c in Unit 2).

**9** The verb *to write*: **я пишу́, ты пи́шешь**

**10** The verb *to be able*: **я могу́, ты мо́жешь**

# 11

## Это зависит от погоды
# It depends on the weather

In this unit you will learn
- *How to talk about future actions and intentions*
- *How to give and seek information about the weather*

## Dialogue

Sasha is trying to persuade Ira to come mushroom picking in the country with him on his day off.

| | |
|---|---|
| **Са́ша** | Йра, каки́е у тебя́ пла́ны на за́втра? |
| **Йра** | На за́втра? |
| **Са́ша** | Да, что ты бу́дешь де́лать за́втра? |
| **Йра** | За́втра я бу́ду свобо́дна, я пойду́ по магази́нам и … |
| **Са́ша** | Хорошо́! За́втра у меня́ выходно́й день. Дава́й пое́дем за́ город! |
| **Йра** | Слу́шай, Са́ша, и у меня́ бу́дет го́стья, англи́йская подру́га, А́нна. |
| **Са́ша** | Тем лу́чше! В лесу́ бу́дет о́чень прия́тно … зна́ешь, там бу́дут грибы́ … |
| **Йра** | (*Uncertainly.*) … Да … но слу́шай, Са́ша … мне ка́жется, что э́то зави́сит от пого́ды. |

*CD 2, TR 1, 00:07*

| | |
|---|---|
| | Кака́я сего́дня пого́да? – хо́лодно, идёт дождь. Собира́ть грибы́ в таку́ю пого́ду я не о́чень хочу́ … |
| Са́ша | (*Thoughtfully.*) … Да, сего́дня пого́да плоха́я. А когда́ прогно́з пого́ды по ра́дио? … Сейча́с? … Нет? … Ну, дава́й послу́шаем прогно́з пого́ды сего́дня ве́чером – е́сли бу́дет хоро́ший прогно́з, тогда́ пое́дем за́ город! |
| Йра | Ла́дно, е́сли бу́дет тепло́ и дождя́ не бу́дет, пое́дем. |
| Са́ша | Хорошо́. Я позвоню́ тебе́ сего́дня ве́чером ча́сов в во́семь. Е́сли бу́дет хоро́шая пого́да, пое́дем на авто́бусе в дере́вню. |
| Йра | В каку́ю дере́вню? В Тарака́новку, да? |
| Са́ша | Да. Недалеко́ отту́да большо́й, краси́вый лес. Там всегда́ ма́сса грибо́в. |
| Йра | Ну, е́сли и пое́дем, где встре́тимся? |
| Са́ша | По-мо́ему, А́нна не зна́ет, где остано́вка авто́буса … но она́ зна́ет, где ста́нция метро́ «Беля́ево», да? |
| Йра | Ду́маю, да. |
| Са́ша | Хорошо́, встре́тимся в метро́, посереди́не платфо́рмы, в семь часо́в. |
| Йра | Договори́лись. Ты позвони́шь мне сего́дня ве́чером, пото́м я позвоню́ А́нне и всё объясню́ ей. |
| Са́ша | Ну, всё! До ско́рого! |

QUICK VOCAB

| | |
|---|---|
| я пойду́ по магази́нам | I'll do the shopping (go to the shops) |
| выходно́й день | day off |
| дава́й пое́дем | let's go |
| за́ город | into the country |
| го́стья | (female) guest |
| подру́га | (female) friend |
| тем лу́чше | so much the better |
| пого́да | weather |

174

| | |
|---|---|
| хо́лодно | *it is cold* |
| дождь (m.) идёт | *it's raining* |
| собира́ть | *to gather, collect* |
| в таку́ю пого́ду | *in such weather* |
| прогно́з пого́ды | *weather forecast* |
| по ра́дио | *on the radio* |
| дава́й послу́шаем | *let's listen* |
| тогда́ | *then, in that case* |
| я позвоню́ тебе́ | *I'll ring you* |
| дере́вня | *village; countryside* |
| ма́сса | *mass* |
| е́сли и пое́дем | *if we do go* |
| где встре́тимся? | *where shall we meet each other?* |
| посереди́не платфо́рмы | *in the middle of the platform* |
| договори́лись | *agreed* |
| объясню́ | *I will explain* |

## Грибы́ *Mushrooms*

We saw in Unit 8 that mushrooms are an important part of Russian cuisine; collecting mushrooms is a favourite weekend pastime for town dwellers, who dry, salt or pickle their mushrooms for later use in a variety of **заку́ски,** soups and main dishes.

## Пого́да *Weather*

In an enormous country like the Russian Federation, it is no surprise that there is considerable variation in the climate. Moscow has a humid continental climate; winter temperatures rarely drop below −15°C and summer temperatures sometimes reach 30°. In Yakutia (in the far east of Siberia) winter temperatures dip to as low as −65 °, but it has relatively short and hot summers (July temperatures in excess of 30°). This temperature range contrasts with the mountainous southern republic of Altai, which has a temperate continental climate with winter temperatures dropping to −30° and summer highs of 19°.

If you want to check Russian weather forecasts on the internet, try www.gismeteo.ru/.

## Questions

**1** *True or false?*

**a** За́втра Са́ша хо́чет сиде́ть весь день до́ма.
**b** Сего́дня пого́да хоро́шая.
**c** Йра не хо́чет собира́ть грибы́, е́сли бу́дет хо́лодно.
**d** Е́сли пого́да бу́дет хоро́шая, они́ пое́дут за́ город в оди́ннадцать часо́в.

**2** *Answer the questions!*

**a** Почему́ Са́ша ду́мает, что в лесу́ бу́дет прия́тно?
**b** Как они́ пое́дут за́ город?
**c** Где они́ встре́тятся?
**d** Во ско́лько они́ встре́тятся?

## How do you say it?

How to:
**1** *Ask about future actions and intentions*

Каки́е у тебя́/вас пла́ны на за́втра?
Что ты бу́дешь де́лать за́втра? Что вы бу́дете де́лать за́втра?

> **Insight**
> In this Dialogue Sasha uses the phrase **пла́ны на за́втра** (*plans for tomorrow*). We first met **на** + accusative, meaning *intended for/planned for* in Unit 5, and it is very useful in time phrases: e.g. **пла́ны на суббо́ту** (*plans for Saturday*).

**2** *Talk about future actions and intentions*

Завтра я буду свободна.
Завтра я пойду по магазинам.
Завтра мы поедем за город.

**3** *Ask about the weather*

Какая сегодня погода?
Какая завтра будет погода?

**4** *Give information about the weather*

Сегодня холодно и идёт дождь.
Завтра будет тепло.

---

## Grammar

### 1 *Talking about the weather*

Answers to the question **Какая сегодня погода?** fall into four different categories:

**a** those that use the verb **идти** – rain, snow and hail all *walk*:

| | |
|---|---|
| идёт дождь | *it's raining* |
| идёт снег | *it's snowing* |
| идёт град | *it's hailing* |

**b** those that use verbs specific to the kind of weather – the sun *shines*, the wind *blows*:

| | |
|---|---|
| светит солнце | *the sun is shining* |
| дует ветер | *the wind is blowing* |

Note the **л** in **солнце** is not pronounced.

**c** those that use an adverb – it's cold, chilly, warm, hot, etc.:

| | | | |
|---|---|---|---|
| хо́лодно | *it's cold* | жа́рко | *it's hot* |
| прохла́дно | *it's chilly* | ду́шно | *it's suffocatingly hot* |
| тепло́ | *it's warm* | па́смурно | *it's overcast* |

## Insight

It might help you to learn the words for *warm* and *cold* by noting the similarities with English: the Russian word for *warm* (**тепло́**) sounds a little like the English word *tepid*, and the first syllable of **хо́лодно** (*cold*) has similarities with its English counterpart.

**NB** If you actually state the word *weather* you must use an adjective (not an adverb) and make it agree with **пого́да**:

| | |
|---|---|
| Сего́дня пого́да жа́ркая. | *The weather's hot today.* |
| Сего́дня жа́рко. | *It's hot today.* |

**d** those that just state a noun – *fog, a blizzard*:

| | |
|---|---|
| Сего́дня тума́н. | *It's foggy today.* |
| За́втра бу́дет мете́ль. | *There will be a blizzard tomorrow.* |

## Insight

In English we use the word *it* frequently: *is it foggy? Is it raining? Is it cold?* Russian likes to be more specific, and the key word (a noun, adverb or adjective) tends to come last in the phrase for emphasis:

Идёт снег
Сего́дня тума́н
Бу́дет тепло́
Сего́дня пого́да жа́ркая

## 2 The future tense

There are two kinds of future tense in Russian; one is used to describe actions in the future that are incomplete, unspecific, repeated, or continuing, e.g.: *When you are in Moscow I will ring you every day* or *Tomorrow I will write some letters, do some gardening and watch some television.*

The second form of the future is used for actions that are specific, single, completed, e.g.: *I will ring you tomorrow at four o'clock* or *I will write to Vanya tomorrow and watch the news at nine.*

The first kind of future tense is sometimes called the compound future, because it is made up of two elements: the future tense of the verb *to be*, which we met in Unit 9, and something called the imperfective infinitive. In Russian, verbs usually have two infinitives (i.e. the *to do* part of the verb). One is called the imperfective and the other the perfective. The present tense is made from the imperfective infinitive:

| | |
|---|---|
| imperfective infinitive: | слу́шать (*to listen to*) |
| present tense: | я слу́шаю, ты слу́шаешь etc. |
| compound (or imperfective) future: | я бу́ду слу́шать |

e.g.: Я бу́ду слу́шать ра́дио ка́ждый ве́чер.
*I will listen to the radio every evening.*

The second kind of future tense is sometimes called the simple future and is made in exactly the same way as the present tense, except that it is formed from the perfective infinitive:

| | |
|---|---|
| perfective infinitive: | послу́шать (*to listen to*) |
| perfective future tense: | я послу́шаю |

e.g.: Я послу́шаю прогно́з пого́ды в шесть часо́в.
*I'll listen to the weather forecast at six o'clock.*

It is important from now on always to learn both infinitives for each verb. They are usually written like this in dictionaries and vocabularies:

слу́шать/послу́шать (i.e. imperfective first, perfective second)

A large number of verbs have a perfective infinitive which looks exactly like the imperfective infinitive, except that it has some sort of prefix – thus, **слу́шать** has the perfective **послу́шать**.

Here are some more examples:

| | |
|---|---|
| ви́деть/уви́деть | *to see* |
| де́лать/сде́лать | *to do, make* |
| звони́ть/позвони́ть | *to ring* |
| писа́ть/написа́ть | *to write* |
| обе́дать/пообе́дать | *to have lunch* |
| смотре́ть/посмотре́ть | *to watch, look at* |

Sometimes the spelling of a verb is changed slightly by the addition of a prefix: **игра́ть/сыгра́ть** (*to play*).

Sometimes it is not the beginning but the ending of a verb which changes:

| | |
|---|---|
| встреча́ться/встре́титься | *to meet one another* |
| получа́ть/получи́ть | *to receive* |
| объясня́ть/объясни́ть | *to explain* |

In these three examples the imperfective infinitive is first conjugation (like **чита́ть**) and the perfective is second conjugation (like **говори́ть**) – this is often the case where the imperfective and perfective infinitives differ in the way they end.

**NB** Note especially the verb *to buy*, whose infinitives differ both at the beginning and at the end – **покупа́ть/купи́ть**.

Sometimes a verb has only one infinitive, e.g.: **быть** (*to be*), and occasionally there is little or no resemblance between the

imperfective and perfective: **говори́ть/сказа́ть** (*to say, tell*);
**возвраща́ться/верну́ться** (*to return*).

The verbs we met in Unit 9 which have two forms of the present tense
have two imperfective infinitives, but only one perfective infinitive.

| **Imperfectives** | **Perfective** |
|---|---|
| ходи́ть/идти́ | пойти́ |
| е́здить/е́хать | пое́хать |
| бе́гать/бежа́ть | побежа́ть |

## Insight

The compound future = future tense of **быть** + the
imperfective infinitive. It is used to talk about actions in the
future which are Repeated, Unspecific or General (RUG!):

**В а́вгусте я бу́ду рабо́тать в саду́ ка́ждый день**
(*In August I will do some gardening every day*).

The simple future = perfective infinitive with present tense
endings. It is used to talk about actions in the future dealing
with Completion And Result of something Specific (CARS!):

**В а́вгусте он вернётся домо́й** (*In August he will return home*).

Note that **дава́й[те]** (*let's*) is always followed by the perfective future:

| **Дава́йте пое́дем за́ город.** | *Let's go into the country.* |
|---|---|

Remember that the future tense of **быть** is needed if you want to
use **мо́жно, на́до, нельзя́** or **пора́** in a future sense, e.g.:

| **За́втра мне на́до бу́дет рабо́тать.** | *Tomorrow I will have to work.* |
|---|---|

Note too that, just as **нет** + genitive is used to express *do not have
any*, **не бу́дет** is used to express *will not have any*:

| **У меня́ не бу́дет вре́мени.** | *I won't have any time.* |
|---|---|

Usually it is quite clear when you need to use the future tense – *will* is the clearest indicator and there are often other clues as well (*tomorrow*, *next week*, etc.). However, English sometimes implies the future tense, but doesn't use it, e.g. *When you are in Moscow, I will ring you every day*. In Russian the future tense *must* be used whenever it is *implied*:

| | |
|---|---|
| Когда́ ты бу́дешь в Москве́, я бу́ду звони́ть тебе́ ка́ждый день. | *When you are (i.e. will be) in Moscow, I will ring you every day.* |

> ## Insight
> This is sometimes called the 'logical future' and the trick is to remember that English does not use the future tense after words such as *after*, *before*, *until* and *when*, but Russian does!

### 3 Звони́ть/позвони́ть *To telephone*

This verb means *to ring, to telephone*. If you are ringing someone remember to use the dative case for the person:

| | |
|---|---|
| Я позвоню́ тебе́ сего́дня ве́чером. | *I'll ring you this evening.* |
| И́ра позвони́т Áнне за́втра. | *Ira will ring Anna tomorrow.* |

If you're ringing a place, use **в** + accusative:

| | |
|---|---|
| Он позвони́т в больни́цу. | *He'll ring the hospital.* |

### 4 Идти́ *To walk, go on foot*

Note that as well as being used when talking about rain, snow and hail, this verb is also used to describe what's on, e.g. Что идёт в Большо́м теа́тре? *What's on at the Bolshoi?*

## 5 За́ го́род *Into the country*

This literally means *beyond the town* – here the preposition **за** (*beyond, behind*), which is normally used with the instrumental case, is used with the accusative case to express motion; *in the country* is **за́ го́родом** (i.e. with the instrumental case).

## 6 *Emphatic* и

The principal meaning of **и** is *and*, but it is also used to give extra emphasis; on such occasions it can be translated by English emphatic terms, such as *do, indeed, even*, e.g. **е́сли и пое́дем** *if we do go*.

---

## Practice

### 11.1 *Read and answer!*

Choose the correct form of the future tense:

- **a** Когда́ она́ бу́дет в Аме́рике, она́ ча́сто бу́дет игра́ть/ сыгра́ет в те́ннис.
- **b** За́втра я бу́ду писа́ть/напишу́ письмо́ Ви́ктору.
- **c** Я всегда́ бу́ду де́лать/сде́лаю поку́пки в универса́ме.
- **d** Я бу́ду звони́ть/позвоню́ вам за́втра в пять часо́в.
- **e** Когда́ они́ бу́дут в Москве́, они́ ча́сто бу́дут обе́дать/ пообе́дают в рестора́не «Кали́нка».

## Insight

As you can see from exercise 11.1, words such as **всегда́** (*always*) and **ча́сто** (*often*), which imply repetition in the future, are useful signposts that the compound future is needed, whereas a specific time such as **за́втра в пять часо́в** indicates that the simple future will be required.

### 11.2 Look and answer!

Look at the pictures below and answer the questions:

**a** Какáя сегóдня погóда?

**b** Какáя сегóдня погóда?

**c** Какáя сегóдня погóда?

**d** Какáя сегóдня погóда?

### 11.3 Look and write!

Look at the list below and make up sentences about where each person lives and what the weather is like there.

| Кто? | Где? | Далеко́ от Москвы́? | Кака́я сего́дня пого́да? |
|------|------|-------------------|-----------------------|
| **a** Óльга | Óбнинск | не о́чень | со́лнце, не хо́лодно |
| **b** Серёжа | Арха́нгельск | о́чень | снег, о́чень хо́лодно |
| **c** Еле́на | Ки́ев | далеко́ | тума́н, тепло́ |
| **d** Ю́рий | Ташке́нт | о́чень далеко́ | со́лнце, ду́шно |
| **e** Га́ля | Екатеринбу́рг | далеко́ | ве́тер, па́смурно |

**a** Óльга живёт в Óбнинске, недалеко́ от Москвы́. Сего́дня све́тит со́лнце, не хо́лодно.

### 11.4 Read, answer and listen!

You're not keen on taking up Petya's invitations! Complete your part of the conversation then listen to the complete conversation on the recording.

| | | |
|---|---|---|
| **Пе́тя** | У меня́ два биле́та на о́перу. Вы хоти́те пойти́ со мной? | **CD 2, TR 1, 02:31** |
| **Вы** | **(a)** Thank him, but say you can't because you've got to work (i.e. it is necessary for you to work) this evening. | |
| **Пе́тя** | Ой, как жаль. Ничего́. У меня́ то́же два биле́та в кино́ на за́втра. Хоти́те пойти́? | |
| **Вы** | **(b)** Say 'sorry', you're going (i.e. will go) to Olga's tomorrow. | |
| **Пе́тя** | Ничего́. В четве́рг бу́дет хокке́йный матч – у меня́ уже́ есть два биле́та. Хоти́те пойти́ со мной? | |
| **Вы** | **(c)** Thank him, but say it's very cold today. If it's cold on Thursday you won't really want to watch a hockey match. | |

| Пётя | Тогда́ дава́йте послу́шаем прогно́з пого́ды в сре́ду. |
|-------|------|
| Вы | **(d)** Say OK, you'll ring him on Wednesday at about eight o'clock. |
| Пётя | А каки́е у вас пла́ны на суббо́ту? |
| Вы | **(e)** Say you don't know, it depends on the weather. |

### 11.5 Read and answer!

Look at the following extract about television programmes and answer the questions.

**a** Which programme is on at 9 o'clock every evening?
**b** What is on at 18.30 on a Monday?
**c** When are there sports programmes?
**d** What are the names of the various music programmes?
**e** Which programmes would interest language students?

# СПРАВКИ: ТВ

| Понедельник – 28 мая | | Вторник – 29 мая | |
|-------|-------|-------|-------|
| 18.30 | Документальный фильм «Суздаль» | 18.30 | Теннис |
| 20.15 | Испанский язык | 19.30 | Итальянский язык |
| 21.00 | Новости | 20.00 | «Здравствуй, музыка!» |
| 23.00 | Конкурсы | 21.00 | Новости |
| **Среда – 30 мая** | | **Четверг – 31 мая** | |
| 18.00 | «Музыкальный киоск» | 18.45 | Фильм – детям |
| 20.00 | Мультфильм (*cartoon*) | 19.15 | Хоккей |
| 21.00 | Новости | 21.00 | Новости |
| 22.05 | «Что, где, когда?» | 22.00 | «Музыкальный телефон» |

## Comprehension

**1** *Conversation*

**Read, listen and answer!**

Misha and Lena are trying to agree about how to spend the weekend.

CD 2, TR 1, 03:40

| | |
|---|---|
| **Ми́ша** | Что мы бу́дем де́лать в суббо́ту? |
| **Ле́на** | Как, что? Мы пое́дем в го́род, ведь нам на́до сде́лать поку́пки. |
| **Ми́ша** | Ой, как ску́чно! Ка́жется, в суббо́ту бу́дет хоро́шая пого́да. Ты не хо́чешь пое́хать за́ город? |
| **Ле́на** | А как же мы мо́жем? В суббо́ту ве́чером мы пое́дем в го́сти к Мари́не. |
| **Ми́ша** | Пра́вда? (*Sighs.*) Ой, как ску́чно! |
| **Ле́на** | Ми́ша, что ты! Мари́на о́чень до́брый, интере́сный челове́к. |
| **Ми́ша** | Тогда́ что мы бу́дем де́лать в воскресе́нье? |
| **Ле́на** | Ве́чером мы пое́дем в теа́тр: у нас биле́ты на пье́су. |
| **Ми́ша** | А днём что бу́дем де́лать? |
| **Ле́на** | Что ты хо́чешь де́лать? |
| **Ми́ша** | Я хочу́ пое́хать за́ город. |
| **Ле́на** | Вре́мени не бу́дет, ведь ве́чером мы пойдём в теа́тр. |
| **Ми́ша** | Зна́ю, зна́ю. Тогда́ дава́й погуля́ем в па́рке … |
| **Ле́на** | Хорошо́, е́сли бу́дет хоро́шая пого́да. |
| **Ми́ша** | … пото́м пообе́даем в рестора́не. |
| **Ле́на** | Хорошо́ … а по́сле обе́да ты напи́шешь письмо́ ма́ме, да? |
| **Ми́ша** | (*Sighs.*) Напишу́, напишу́ … |

| как же? | how on earth? |
| ездить/ехать/поехать в гости (к + dative) | to visit (lit. to go as a guest) |
| добрый | good, kind |

**1** В субботу Лена хочет

**a** сидеть дома
**b** поехать за город
**c** делать покупки
**d** гулять в парке

**2** Миша думает, что у Марины

**a** не будет скучно
**b** будет скучно
**c** будет интересно
**d** будет приятно

**3** У них билеты

**a** на оперу
**b** на фильм
**c** на балет
**d** на пьесу

**4** Когда Миша напишет письмо маме?

**a** в субботу после обеда
**b** в воскресенье утром
**c** в воскресенье после обеда
**d** в воскресенье вечером

## 2 Reading

🔊 **CD 2, TR 1, 05:03**

**Read and listen to the text and answer the questions in English.**

**a** How much rain will there be in the Crimea this week?
**b** What news is there for swimmers?
**c** Will it be colder in Moscow or St Petersburg during the night according to forecast **A**?
**d** Which is the only place in forecast **A** to be unaffected by rain?
**e** Where is there a risk of fire?
**f** Where will there be snow according to forecast **Б**?
**g** Which place will be affected by strong wind according to forecast **Б**?

## А

В Крыму́ в нача́ле неде́ли без оса́дков, но́чью 12–17 гра́дусов тепла́, днём 22–27. В дальне́йшем кратковре́менные дожди́, гро́зы, но́чью 9–14, днём 18–24 гра́дуса. Температу́ра воды́ у берего́в Кры́ма 16–18 гра́дусов.

В Санкт-Петербу́рге в отде́льные дни кратковре́менные дожди́, но́чью 4–9, днём 13–18 гра́дусов.

В Москве́ и Подмоско́вье кратковре́менные дожди́, но́чью 7–12, днём 14–19, в отде́льные дни до 22 гра́дусов.

В Сре́дней А́зии бу́дет суха́я и жа́ркая пого́да, без оса́дков – там ожида́ется высо́кая пожа́рная опа́сность в леса́х.

## Б

В Арха́нгельске в нача́ле неде́ли температу́ра днём бу́дет 2–6 гра́дусов моро́за.

На восто́ке Украи́ны 2–7, места́ми 9 гра́дусов моро́за.

Снег и мете́ли на се́вере Ура́ла. Днём от 1–6 до 7–12 гра́дусов моро́за.

В Санкт-Петербу́рге в нача́ле неде́ли оса́дки; днём 1–5 гра́дусов моро́за, си́льный ве́тер.

В Москве и Подмоско́вье днём 3–7 гра́дусов моро́за.

| | |
|---|---|
| **в дальне́йшем** | later on, subsequently |
| **вода́** | water |
| **12 гра́дусов тепла́** | 12 degrees above zero |
| **гроза́** | (thunder)storm |
| **кратковре́менные дожди́** | showers |
| **места́ми** | in places |
| **моро́з** | frost |
| **нача́ло** | beginning |
| **ожида́ться** | to be expected |
| **опа́сность** (f.) | danger |
| **оса́дки** | precipitation |
| **отде́льный** | separate |

QUICK VOCAB

| | |
|---|---|
| | |

| | |
|---|---|
| **сильный** | *strong* |
| **Сре́дняя А́зия** | *Central Asia* |
| **сухо́й** | *dry* |
| **тепло́** | *warmth* |
| **Ура́л** | *Urals* |

## Key phrases

◀) **CD 2, TR 1, 06:36**

Can you remember how to say the following in Russian? Listen to the recording and practise saying each phrase.

**a** What are your plans for tomorrow?
**b** What's the weather like today?
**c** Tomorrow it will be hot.
**d** I will ring you tomorrow evening.
**e** Where shall we meet?

## Test yourself

**1** If you were told that the temperature tomorrow was expected to reach **три́дцать гра́дусов моро́за** would you opt for your fur hat or your sun hat?

**2** If you wanted to say *I will ring you tomorrow*, which case would you need for the word *you*?

**3** You have tickets for the theatre. How would you ask your friend if he/she wants to come with you?

**4** What question would you ask to find out what the weather is like today?

**5** What question would you ask to find out your friend's plans for Tuesday?

**6** Do you know why the following phrase uses the compound future? **Я всегда́ бу́ду де́лать поку́пки здесь.**

**7** If **э́то зави́сит от пого́ды** means *it depends on the weather*, how would you say *it depends on Anna*?

**8** What would you need to change and add to make the following phrase refer to tomorrow, instead of today? **Сего́дня мо́жно смотре́ть телеви́зор.**

**9** When would you need to use the word **дава́й** or **дава́йте**?

**10** If you were invited to spend a day **за́ го́родом** would you be more likely to be going for a stroll or window-shopping?

# 12

## Ира дома?
# Is Ira at home?

In this unit you will learn
- *How to hold a conversation on the telephone (how to identify yourself, ask for the person you want to speak to and how to deal with wrong numbers)*
- *How to talk about past events and actions*

## Dialogue

Anna decides to ring Ira from a call box to thank her for the trip into the country with Sasha, but she has some trouble getting through ...

CD 2, TR 2, 00:05

| | |
|---|---|
| **Áнна** | Алло́! Йра, э́то ты? |
| **Го́лос 1** | А? ... Како́й но́мер вы набра́ли? |
| **Áнна** | 428-39-56. |
| **Го́лос 1** | Нет, э́то не тот. |
| **Áнна** | Прости́те. (*Dials again.*) ... Алло́! |
| **Го́лос 2** | Магази́н «Де́тский мир». Слу́шаю вас. |
| **Áнна** | Извини́те. Опя́ть я не туда́ попа́ла! (*Dials again.*) ... Алло́! Йра до́ма? |
| **Йра** | Кто э́то говори́т? |
| **Áнна** | Говори́т А́нна ... А́нна Принс. |

| | |
|---|---|
| **Йра** | А́нна, приве́т! Отку́да ты звони́шь? |
| **А́нна** | Я в автома́те. Йра, я о́чень хочу́ тебя́ поблагодари́ть за на́шу пое́здку за́ город! |
| **Йра** | Интере́сно бы́ло, да? |
| **А́нна** | Да, всё бы́ло о́чень интере́сно! Спаси́бо большо́е! |
| **Йра** | Ну, что ты, А́нна. Нам то́же бы́ло о́чень прия́тно. |
| **А́нна** | Скажи́ Са́ше, пожа́луйста, что пое́здка мне о́чень понра́вилась. |
| **Йра** | Обяза́тельно скажу́. Он бу́дет о́чень рад ... А́нна, у меня́ два биле́та в Большо́й теа́тр на послеза́втра. Ты хо́чешь пойти́ со мно́й на о́перу? |
| **А́нна** | Коне́чно, о́чень хочу́! |
| **Йра** | Хорошо́, уви́димся послеза́втра на о́пере в Большо́м теа́тре, да? |
| **А́нна** | Как хорошо́! |
| **Йра** | Встре́тимся у вхо́да в теа́тр, полседьмо́го. Поня́тно? |
| **А́нна** | Да, всё поня́тно. Ещё раз спаси́бо! До ско́рого. |
| **Йра** | Всего́ до́брого, А́нна. До свида́ния. |

| | |
|---|---|
| **како́й но́мер вы набра́ли?** | *what number did you dial?* |
| **э́то не тот** | *it's not the right one* |
| **прости́те** | *sorry, forgive me* |
| **Де́тский мир** | *Children's World (name of a store)* |
| **опя́ть** | *again* |
| **я не туда́ попа́ла** | *I've got the wrong number* |
| **отку́да ты звони́шь?** | *where are you ringing from?* |
| **благодари́ть/поблагодари́ть (за + accusative)** | *to thank (for)* |
| **всё бы́ло** | *everything was* |
| **пое́здка мне о́чень понра́вилась** | *I really enjoyed the excursion* |
| **обяза́тельно скажу́** | *I'll tell him without fail/I'll be sure to tell him* |

QUICK VOCAB

| послеза́втра | the day after tomorrow |
| увидимся | we will see one another |
| всего́ до́брого | all the best |

### Телефо́н *Telephone*

When answering the telephone, it is usual to say **Алло́! Слу́шаю вас** (or just **слу́шаю**) or **Кто э́то говори́т?** If you are ringing a person's home telephone number you can ask for the person you want to speak to by asking if they are at home (**Ири́на до́ма?**); in more formal situations you might say **Мо́жно Ири́ну Никола́евну к телефо́ну?** (lit. *Is it possible [to call] Irina Nikolaevna to the telephone?*) or **Позови́те Ири́ну Никола́евну к телефо́ну, пожа́луйста** (lit. *Call Irina Nikolaevna to the telephone please*). To identify yourself say **С ва́ми говори́т …** or just **Говори́т …**; if someone asks for you and you want to say *speaking*, simply say **Э́то я** or **Я у телефо́на**. When you are dealing with wrong numbers, use **Э́то не тот** (lit. *It is not that one/that number*), **Вы не туда́ попа́ли** (lit. *You have turned up not to there*) or **Вы непра́вильно набра́ли но́мер** (lit. *You have dialled wrongly*). Look back to Unit 3 for more information on using telephones and remember that a mobile phone is either **моби́льный телефо́н** or **со́товый телефо́н**.

---

### Insight

A seven-digit telephone number will usually be split up and spoken as follows:

| 346-32-25 | три́ста три́дцать шесть – три́дцать два – два́дцать пять |
| | (i.e. three hundred and thirty six, thirty-two, twenty-five) |

---

However, if you find it easier to say each digit separately, you would be understood.

# Questions

## 1 *True or false?*

**a** А́нна не туда́ попа́ла два ра́за (*twice*).
**b** А́нна звони́т из гости́ницы.
**c** Послеза́втра А́нна и И́ра пойду́т в кинотеа́тр.
**d** А́нна и И́ра встре́тятся полседьмо́го.

## 2 *Answer the questions!*

**a** А́нна хо́чет позвони́ть в магази́н «Де́тский мир»?
**b** Как А́нне понра́вилась пое́здка за́ город?
**c** Когда́ И́ра и А́нна опя́ть уви́дятся?
**d** Где они́ встре́тятся?

# How do you say it?

How to:
**1** *Identify yourself on the telephone*

(С ва́ми) говори́т Ири́на Никола́евна.
Говори́т А́нна.
Э́то я.
Я у телефо́на.

**2** *Answer the telephone*

Алло́. Слу́шаю вас.
Кто э́то говори́т?

**3** *Deal with wrong numbers*

Это не тот.
Вы не туда́ попа́ли.
Вы непра́вильно набра́ли но́мер.

**4** *Talk about past events and actions*

Всё бы́ло о́чень интере́сно.
Пое́здка мне о́чень понра́вилась.
Нам то́же о́чень понра́вилось.

## Grammar

### 1 Благодари́ть/поблагодари́ть *to thank*

Note that this verb is followed by **за** + accusative: **благодарю́ тебя́ за экску́рсию**. Note also **Спаси́бо за** + accusative (**Спаси́бо за пода́рок**, *thank you for the present*) and **плати́ть/заплати́ть за** + accusative (*to pay for*).

> ## Insight
> Learning these useful ways of saying thank you and talking about payment will also help you to revise the accusative case:
>
> **Спаси́бо за но́вую кни́гу!** (*Thank you for the new book*).
> **На́до плати́ть за на́ши театра́льные биле́ты**
> (*It is necessary to pay for our theatre tickets*).

### 2 *Past tense*

In English we have various forms of the past tense:

*I was reading, I used to read, I have read, I read, I had read*

In Russian there are only two forms of the past tense; one is made from the imperfective infinitive (or imperfective aspect) and the other from the perfective infinitive (or perfective aspect).

The imperfective past tense is used for actions which are repeated, continuing or incomplete:

I *used to read* the newspaper every day.
I *was reading* the newspaper when the telephone rang.
I *was reading/read* the newspaper yesterday (but I didn't finish it).
I *read* for two hours yesterday.

Note that in a sentence such as *I read for two hours yesterday*, there is a sense of continuation – we are not informed whether the reading was finished or not, but that it went on for two hours – so we need to use the imperfective past tense.

The perfective past tense is used for single, completed actions:

I *read* the newspaper all the way through yesterday morning.
I had *already read* the newspaper when the telephone rang.

## Insight

Just as for the future tense (Unit 11), you have a choice in Russian for the past tense: use the IMPERFECTIVE if you are talking about the PROCESS of an action (habitual, repeated, continuing, general, unspecific), and the PERFECTIVE for the RESULT of an action (single, specific, completed).

Formation of the past tense is the same for both imperfective and the perfective. Take the infinitive, remove -ть and add the following:

| Subject of verb | Add | Example | Meaning |
|---|---|---|---|
| *Masculine singular* (verb: читáть/ прочитáть) | **л** | Вúктор читáл ромáн | *Viktor was reading a novel* |

| Feminine singular (verb: писа́ть/ написа́ть) | ла | О́ля написа́ла письмо́ | Olya has written the letter |
|---|---|---|---|
| Neuter singular (verb: свети́ть/ [no perf.]) | ло | Со́лнце свети́ло | The sun was shining |
| Plural (verb: слу́шать/ послу́шать) | ли | Мы слу́шали му́зыку | We were listening to music |

In other words, past tense endings are rather like adjective endings – they have to agree with the number (singular or plural?) and gender (masculine, feminine, neuter?) of the subject. (Note that when you are forming the past tense to agree with **вы** the ending will always be **-ли**, whether **вы** is referring to a group of people or whether it is being used as the polite form to one person only.) Most irregular verbs form their past tenses in this way too, e.g.: **жить** (жил, жила́, etc)., **хоте́ть** (хоте́л, хоте́ла, etc.). The only exceptions among the verbs we have met so far are:

| | |
|---|---|
| **вести́** (to lead, take on foot) | вёл, вела́, вело́, вели́ |
| **везти́** (to transport) | вёз, везла́, везло́, везли́ |
| **есть** (to eat) | ел, е́ла, е́ло, е́ли |
| **идти́** (to go on foot, to walk) | шёл, шла, шло, шли |
| **мочь** (to be able) | мог, могла́, могло́, могли́ |
| **нести́** (to carry) | нёс, несла́, несло́, несли́ |

Verbs of motion have three possible past tenses (since they have three infinitives – two imperfectives and one perfective). The past tense of the first imperfective can imply a habit or a return journey; the past tense of the second imperfective indicates an action which was in progress; the past tense of the perfective implies one single action in the past; this form often also means to *set off*:

| Imperfective | Imperfective | Perfective |
|---|---|---|
| ходи́ть | идти́ | пойти́ |
| он ходи́л *he used to go* (habit) | он шёл *he was going* (action in progress) | он пошёл *he has gone, has set off* |
| он ходи́л *he has been* (return journey) | | |

Note that the past tense of **быть** (*to be*) is required if you want to give **мо́жно, на́до, нельзя́, пора́**, a past meaning: **Вчера́ мне на́до бы́ло рабо́тать** (*Yesterday I had to work*). Similarly the past tense of **быть** is required if you need to use phrases like **У меня́ нет де́нег** (*I have no money*) in the past tense: **У меня́ не́ было де́нег** (*I had no money*).

## Insight

Only four endings for the past tense!
**Он быЛ в теа́тре и она́ быЛА́ в рестора́не. Мы бы́ЛИ до́ма – бы́ЛО ску́чно!** He was at the theatre, and she was at the restaurant. We were at home – it was boring!

### 3 Мы уви́димся *We'll see each other*

Note that the addition of reflexive endings to the verb **ви́деть/ уви́деть** (*to see*) produces the verb meaning *to see one another*: **уви́димся за́втра** (lit. *we will see one another tomorrow*) is frequently heard when people are saying goodbye. In Unit 11 we saw that **Где мы встре́тимся?** means *Where shall we meet [one another]?* – here the verb **встреча́ть/встре́тить** (*to meet*) has been made reflexive in the same way.

### 4 *Prepositional case*

We have already met some of the uses of the prepositional case and learnt how to form the prepositional singular of nouns; in **в Большо́м теа́тре** (*at the Bolshoi Theatre*) the prepositional singular of the adjective **большóй** is used. To form the prepositional of masculine and neuter singular adjectives add **-ом**, unless the rule about the unstressed **о** applies, in which case add **-ем**. Feminine singular adjectives add **-ой**, unless the rule about the unstressed **о** applies, in which case add **ей**:

| | |
|---|---|
| в нó вом музéе | *in the new museum* |
| в хорóшей кни́ге | *in a good book* |
| в стáром здáнии | *in the old building* |

## Insight

We have now covered all six singular case endings for adjectives. Have you noticed that there aren't many different feminine ones to learn? Just **-ая** for nominative and **-ую** for accusative; **-ой** or **-ей** for all the rest (genitive, dative instrumental and prepositional)!

## Practice

### 12.1 Read and answer!

Match the questions with the answers:

| | |
|---|---|
| **1** Комý онá звони́т? | **a** По срéдам. |
| **2** Когдá он обы́чно дéлает покýпки? | **b** Нет, не óчень. |
| **3** Когдá он позвони́л тебé? | **c** В универсáме. |
| **4** Где он обы́чно покупáет продýкты? | **d** И́ре. |
| **5** Вам понрáвилась экскýрсия? | **e** В срéду. |

### 12.2 Read and answer!

Which is the correct alternative (imperfective past or perfective past?)

**a** Когдá он жил в Гермáнии, он чáсто игрáл/сыгрáл в футбóл.

**b** Вчерá онá писáла/написáла письмó Ви́ктору.

**c** Ра́ньше Ни́на всегда́ де́лала/сде́лала поку́пки в це́нтре го́рода.

**d** Вчера́ мы смотре́ли/посмотре́ли телеви́зор, когда́ вдруг кто́-то звони́л/позвони́л в дверь.

**e** Снача́ла я чита́ла/прочита́ла газе́ту, пото́м я обе́дала/пообе́дала.


## 12.3 Look and answer!

What sort of career would you be interested in if you applied for a place on the course outlined in this extract from an advertisement?

> **Факультет административного менеджмента предлагает ...**
>
> ## Курсы МЕНЕДЖЕРОВ – МАРКЕТОЛОГОВ
>
> **В программе обучения – информационные ресурсы ИНТЕРНЕТ для маркетинга**


## 12.4 Look and write!

You are a 'telephone addict' – describe all the telephone calls you made yesterday, using the following information:

| Кому́? | О чём? |
|--------|--------|
| **a** Са́ша | его́ но́вая маши́на |
| **b** И́ра | пое́здка в Се́ргиев Поса́д |
| **c** Макси́м | францу́зский фи́льм |
| **d** А́лла | но́вый уче́бник (*textbook*) |
| **e** Воло́дя | плоха́я пого́да |

**a** Вчера́ я позвони́л(а) Са́ше. Мы говори́ли о его́ но́вой маши́не.

### 12.5 Read and answer!

Read what Nina did yesterday, then answer the questions that follow.

Вчера́ я была́ о́чень занята́. Я вста́ла в семь часо́в и поза́втракала на ку́хне. У́тром я рабо́тала два часа́ в библиоте́ке, пото́м я пообе́дала в буфе́те. По́сле обе́да я сде́лала поку́пки в универса́ме. Ве́чером я пригото́вила у́жин, написа́ла письмо́ ма́ме, пото́м смотре́ла телеви́зор.

**a** Во ско́лько Ни́на вста́ла?
**b** Где она́ поза́втракала?
**c** Что она́ де́лала у́тром?
**d** Где она́ пообе́дала?
**e** Что она́ де́лала ве́чером?

| | |
|---|---|
| встава́ть/встать | to get up |
| гото́вить/пригото́вить | to prepare, cook |

**f** The following information tells you what Vadim did yesterday. Use it to write a paragraph following the model about Nina above:

| У́тром | По́сле обе́да | Ве́чером |
|---|---|---|
| Встать: полшесто́го | рабо́тать: | игра́ть: футбо́л |
| поза́втракать: ку́хня | 3 часа́/заво́д | смотре́ть: телеви́зор |
| рабо́тать: 5 часо́в/заво́д | | чита́ть: газе́та |
| пообе́дать: рестора́н | | |

Now answer these questions about yourself.

**a** Во ско́лько вы вста́ли вчера́?
**b** Где вы поза́втракали?
**c** Что вы де́лали у́тром?
**d** Где вы пообе́дали?
**e** Что вы де́лали ве́чером?

---

## Comprehension

### 1 *Conversation*

**Read, listen and answer!**

Maxim is very absent-minded and has forgotten the essential details about an important meeting. He rings Lena for help.

| | |
|---|---|
| **Го́лос** | Алло́. |
| **Макси́м** | Алло́. Мо́жно Ле́ну к телефо́ну, пожа́луйста? |
| **Го́лос** | Мину́точку ... она́ сейча́с подойдёт. |
| **Макси́м** | Алло́. Ле́на? |
| **Ле́на** | Да, э́то я. Кто э́то говори́т? |
| **Макси́м** | Э́то Макси́м. |
| **Ле́на** | Здра́вствуй, Макси́м. Как дела́? |
| **Макси́м** | Ничего́, спаси́бо ... Скажи́, Ле́на, ты за́втра бу́дешь на совеща́нии у дире́ктора? |
| **Ле́на** | Коне́чно, ведь э́то о́чень ва́жное совеща́ние. |
| **Макси́м** | Зна́ю, зна́ю ... то́лько я забы́л ... во ско́лько э́то бу́дет? |
| **Ле́на** | Полоди́ннадцатого утра́. |
| **Макси́м** | Ах, да, коне́чно ... |
| **Ле́на** | Э́то всё? ... Я сейча́с о́чень занята́, Макси́м. |
| **Макси́м** | Извини́, Ле́на ... а я не о́чень хорошо́ по́мню, о чём мы бу́дем говори́ть на совеща́нии. |

CD 2, TR 2, 02:27

| Ле́на | Что ты, Макси́м! Мы коне́чно бу́дем говори́ть о но́вом догово́ре с францу́зской автомоби́льной компа́нией. |
|---|---|
| Макси́м | Ах, да, коне́чно ... Спаси́бо, Лена ... э́то всё! До за́втра. |
| Ле́на | Всего́ до́брого, Макси́м. До свида́ния. |

| | |
|---|---|
| она́ сейча́с подойдёт | she's just coming |
| совеща́ние | meeting |
| дире́ктор | director |
| ва́жный | important |
| забыва́ть/забы́ть | to forget |
| по́мнить/вспо́мнить | to remember |
| догово́р | agreement, contract |
| автомоби́льная компа́ния | car company |

**1** Ва́жное совеща́ние бу́дет

**a** сего́дня в 10ч30 у́тра
**b** за́втра в 10ч30 у́тра
**c** за́втра в 11 часо́в
**d** сего́дня у́тром

**2** Ле́на сейча́с

**a** отдыха́ет
**b** свобо́дна
**c** о́чень занята́
**d** не о́чень занята́

**3** На совеща́нии они́ бу́дут говори́ть о

**a** но́вом догово́ре с италья́нской компа́нией
**b** ста́ром догово́ре с францу́зской компа́нией
**c** но́вом догово́ре с францу́зской компа́нией
**d** нева́жном догово́ре с францу́зской компа́нией

## 2 Reading

Read the text and answer the questions in English.

**a** What did 46% of people between the ages of 25 and 34 say they could not do?

**b** What do young people not remember?

**c** What does the mobile phone help them to organize?

**d** How much time do young people say their spend on their mobiles per day?

**e** What are the two most popular mobile services?

Что такóе моби́льный телефóн для совремéнного человéка? Результáты опрóса покáзывают, что 46% опрóшенных в вóзрасте от 25 до 34 лет сказáли, что не мóгут жить без моби́льных телефóнов. Молоды́е, конéчно, не пóмнят жизнь без моби́льников для организáции ли́чной и социáльной жи́зни. Нéкоторые молоды́е лю́ди сказáли, что они́ провóдят в общéнии со свои́м

моби́льным часá три в день. Для 40% респондéнтов сáмые популя́рные услýги – моби́льный шóппинг и отпрáвка СМС.

| | |
|---|---|
| **вóзраст** | *age* |
| **жизнь** (f.) | *life* |
| **ли́чный** | *personal* |
| **нéкоторые молоды́е лю́ди** | *some young people* |
| **общéние** | *communication* |
| **опрóс** | *questionnaire, survey* |
| **опрóшенный** | *person who answers a questionnaire* |
| **отпрáвка СМС (эс-эм-эс)** | *texting* |
| **покáзывать/показáть** | *to show* |
| **пóмнить** | *to remember* |
| **проводи́ть/провести́** | *to spend (of time)* |
| **совремéнный** | *modern* |

**QUICK VOCAB**

## Key phrases

◄) CD 2, TR 2, 03:53

Can you remember how to say the following in Russian? Listen to the recording and practise saying each phrase.

**a** Who's speaking?
**b** Is Viktor at home?
**c** Everything was very interesting.
**d** Thanks again!
**e** All the best.

## Ten things to remember

1 **Всего доброго** (*all the best*) is a good phrase to use at the end of a telephone conversation with a friend; the phrase is in the genitive case because the verb **желать** (*to wish*) is understood (see Unit 9).

2 **Увидимся** (literally: *we'll see each other*) can often be a useful phrase when making arrangements for the next meeting with a friend and is usually followed by the relevant time phrase (e.g. **завтра** – *tomorrow*).

3 When saying goodbye to someone, phrases such as *until tomorrow* (**до завтра**), *until Monday* (**до понедельника**) can be useful.

4 Remember to use the accusative after **за** when you are thanking someone for something: **спасибо за вкусный ужин** (*thank you for the delicious supper*).

5 When making the past tense, you must chose whether to make it from the imperfective or the perfective infinitive. Remember

that the imperfective will deal with PROCESS and the perfective with RESULT.

**6** Now we have covered the past tense, you will find time phrases even more useful; remember that many of these use the instrumental case (e.g. **ле́том** – *in the summer*, see Unit 9).

**7** Now we have done the prepositional case of singular adjectives (masculine and neuter: **-ом/-ем**; feminine: **-ой/-ей**), you will be able to give more details about where you live, for example: **я живу́ в ма́леньком до́ме в краси́вой дере́вне** (*I live in a small house in a beautiful village*).

**8** When answering the telephone it is usual to say **Алло́!** Note that this is pronounced *аллё*.

**9** A mobile phone is either **со́товый телефо́н, моби́льный телефо́н** or **моби́льник**.

**10** The dative case is needed for the person you telephone: **Вчера́ ве́чером я позвони́ла Ви́ктору и О́льге** (*Yesterday I rang Viktor and Olga*).

# 13

## Мне нужно к врачу?
## Must I go to the doctor's?

In this unit you will learn
- *How to say how you feel*
- *How to ask others how they feel*
- *How to seek and give advice*
- *How to talk about necessity*

### Dialogue

Ira has called for Anna at her hotel room, to go on their trip to Sergiev Posad, but finds Anna is not well.

CD 2, TR 3, 00:07

| Йра | Áнна, ты сегóдня невáжно выглядишь. Что с тобóй? Ты больнá? |
|---|---|
| Áнна | Да, мне кáжется, я заболéла. Мне плóхо. У меня болит гóрло. |
| Йра | И головá болит? |
| Áнна | Кáжется, да. |
| Йра | Гм, мóжет быть у тебя начинáется грипп. |
| Áнна | Что мне дéлать? Что ты совéтуешь? Мне нýжно к врачý? |
| Йра | Нет, тебé лýчше лежáть в постéли. Я сейчáс позвоню в бюрó обслýживания. Врач скóро придёт. |
| Áнна | Знáчит, нам сегóдня нельзя в Сéргиев Посáд? |

| Йра | Да, Áнна, я дýмаю, что сегóдня нельзя́. |
|---|---|
| Áнна | Ой, как жаль. Извини́, Йра. |
| Йра | Ничегó, Áнна. Не беспокóйся об э́том. Сегóдня ты должна́ отдыха́ть. |
| Áнна | Спаси́бо, Йра, ты óчень добра́. |
| Йра | Не́ за что! Скажи́, Áнна, что тебе́ нýжно? Тебе́ хóчется пить? |
| Áнна | Да, óчень хочý. |
| Йра | Хорошó ... я закажý че́рез дежýрную чай с лимóном. Э́то всегда́ помога́ет. Тебе́ скóро бýдет лýчше. |

| | |
|---|---|
| ты нева́жно вы́глядишь | you don't look too well |
| что с тобóй? | what's wrong with you? |
| ты больна́? | are you ill? |
| я заболе́ла | I'm ill (lit. I've been taken ill) |
| мне плóхо | I feel unwell |
| у меня́ боли́т гóрло | I have a sore throat |
| головá | head |
| грипп | flu |
| что ты сове́туешь? | what do you advise? |
| мне нýжно к врачý? | must I go to the doctor's? |
| тебе́ лýчше лежа́ть в посте́ли | you'd better stay in bed |
| врач скóро придёт | the doctor will soon be here |
| не беспокóйся об э́том! | don't worry about it |
| ты должна́ | you must |
| ты óчень добра́ | you're very kind |
| не́ за что! | think nothing of it! |
| тебе́ хóчется пить? | are you thirsty? |
| я закажý (зака́зывать/заказа́ть) | to order |
| помога́ть/помóчь | to help |
| тебе́ скóро бýдет лýчше | you'll soon feel better |

QUICK VOCAB

## Insight

**Нам сегóдня нельзя́** (for us today it is not possible). Remember that you need to use the dative case to explain who can't/must do something: **Тебе́ на́до отды́хать!** (You must rest!).

## Врач *The doctor*

Visitors to Russia can arrange to see a doctor by contacting the hotel service bureau; the doctor may visit you in your hotel room, or you may be referred to the hotel's own treatment centre – **медпу́нкт**. The **дежу́рная** (literally *woman on duty*) is responsible for the organization of her floor/corridor in the hotel.

Russian citizens would normally ring a polyclinic – **поликли́ника** – to arrange for the doctor to make a home visit or they might go to the polyclinic themselves.

When patients make appointments at a polyclinic they are given a **тало́н** (*coupon/card*) for a particular doctor's surgery at a particular time. The doctor may give the patient a **реце́пт** (*prescription*), to be bought at the **апте́ка** (*chemist's*). Note that there are two words for doctor – **врач** (to denote the profession) and **до́ктор** (for when you're talking to one). In the event of an emergency, an ambulance can be summoned by dialling 03 (**ноль три**). For some, a stay in the **больни́ца** (*hospital*) may be necessary or a spell in a **санато́рий** (*convalescent home*) or **дом о́тдыха** (*rest home*).

### Sergiev Posad

The town of Sergiev Posad (known as Zagorsk during the Soviet era) lies some 75 kilometres from Moscow; it is an important centre of the Russian Orthodox Church and site of the Trinity Monastery of St Sergii.

---

## Questions

### 1 *True or false?*

**a** А́нне сего́дня пло́хо.
**b** Сего́дня А́нна и И́ра пое́дут в Се́ргиев Поса́д.
**c** И́ра звони́т в поликли́нику.
**d** И́ра рекоменду́ет чай с лимо́ном.

## 2 Answer the questions!

**a** Как Áнна сегóдня вы́глядит?
**b** Что у Áнны боли́т?
**c** Как мóжно заказáть чай с лимóном?
**d** Кудá Áнна хотéла сегóдня поéхать?

---

# How do you say it?

How to:
**1** *Say how you feel*

Мне плóхо.

**2** *Ask others how they feel*

Что с тобóй?                    Что с вáми?
Ты больнá?                      Ты бóлен? Вы больны́?

**3** *Ask for advice*

Что мне дéлать?
Что ты совéтуешь?              Что вы совéтуете?

**4** *Giving advice*

Тебé лýчше.                      Вам лýчше.
Я совéтую.
Не беспокóйся!                  Не беспокóйтесь!

**5** *Talk about necessity*

Мне нýжно к врачý?
Что тебé нýжно?
Ты должнá.        Ты дóлжен.        Вы должны́.

## Grammar

### 1 *Dative case*

In Unit 6 we saw that the dative case is used to mean *to*, *for* and after verbs such as *to give*, *to say*. The dative case is also very useful when describing how you feel; it is used in impersonal expressions made up of the dative case and the short form of the neuter adjective:

| | |
|---|---|
| **Мне жа́рко.** | *I feel hot* (lit. *it is hot for me*). |
| **Вам не хо́лодно?** | *Are you cold?* |
| **Ему́ бы́ло пло́хо.** | *He felt ill.* |

This construction is useful not only when you are describing physical feelings – you can also use it to talk about boredom and interest:

| | |
|---|---|
| **Мне бы́ло о́чень скучно на ле́кции.** | *I found it very boring at the lecture.* |
| **Ему́ о́чень интере́сно чита́ть ру́сские газе́ты.** | *He finds it very interesting to read Russian newspapers.* |

The dative case is also used after certain verbs, some of which we have already met. Here is a list of the most common:

| | |
|---|---|
| **звони́ть/позвони́ть** (*to ring*) | **Óля позвони́ла врачу́** *Olya rang the doctor* |
| **каза́ться/показа́ться** (*to seem*) | **Мне ка́жется, что у тебя́ грипп** *I think (it seems to me) you've got the flu* |
| **нра́виться/ по-нра́виться** (*to please*) | **Ей не нра́вятся э́ти табле́тки** *She doesn't like these tablets* |
| **помога́ть/помо́чь** (*to help*) | **Э́ти табле́тки помо́гут вам** *These tablets will help you* |
| **рекомендова́ть/ порекомендова́ть** (*to recommend*) | **Что вы рекоменду́ете мне?** *What do you recommend for me?* |

| советовать/ посоветовать (to advise) | Врач посоветовал ей отдыхать *The doctor advised her to rest* |
| хотеться/захотеться (to want, feel like) | Мне хочется спать *I want to sleep/I feel like a sleep* |

Note that the dative case is also found in time expressions with the preposition **к**:

| **к часу** | *at about one o'clock, towards one o'clock* |
| **к шести часам** | *at about six o'clock, towards six o'clock* |

Finally, the dative case is very useful when you are talking about necessity:

| **Что мне делать?** | *What should I do?* (lit. *What to me to do?*) |
| **Когда мне принимать таблетки?** | *When should I take the tablets?* |

························································································
## Insight

You have now met various ways of stating how you think/ feel:

| **Я думаю, что здесь скучно** | *I think it's boring here* |
| **Мне кажется, что здесь скучно** | *It seems to me that it's boring here* |
| **Мне здесь скучно** | *I feel bored here* |
| **По-моему здесь скучно** | *In my opinion it's boring here* |
························································································

### 2 Short adjectives

In Unit 8 we saw that most Russian adjectives have a long and a short form and we met some commonly used short forms – note the following further examples of short form adjectives:

| Meaning | Masc. | Fem. | Neut. | Pl. |
|---|---|---|---|---|
| ill | бóлен | больнá | бóльно | больны́ |
| duty-bound (must, have to, should) | дóлжен | должнá | должнó | должны́ |
| necessary | нýжен | нужнá | нýжно | нужны́ |

**Дóлжен** agrees with the person who must do something, e.g.:

| | |
|---|---|
| Сегóдня Áнна должнá отдыхáть. | *Anna must rest today.* |
| Вчерá Алексéй дóлжен был отдыхáть. | *Yesterday Alexei had to rest.* |
| Зáвтра мы должны́ бýдем отдыхáть. | *We must/will have to rest tomorrow.* |

**Нýжен** must agree with the thing that is needed e.g.:

| | |
|---|---|
| Тебé нужнá э́та кни́га? | *Do you need this book? (lit. is this book necessary to you?)* |

The neuter form **нýжно** is identical in meaning to **нáдо**.

## Insight

In English, verbs express the idea of *must* and *need*, but Russian uses short adjectives:

- **Дóлжен** agrees with the *person* who *must* do something – **Они́ должны́ рабóтать** (*They must work*).

- **Нýжен** agrees with the *item* which is *necessary*: **Мне нужнá вáша кни́га** (*I need your book*).

Note that there is a difference in meaning between the short form **бóлен** and the long form adjective **больнóй**:

| бо́лен (больна́, больны́) | sick, ill (temporarily) |
| больно́й | chronically ill, an invalid; a patient |

Note also:

| прав | right, correct | жив | alive |
| пра́вый | right-wing | живо́й | lively |

'The customer is always right ...'

> **покупа́тель** (m.)   customer

## 3 Verbs ending in -овать and -евать

The infinitive of these verbs looks like the infinitive of a first conjugation verb, but beware! In the present tense the -ова and -ева change to -у, e.g.:

| рекомендова́ть | рекоменду́ю | рекоменду́ем |
| (to recommend) | рекоменду́ешь | рекоменду́ете |
| | рекоменду́ет | рекоменду́ют |

Many of these verbs are imported from other languages, e.g.:

| танцева́ть | to dance (from German) |
| интересова́ться | to be interested |
| нокаути́ровать | to knock out |

In the context of health, the following are very common:

| | |
|---|---|
| жа́ловаться (на + accusative) | *to complain (of, about)* |
| На что вы жа́луетесь? | *What's the problem? (lit. What are you complaining of?)* |
| чу́вствовать себя́ | *to feel* |
| Как вы себя́ чу́вствуете? | *How are you feeling?* |

(Note that with the verb *to feel* the **себя́** never changes.)

---

**Insight**

Verbs ending in **-евать/овать** 'lose their middle', like verbs ending in **-авать** (e.g. **дава́ть**, to give – see Unit 2):

**Балери́на танцу́ет и жа́луется, что ей бо́льно; врач даёт ей сове́ты и рекоменду́ет по́лный покой.**
(*The ballerina dances and complains that she's in pain; the doctor gives her advice and recommends complete rest.*)

---

**4 'To be ill'; 'to hurt'; 'to be sore'**

**a** The verb **боле́ть** (present tense **боле́ю, боле́ешь**) means *to be ill* (*with*), e.g.:

Áнна боле́ет гри́ппом.          *Anna is ill with the flu.*

**b** The verb **заболева́ть/заболе́ть** means *to fall ill with*, *to catch*, e.g.:

Áнна заболе́ла гри́ппом.          *Anna has caught flu.*

(NB **Заболева́ть**, exceptionally, *does* work like a first conjugation verb – i.e. **заболева́ю, заболева́ешь**).

**c** The verb **боле́ть** (second conjugation, like **говори́ть**) is found only in the third person singular and the third person plural:

| | |
|---|---|
| У меня́ боли́т голова́. | *My head aches.* |
| У меня́ боля́т но́ги. | *My legs/feet ache.* |

The perfective form **заболе́ть** has the meaning *to begin to hurt*:

| | |
|---|---|
| Когда́ у вас заболе́л зуб? | *When did your tooth begin to hurt?* |

Note that Russian does not use possessive adjectives with parts of the body (i.e. to say *your tooth*, use **у вас зуб**).

### 5 *Verbs ending in* -**казать**

This ending is found in the verb for *to seem* (**каза́ться/показа́ться**) and also in the perfective infinitive of a number of common verbs:

| | |
|---|---|
| говори́ть/сказа́ть | *to say, tell* |
| зака́зывать/заказа́ть | *to order, book, reserve* |
| пока́зывать/показа́ть | *to show* |

Note that verbs which end in this way are not regular first conjugation:

| | |
|---|---|
| я скажу́ (*I will say*) | мы ска́жем |
| ты ска́жешь | вы ска́жете |
| он ска́жет | они́ ска́жут |

---

## Practice

### 13.1 *Look and answer!*

Как они́ себя́ чу́вствуют?

**a** Ива́н

*hot*   Ива́ну жа́рко

**b** Óля

cold

**c** Серёжа

bad/unwell

**d** Ви́ктор

bored

### 13.2  Read and answer!

Look at the doctor's question and the patient's answer:

Зуб
– На что вы жа́луетесь?
– У меня́ боли́т зуб.

Answer in a similar way, using the words given below:

**a** голова́
**b** го́рло
**c** ру́ки (*hands/arms*)
**d** живо́т (*stomach*)
**e** спина́ (*back*)

### 13.3  Read, answer and listen!

You are on holiday in Yalta. You are feeling unwell and the doctor has come to visit you. Complete your part of this conversation, then listen to the complete conversation on the recording.

CD 2, TR 3, 01:41

| | |
|---|---|
| **Врач** | Здра́вствуйте! Сади́тесь, пожа́луйста. На что вы жа́луетесь? |
| **Вы** | **(a)** Say 'hello' to the doctor. Explain that you have a sore throat. |
| **Врач** | А кака́я у вас температу́ра? |
| **Вы** | **(b)** Say you think you have a high temperature. |
| **Врач** | Ну, откро́йте, пожа́луйста, рот … да, го́рло кра́сное. У вас анги́на. |
| **Вы** | **(c)** Ask what you should do. |
| **Врач** | Вы должны́ отдыха́ть. Вот вам табле́тки. |
| **Вы** | **(d)** Ask when you should take the tablets. |
| **Врач** | Принима́йте по табле́тке два ра́за в день. Заходи́те ко мне за́врта в медпу́нкт. |

| | |
|---|---|
| температу́ра | *temperature* |
| высо́кий | *high* |
| откро́йте! | *open!* |
| рот | *mouth* |
| анги́на | *tonsillitis* |
| принима́ть | *to take* |
| по табле́тке два ра́за в день | *one tablet twice a day* |
| заходи́ть/зайти́ | *to call in/pop in* |

QUICK VOCAB

## Insight

Two useful formulae:

- **y** + *genitive of person* + **боли́т/боля́т** *(for plural)* + *part of the body:* **У меня́ боли́т го́рло и боля́т глаза́** *(I have a sore throat and my eyes hurt).*

- *dative of the person* + *adverb* to describe the feeling: **мне пло́хо** *(I feel ill).*

### 13.4 Look and answer!

Look at the pictures and decide what the doctor is advising:

**a** Что рекомендует врач?

Врач рекомендует мне не курить.

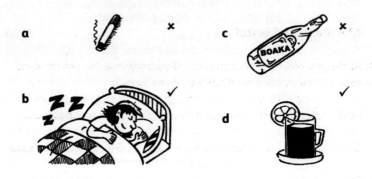

### 13.5 Read and answer!

Choose the most appropriate 'prescription' for each of the following:

**1** Аркадий чувствует себя нехорошо. У него болит зуб. Что ему надо делать?

**a** купить мороженое; **b** пойти в бассейн; **c** принимать таблетки

**2** У Светы болит горло. Что ей надо делать?

**a** смотреть футбольный матч; **b** отдыхать дома; **c** петь на концерте

**3** У Бориса голова болит. Что ему надо делать?

**a** читать «Войну и мир»; **b** идти на дискотеку; **c** лежать в постели

**4** У вас боли́т нога́. Что вам на́до де́лать?

**a** игра́ть в хокке́й; **b** сиде́ть до́ма; **c** гуля́ть с соба́кой

| | |
|---|---|
| **петь (пою́, поёшь)** | *to sing* |
| **дискоте́ка** | *disco* |
| **Война́ и мир** | *War and Peace* |

### 13.6 Read and write!

Read the symptoms, advice and conclusions in the list below, then write a sentence about each following the model.

| | Кто? | Что боли́т? | Что де́лать? | Зна́чит, нельзя́ ... |
|---|---|---|---|---|
| **a** | О́ля | живо́т | позвони́ть в поликли́нику | обе́дать в рестора́не |
| **b** | Та́ня | нога́ | сиде́ть до́ма | игра́ть в те́ннис |
| **c** | Вы | спина́ | лежа́ть в посте́ли | рабо́тать в саду́ |
| **d** | А́лла | го́рло | пить чай с лимо́ном | петь на конце́рте |
| **e** | Он | глаз | отдыха́ть | смотре́ть телеви́зор |

**a** У О́ли боли́т живо́т. Она́ должна́ позвони́ть в поликли́нику. Зна́чит ей нельзя́ обе́дать в рестора́не.

Now write similar sentences about the others listed above.

## Insight

Different ways of seeking advice:

* Question word + dative of the person needing advice + infinitive: **Что нам де́лать?** (*What should we do?*) **Когда́ ему́ принима́ть табле́тки?** (*When should he take the tablets?*)

* Use the verbs *to recommend, to advise*: **Что вы рекоменду́ете/сове́туете, до́ктор?** (*What do you recommend/advise, doctor?*).

## Comprehension

### 1 *Conversation*

**Read, listen and answer!**

Sasha is at the doctor's.

| | |
|---|---|
| **Врач** | На что вы жа́луетесь? |
| **Са́ша** | У меня́ о́чень боли́т живо́т. |
| **Врач** | Когда́ э́то начало́сь? |
| **Са́ша** | Вчера́ то́лько. |
| **Врач** | Покажи́те мне, где у вас боли́т? |
| **Са́ша** | Вот здесь, с пра́вой стороны́. |
| **Врач** | Си́льно боли́т? |
| **Са́ша** | Да, до́ктор, о́чень бо́льно. |
| **Врач** | Гм. Аппети́т есть? |
| **Са́ша** | Нет. Вчера́ я ничего́ не ел. Сего́дня то́же не хочу́ есть. Что де́лать, до́ктор? Табле́тки мне помо́гут? |
| **Врач** | Я не ду́маю. У вас, ка́жется, аппендици́т. |
| **Са́ша** | За́втра мне ну́жно пое́хать в Новосиби́рск! |
| **Врач** | Ни в ко́ем слу́чае! Вам ну́жно неме́дленно в больни́цу. |

| QUICK VOCAB | |
|---|---|
| **си́льно** | *strongly* |
| **бо́льно** | *painful* |
| **ничего́ не ел** | *I ate nothing* |
| **ни в ко́ем слу́чае** | *on no account* |
| **неме́дленно** | *immediately* |

**True or false?**

**a** У Са́ши боли́т рука́.
**b** Он бо́лен уже́ четы́ре дня.

**c** У него́ си́льные бо́ли (*pains*) в живо́те.
**d** Са́ше не хо́чется есть.
**e** Са́ша до́лжен принима́ть табле́тки.
**f** Са́ше нельзя́ за́втра пое́хать в Новосиби́рск.


## 2 *Reading*

Read and listen to the text, and answer the questions in English.

◄⅃) CD 2, TR 3, 03:29

**a** What cannot be bought?
**b** For whom is illness particularly unpleasant?
**c** From what illness does Tamara's child suffer?
**d** Why are medicines a problem for Tamara?
**e** What takes her a great deal of time every day?
**f** What must her child do four or five times every day?

Уважа́емый реда́ктор!

«Всё мо́жно купи́ть, кро́ме здоро́вья». Боле́ть всегда́
неприя́тно. Де́тям осо́бенно неприя́тно. У моего́ ребёнка
са́харный диабе́т. Это стра́шная боле́знь. А где прогре́сс
в лече́нии диабе́та? Сейча́с все говоря́т по ра́дио, по
телеви́зору, в газе́тах о СПИДе. А что же диабе́т?

Сейча́с в Росси́и ещё возмо́жно лечи́ться беспла́тно.
Но у меня́ така́я пробле́ма: кро́ме инсули́на, не все ну́жные
лека́рства беспла́тны. Ещё пробле́ма. Ка́ждый день я теря́ю
ма́ссу вре́мени в по́исках ну́жных овоще́й и фру́ктов, а
ребёнок до́лжен 4–5 раз в день принима́ть пи́щу. Что же
мне де́лать?

Тама́ра Ива́новна Кузнецо́ва, г. Пермь

(«Литерату́рная газе́та»)

| | |
|---|---|
| беспла́тный | *free* |
| боле́знь | *illness* |
| возмо́жно | *possible* |
| в по́исках (+ gen.) | *in search (of)* |
| здоро́вье | *health* |
| кро́ме (+ gen.) | *except* |
| лека́рство | *medicine* |
| лече́ние | *treatment* |
| лечи́ться | *to be treated* |
| осо́бенно | *especially* |
| пи́ща | *food* |
| СПИД | *AIDS* |
| стра́шный | *dreadful* |
| теря́ть/потеря́ть | *to lose* |
| Уважа́емый реда́ктор | *Dear Editor* |

## Key phrases

◀) CD 2, TR 3, 04:40

Can you remember how to say the following in Russian? Listen to the recording and practise saying each phrase.

  **a** What's wrong with you?
  **b** I feel ill.
  **c** Do you feel better?
  **d** Don't worry.
  **e** Are you thirsty?

## Test yourself

**1** How would you tell someone that you feel cold?

**2** If someone says **спасибо** to you, you could reply **пожалуйста**. What else could you say? Have another look at the Dialogue in Unit 13 if you can't remember.

**3** Your head aches. How will you explain this to the doctor?

**4** The verb **интересоваться** is followed by the instrumental case. How will you explain to someone that you are interested in Russian literature – **русская литература**? See Unit 8 to remind yourself of the case endings for the instrumental case.

**5** The verb **жаловаться** is followed by **на** and the accusative case. How would you complain about a *boring excursion* – **скучная экскурсия**? (Units 3 and 10 can help you with accusative endings.)

**6** **Мне нужны таблетки!** (*I need some tablets!*). Can you explain the ending of **нужны?** See Grammar section 2 if you need help.

**7** Which word will you need to put into this sentence to explain that you can't go to the theatre today? **Извините, мне сегодня —— в театр.**

**8** You have a sore throat. How will you ask for lemon tea?

**9** **Не беспокойтесь!** What advice is being given here?

**10** Good news! You feel better. How will you explain this to the doctor?

# 14

## Свитер тебе очень идёт
## The sweater really suits you

In this unit you will learn
- *How to talk about clothes and appearance*
- *How to ask for and give advice about size and colour*
- *How to express simple comparisons and negatives*

### Dialogue

Ira is shopping for a new sweater and Anna has gone with her.

CD2, TR 4, 00:07

| | |
|---|---|
| **Áнна** | Что ты хóчешь купи́ть, Йра? Куда́ мы идём? |
| **Йра** | Я хочу́ купи́ть сви́тер. Зна́чит, мы пойдём снача́ла в универма́г, а éсли там ничегó не найду́, пойдём в магази́н «Одéжда», а потóм в «Мóдный трикота́ж». |
| **Áнна** | А до магази́на «Мóдный трикота́ж» далекó? |
| **Йра** | Нет, не óчень – э́тот магази́н нахóдится недалекó от ста́нции метрó Академи́ческая ... ты не уста́ла? |
| **Áнна** | Нет, что ты! |
| **Йра** | (*Looking at sweaters in* «Мóдный трикота́ж».) Ты ду́маешь, что э́тот сви́тер мне идёт, Áнна? Такóй краси́вый, я́рко-кра́сный цвет! |

| | |
|---|---|
| **Áнна** | (*Uncertainly.*) Да, о́чень я́ркий ... то́лько немно́жко мал, по-мо́ему. |
| **Йра** | (*Sighs.*) Да, ты права́ ... |
| **Áнна** | А посмотри́ на э́тот сви́тер, он на разме́р бо́льше. Ты не хо́чешь его́ приме́рить? |
| **Йра** | Да ... (*Tries it on.*) Ты не ду́маешь, что э́тот сви́тер вели́к? |
| **Áнна** | Нет, нет. Э́то лу́чше. Сви́тер тебе́ о́чень идёт. Како́го цве́та твоя́ ю́бка? Зелёная, да? |
| **Йра** | Да, све́тло-зелёная. |
| **Áнна** | Я уве́рена, что э́тот чёрный сви́тер о́чень хорошо́ подойдёт к твое́й ю́бке. |
| **Йра** | Ну, а я хоте́ла купи́ть сви́тер бо́лее весёлого цве́та. |
| **Áнна** | Я сове́тую тебе́ купи́ть вот э́тот чёрный сви́тер. |
| **Йра** | Но я обы́чно ношу́ бо́лее я́ркие цвета́ ... |
| **Áнна** | Заче́м? Чёрный цвет так хорошо́ тебе́ идёт – ведь у тебя́ тёмные глаза́, тёмные во́лосы. Ты в нём о́чень шика́рно вы́глядишь. |
| **Йра** | Пра́вда? Да, мо́жет быть ты и права́. Хорошо́, я возьму́ вот э́тот. |
| **Áнна** | О́чень хорошо́ ... Скажи́, Йра, у нас вре́мя ещё есть? ... Я о́чень хочу́ приме́рить мехову́ю ша́пку ... |
| **Йра** | Коне́чно! Како́й у тебя́ разме́р? |
| **Áнна** | Не зна́ю. |
| **Йра** | Ничего́. Продавщи́ца нам помо́жет. |

| | |
|---|---|
| **универма́г** | *department store* |
| **ничего́** | *nothing; never mind* |
| **найду́ (находи́ть/найти́)** | *to find* |
| **оде́жда** (singular only) | *clothes* |
| **Мо́дный трикота́ж** | *Fashionable Knitwear (name of a store)* |
| **уста́ла (устава́ть/уста́ть)** | *tired (to get tired)* |

QUICK VOCAB

| | |
|---|---|
| сви́тер мне идёт | the sweater suits me |
| я́рко-кра́сный | bright red |
| цвет (pl. цвета́) | colour |
| мал | too small |
| на разме́р бо́льше | a size bigger |
| приме́ривать/приме́рить | to try on |
| вели́к | too big |
| лу́чше | better |
| зелёная (зелёный) | green |
| све́тло-зелёная | light green |
| уве́рена (уве́ренный) | certain, sure |
| чёрный | black |
| подойдёт к (подходи́ть/подойти́) | (here) will go with |
| весёлый | cheerful |
| я обы́чно ношу́ (носи́ть) | I usually wear |
| тёмный | dark |
| во́лосы | hair |
| шика́рно вы́глядишь | you look smart |
| мо́жет быть | perhaps |
| возьму́ (брать/взять) | to take |
| мехова́я ша́пка | fur hat |
| продавщи́ца нам помо́жет (помога́ть/помо́чь) | the shop assistant will help us |

## Insight

**Ты не уста́ла?** means *Are you tired?* Ira used the perfective past tense (literally *have not you got tired?*). To say *I'm tired*, use **я уста́л** if you are a man, or **я уста́ла** if you are a women (and *we are tired* would be **мы уста́ли**).

### Универма́г: a department store

**Универма́г** is a department store; the most famous of all Russian department stores is **ГУМ** (**Гла́вный универса́льный магази́н**), situated just off Red Square in Moscow (for a virtual visit, have a look at www.gum.ru). Smaller Russian shops tend to have names describing their goods (Товáры): **Óбувь** (*footwear*), **Одéжда** (*clothes*), **Товáры для детéй** (*children's goods*), **Хозтовáры** (*household goods*).

## Questions

**1** *True or false?*

**a** Йра хóчет купи́ть ю́бку.
**b** Снача́ла Йра и А́нна иду́т в «Мóдный трикота́ж».
**c** Йре нра́вится я́рко-кра́сный сви́тер.
**d** А́нна ду́мает, что чёрный сви́тер ей идёт лу́чше.
**e** А́нна хóчет приме́рить чёрный сви́тер.

**2** *Answer the questions!*

**a** Где нахóдится «Мóдный трикота́ж»?
**b** Почему́ А́нна ду́мает, что Йре не на́до покупа́ть я́рко-кра́сный сви́тер?
**c** Почему́ А́нна ду́мает, что Йре на́до купи́ть чёрный сви́тер?
**d** Каки́е цвета́ Йра обы́чно предпочита́ет?
**e** Какой сви́тер Йра покупа́ет наконéц (*finally*, *in the end*)?

## How do you say it?

How to:
**1** *Talk about size*

Какóй у тебя́ разме́р? Какóй у вас разме́р?
Э́тот сви́тер на разме́р бóльше.
Э́тот сви́тер мал.
Э́тот сви́тер вели́к.

**2** *Talk about colour*

Какого цвёта твоя юбка?
Ярко-красный свитер.
Свётло-зелёный свитер.

**3** *Make comparisons*

Это лучше.
Более яркий свитер.

**4** *Give advice*

Я совётую тебё. Я совётую вам.

**5** *Talk about appearance*

Ты очень шикарно выглядишь. Вы очень шикарно выглядите.

Свитер тебе́ о́чень идёт.

Свитер подойдёт к твое́й ю́бке.

У тебя́ тёмные глаза́, тёмные во́лосы. У вас тёмные глаза́, тёмные во́лосы.

---

## Grammar

### 1 Negative expressions

The most important thing to remember about the negative expressions (*nothing*, *no one*, *nowhere*, etc.) below is that when they are used with a verb (in a tense or command form), and that **не** must always be added before the verb:

| | |
|---|---|
| Я ничего́ не понима́ю. | *I understand nothing/I don't understand anything.* |
| Я никогда́ не смотрю́ телеви́зор. | *I never watch television.* |
| Она́ нигде́ не рабо́тает. | *She doesn't work anywhere.* |
| Мы никуда́ не идём. | *We're not going anywhere.* |
| Никто́ не зна́ет об э́том. | *No one knows about this.* |

The words **ничто́** (*nothing*) and **никто́** (*no one*) decline (i.e. have case endings) like **кто** and **что**; note that **ничего́** is the accusative of **ничто́**:

| | |
|---|---|
| Он ничего́ не сказа́л об э́том. | *He didn't say anything about this.* |
| Она́ никого́ не зна́ет в э́том го́роде. | *She doesn't know anyone in this town.* |

If you need to use a preposition with *nothing* and *no one* it splits them up and the two parts are written separately:

| | |
|---|---|
| Он ни о чём не говори́л. | *He didn't speak about anything.* |

| Она́ ни с кем не говори́ла | She didn't speak |
|---|---|
| об э́том. | with anyone about this. |

---

## Insight

In English negative phrases we have one negative word, followed by positives: *No one (negative) ever (positive) does anything (positive) for me*; in the Russian version of this phrase there is a whole string of negatives: **Никто́ никогда́ ниче́го не дела́ет для меня́** (literally: 'No one never nothing does not do for me').

---

### 2 *Dative case*

Note the use of the dative case in the expression *to suit*:

| Э́тот сви́тер Ви́ктору | *This sweater really suits* |
|---|---|
| (dative) о́чень идёт. | *Viktor.* |

### 3 *Colours*

If you want to ask about the colour of something, say *of what colour is …*: **Како́го цве́та твоя́ ю́бка?** *What colour is your skirt?* The most common colour words are:

| | | | | | |
|---|---|---|---|---|---|
| **бе́лый** | white | **кори́чневый** | brown | **се́рый** | grey |
| **голубо́й** | light blue | **кра́сный** | red | **си́ний**[*] | dark blue |
| **жёлтый** | yellow | **ора́нжевый** | orange | **чёрный** | black |
| **зелёный** | green | **ро́зовый** | pink | | |
| **ка́рий**[*] | brown (eyes) | **седо́й** | grey (hair) | | |

To qualify shades of colour use the prefixes **я́рко-** (*bright-*), **тёмно-** (*dark-*), **све́тло-** (*light-*), **бле́дно-** (*pale-*):

---

[*]See Unit 16 for an explanation of this kind of adjective ending.

| | |
|---|---|
| Вы предпочита́ете я́рко-кра́сное пла́тье и́ли бле́дно-ро́зовое? | *Do you prefer the bright red dress or the pale pink?* |

## 4 Short adjectives

The short form of one group of adjectives is used to suggest *too big*, *too small*, etc:

| | |
|---|---|
| **вели́к, велика́, велико́, велики́** | *(too big):* |
| Э́то пла́тье (мне) велико́ | *The dress is too big (for me)* |
| **дли́нен, длинна́, дли́нно, дли́нны** | *(too long):* |
| Э́то пла́тье (мне) дли́нно | *This dress is too long (for me)* |
| **ко́роток, коротка́, ко́ротко, коротки́** | *(too short):* |
| Э́ти брю́ки (мне) коротки́ | *These trousers are too short (for me)* |
| **мал, мала́, мало́, малы́** | *(too small):* |
| Э́та ю́бка (мне) мала́ | *This skirt is too small (for me)* |
| **у́зок, узка́, у́зко, узки́** | *(too narrow):* |
| Э́ти брю́ки (мне) узки́ | *These trousers are too narrow (for me)* |
| **широ́к, широка́, широко́, широки́** | *(too wide):* |
| Э́та руба́шка (мне) широка́ | *This shirt is too wide (for me)* |

## 5 'To wear'

The verb **носи́ть** can only be used to mean *to wear* when you are talking about habit:

| | |
|---|---|
| Я всегда́ ношу́ костю́м на рабо́те. | *I always wear a suit when I'm at work.* |
| В саду́ он обы́чно но́сит ста́рые брю́ки. | *He usually wears old trousers in the garden.* |

If you want to describe what someone wears/wore on a specific occasion, either use **на** + prepositional (of the person), or **в** + prepositional (of the item of clothing):

| | |
|---|---|
| Сего́дня на ней бе́лое пла́тье. | *Today she's wearing a white dress.* |
| Вчера́ он был в чёрном костю́ме. | *Yesterday he wore a black suit.* |

## Insight

Two ways of saying to wear:

- habit, repetition – indicated, e.g., by **всегда́** (*always*), **иногда́** (*sometimes*), **ка́ждый день** (*every day*), **обы́чно** (*usually*), **ча́сто** (*often*) – use **носи́ть** + accusative. Example: Он всегда́ но́сит костю́м (*He always wears a suit*).

- referring to a specific occasion – (indicated, e.g., by **сего́дня у́тром** (*this morning*), **на сва́дьбе** (*at the wedding*) – use **на** + prepositional case of the person + nominative case of the item of clothing, or nominative case of the person + **в** + prepositional case of the item of clothing. Examples: **Сего́дня у́тром на ней кра́сное пла́тье** (*This morning she is wearing a red dress*; lit., *this morning on her a red dress*). **На сва́дьбе она́ была́ в ро́зовое пла́тье** (*At the wedding she wore a pink dress*; lit., *At the wedding she was in a pink dress*).

### 6 Брать/взять *To take*

This is a very common verb meaning to take, and both the imperfective and perfective are irregular:

брать (present) я беру́, ты берёшь, он берёт, мы берём, вы берёте, они́ беру́т

взять (future) я возьму́, ты возьмёшь, он возьмёт, мы возьмём, вы возмёте, они́ возьму́т

The future (*I will take*) is very often used in the context of shopping:

> Я возьму́ голубу́ю руба́шку.     *I'll take the pale blue shirt.*

The command form of **взять** is also commonly used: **Возьми́те!**


## 7 Comparison

In English the comparative is formed by adding *-er* to an adjective or by using *more* – a *bigger* book, a *more interesting* book. In Russian, the easiest way to form the comparative is simply to use the word **бо́лее** (*more*) in front of an adjective:

> Я хочу́ купи́ть бо́лее     *I want to buy a more*
> мо́дную блу́зку.     *fashionable blouse.*

The word **ме́нее** (*less*) can be used in a similar way:

> Я хочу́ купи́ть ме́нее     *I want to buy a less bright*
> я́ркую ю́бку.     *skirt.*

These forms of the comparative must be used when you are using an adjective before the noun (called an attributive adjective), but note that there are several common adjectives which cannot form the comparative with **бо́лее**:

| | |
|---|---|
| бо́льший/ме́ньший | *bigger/lesser* |
| лу́чший/ху́дший | *better/worse* |
| ста́рший/мла́дший | *older/younger; senior/junior* |
| Я хочу́ купи́ть лу́чшую блу́зку. | *I want to buy a better blouse.* |

A short form of the comparative adjective exists and can be used after the noun (called a predicative adjective) and this is formed by adding **-ee** to the stem of the adjective:

> Э́та блу́зка модне́е.     *This blouse is more fashionable.*

The short form of the comparative adjective is also the comparative adverb, so, for example, **быстре́е** means both *quicker* and *more quickly*.

There are a number of common short comparative adjectives which are irregular (a full list is given in Appendix 1):

| | | |
|---|---|---|
| бли́зкий | бли́же | (*nearer*) |
| большо́й (*big*) | бо́льше | (*bigger, more*) |
| высо́кий (*tall, high*) | вы́ше | (*taller, higher*) |
| далёкий (*far, distant*) | да́льше | (*further*) |
| | (*or* да́лее) | |
| дешёвый (*cheap*) | деше́вле | (*cheaper*) |
| дорого́й (*dear, expensive*) | доро́же | (*dearer, more expensive*) |
| ма́ленький (*small*) | ме́ньше | (*smaller, less*) |
| молодо́й (*young*) | моло́же | (*younger*) |
| плохо́й (*bad*) | ху́же | (*worse*) |
| по́здний (*late*) | по́зже/поздне́е | (*later*) |
| просто́й (*simple, easy*) | про́ще | (*simpler, more simply*) |
| ра́нний (*early*) | ра́ньше | (*earlier, previously*) |
| ста́рый (*old*) | ста́рше | (*older*) |
| хоро́ший (*good*) | лу́чше | (*better*) |
| ча́стый (*frequent*) | ча́ще | (*more often*) |
| я́ркий (*bright*) | я́рче | (*brighter*) |

**Чем** (*than*) is useful when comparing two items and must be used if you are using the long comparative (i.e. with **бо́лее**):

Э́то бо́лее мо́дная ю́бка, чем её ю́бка. *This is a more modern skirt than hers.*

With short comparatives the second part of the comparative can be put into the genitive case or **чем** can be used:

Э́то пла́тье модне́е, чем твоё.
Э́то пла́тье модне́е твоего́. } *This dress is more modern than yours.*

Note that if you are expressing degrees of comparison (i.e. by saying something is bigger or smaller), the preposition **на** is needed:

Этот свитер на размер        *This sweater is one size*
 бо́льше.                     *bigger.*
Эта ю́бка намно́го лу́чше.    *This skirt is a lot better.*

## Insight

For the irregular short comparatives, try learning them in pairs of opposites:

- **бли́же**   (*nearer*)          **да́льше**   (*further*)
- **бо́льше**  (*bigger, more*)     **ме́ньше**   (*smaller, less*)
- **деше́вле** (*cheaper*)          **доро́же**   (*dearer*)
- **лу́чше**   (*better*)           **ху́же**     (*worse*)
- **ра́ньше**  (*earlier*)          **по́зже**    (*later*)

## Practice

### 14.1 Read and answer!

Complete the negative answers of the pessimist:

- **a** Оптими́ст: Вы всё понима́ете? Пессими́ст: (*nothing*) Нет, я _____ понима́ю.
- **b** Оптими́ст: Вы уже́ зна́ете дире́ктора заво́да? Пессими́ст: (*no one*) Нет, я здесь _____ зна́ю.
- **c** Оптими́ст: Он уже́ рабо́тает в больни́це? Пессими́ст: (*nowhere*) Нет, он _____ рабо́тает.
- **d** Оптими́ст: Вы ча́сто хо́дите в теа́тр? Пессими́ст: (*never*) Нет, мы _____ хо́дим в теа́тр.
- **e** Оптими́ст: Вы бу́дете на ве́чере (*party*)? Пессими́ст: (*nowhere*) Нет, мы _____ идём.

## 14.2 Read, answer and listen!

You are buying a fur hat. Complete your part of the conversation with the shop assistant, then listen to the complete conversation on the recording.

CD2, TR 4, 02:44

| Вы | (a) Say 'excuse me, please, do you have any fur hats?' |
|---|---|
| Продавщи́ца | Коне́чно. Вот они́. |
| Вы | (b) Ask the assistant to show you that fur hat ... over there, on the left. |
| Продавщи́ца | Пожа́луйста. |
| Вы | (c) Ask if you can try it on. |
| Продавщи́ца | Пожа́луйста. |
| Вы | (d) Say you think it's too big. |
| Продавщи́ца | Да, мо́жет быть вы пра́вы. Хоти́те приме́рить э́ту ша́пку? |
| Вы | (e) Say 'yes, please'. |
| Продавщи́ца | Да, по-мо́ему э́то лу́чше. |
| Вы | (f) Say 'yes, you're right'. Say you'll take this one. |
| Продавщи́ца | Пожа́луйста. |

## 14.3 Read and answer!

Look at the following information about shops situated near the stations of Moscow's Circle Line and answer the questions:

**a** How many department stores are accessible from the Circle Line?
**b** Which different clothes shops are mentioned?
**c** At which metro station would you have to get off if you wanted to buy household items?
**d** How many shoe shops are mentioned?

# МОСКВА – СПРАВКА
# МЕТРОПОЛИТЕН
# МАГАЗИНЫ

**Кольцевая линия**

| | | |
|---|---|---|
| Станция метро Краснопресненская | – | «Олимп» (спорттовары), «Товары для детей», «Универмаг Краснопресненская» |
| Станция метро Киевская | – | «Русский сувенир», «Обувь», «Товары для дома» |
| Станция метро Таганская | – | «Цветы», «Обувь», «Товары для детей», «Мужская одежда» |
| Станция метро Новослободская | – | «Молодость» (детская одежда), «Обувь», «Универмаг» |

**де́тский** (adj.)   *children's*
**мужско́й** (adj.)   *men's*

### 14.4 Read and answer!

Complete the phrases below:

| | | | |
|---|---|---|---|
| **1** | _____ вы идёте сейча́с? | **a** | Как |
| **2** | _____ вам нра́вится э́тот костю́м? | **b** | Ско́лько |
| **3** | _____ вы обы́чно де́лаете поку́пки? | **c** | Куда́ |
| **4** | _____ у вас разме́р? | **d** | Како́й |
| **5** | _____ сто́ит э́тот сви́тер? | **e** | Где |

**де́лать/сде́лать поку́пки**   *to do the shopping*

### 14.5 Read and write!

Read the information about each person, then make up sentences to describe their preferences:

**a** Ви́ктор–голуба́я руба́шка–мо́дный–бе́лая руба́шка
**b** Ма́ша–чёрная ю́бка–краси́вый–кра́сная ю́бка
**c** Вади́м–зелёный сви́тер–дешёвый–чёрный сви́тер
**d** Йра–кра́сное пла́тье–я́ркий–се́рое пла́тье
**e** Серге́й–но́вый га́лстук (*tie*)–весёлый–ста́рый га́лстук

**a** Ви́ктор предпочита́ет голубу́ю руба́шку, потому́ что она́ модне́е бе́лой руба́шки.

## Insight

In exercise 14.5 the accusative case is needed for the item each person prefers and the genitive case for the less favoured item:

Viktor prefers the pale blue shirt (accusative because it is the object of the verb) because it is more modern than the white shirt (genitive of comparison).

### 14.6 Read and answer!

Read this passage about Alla, then answer the questions:

В свобо́дное вре́мя А́лла о́чень лю́бит чита́ть рома́ны. Она́ ду́мает, что э́то интере́снее, чем смотре́ть телеви́зор. Обы́чно она́ чита́ет романти́ческие кни́ги, но вчера́ в кни́жном магази́не она́ купи́ла бо́лее серьёзную кни́гу – биогра́фию. На́до сказа́ть, что ей не о́чень нра́вится э́та кни́га. Она́ ду́мает, что э́то ску́чнее, чем рома́ны. Она́ ча́сто хо́дит в кни́жный магази́н – иногда́ два ра́за в неде́лю. За́втра она́ ещё раз пойдёт в кни́жный магази́н, потому́ что она́ хо́чет купи́ть бо́лее интере́сную кни́гу.

| биогра́фия | biography |
|---|---|
| кни́жный магази́н | bookshop |
| рома́н | novel |

**a** Что А́лла лю́бит де́лать в свобо́дное вре́мя?
**b** Каки́е кни́ги она́ предпочита́ет?
**c** Что она́ купи́ла вчера́?
**d** В како́м магази́не мо́жно купи́ть кни́ги?

Now answer these questions about yourself:

**a** Вы ду́маете, что интере́снее смотре́ть телеви́зор и́ли чита́ть кни́ги?
**b** Каки́е рома́ны вы предпочита́ете? Романти́ческие, истори́ческие … и́ли вы предпочита́ете биогра́фии?
**c** Вы ча́сто хо́дите в кни́жный магази́н?

---

## Comprehension

### 1 *Conversation*

**Read, listen and answer!**

Vadim has gone to the department store to buy a suit.

| Продавщи́ца | Вам помо́чь? |
|---|---|
| Вади́м | Я ищу́ костю́м. |
| Продавщи́ца | Како́го цве́та? |
| Вади́м | У вас есть тёмно-си́ние? |
| Продавщи́ца | Есть … то́лько вы́бор не о́чень большо́й. Како́й у вас разме́р? |
| Вади́м | Я не уве́рен. Пятидеся́тый, ка́жется. |
| Продавщи́ца | Гм, посмо́трим … Есть чёрный пятидеся́того, и́ли тёмно-си́ний пятьдеся́т второ́го разме́ра. Вы хоти́те приме́рить их? |

| | |
|---|---|
| **Вади́м** | Да, пожа́луйста … (*Tries them on.*) … Вам не ка́жется, что тёмно-си́ний костю́м мне вели́к? |
| **Продавщи́ца** | Нет, наоборо́т, тёмно-си́ний вам о́чень идёт, а чёрный, по-мо́ему, мал. |
| **Вади́м** | Ско́лько сто́ит тёмно-си́ний костю́м? |
| **Продавщи́ца** | Две́сти пятьдеся́т рубле́й. |
| **Вади́м** | Ой, о́чень до́рого! |
| **Продавщи́ца** | Да, до́рого. Но зато́ о́чень краси́вый шерстяно́й костю́м. |
| **Вади́м** | Да, вы пра́вы … хорошо́, я возьму́ тёмно-си́ний костю́м. |
| **Продавщи́ца** | Э́то всё? |
| **Вади́м** | Нет. У вас есть бе́лые руба́шки? |
| **Продавщи́ца** | Да, … вот бе́лые руба́шки по со́рок рубле́й. Како́й разме́р? |
| **Вади́м** | Сороково́й, со́рок второ́й – я не уве́рен … что вы посове́туете? |
| **Продавщи́ца** | Я вам рекоменду́ю со́рок второ́й. |
| **Вади́м** | Хорошо́ … Я возьму́ тёмно-си́ний костю́м и одну́ бе́лую руба́шку. Ско́лько с меня́? |
| **Продавщи́ца** | С вас две́сти девяно́сто рубле́й. |

**QUICK VOCAB**

| | |
|---|---|
| **я ищу́ (иска́ть: ищу́, и́щешь … и́щут)** | *to look for* |
| **вы́бор** | *choice* |
| **наоборо́т** | *on the contrary* |
| **зато́** | *on the other hand* |
| **шерстяно́й** | *wool(len)* |
| **сороково́й** | *fortieth* |
| **девяно́сто** | *ninety* |

**1** Вади́м хо́чет купи́ть
 **a** тёмно-синий сви́тер
 **b** чёрный костю́м

**2** Продавщи́ца говори́т, что
 **a** чёрный костю́м широ́к
 **b** чёрный костю́м вели́к

| c | се́рый костю́м | c | чёрный костю́м мал |
|---|---|---|---|
| d | тёмно-си́ний костю́м | d | чёрный костю́м у́зок |

**3** Вади́м покупа́ет костю́м, потому́ что

  **a** он до́рого сто́ит
  **b** э́то краси́вый костю́м
  **c** э́то дешёвый костю́м

**4** Вади́м покупа́ет та́кже

  **a** кра́сный га́лстук
  **b** чёрную руба́шку
  **c** бе́лую руба́шку

## 2 Reading

Read the text and answer the questions in English.

**a** What is the relationship between Viacheslav and Egor Zaitsev?
**b** Where did Egor study?
**c** In which countries is Egor Zaitsev already famous?
**d** What is Viacheslav's preference in fashion?
**e** To what does Egor compare fashion?
**f** What does Egor consider Viacheslav to be?

В Москве́ есть я́ркая, тала́нтливая дина́стия модельеров – широко́ изве́стный Вячесла́в За́йцев и его́ сын, Его́р. По́сле оконча́ния Моско́вского тексти́льного институ́та Его́р пошёл рабо́тать к отцу́.

Клие́нты и посети́тели Моско́вского до́ма мо́ды на проспе́кте Ми́ра уже́ хорошо́ зна́ют его́ моде́ли. Зна́ют его́ моде́ли та́кже и в Япо́нии, Австра́лии, И́ндии … везде́, где моде́ли мла́дшего За́йцева бы́ли вме́сте с колле́кциями отца́.

Вячесла́в За́йцев бо́льше всего́ лю́бит кла́ссику: «Класси́ческий костю́м прове́рен вре́менем, э́то не мо́да, а стиль».

Его́р счита́ет, что мо́да – э́то иску́сство, сродни́ му́зыке и́ли жи́вописи. Он занима́ется молодёжной мо́дой. Е́сли осно́ва моделе́й ста́ршего За́йцева англи́йский костю́м, то мла́дший предпочита́ет аванга́рд. Одна́ко, оте́ц для Его́р – учи́тель и постоя́нный приме́р.

(«Огонёк»)

| | |
|---|---|
| **аванга́рд** | *avant garde* |
| **вме́сте с** (+ instr.) | *together with* |
| **дина́стия** | *dynasty* |
| **жи́вопись** (f.) | *painting* |
| **клие́нт** | *customer* |
| **колле́кция** | *collection* |
| **мо́да** | *fashion* |
| **моде́ль** (f.) | *model* |
| **модельéр** | *modeller, fashion designer* |
| **молодёжный** | *young people's* (adjective) |
| **оконча́ние** | *finishing, graduation* |
| **осно́ва** | *basis, foundation* |
| **посети́тель** (m.) | *visitor* |
| **постоя́нный** | *constant* |
| **приме́р** | *example* |
| **прове́рен** | *tested, checked* |
| **сродни́** (+ dative) | *related to* |
| **стиль** (m.) | *style* |
| **тексти́льный** | *textile* (adjective) |

---

## Key phrases

🔊 **CD 2, TR 4, 05:11**

Can you remember how to say the following in Russian? Listen to the recording and practise saying each phrase.

- **a** I never watch television.
- **b** Yes, perhaps you're right.
- **c** Would you like (do you want) to try this fur hat on?
- **d** The green sweater really suits you.
- **e** This skirt is a lot better.

## Test yourself

**1** You've seen just the fur hat you'd like. How would you ask to try it on?

**2** If you are asking for a grey suit, would you use **седо́й** or **се́рый**?

**3** What is missing from the following sentence? **Я ничего́ — понима́ю!**

**4** Which word would you insert in the following sentence to make it mean *I prefer the more abstract design*? **Я предпочита́ю — абстра́ктную моде́ль.**

**5** Which case of *you* would you need to use if you ask Anna if she feels better?

**6** You are unsure about the red shirt – how would you ask if it suits you?

**7** If the reply is **Я сове́тую вам взять зелёную руба́шку,** what advice are you being given?

**8** You decide to buy the red shirt anyway. How will you say *I'll take it*?

**9** What will you add to the following sentence to make it mean *I am sure you are right*? **Я —, что ты —.**

**10** How would you make this sentence negative? **Я всегда́ понима́ю всё** (*I always understand everything*).

# 15

## С днём рождения!

## Happy birthday!

In this unit you will learn

* *How to talk about dates*
* *How to say when and where you were born and state your age*
* *How to ask other people about their age, and place and date of birth*
* *How to greet people on special occasions*

### Dialogue

Ira has taken Anna to Volodya's birthday celebrations.

CD 2, TR 5, 00:05

| Йра | Воло́дя, приве́т. С днём рожде́ния! Жела́ю тебе́ всего́ са́мого наилу́чшего, ... сча́стья, здоро́вья и успе́хов во всех твои́х дела́х! |
| Анна | С днём рожде́ния, Воло́дя! |
| Воло́дя | Спаси́бо. Пожа́луйста, входи́те! |
| Йра | Вот тебе́ пода́рок ... извини́, э́то не о́чень оригина́льно! |
| Воло́дя | Ну, что ты, Йра ... мне о́чень нужны́ носки́. |
| Анна | А вот пода́рок от меня́ ... наде́юсь, что он тебе́ понра́вится ... э́то кни́га об изве́стных англи́йских спортсме́нах. Я зна́ю, что ты лю́бишь спорт. |

246

| | |
|---|---|
| **Воло́дя** | Спаси́бо большо́е, А́нна. Я о́чень люблю́ чита́ть таки́е кни́ги. (*Starts leafing through book.*) |
| **И́ра** | Ну, Воло́дя, мы бу́дем весь ве́чер стоя́ть в прихо́жей, что ли? Где же шампа́нское, где заку́ски? |
| **Воло́дя** | Пожа́луйста, проходи́те в гости́ную. Там всё есть. |
| **И́ра** | (*Sips champagne.*) ... Хоро́шее шампа́нское ... Я предлага́ю тост за Воло́дю! |
| **А́нна** | За Воло́дю! |
| **И́ра** | Скажи́, Воло́дя, е́сли не секре́т, ско́лько тебе́ лет? |
| **Воло́дя** | Мне? Ну, лет три́дцать. |
| **И́ра** | Е́сли я не ошиба́юсь, тебе́ уже́ три́дцать семь лет ... ведь ты на три го́да ста́рше меня́ ... зна́чит ты роди́лся в како́м году́? |
| **Воло́дя** | (*Sighs.*) В пятьдеся́т четвёртом. |
| **А́нна** | (*Embarrassed.*) Тебе́ легко́ даётся матема́тика, И́ра! ... А где ты роди́лся, Воло́дя? |
| **Воло́дя** | На Украи́не, в Ки́еве ... Ну, всё обо мне. Како́го числа́ твой день рожде́ния, А́нна? |
| **А́нна** | Восьмо́го ма́рта. |
| **И́ра** | Восьмо́го ма́рта! ... Ты ведь зна́ешь, что э́то у нас пра́здник? |
| **А́нна** | Нет, не зна́ла. Како́й э́то пра́здник? |
| **И́ра** | Э́то междунаро́дный же́нский день. В э́тот день же́нщинам де́лают мно́го комплиме́нтов, да́рят им цветы́, пода́рки. |
| **А́нна** | Пра́вда? ... И́ра, ты права́, шампа́нское о́чень вку́сное ... |
| **Воло́дя** | Да, в буты́лке есть ещё немно́жко ... переда́й мне твой бока́л, А́нна! |

| | |
|---|---|
| с днём рожде́ния! | *happy birthday!* |
| жела́ю тебе́ всего́ са́мого наилу́чшего | *I wish you all the very best* |
| сча́стье | *happiness* |
| успе́х | *success* |
| входи́ть/войти́ | *to enter, come/go in* |
| оригина́льно | *original* |
| носки́ (носо́к) | *socks (sock)* |
| наде́яться | *to hope* |
| об изве́стных англи́йских спортсме́нах | *about famous English sportsmen* |
| прихо́жая | *(entrance) hall* |
| что ли? | *eh?, perhaps?* |
| проходи́ть/пройти́ | *to go through, past* |
| тост за (+ accusative) | *toast to* |
| секре́т | *secret* |
| ско́лько тебе́ лет? | *how old are you?* |
| ошиба́ться/ошиби́ться | *to make a mistake* |
| ты роди́лся (роди́ться) | *you were born (to be born)* |
| тебе́ легко́ даётся матема́тика | *you're good at maths (lit. maths gives itself to you easily)* |
| обо мне | *about me* |
| како́го числа́ (число́) | *on what date? (date)* |
| март | *March* |
| пра́здник | *holiday, festive occasion* |
| междунаро́дный же́нский день | *International Women's Day* |
| же́нщина | *woman* |
| комплиме́нт | *compliment* |
| дари́ть/подари́ть | *to give as a present* |
| передава́ть/переда́ть | *to pass, pass on* |

QUICK VOCAB

## Insight

Toasts are a key part of Russian social occasions – so **предлага́ть тост за + accusative** is a useful phrase! Sometimes the animate accusative is needed: **Я предлага́ю тост за мои́х ру́сских друзе́й!** (*I propose a toast to my Russian friends*). See Units 5 and 7 for the animate accusative.

248

## Пра́здник *A holiday*

International Women's Day (8 March) is one of a range of major public holidays celebrated in Russia – New Year (**Но́выи год**), Day of Spring and Labour (1 May) and Victory Day (9 May, marking the end of the 'Great Patriotic War', i.e. the Second World War). There is also an impressive range of special days to mark the work of particular professions – e.g. Day of the Teacher (5 October), Day of the Medical Worker (third Sunday in June), Fisherman's Day (second Sunday in July). Russian is rich in greetings, but perhaps the most useful (to cover all occasions!) is **С пра́здником!** (literally *with the holiday* – actually a shortened form of *I congratulate you on the holiday*, **Поздравля́ю вас с пра́здником!**). Similar constructions are used for *Happy New Year* (**С Но́вым го́дом!**), *Welcome!* – after a journey – (**С прие́здом!**) and, of course, **С днём рожде́ния!**

**Insight**

Two tips about greetings:

- the instrumental case is used for greetings which name the special day (**С днём учи́теля!** – *Happy Teachers' Day!*)
- the genitive case is needed for wishes expressed on a special day (**Жела́ю вам/тебе́ успе́ха!** – *I wish you success!*); see Unit 9.

## Questions

### 1 *True or false?*

**a** И́ра да́рит Воло́де носки́.
**b** Воло́дя моло́же И́ры.
**c** Воло́дя роди́лся в Москве́.
**d** А́нна роди́лась восьмо́го ма́рта.
**e** А́нна лю́бит шампа́нское.

## 2 *Answer the questions!*

**a** Почему́ А́нна да́рит Воло́де кни́гу об изве́стных спортсме́нах?

**b** Како́й тост И́ра предлага́ет?

**c** Ско́лько лет Воло́де?

**d** Где он роди́лся?

**e** Како́й пра́здник восьмо́го ма́рта?

---

# How do you say it?

How to:

**1** *Greet people on special occasions*

[Поздравля́ю тебя́/вас] с пра́здником!
С днём рожде́ния!
Жела́ю тебе́/вам всего́ са́мого наилу́чшего!

**2** *Ask on what date*

Како́го числа́?

**3** *Ask when a person was born*

Когда́ ты роди́лся/ты родила́сь/вы роди́лись?
В како́м году́ ты роди́лся/ты родила́сь/вы роди́лись?

**4** *Ask where a person was born*

Где ты роди́лся/ты родила́сь/вы роди́лись?

**5** *Seek and give information about age*

Ско́лько тебе́/вам лет?
Мне три́дцать семь лет.

**6** *Ask about a special occasion*

Какóй э́то пра́здник?

## Grammar

### 1 *Prepositional case*

In the phrase **об изве́стных англи́йских спортсме́нах**, the prepositional plural of the adjectives (**изве́стный** and **англи́йский**) and noun (**спортсме́н**) is used. Note that **об** (not **о**) is used before a word beginning with a vowel; note also **обо мне** (*about me*) and **обо всём** (*about everything*).

The prepositional plural of nouns is formed as follows, irrespective of gender.

Add **-ах** (to all nouns ending in consonant, **-а**, **о**) or **-ях** (to all others). The prepositional plural of adjectives is formed by adding **-ых** unless the stem of an adjective ends in **г, к, х, ж, ч, ш, щ**, in which case add **-их**:

| | |
|---|---|
| **в больши́х ру́сских города́х** | *in large Russian towns* |
| **в э́тих ста́рых кни́гах** | *in these old books* |
| **Он говори́л о но́вых учителя́х.** | *He was talking about the new teachers.* |
| **в твои́х интере́сных пи́сьмах** | *in your interesting letters* |

### Insight

A phrase to help you remember the prepositional plural: **Расскажи́те мне о ва́ших но́вых друзья́х** (*Tell me about your new friends*). Have you spotted that the prepositional plural adjective endings are the same as genitive plural adjectives?

## 2 Dates

Months of the year in Russian are as follows:

| | | | |
|---|---|---|---|
| янва́рь | апре́ль | ию́ль | октя́брь |
| февра́ль | май | а́вгуст | ноя́брь |
| март | ию́нь | сентя́брь | дека́брь |

Note that months are written with a small letter in Russian (except at the beginning of a sentence) and that **all** months are masculine. To say *in* a month, simply use **в** + prepositional:

**в январе́** *(in January)*      **в ма́рте** *(in March)*
**в а́вгусте** *(in August)*

Note that **янва́рь, февра́ль, сентя́брь, октя́брь, ноя́брь, дека́брь** are all stressed on the last syllable in the prepositional case, e.g.: **в январе́**.

Ordinal numerals (see Unit 9) are used when talking about specific dates – i.e. Russian, like English, talks about the 18th (i.e. ordinal numeral) of October (i.e. genitive case) – **восемна́дцатое октября́**. The neuter form of the ordinal is used because the word for date – **число́** – is understood, but not stated. To say *on* a date, put the ordinal into the genitive case:

| | |
|---|---|
| **Како́е сего́дня число́? –** | *What is the date today? –* |
| **Сего́дня восемна́дцатое** | *Today is the 18th of* |
| **октября́.** | *October.* |
| **Како́го числа́ ваш день** | *On what date is your* |
| **рожде́ния? – Два́дцать** | *birthday? – On the 27th* |
| **седьмо́го февраля́.** | *of February.* |

The ordinal numerals are also important if you want to talk about a particular year. For 1991, for example, what Russian says literally is *the one thousand, nine hundred and ninety-first year*: **ты́сяча девятьсо́т девяно́сто пе́рвый год**. If you want to say in what year something happened, then **в** + prepositional is used, but only the very last digit (i.e. the ordinal numeral) has to be put into the prepositional case:

**В како́м году́ А́нна**      *In what year did Anna*
**познако́милась с И́рой?**      *meet Ira?*
**В ты́сяча девятьсо́т**      *In 1991.*
**девяно́сто пе́рвом году́.**

**NB** *2000* is двухты́сячный год. *In 2000* is в двухты́сячном году́.

A simpler way of expressing the year in writing is:

**1991 г** *1991*      **в 2000-ом году́** *in 2000*
**в апре́ле 1991-ого го́да**      *in April 1991 – i.e. in April*
                          *of the 1991st year*

## Insight

To help remember how to express dates in Russian, try working out in Russian some birthdays which are significant for you:

- **Моя́ дочь родила́сь в две ты́сячи девя́том году́**
  (*My daughter was born in 2009*).
- **День рожде́ния моего́ му́жа тре́тьего октября́**
  (*My husband's birthday is on 3rd October*).

### 3 *Time expressions*

Note the different ways in which units of time are treated in Russian:

**a** If you are dealing with units of time from a second to a day, use **в** + accusative case:

**в э́тот моме́нт**      *at this/that moment*
**в час**      *at one o'clock*
**в пя́тницу**      *on Friday*

**b** If you are dealing with a week, **на** + prepositional must be used:

| | |
|---|---|
| **на э́той неде́ле** | *this week* |
| **на про́шлой неде́ле** | *last week* |
| **на бу́дущей неде́ле** | *next week* |

**c** As we saw in section 2 above, months and years take **в** + prepositional case:

| | |
|---|---|
| **в декабре́** | *in December* |
| **в како́м ме́сяце?** | *in which month?* |
| **в э́том году́** | *this year* |

### 4 Verbs of motion

In the dialogue we saw two verbs which look very similar: **входи́ть** (*to enter, go in*) and **проходи́ть** (*to go past, through*).

These are two of a very useful family of verbs of motion whose special feature is that prefixes are used to give more specific meanings (e.g. *to go in, to go as far as,* etc.). These verbs have one imperfective form, ending in **-ходи́ть** and a perfective ending in **-йти**. With prefixed verbs of motion it is important to remember both the meaning of the prefix and the preposition most likely to be used after the verb; e.g. **входи́ть/войти́** means *to go into* and this is usually followed by **в** + accusative:

| | |
|---|---|
| **Он открыва́ет дверь и входи́т в библиоте́ку.** | *He opens the door and goes into the library.* |

The most important prefixed verbs of motion include the following (note that the perfective future and perfective past are formed like the future and past of **идти́**):

| | | |
|---|---|---|
| to approach | подходи́ть/подойти́<br>к + dat. | Официа́нт подошёл<br>к на́шему сто́лику<br>*The waiter approached<br>our table* |
| to arrive,<br>come | приходи́ть/прийти́<br>в + acc. | Я наде́юсь, что он<br>во́время придёт!<br>*I hope that he will arrive<br>on time!* |
| to cross | переходи́ть/перейти́<br>че́рез + acc. | Он бы́стро перехо́дит<br>че́рез у́лицу<br>*He quickly crosses the<br>street* |
| to enter | входи́ть/войти́<br>в + acc. | Врач вошёл в ко́мнату<br>*The doctor entered the<br>room* |
| to exit | выходи́ть/вы́йти<br>из + gen. | Тури́сты сейча́с<br>выхо́дят из музе́я<br>*The tourists are going out<br>of the museum now* |
| to get off | сходи́ть/сойти́<br>с + gen. | Все де́ти сойду́т с<br>авто́буса<br>*All the children will get<br>off the bus* |
| to leave | уходи́ть/уйти́<br>из + gen. | Воло́дя уже́ ушёл<br>*Volodya has already left* |
| to pass | проходи́ть/пройти́<br>ми́мо + gen. | Она́ всегда́ прохо́дит<br>ми́мо шко́лы<br>*She always goes past<br>the school* |
| to pop into | заходи́ть/зайти́<br>в + acc.; к + dat. | Я обы́чно захожу́<br>в универса́м<br>*I usually pop into the<br>supermarket*<br>Вчера́ Воло́дя зашёл<br>к Вади́му<br>*Yesterday Volodya popped<br>into Vadim's* |

## Insight

Useful nouns related to prefixed verbs of motion include:

| | |
|---|---|
| • **вход** | *entrance* |
| • **вы́ход** | *exit* |
| • **перехо́д** | *crossing, subway* |
| • **отъе́зд/отхо́д** | *departure – on foot or by transport* |
| • **прие́зд/прихо́д** | *arrival – on foot or by transport* |

Two not so obviously related to travel:

| | |
|---|---|
| • **дохо́д** | *income* |
| • **захо́д со́лнца** | *sunset* |

---

## Practice

### 15.1 Read and answer!

Match the question with the answer:

| | | | |
|---|---|---|---|
| **1** | Как вас зову́т? | **a** | Идёт снег. |
| **2** | Когда́ вы родили́сь? | **b** | Два́дцать пе́рвое сентября́. |
| **3** | Где вы живёте? | **c** | В три часа́. |
| **4** | Кем вы рабо́таете? | **d** | В 1964-ом году́. |
| **5** | Како́е сего́дня число́? | **e** | Ви́ктор. |
| **6** | Кака́я сего́дня пого́да? | **f** | Учи́телем. |
| **7** | Во ско́лько отхо́дит по́езд? | **g** | В Новосиби́рске. |

(**NB: Кем** (instr. of **кто**) **вы рабо́таете?** – lit. *as whom do you work?*)

### 15.2 Look and answer!

Look at the two cards below and explain what each is for:

**a**                               **b**

*С новым годом!*

*С днём рождения!*

### 15.3 Read and write!

Read the following paragraph about Валенти́на Серге́евна Я́блокова:

> Валенти́на Серге́евна Я́блокова ру́сская, родила́сь в Новгороде 15-ого января́ 1968-ого го́да. Валенти́на живёт в Санкт-Петербу́рге, где она рабо́тает врачо́м.

Now look at the following information and use it to write a paragraph like the one above:

| | |
|---|---|
| Фами́лия: | Быко́в |
| И́мя, о́тчество: | Оле́г Петро́вич |
| Национа́льность: | ру́сский |
| Да́та рожде́ния: | 12-ого апре́ля 1972-ого го́да |

| Ме́сто рожде́ния: | Я́лта |
| Местожи́тельство: | Краснода́р |
| Профе́ссия: | учи́тель |

qv **о́тчество** *patronymic*
**местожи́тельство** *place of residence*

### 15.4 Read and answer!

Complete the sentences with an appropriate phrase from the list which follows:

**a** Англи́йские тури́сты о́чень лю́бят обе́дать в _____.
**b** Анато́лию о́чень нра́вится _____.
**c** Официа́нт рекоменду́ет _____ грибы́ со смета́ной.
**d** В _____ есть о́чень интере́сные карти́ны.
**e** Извини́те, у нас сего́дня нет _____.
**f** Они живу́т в _____.

| больши́х рестора́нах | но́вых кварти́рах |
| иностра́нным тури́стам (*foreign*) | ру́сских музе́ях |
| кни́га о спортсме́нах | све́жего (*fresh*) молока́ |

### 15.5 Read, answer and listen!

You have gone to see the doctor, who is filling in a form with all your details. Complete your part of the conversation, then listen to the complete conversation on the recording.

CD 2, TR 5, 02:35

| **Врач** | Как ва́ша фами́лия? |
| **Вы** | **(a)** Say that your surname is Brown. |
| **Врач** | Национа́льность? |
| **Вы** | **(b)** Say that you are English. |
| **Врач** | Да́та рожде́ния? |
| **Вы** | **(c)** Say that you were born on 12 April 1968. |

| Врач | Где вы родили́сь? |
| Вы | **(d)** Say that you were born in Leeds, in the north of England. |
| Врач | Кем вы рабо́таете? |
| Вы | **(e)** Say that you work as a journalist. |

## 15.6 Read and answer!

Complete the following descriptions of Boris's movements:

Ча́сто Бори́с по́здно _____ (arrives) на рабо́ту. Де́ло в том, что он далеко́ живёт от музе́я, где он рабо́тает. Обы́чно он _____ (goes out of) из кварти́ры в 8 ч., _____ (approaches) к остано́вке и ждёт трамва́я. Он _____ (gets off) с трамва́я недалеко́ от музе́я, _____ (crosses) че́рез у́лицу и _____ (goes into) в музе́й. Он ти́хо _____ (passes) ми́мо кабине́та дире́ктора и _____ (enters) в свой кабине́т.

| | |
| --- | --- |
| ждать (жду, ждёшь … ждут) | to wait for |
| де́ло в том, что | the thing is that |
| ти́хо | quietly |
| кабине́т | office; study |

## Comprehension

### 1 *Conversation*

**Read, listen and answer!**

Valentina and Oleg are deciding how best to celebrate their daughter's birthday.

| Валенти́на | Седьмо́го а́вгуста день рожде́ния Ма́ши. Ты уже́ поду́мал об э́том? |
|---|---|
| Оле́г | Я не понима́ю, почему́ на́до об э́том ду́мать! Ведь мы, коне́чно, ку́пим ей пода́рок, приглаḿим друзе́й на ве́чер. Всё о́чень про́сто. |
| Валенти́на | Ну что ты, Оле́г, э́то далеко́ не просто́е де́ло! Что и́менно на́до купи́ть ей? Кого́ и́менно на́до пригласи́ть на ве́чер? |
| Оле́г | Ты же намно́го лу́чше меня́ понима́ешь, что на́до купи́ть! |
| Валенти́на | Мо́жет быть, но на э́той неде́ле я так занята́! Помоги́ мне, пожа́луйста! |
| Оле́г | Ну, насчёт пода́рка не беспоко́йся … я куплю́ ей духи́ и́ли кассе́ты. |
| Валенти́на | Спаси́бо. А кого́ пригласи́ть? |
| Оле́г | Са́шу, коне́чно, да … и А́ню, и … |
| Валенти́на | Мину́точку! Я запи́сываю … |
| Оле́г | И Све́ту, и Бо́рю … |
| Валенти́на | А почему́ Бо́рю? Он мне не о́чень нра́вится. |
| Оле́г | Мо́жет быть, но он так хорошо́ игра́ет на гита́ре … с ним бу́дет веселе́е. |
| Валенти́на | Ла́дно … а ещё пробле́ма: на́до купи́ть хоро́шее шампа́нское, а у меня́ так ма́ло вре́мени … |
| Оле́г | Не беспоко́йся об э́том. Я куплю́ шампа́нское, а ты пригото́вишь заку́ски. Договори́лись, да? |
| Валенти́на | Договори́лись. Спаси́бо тебе́ за по́мощь, Оле́г. |

| и́менно | precisely |
| насчёт (+ gen.) | as regards, concerning |
| духи́ (m.) | perfume |

| кассе́та | *cassette* |
| запи́сывать/записа́ть | *to note down* |
| по́мощь (f.) | *help* |

Complete the following sentences:

**1** День рожде́ния Ма́ши _____.
**2** _____ счита́ет, что э́то не сло́жное де́ло.
**3** Оле́г ку́пит Ма́ше _____.
**4** Оле́г хо́чет пригласи́ть Бо́рю, потому́ что _____.

## 2 *Reading*

◀) **CD 2, TR 5, 04:52**

**Read and listen to the text and answer the questions in English.**

**a** What is considered the most important purchase in preparation for New Year's Eve?
**b** Describe Grandfather Frost.
**c** Who usually accompanies him?
**d** What is traditionally the first toast to be made on New Year's Eve?
**e** What do people wish one another at midnight?

Как ру́сские встреча́ют Но́вый год? К концу́ декабря́ они́ гото́вятся к э́тому пра́зднику. На́до коне́чно купи́ть пода́рки де́тям, родны́м, друзья́м, но важне́е всего́ – купи́ть нового́днюю ёлку. Вот почему́ на ёлочных база́рах всегда́ мно́го наро́ду. И де́ти и взро́слые лю́бят украша́ть ёлку шара́ми, игру́шками, конфе́тами. Де́ти с нетерпе́нием ждут прихо́да одного́ о́чень ва́жного го́стя ... до́брого старика́, Де́да Моро́за. Дед Моро́з – стари́к с бе́лой бородо́й, в бе́лой шу́бе и с больши́м мешко́м. В мешке́, коне́чно, пода́рки для дете́й. Дед Моро́з обы́чно прихо́дит вме́сте со свое́й вну́чкой, Снегу́рочкой. Она́ то́же в бе́лой шу́бе и помога́ет Де́ду Моро́зу, когда́ он раздаёт пода́рки де́тям. Ве́чером 31-ого декабря́ взро́слые собира́ются за столо́м, предлага́ют то́сты … пе́рвый тост по тради́ции за ста́рый год. В 12 часо́в бьют Кремлёвские кура́нты. Лю́ди встаю́т, пьют шампа́нское, поздравля́ют друг дру́га с Но́вым го́дом, жела́ют друг дру́гу сча́стья, здоро́вья и успе́хов.

| | |
|---|---|
| **бить/проби́ть (бью, бьёшь … бьют)** | *to strike* (of clock) |
| **борода́** | *beard* |
| **важне́е всего́** | *most important of all* |
| **взро́слый** | *adult* |
| **вну́чка** | *granddaughter* |
| **Дед Моро́з** | *Grandfather Frost* (i.e. Father Christmas) |
| **друг дру́га** | *one another* |
| **игру́шка** | *toy* |
| **коне́ц** | *end* |
| **конфе́та** | *sweet* |
| **Кремлёвские кура́нты** | *Kremlin chimes* |
| **мешо́к** | *sack* |
| **мно́го наро́ду** | *a lot of people* |
| **нетерпе́ние** | *impatience* |
| **нового́дняя ёлка** | *New Year (fir) tree* |
| **по тради́ции** | *according to tradition* |
| **прихо́д** | *arrival* |
| **раздава́ть/разда́ть** | *to distribute* |
| **родны́е** | *relatives* |
| **Снегу́рочка** | *Snow Maiden* |
| **собира́ться/собра́ться** | *to gather* |
| **стари́к** | *old man* |
| **сча́стье** | *happiness* |
| **украша́ть/укра́сить** | *to decorate* |
| **шар** | *ball* |
| **шу́ба** | *fur coat* |

## Insight

'One another': the ending of the second word changes depending on what is being said:

- accusative: **они понима́ют друг дру́га** (*they understand one another*)
- dative: **они пи́шут друг дру́гу** (*they write to one another*)
- prepositional: **они ду́мают друг о дру́ге** (*they think about one another*)

---

## Key phrases

🔊 **CD 2, TR 5, 06:08**

Can you remember how to say the following in Russian? Listen to the recording and practise saying each phrase.

  **a** Happy birthday!
  **b** Happy New Year!
  **c** How old are you?
  **d** I was born in 1968.
  **e** Congratulations!

---

## Test yourself

**1** There is a word missing in the following sentence – what is it?
**Я наде́юсь, __ тебе́ лу́чше.** (*I hope you are feeling better*).

**2** What is the gender of all months of the year?

**3** What happens to the stress on the following months when you put them into the prepositional case (e.g. in October): **янва́рь, февра́ль, сентя́брь, октя́брь, ноя́брь, дека́брь?**

**4** How would you ask the question *on what date?*

**5** Which preposition would you add to complete the following sentence? **Он обы́чно выхо́дит __ музе́я в 5 часо́в** (*He usually leaves the museum at 5 o'clock*).

**6** Which preposition would you add to complete the following sentence? **Вчера́ она́ по́здно пришла́ __ теа́тр** (*Yesterday she arrived late at the theatre*).

**7** What is the difference between **в пя́тницу** and **по пя́тницам**?

**8** How would you ask someone what job they do?

**9** How would you propose a toast to your friend, Viktor?

**10** Put the correct endings on the last two words in the following sentence: **Они́ хотя́т обе́дать в лу́чш__ рестора́н__** (*They want to have lunch in the best restaurant*).

# 16

# Было бы лучше ...
## It would be better ...

In this unit you will learn
- *How to express your opinion about arrangements and events*
- *How to indicate preference in arrangements*
- *How to express hopes and intentions about arrangements*
- *How to make hypothetical statements*
- *How to express statements contrary to fact*

## Dialogue

The end of Anna's stay in Moscow is approaching. Ira and Sasha are trying to agree about where to take Anna on one of her last free evenings.

| | | |
|---|---|---|
| **Cáша** | Éсли я не ошибáюсь, А́нна бу́дет свобóдна во вто́рник вéчером. | CD 2, TR 6, 00:05 |
| **Йра** | Ты ошибáешься. Как я ужé сказáла, во вто́рник онá должнá пойти́ на лéкцию о ру́сской жи́вописи. | |
| **Cáша** | Ой, как серьёзно! Бéдная А́нна! Знáчит, бы́ло бы лу́чше пригласи́ть её в теáтр в четвéрг? | |
| **Йра** | Да. Давáй посмóтрим послéдний нóмер «Театрáльно-концéртной Москвы́» ... агá, в Большóм идёт óпера Вéрди «Отéлло» ... | |

| | |
|---|---|
| **Са́ша** | Но она́ уже́ была́ с тобо́й в Большо́м на о́пере «Князь И́горь» – я ду́маю, что она́ бы предпочла́ что́-нибудь поле́гче, посмешне́е … посмотри́, в Центра́льном теа́тре ку́кол идёт пье́са «Кот в сапога́х». |
| **И́ра** | Я уве́рена, что она́ бы сама́ вы́брала коме́дию, кото́рая идёт в теа́тре и́мени Го́голя. |
| **Са́ша** | Кака́я это коме́дия? |
| **И́ра** | Михаи́л Зо́щенко: «Уважа́емый това́рищ». |
| **Са́ша** | Да, И́рочка, мо́жет быть ты права́. Смешна́я пье́са, должно́ быть. Я э́то запи́сываю. А что ещё ты предлага́ешь? |
| **И́ра** | В Большо́м за́ле консервато́рии … игра́ет симфони́ческий орке́стр, а в Музыка́льном теа́тре идёт бале́т «Снегу́рочка». |
| **Са́ша** | Гм, на конце́рте симфони́ческого орке́стра бы́ло бы немно́жко ску́чно, а бале́т, по-мо́ему, ей о́чень понра́вился бы. Это бале́т на му́зыку Чайко́вского, не пра́вда ли? |
| **И́ра** | Пра́вильно. |
| **Са́ша** | Хорошо́ … я постара́юсь доста́ть биле́ты и́ли на коме́дию «Уважа́емый това́рищ» и́ли на бале́т «Снегу́рочка», на четве́рг. |
| **И́ра** | Всё пра́вильно. Жела́ю тебе́ успе́ха. |
| **Са́ша** | Спаси́бо … да, действи́тельно, бы́ло бы лу́чше, е́сли бы мы об э́том поду́мали пора́ньше. |
| **И́ра** | Да, э́то пра́вда. Мы должны́ бы́ли бы доста́ть биле́ты до э́того. Ничего́. Бу́дем наде́яться на лу́чшее. Позвони́ мне, как то́лько доста́нешь биле́ты! |

| | |
|---|---|
| ле́кция | *lecture* |
| серьёзно (серьёзный) | *serious* |
| бе́дная (бе́дный) | *poor* |
| после́дний но́мер | *latest edition* |
| «Князь И́горь» | *'Prince Igor'* |
| предпочла́ бы | *she would prefer* |
| что́-нибудь | *something* |
| поле́гче (лёгкий) | *a bit lighter (light)* |
| посмешне́е (смешно́й) | *a bit more amusing (amusing)* |
| теа́тр ку́кол | *puppet theatre* |
| «Кот в сапога́х» | *'Puss in Boots'* |
| она́ бы сама́ вы́брала | *she herself would choose* |
| коме́дия | *comedy* |
| кото́рая (кото́рый) | *which* |
| теа́тр и́мени Го́голя | *Gogol Theatre* |
| уважа́емый | *respected* |
| должно́ быть | *probably (lit. it must be)* |
| не пра́вда ли? | *isn't that right?* |
| пра́вильно | *right, correct* |
| постара́юсь (стара́ться/постара́ться) | *I'll try (to try)* |
| достава́ть/доста́ть (доста́ну, доста́нешь) | *to get, obtain* |
| и́ли ... и́ли | *either ... or* |
| действи́тельно | *really* |
| бы́ло бы лу́чше | *it would be better/ it would have been better* |
| пора́ньше | *a bit sooner* |
| бу́дем наде́яться на лу́чшее | *let's hope for the best* |
| как то́лько | *as soon as* |

This dialogue revises **в** and **на** (see Units 2, 3 and 5) – usually **на** for events and **в** for places (+ accusative for motion; + prepositional for position): **пойти́ на о́перу/в теа́тр** (to go to see an opera/to the theatre); **в Большо́м на о́пере** (at the Bolshoi theatre at the opera).

## Moscow's theatres

With over forty professional theatres and many more amateur ones, visitors have a vast variety of performances. The most famous Moscow theatres include the Bolshoi (for opera and ballet), the Taganka Theatre of Drama and Comedy, and the Moscow Arts Theatre (**МХАТ**), which is named after Anton Chekhov. Many theatres and concert halls are named after famous writers, composers and directors – this is indicated by the letters **им.** (an abbreviation of **и́мени**, *of the name of*) – thus **Конце́ртный зал им. П.И. Чайко́вского, Теа́тр и́мени Н.В. Го́голя, Драмати́ческий теа́тр и́мени** К.С. **Станисла́вского. Теа́тр и́мени** А.С. **Пу́шкина** is named after Alexander Pushkin, widely regarded as Russia's greatest poet. Moscow's **Теа́тр эстра́ды** stages shows, musicals and rock bands, whilst the Central State Puppet Theatre also houses the Russian State Museum of Theatrical Puppets, with over 3,000 theatrical puppets from some 50 countries.

## Diminutive forms of names

When Sasha addresses Ira as **Йрочка** he is using a diminutive form of her name. Spoken Russian makes considerable use of diminutive forms; sometimes the diminutive indicates affection or endearment: thus, for example, **мать** (*mother*) becomes **ма́ма, мам** or **ма́мочка.** The use of diminutives is frequent with first names – here are some typical examples:

| Full name | Diminutives |
| --- | --- |
| Алекса́ндр | Са́ша, Шу́ра, Са́шенька, Шу́рочка |
| Бори́с | Бо́ря, Бо́ренька |
| Влади́мир | Воло́дя, Во́ва, Воло́денька, Во́вочка |
| Еле́на | Ле́на, Ле́ночка |
| Ири́на | Йра, Йрочка, Ири́ша |
| Ната́лья | Ната́ша, Ната́шенька |
| О́льга | О́ля, О́ленька |

Requests and statements which use diminutives sound gentler, because they tend to imply that the request is only a small one or that the opinion is not too harsh; some useful diminutives in this context are:

| | |
|---|---|
| Да́йте, пожа́луйста, кусо́чек сы́ра. | *Give me a piece of cheese, please* (**кусо́к**, *a piece*). |
| Бы́ло немно́жко ску́чно. | *It was a bit boring* (**немно́го**, *a little*). |

The diminutive of nouns is commonly used when talking with or about children; the most common diminutive ending for masculine nouns is **-ик** and for feminine nouns **-ка** or **-очка**.

---

## Questions

### 1 *True or false?*

**a** А́нна бу́дет свобо́дна во вто́рник ве́чером.

**b** Са́ша ду́мает, что бу́дет ску́чно на ле́кции о жи́вописи.

**c** У И́ры нет после́днего но́мера «Театра́льно-концертной Москвы́».

**d** «Уважа́емый това́рищ» – коме́дия.

**e** «Снегу́рочка» – о́пера на му́зыку Чайко́вского.

**f** Са́ша ду́мает, что тру́дно (*difficult*) бу́дет доста́ть биле́ты на четве́рг.

### 2 *Answer the questions!*

**a** Когда́ А́нна бу́дет свобо́дна?

**b** Что идёт в Большо́м теа́тре?

**c** В како́м теа́тре идёт «Кот в сапога́х»?

**d** Почему́ Са́ша не хо́чет пойти́ на конце́рт в консервато́рию?

**e** Когда́ Са́ша до́лжен позвони́ть И́ре?

## How do you say it?

How to:

**1** *Ask and state when someone will be free*

Когда́ она́ бу́дет свобо́дна?
Она́ бу́дет свобо́дна в четве́рг.

**2** *Indicate preference in arrangements*

Бы́ло бы лу́чше …

**3** *Make hypothetical statements – what might be the case*

Она́ бы предпочла́ …
Смешно́, должно́ быть …
Ей понра́вился бы …
Бы́ло бы немно́жко ску́чно …

**4** *Express statements contrary to fact (what ought to have been done)*

Бы́ло бы лу́чше, е́сли бы мы об э́том поду́мали пора́ньше.
Мы должны́ бы́ли бы доста́ть биле́ты до э́того.

**5** *Express intentions and hope*

Я постара́юсь …
Бу́дем наде́яться на лу́чшее.

## Grammar

### 1 Кото́рый *Who or which*

**Кото́рый** means *who* or *which* (it is a relative pronoun). It is
always preceded by a comma and its endings work like those of an

adjective. The important point to remember is that **котóрый** must agree with the noun it refers to in number (singular or plural?) and gender (masculine, feminine or neuter?), but its case is determined by what follows:

> Óльга, котóрая рабóтает в музéе, на пять лет стáрше меня́.
> *Olga, who works at the museum, is 5 years older than me.*

In this sentence, **котóрая** has a feminine singular adjective ending because **Óльга** is feminine singular and it is in the nominative because *who* here is the subject of *to work* (it is the subject of the relative clause).

> Óльга, котóрую вы ужé знáете, рабóтает в музéе.
> *Olga, whom you already know, works at the museum.*

In this sentence, **котóрую** is once again a feminine singular adjective, but this time it is in the accusative case, because here it is the object of the verb *to know*:

> Óльга, с котóрой вы познакóмились на лéкции, прилáсила нас в теáтр.
> *Olga, whom you met at the lecture, has invited us to the theatre.*

In this sentence, **котóрой** is feminine singular instrumental form after the preposition **с** (**познакóмиться с** + instrumental, *to become acquainted with, to meet*).

Take care not to confuse **котóрый** and **какóй** – the latter means *which* or *what* but is only used in questions and exclamations:

| | |
|---|---|
| В какóм теáтре идёт «Снегýрочка»? | *At which theatre is the Snow Maiden on?* |
| Какáя интерéсная пьéса! | *What an interesting play!* |

## 2 Soft adjectives

A soft adjective is one whose masculine singular ends in **-ий**, for no apparent reason – i.e. the stem of the adjective does not end in a letter (**г, к, х, ж, ч, ш, щ**) which would prevent **-ый** being used. The vast majority of soft adjectives have a masculine singular ending in **-ний**, such as **после́дний** (*last, most recent*). The nominative forms of a soft adjective are:

| | | |
|---|---|---|
| Masc. sing. | после́дний авто́бус | *the last bus* |
| Fem. sing. | после́дняя страни́ца | *the last page* |
| Neut. sing. | после́днее письмо́ | *the last letter* |
| Plural: | после́дние изве́стия | *the latest news* |

In the accusative, genitive, dative, instrumental and prepositional (like the possessive adjectives **мой, твой, наш, ваш**) soft adjectives take the alternative adjectival endings – i.e. the **н** at the end of the stem is never followed by **ы**, but always by **и**; it is never followed by **о**, but always by **е**:

| | |
|---|---|
| **дома́шний** (*domestic*) | По суббо́там обы́чно она́ занима́ется дома́шним хозя́йством. |
| | *She's usually busy with housework on Saturdays.* |

| **рáнний** (early) | Он всегдá éздит на рабóту рáнним пóездом. |
| | *He always travels to work on the early train.* |
| **сúний** (dark blue) | Сегóдня онá в сúней юбке и сúней блýзке. |
| | *She's wearing a dark blue skirt and blouse today.* |
| **вечéрний** (evening) | Он всегдá читáет вечéрнюю газéту. |
| | *He always reads the evening paper.* |

Note that many soft adjectives are connected with time e.g.:

| **весéнний** | *spring* |
| **дрéвний** | *ancient* |
| **зúмний** | *winter* |
| **лéтний** | *summer* |
| **осéнний** | *autumn* |
| **пóздний** | *late* |
| **сегодняшний** | *today's* |

## Insight

A number of soft adjectives deal with location – e.g. on a long-distance train: **вéрхняя/нúжняя пóлка** (*upper/lower bunk*), **сосéднее купé** (*neighbouring compartment*).

Notice that there is one soft adjective which does not end in **-ний: кáрий** (*hazel/brown used to describe eyes*) – **у негó кáрие глазá** (*he has got brown eyes*).

### 3 Как тóлько *As soon as*

This phrase means *as soon as*; remember that in English this can hide a future meaning – *I will ring you as soon as I [will] get the tickets*. In a case like this, the verb *must* be in the future tense in Russian: **Я тебé позвоню**, как тóлько **достáну билéты**.

## 4 Conditional

In English we have various ways of expressing the conditional:

*I **would** read the evening paper if I had the time.*
*She **would be** feeling better if she hadn't eaten so much caviare.*
*He **would have** bought the tickets if he had remembered.*

In Russian, there is only one form of the conditional (i.e. the same form covers *would*, *would be*, *would have*).

It is formed very simply, by adding **бы** to the past tense of the verb (either imperfective or perfective, depending on the normal rules which determine choice of aspect):

| | |
|---|---|
| Я прочита́л[а] **бы** газе́ту … | *I would read the paper …* |
| Она́ чу́вствовала **бы** себя́ лу́чше … | *She would be feeling better …* |
| Он купи́л **бы** биле́ты … | *He would have bought the tickets …* |

**Бы** usually follows the verb, but this is not a strict rule; it *can* follow any word in the sentence which requires special emphasis:

| | |
|---|---|
| Он ду́мает, что пье́са «Кот в сапога́х» смешна́я, а И́ра **бы** сказа́ла, что э́то не о́чень интере́сный спекта́кль. | *He thinks that the play 'Puss in Boots' is funny, but **Ira** would say that it's not a very interesting show/performance.* |

Note how Russian deals with conditions introduced by *if*; where a condition is still possible, the conditional is not used at all:

**1** Е́сли + future …      + future
*If I get [i.e. will get] tickets,*      *I will ring you.*
Е́сли я доста́ну биле́ты,      я позвоню́ тебе́.

If the condition is hypothetical, or no longer possible, then the conditional must be used in both halves of the sentence:

**2** Éсли + conditional        + conditional
*If he had got the tickets*        *he would have rung you.*
Éсли бы он доста́л биле́ты,        он позвони́л бы тебе́.

---

## Insight
The conditional:

- is easy to form: use the imperfective or perfective past tense, as appropriate, followed by **бы**
- **бы** never changes
- has only one form, so **бы́ло бы лу́чше** can mean either *it would be better* or *it would have been better.*

---

### 5 Сам *Self*

This is a determinative pronoun, meaning *self*. It declines like **э́тот** and is used to emphasize subject pronouns or nouns, stressing that one particular person is indicated and no other:

Она́ сама́ вы́брала бы …        *She herself would choose …*
Он позвони́л самому́        *He rang the director himself.*
  дире́ктору.

---

## Practice

### *16.1 Read and answer!*

Fill in the gaps by choosing the appropriate form of **кото́рый** from the list below:

кото́рого, кото́рой, кото́ром, кото́рую, кото́рый, кото́рыми

**a** Пианист, _____ даёт концерт в большом зале консерватории, известен во всём мире.

**b** Пьеса, о _____ вы говорите, не очень смешная.

**c** Театр, в _____ идёт опера «Князь Игорь», очень старый.

**d** Актёр, _____ мы смотрели вчера, неплохо играл роль князя.

**e** Туристам, с _____ мы были в театре, очень понравился балет.

**f** Балерина, _____ вы очень любите, действительно талантлива.

### *16.2 Read and answer!*

Look at the extract from a theatre's calendar and answer the questions which follow:

**ПЕРМСКИЙ ТЕАТР "У МОСТА"**

13-й театральный сезон

**РЕПЕРТУАР НА НОЯБРЬ 2009 ГОДА**

Ф.М. ДОСТОЕВСКИЙ

**ПРЕМЬЕРА ПРЕСТУПЛЕНИЕ И НАКАЗАНИЕ**

Версия театра "У МОСТА"

продолжительность 2.50

режиссер-постановщик С.ФЕДОТОВ

ПЕРМСКИЙ театр У МОСТА

12 воскресенье, начало в 14.00 и в 18.00.
13 понедельник, начало в 18.00.
14 вторник, начало в 19.00.

**a** The extract gives information about the month of _____.
**b** This is the theatre's _____ season.
**c** The play to be performed on 12th, 13th, 14th is based on a novel by _____.
**d** On Tuesday 14th the play begins at _____.


### 16.3 Read and write!

Which activity would you choose under the following circumstances?

Write a sentence for each one:

**a** Если бы вы бы́ли свобо́дны по́сле обе́да, что бы вы де́лали?

   **i** игра́ть в футбо́л
   **ii** игра́ть в ша́хматы
   **iii** смотре́ть телеви́зор

Е́сли бы я был[а́] свобо́ден[свобо́дна] по́сле обе́да, я бы смотре́л[а] телеви́зор.

**b** Е́сли бы у вас бы́ло мно́го де́нег, что бы вы сде́лали?

   **i** купи́ть но́вую маши́ну
   **ii** купи́ть пода́рки друзья́м
   **iii** купи́ть но́вый дом

**c** Е́сли бы вы пло́хо чу́вствовали себя́, что бы вы сде́лали?

   **i** пожа́ловаться дру́гу
   **ii** пойти́ в поликли́нику
   **iii** пойти́ на хокке́йный матч

**d** Е́сли бы вы потеря́ли соба́ку, что бы вы сде́лали?

   **i** купи́ть ко́шку
   **ii** позвони́ть в полице́йский уча́сток (*police station*)
   **iii** пойти́ в кино́

### 16.4 Read, look and answer!

Make up dialogues explaining which activity/entertainment you prefer:

– Что вы лю́бите бо́льше, чте́ние (✓), спорт или ку́хню?
– Бо́льше всего́ я люблю́ чте́ние.

Now make up similar dialogues for each set of pictures below:

**a** спорт        му́зыка ✓        жи́вописЬ

**b** теа́тр        кино́ ✓        цирк

**c** о́пера ✓        бале́т        футбо́л

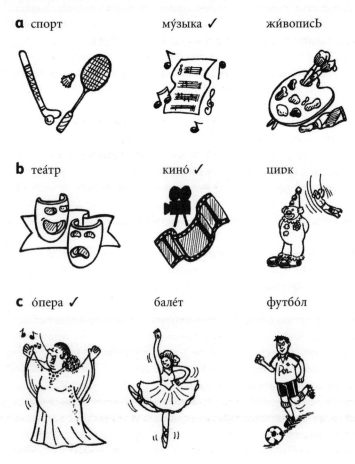

## 16.5 Read and write!

Read the information given about each person and their present job.
Write sentences explaining what sort of job would be better for each one.

| Кто? | Какой это человек? | Профессия | Совет |
|---|---|---|---|
| **a** Лена | тихий | учительница | библиотекарша |
| **b** Виктор | не очень энергичный | гимнаст | администратор |
| **c** Вадим | творческий | шофёр | журналист |
| **d** Наташа | добрый, энергичный | телефонистка | медсестра |
| **e** Миша | очень серьёзный | футболист | адвокат |

**a** Лена тихий человек. Она учительница. Было бы лучше, если бы она работала библиотекаршей.

| | |
|---|---|
| **совет** | *advice* |
| **библиотекарша** | *librarian* |
| **энергичный** | *energetic* |
| **гимнаст** | *gymnast* |
| **творческий** | *creative* |
| **шофёр** | *driver* |
| **телефонистка** | *telephonist* |
| **медсестра** | *nurse* |
| **адвокат** | *solicitor* |

QUICK VOCAB

## 16.6 Read and answer!

Match the question with the answer:

**1** Как вы ездите на работу?
**2** Чем вы занимаетесь по субботам?
**3** Какую газету он читает?
**4** Какой галстук он обычно носит?
**5** Какую юбку она обычно носит в августе?

**a** вечернюю
**b** летнюю
**c** домашним хозяйством
**d** ранним автобусом
**e** синий

## Comprehension

### 1 *Read, listen and answer!*

Boris has found his seat at the theatre and is waiting for the play to begin.

CD2, TR 6, 02:45

| | |
|---|---|
| **Де́вушка** | Извини́те, пожа́луйста, како́е э́то ме́сто? |
| **Бори́с** | Со́рок пя́тое. |
| **Де́вушка** | Прости́те, но э́то моё ме́сто. Я ду́маю, что вы оши́блись ме́стом. |
| **Бори́с** | Мину́точку … мо́жет быть я и оши́бся … вот мой биле́т … восьмо́й ряд, со́рок шесто́е ме́сто … Ой, прости́те, вы пра́вы. |
| **Де́вушка** | Ничего́, ничего́. Э́то нева́жно. |
| **Бори́с** | Кака́я глу́пость! Я до́лжен был бы наде́ть очки́. |
| **Де́вушка** | Не беспоко́йтесь. Тепе́рь всё в поря́дке. |
| **Бори́с** | Но бы́ло бы лу́чше, е́сли бы я повнима́тельнее посмотре́л на биле́т. |
| **Де́вушка** | Пожа́луйста, не беспоко́йтесь. Ведь э́то нева́жно … А вы не зна́ете, кто в ро́ли Ма́ши сего́дня ве́чером? Я купи́ла бы програ́мму, е́сли бы зна́ла, где. |
| **Бори́с** | Пожа́луйста, вот моя́ програ́мма … посмотри́те … |
| **Де́вушка** | Спаси́бо, вы о́чень добры́. |
| **Бори́с** | Не́ за что. |
| **Де́вушка** | Как хорошо́! Игра́ет Жу́кова! |
| **Бори́с** | Жу́кова? Я её не зна́ю … |
| **Де́вушка** | О́чень да́же тала́нтливая актри́са, кото́рая так хорошо́ игра́ла О́лю в фи́льме «Ле́тним у́тром». Вы, должно́ быть, зна́ете э́тот фильм? |
| **Бори́с** | Нет, не зна́ю. Я не о́чень ча́сто хожу́ в кинотеа́тр. |

| Де́вушка | Почему́? |
|---|---|
| Бори́с | Ну, не зна́ю … немно́жко ску́чно. |
| Де́вушка | Вы мно́го теря́ете. Е́сли вы хоти́те, я объясню́ вам в антра́кте, каки́е фи́льмы сто́ит посмотре́ть. |

| | |
|---|---|
| ряд | row |
| кака́я глу́пость! | what stupidity! |
| надева́ть/наде́ть | to put on |
| очки́ | spectacles |
| всё в поря́дке | everything is in order |
| повнима́тельнее (внима́тельный) | a bit more carefully (attentive, careful) |
| роль (f.) | role |
| антра́кт | interval |
| сто́ит посмотре́ть | it is worth watching |

**1** Бори́с оши́бся
  **a** ря́дом
  **b** теа́тром
  **c** число́м
  **d** ме́стом

**2** Бори́с до́лжен был бы
  **a** прочита́ть всю програ́мму
  **b** посмотре́ть на биле́т бо́лее внима́тельно
  **c** наде́ть га́лстук
  **d** бы́стро посмотре́ть на биле́т

**3** Де́вушка ду́мает, что
  **a** Жу́кова о́чень хоро́шая актри́са
  **b** Жу́кова совсе́м (quite, entirely; at all) нетала́нтливая актри́са
  **c** не сто́ит смотре́ть фильм «Ле́тним у́тром»
  **d** в кинотеа́тре немно́жко ску́чно

## Insight

It is worth learning the perfective past tense of the verb **ошиба́ться/ошиби́ться** (to be mistaken, to be wrong about something): **он оши́бся, она́ оши́блась, они́ оши́блись**; the instrumental case is needed to explain what you are mistaken/wrong about: **он оши́бся ме́стом** (he's got the wrong seat).

## 2 Reading

🔊 **CD 2, TR 6, 04:25**

Read and listen to the text and answer the questions in English.

**a** What happened on 7 May 1840?
**b** How old was Tchaikovsky when he died?
**c** How long did he live in Klin?
**d** How many people visit the museum every year?
**e** Why is it generally considered that the museum first opened in October 1894?
**f** Why do visitors feel that they are going back into the past when they enter the museum?
**g** When is Tchaikovsky's grand piano used nowadays?

Седьмо́го ма́я 1840-ого го́да роди́лся ма́льчик, кото́рый стал го́рдостью и сла́вой ру́сской музыка́льной культу́ры – Пётр Ильи́ч Чайко́вский. Вели́кий музыка́нт у́мер в октябре́ 1893-ого го́да. Ему́ бы́ло пятьдеся́т три го́да.

282

Дом-музе́й П.И.Чайко́вского нахо́дится в Клину́, стари́нном го́роде в 80 киломе́трах от Москвы́. В Клину́ вели́кий ру́сский компози́тор провёл после́дние де́вять лет свое́й жи́зни, в тече́ние кото́рых он написа́л, наприме́р, о́перу «Пи́ковая да́ма», бале́т «Спя́щая краса́вица», симфо́нии («Манфред», Пя́тую и Шесту́ю). Ежего́дно дом-музе́й принима́ет сто ты́сяч посети́телей. Традицио́нно днём откры́тия музе́я счита́ется 9 декабря́ 1894-ого го́да – да́та пе́рвой за́писи в кни́ге регистра́ции посети́телей. Когда́ вхо́дишь в э́тот ста́рый дом, ка́жется, что попада́ешь в про́шлое … Ка́ждая вещь – но́ты, кни́ги, портре́ты, ме́бель – на том же ме́сте, что и при жи́зни компози́тора. Роя́ль всё ещё занима́ет центра́льное ме́сто кабине́та-гости́ной. Два ра́за в год – в день рожде́ния компози́тора и в день его́ па́мяти – изве́стные пиани́сты сно́ва игра́ют на э́том роя́ле.

(Дом-музе́й П.И.Чайко́вского в Клину́)

| вещь (f.) | thing |
|---|---|
| в тече́ние (+ genitive) | during |
| го́рдость (f.) | pride |
| ежего́дно | annually |
| за́пись (f.) | entry |
| на том же ме́сте | in the very same place |
| но́ты | (sheet) music |
| па́мять (f.) | memory, remembrance (here: anniversary of his death) |
| «Пи́ковая да́ма» | 'Queen of Spades' |
| попада́ть/попа́сть | to turn up, to find oneself |
| посети́тель (m.) | visitor |
| при жи́зни компози́тора | in the composer's lifetime |
| проводи́ть/провести́ | to spend (time) |
| роя́ль (m.) | grand piano |
| свое́й жи́зни | of his life |
| сла́ва | glory, fame |
| сно́ва | again |

QUICK VOCAB

| «Спя́щая краса́вица» | 'Sleeping Beauty' |
|---|---|
| станови́ться/стать | to become |
| (+ instrumental) | |
| стари́нный | ancient |
| умира́ть/умере́ть (past tense: | to die |
| у́мер, умерла́) | |

## Key phrases

🔊 **CD 2, TR 6, 06:10**

Can you remember how to say the following in Russian? Listen to the recording and practise saying each phrase.

- **a** Let's hope for the best.
- **b** When will she be free?
- **c** It would be better …
- **d** Isn't that right?
- **e** It would be a bit boring.

## Ten things to remember

**1** **Како́й** (*which, what*) is only used in questions and exclamations.

**2** **Кото́рый** (*who, which*) works like an adjective.

**3** **Е́сли** + future + future if what you're talking about is still possible: **За́втра я пое́ду к врачу́, е́сли мне не бу́дет лу́чше** (*Tomorrow I'll go to the doctor's if I don't feel better*).

**4** **Е́сли** + conditional + conditional if what you're talking about is no longer possible: **Он пригласи́л бы её в теа́тр, е́сли бы не потеря́л её а́дрес** (*He would invite/would have invited her to the theatre if he hadn't lost her address*).

**5** How to say you're wrong about something: use **ошиба́ться/ ошиби́ться** + instrumental case: **К сожале́нию, они́ ошибли́сь число́м** (*Unfortunately they got the wrong date/mistook the date*).

**6** **Чайко́вский стал го́рдостью и сла́вой ру́сской музыка́льной культу́ры** (*Tchaikovsky became the pride and glory of Russian musical culture*). Remember that the verb **станови́ться/ стать** takes the instrumental case, e.g. **Мой сын хо́чет стать программи́стом** (*My son wants to become a computer programmer*).

**7** As well as being useful when finding out the price of things, the verb **сто́ить** (*to cost*) also means *to be worth*, so you might find it useful when expressing opinion: **По-мо́ему, не сто́ит покупа́ть биле́ты на э́ту пье́су** (*In my opinion, it's not worth buying tickets for that play*).

**8** Use **на** + accusative if you are buying tickets for an event: **биле́ты на вы́ставку, на бале́т, на конце́рт** (*tickets for an exhibition, a ballet, a concert*).

**9** If you want to thank someone formally for their kindness, use the short form of the adjective *kind*: **вы о́чень добры́**(*you are very kind*). Remember that even if **вы** only refers to one person, the plural ending must be used. See Unit 8 for short adjectives.

**10** Two useful phrases: **мо́жет быть** (*perhaps, maybe*) and **должно́ быть** (*it must be*), for example: **Мо́жет быть она́ ошибла́сь число́м** (*Perhaps she got the wrong date*); or **Она́, должно́ быть, ошибла́сь число́м** (*She must have got the wrong date*: literally *she, it must be, got the wrong date*).

# 17

# Давай заглянем в бюро путешествий
## Let's pop into the travel agent's

In this unit you will learn
- *How to talk about holidays and holiday accommodation*
- *How to talk about what is best and most comfortable*
- *How to give more information in the negative*

## Dialogue

Ira's mother has not been well and Ira is trying to persuade her to take a holiday.

CD 2, TR 7, 00:08

| Йра | Мáма, как ты себя́ чýвствуешь сего́дня? Тебé лýчше? |
|---|---|
| Мáма | Немнóжко. Йра, не беспокóйся обо мне. Я немнóжко устáла, и всё. |
| Йра | Но ты всё врéмя кáшляешь, вот что беспокóит меня́ … |
| Мáма | Тебé нé о чем беспокóиться, ведь кáшель скóро пройдёт. |
| Йра | Надéюсь … но слýшай, мáма, тебé нýжно отдохнýть. Ты ужé подýмала об óтпуске? Кудá ты поéдешь? |

| | |
|---|---|
| **Мáма** | Никудá не поéду. |
| **Йра** | Не понимáю, а почемý? |
| **Мáма** | Мне нé с кем поéхать в óтпуск, а éхать однá не хочý. |
| **Йра** | Мáмочка, э́то не прáвда … Ведь у меня́ скóро бýдет óтпуск. Я с удовóльствием поéду с тобóй в Сóчи … |
| **Мáма** | … Агá, всё поня́тно. Знáчит ты ужé реши́ла, кудá мы поéдем? Ну, скажи́, какóй э́то курóрт? |
| **Йра** | Да, я слы́шала, что Сóчи э́то лýчший курóрт, éсли хóчешь и отдохнýть и вы́лечиться. Там мя́гкий клúмат и морскóй вóздух, тёплое мóре и сáмые комфортáбельные гости́ницы, экзоти́ческие ресторáны … и |
| **Мáма** | Знáчит, ты ужé былá в бюрó путешéствий? |
| **Йра** | Да, оди́н раз тóлько … а зáвтра ýтром я бýду свобóдна, éсли … |
| **Мáма** | Ну, лáдно, давáй заглянем в бюрó путешéствий зáвтра ýтром. Спрóсим об авиабилéтах. |
| **Йра** | Хорошó! Закáжем нóмер на двои́х, … с дýшем, конéчно … на две недéли в гости́нице «Дагомы́с». |
| **Мáма** | Э́то лýчшая гости́ница, что ли? |
| **Йра** | Конéчно! … Вот у меня́ в сýмке брошю́ра … «Дагомы́с – туристи́ческий центр на Чёрном мóре, отли́чные услóвия для тури́зма, óтдыха и лечéния». |

| | |
|---|---|
| **кáшлять** | *to (have a) cough* |
| **вот что беспокóит меня́** | *that's what's worrying me* |
| **кáшель** (m., fleeting **е**) | *cough* |
| **тебé нýжно отдохнýть** | *you need a holiday* |
| (**отдыхáть/отдохнýть**) | |
| **мне нé с кем поéхать** | *I've no one to go with* |

| | |
|---|---|
| **о́тпуск** | *holiday, leave* |
| **одна́ (оди́н)** | *alone* (lit. *one*) |
| **реша́ть/реши́ть** | *to decide* |
| **куро́рт** | *resort* |
| **лу́чший** | *best* |
| **слы́шать/услы́шать** (2nd conjugation) | *to hear* |
| **выле́чиваться/вы́лечиться** | *to be cured, recover* |
| **мя́гкий кли́мат** | *mild climate* |
| **морско́й во́здух** | *sea air* |
| **мо́ре** | *sea* |
| **са́мые комфорта́бельные гости́ницы** | *the most comfortable hotels* |
| **экзоти́ческий** | *exotic* |
| **давай загля́нем** | *let's pop into* |
| **бюро́ путеше́ствий** | *travel bureau/agency* |
| **спра́шивать/спроси́ть** | *to ask* |
| **авиабиле́т** | *air ticket* |
| **но́мер на двои́х** | *a double room* |
| **усло́вие** | *condition* |
| **лече́ние** | *(medical) treatment* |

> ## Insight
>
> In the dialogue **вот** is used with **что** to give emphasis to Ira's concerns (*that's what …*). You can also use **вот** with *why*: **вот почему́ он не хоте́л купи́ть биле́ты!** (*that's why he didn't want to buy the tickets!*).

### О́тпуск *Holiday/leave*

This is the word for annual holiday/leave from work, as distinct from school holidays (**кани́кулы**) and holiday in the general sense of rest, relaxation from work (**о́тдых**).

With their Mediterranean climate and spectacular scenery, resorts on the Black Sea Coast are a popular holiday destination. Camping and caravanning holidays are not as common as they are in

Western Europe, but there are a number of campsites (**ке́мпинг**, *a campsite*) near major tourist centres where tourists can have accommodation in a chalet (**ле́тний до́мик**) or a tent (**пала́тка**), or where they can park their caravan (**жило́й автоприце́п** or **ке́мпер**). The camping season is not a long one, usually running from 1 June until 30 September.

In hotels (**гости́ницы** or **оте́ли**) the tourist has perhaps the most contact with the personnel at the **бюро́ обслу́живания** (service desk) or with the person in charge of their floor, the 'lady on duty' – **дежу́рная** (the person to ask if you have a difficulty with your room, for example). Note that, in Russia, the **пе́рвый эта́ж** (lit. *first floor*) is the ground floor, **второ́й эта́ж** (lit. *second floor*) is the first floor and so on.

In addition to the hotels and campsites, there are also holiday homes (**дома́ о́тдыха**) and convalescent homes (**санато́рии**).

## Insight

**Куро́рт** (*resort*) must be used with **на** (not **в**) and the prepositional case if you want to say *in* or *at* the resort: **на популя́рных куро́ртах** (*at popular resorts*). See Unit 3 (Grammar section 2) or Appendix 2 for fuller lists of nouns which must be used with **на**.

## Questions

**1** *True or false?*

**a** Йра беспоко́ится о ма́ме.
**b** Ма́ма хо́чет отдыха́ть одна́.
**c** Йра хо́чет пое́хать в Новосиби́рск.
**d** Йра бу́дет свобо́дна за́втра у́тром.
**e** Йра ничего́ не зна́ет о гости́нице «Дагомы́с».

## 2 Answer the questions!

**a** Как ма́ма себя́ чу́вствует сего́дня?
**b** Что ей ну́жно?
**c** Кто мо́жет пое́хать с ма́мой в о́тпуск?
**d** Како́й куро́рт И́ра вы́брала (**choose**)?
**e** Когда́ они́ пойду́т в бюро́ путеше́ствий?

---

## How do you say it?

How to:
**1** *Ask about holidays*

Куда́ ты пое́дешь/вы пое́дете в о́тпуск?

**2** *Ask about holiday accommodation*

Како́й э́то куро́рт?
Кака́я э́то гости́ница?
Како́й э́то ке́мпинг?

**3** *Book holiday accommodation*

Заказа́ть но́мер на двои́х/но́мер на одного́.
Заказа́ть но́мер с ду́шем.
Заказа́ть но́мер на две неде́ли.

**4** *Say what is best; most comfortable*

Э́то лу́чшая гости́ница.
Са́мые комфорта́бельные гости́ницы.

**5** *Say 'no one to go with'*

Мне не́ с кем пое́хать.

**6** *Say 'nothing to worry about'*

Тебе́ не́ о чем беспоко́иться.

---

## Grammar

### 1 *Superlative*

The superlative in English is formed by using *most* with an adjective
or by adding *-est* to an adjective: *the **most** expensive hotel, the dearest
hotel*. In Russian the superlative is formed by using the adjective
**са́мый** in front of the adjective you wish to make superlative:

| | |
|---|---|
| Э́то **са́мый** краси́вый<br>куро́рт в Ита́лии. | *It's the most beautiful<br>resort in Italy.* |
| Э́то **са́мая** комфорта́бельная<br>гости́ница на куро́рте. | *It's the most comfortable<br>hotel in the resort.* |

Note that for adjectives *big/small, good/bad, old/young, high/low*,
the superlative can be made in any of the following ways:

| | |
|---|---|
| using **са́мый** + ordinary adjective: | Э́то **са́мая** хоро́шая<br>гости́ница. |
| using **са́мый** + comparative adjective: | Э́то **са́мая** лу́чшая<br>гости́ница. |
| using just the comparative: | Э́то **лу́чшая**<br>гости́ница. |

All three variants mean: *This is the best hotel*.

If you want to say *This is one of the best hotels*, **из** + genitive must
be used:

Э́то одна́ из лу́чших гости́ниц.  *This is one of the best hotels.*

(See Appendix 1 for further notes on the superlative.)

### 2 Беспоко́ить(ся)/побеспоко́ить(ся) *To be/make anxious*

Note how this verb is used reflexively (i.e. with the endings **-сь, -ся**) when it means *to worry* in the sense of *to be anxious*; when it means *to worry* in the sense of *to make anxious* (i.e. when it has an object), it must be used without the reflexive endings:

| | |
|---|---|
| **Йра беспоко́ится о ма́ме.** | *Ira is worried about her mother.* |
| **Ка́шель беспоко́ит её.** | *The cough is worrying her.* |

The principle applies to a number of common verbs (e.g. *to begin, to finish, to return*) – i.e. they can be used reflexively (if they do not have an object) or non-reflexively (if they do have an object):

| | |
|---|---|
| **Ле́кция начина́ется в семь часо́в ве́чера.** | *The lecture begins at 7 p.m.* |
| **Он всегда́ начина́ет ле́кцию шу́ткой.** | *He always starts the lecture with a joke.* |

### 3 *Negatives*

In Unit 14 we met a group of negative expressions which all begin with **ни-** and which are all used with **не** + verb in a tense or command form, e.g.:

| | |
|---|---|
| Я никуда́ не пое́ду в о́тпуск. | *I'm not going on holiday anywhere.* |
| Я ничего́ не зна́л[а] об э́той гости́нице. | *I didn't know anything about this hotel.* |
| Никому́ не говори́те об э́том! | *Don't tell anyone about this!* |

In this unit we have seen some rather different kinds of negative, e.g.:

| | |
|---|---|
| Тебе́ не́ о чем беспоко́иться. | *There is nothing for you to worry about.* |

This type of negative is always used with an infinitive and is actually a very economical way of saying quite a lot. Note how all the following start with **не́** and are all followed by an infinitive:

| | |
|---|---|
| Не́где рабо́тать. | *There is nowhere to work.* |
| Не́куда идти́. | *There is nowhere to go.* |
| Не́когда смотре́ть телеви́зор. | *There is no time to watch television.* |
| Не́чего пить. | *There is nothing to drink.* |
| Не́кого приглаша́ть на у́жин. | *There is no one to invite to supper.* |

If you want to say, for example, *I have no time to watch the television/there is no time **for me** to watch the television*, simply use the dative of **я**, *for me*: **Мне не́когда смотре́ть телеви́зор**. Note that **не́что** and **(не́)кто** must be used in the correct case form; if a preposition is used with them, it splits them up:

| | |
|---|---|
| Ива́ну не́ на что жа́ловаться. | *Ivan has nothing to complain about.* |
| Мне не́ с кем говори́ть. | *I've no one to talk to.* |

## Insight

A negative starting with:

- **ни-** and is followed by **не** and a verb in a tense
- **не́** is followed by an infinitive has the stress

**Она́ никогда́ не звони́т мне: ей не́когда говори́ть.**
(*She never rings me: she's got no time to talk.*)

### 4 One

To say *one* (i.e. as the subject of the verb), use the **ты** form of the verb, without the pronoun **ты**, or the **вы** form of the verb:

éсли хо́чешь [вы хоти́те]       *if one wishes to have a rest/*
  отдохну́ть                     *holiday*

---

## Practice

### 17.1 Read and answer!

Match the questions with the answers:

| | | | |
|---|---|---|---|
| **1** | Куда́ вы пое́дете в о́тпуск? | **a** | На две неде́ли |
| **2** | Како́й э́то куро́рт? | **b** | В Оде́ссу |
| **3** | Где вы обы́чно отдыха́ете? | **c** | С ва́нной и с телефо́ном |
| **4** | На ско́лько неде́ль? | **d** | Са́мый краси́вый в Росси́и |
| **5** | Како́й но́мер вы хоти́те заказа́ть? | **e** | На бе́регу мо́ря (*at the seaside*) |

294

## 17.2 Look, read and answer!

Look at the following advertisement and complete the following statements:

**a** This company offers a large choice of _____ and apartments.
**b** Holidays can be spent either by the sea or _____.
**c** Holidays are offered in the following countries:
_____, _____, _____, United Arab Emirates (ОАЭ),
_____, _____, Czech Republic (Чехия).

| выходнóй | *day off* |
|---|---|
| вы́бор | *choice* |
| горá | *mountain* |
| мечтá | *dream* |
| побере́жье | *coast* |

ΩV

## 17.3 Read and write!

You're feeling enthusiastic about your holiday plans! Answer the questions according to the model:

**a** Какáя э́то гости́ница? (хорóший) Э́то однá из сáмых хорóших гости́ниц в странé (*country*).
**b** Какóй э́то курóрт? (прия́тный)

**c** Какóй э́то пóезд? (бы́стрый)

**d** Какóй э́то клúмат? (мя́гкий)

**e** Какáя э́то прогрáмма? (интерéсный)

**f** Какóй э́то здание (красúвый)

### 17.4 Read, answer and listen!

You are trying to book a hotel room. Complete your part of the conversation, then listen to the complete conversation on the recording.

CD 2, TR 7, 0226

| | |
|---|---|
| **Администрáтор** | Вам помóчь? |
| **Вы** | **(a)** Say 'hello' and ask if there are any free (свобóдный) rooms. |
| **Администрáтор** | Есть. |
| **Вы** | **(b)** Say you want to book a room. |
| **Администрáтор** | Какóй нóмер вы хотúте заказáть? |
| **Вы** | **(c)** Say you want to book a single room with a shower, telephone and television. |
| **Администрáтор** | На скóлько дней? |
| **Вы** | **(d)** Say 'for five days, until (до + genitive) Friday'. |
| **Администрáтор** | Хорошó. Нóмер 227 свобóден. Э́то на вторóм этажé. Заполнúте, пожáлуйста, бланк. |
| **Вы** | **(e)** Say 'thank you' and ask where you can get (взять) your key (клюю). |
| **Администрáтор** | У дежýрной. |

QV

**заполня́ть/запóлнить бланк**　　*to fill in a form*
**на вторóм этажé**　　*on the first floor* (lit. *on the second floor*)

### 17.5 Read and write!

Look at the list below, then make up sentences explaining why none of the people is able to do the things listed below (think about what forms of **нéчто** and **нéкто** will be needed):

| Кто? | Заня́тие | Почему́ нельзя́? |
|---|---|---|
| **a** Ива́н | пойти́ в теа́тр за́втра | не́кто/с |
| **b** На́дя | смотре́ть телеви́зор | не́когда |
| **c** Ва́ля | писа́ть письмо́ | не́что |
| **d** Бори́с | идти́ сего́дня ве́чером | не́куда |
| **e** Мари́на | рабо́тать | не́где |
| **f** И́горь | жа́ловаться | не́что/на |
| **g** Со́ня | подари́ть кассе́ту | не́кто |

**a** Ива́ну не́ с кем пойти́ в теа́тр за́втра.

---

## Comprehension

### 1 *Conversation*

**Read, listen and answer!**

Nina is having problems with her hotel room and has gone to the
**дежу́рная** for help:

| | |
|---|---|
| **Ни́на** | Извини́те, пожа́луйста … |
| **Дежу́рная** | Здра́вствуйте. Как вам помо́чь? |
| **Ни́на** | Я пло́хо спала́ но́чью. У меня́ в но́мере хо́лодно. Мо́жно ещё одея́ло? |
| **Дежу́рная** | Коне́чно … Вот, пожа́луйста, возьми́те. |
| **Ни́на** | Спаси́бо. |
| **Дежу́рная** | Пожа́луйста. Ещё что-нибудь? |
| **Ни́на** | У меня́ в но́мере почему́-то нет полоте́нца. |
| **Дежу́рная** | Ой, извини́те … вот вам полоте́нце. Всё, да? |
| **Ни́на** | Спаси́бо. Да, тепе́рь всё в поря́дке … То́лько, зна́ете, телеви́зор не о́чень хорошо́ рабо́тает. Но э́то не о́чень ва́жно. |
| **Дежу́рная** | Хорошо́. Я сейча́с пойду́ посмотрю́. |
| **Ни́на** | А у меня́ ещё к вам про́сьба. |

*CD 2, TR 7, 03:07*

| | |
|---|---|
| **Дежу́рная** | Пожа́луйста. |
| **Ни́на** | Вы не мо́жете заказа́ть для меня́ такси́? |
| **Дежу́рная** | Могу́. На когда́? |
| **Ни́на** | На послеза́втра, на оди́ннадцать часо́в утра́. |
| **Дежу́рная** | Куда́ хоти́те пое́хать? |
| **Ни́на** | В аэропо́рт. |
| **Дежу́рная** | Хорошо́. Всё поня́тно. Я сейча́с закажу́. |
| **Ни́на** | Спаси́бо за по́мощь. |
| **Дежу́рная** | Не́ за что. |

| | |
|---|---|
| **одея́ло** | *blanket* |
| **что́-нибудь** | *anything* |
| **почему́-то** | *for some reason or other* |
| **полоте́нце** | *towel* |
| **про́сьба** | *request* |

## Insight

**Я пойду́ посмотрю́** (*I will come and look*); literally this phrase means *I will come I will look* – in other words you need to use the future tense for both verbs, and **и** (*and*) is not used.

**1** Ни́на пло́хо спала́, потому́ что

  **a** в но́мере жа́рко
  **b** но́мер бли́зко от ли́фта
  **c** в но́мере хо́лодно
  **d** в но́мере шу́мно (**noisy**)

**2** В но́мере нет

  **a** посте́ли
  **b** телеви́зора
  **c** полоте́нца
  **d** телефо́на

**3** Ни́на хо́чет пое́хать в аэропо́рт

  **a** по́сле за́втрака
  **b** послеза́втра
  **c** за́втра
  **d** по́сле обе́да

## 2 Reading

**Read the text and answer the questions in English.**

**a** Name the different types of transport used by Russian tour operators.
**b** What different types of tour do they organize?
**c** What is the starting point for the 'Golden Ring' tour?
**d** Which resorts are visited in the 'Great Northern Ring' tour?
**e** How long do the tracking holidays in Siberia last?
**f** Which different sporting activities are offered in the 'Sochi, Yalta, Kherson' tour?

Ру́сские бюро́ путеше́ствий предлага́ют все ви́ды путеше́ствий: самолётом, теплохо́ дом и по́ездом, на авто́бусе и на автомоби́ле – на традицио́ нные фестива́ли иску́сств, на о́тдых и лече́ние, организу́ют пое́здки для делов́ых люде́й – «бизнес-ту́ры», речны́е и морски́е круи́зы. Вот некото́рые из ту́ров и програ́мм, кото́рые предлага́ют ру́сские туропера́торы:

АВТО́БУСНЫЕ И АВТОМОБИ́ЛЬНЫЕ
ТУ́РЫ И МАРШРУ́ТЫ

«Золото́е кольцо́ Росси́и» – четы́ре вариа́нта авто́бусных ту́ров по дре́вним ру́сским города́м: Се́ргиев Поса́д, Росто́в Вели́кий, Су́здаль, Влади́мир. Ту́ры начина́ются и зака́нчиваются в Москве́. «Большо́е Се́верное кольцо́» – путеше́ствие на авто́бусах из столи́цы Росси́и Москвы́ на се́веро-за́пад страны́ к Балти́йскому мо́рю в Санкт-Петербу́рг и да́лее в столи́цу и куро́ртные города́ Эсто́нии.

ТУ́РЫ «АКТИ́ВНЫЙ О́ТДЫХ»

«Тре́кинг по сиби́рской тайге́» – (5–7 дней) – ь окре́стностях о́зера Байка́ла. В програ́мме 25-киломе́тровый похо́д – незабыва́емые встре́чи с фло́рой и фа́уной Сиби́ри.

«Со́чи, Я́лта и Херсо́н» – спорти́вные заня́тия на куро́ртах Чёрного мо́ря – те́ннис, ви́ндсерфинг, па́русный спорт, ры́бная ло́вля, волейбо́л, баскетбо́л, насто́льный те́ннис, тури́стские похо́ды в го́ры Кавка́за и Кры́ма.

| | |
|---|---|
| акти́вный | active |
| Балти́йское мо́ре | Baltic Sea |
| в окре́стностях (+ genitive) | in the vicinity of |
| ви́ндсерфинг | windsurfing |
| встре́ча | meeting |
| гора́ | mountain |
| зака́нчивать(ся)/зако́нчить(ся) | to finish |
| Кавка́з | Caucasus |
| маршру́т | route, itinerary |
| насто́льный те́ннис | table tennis |
| незабыва́емый | unforgettable |
| не́который | some, certain |
| о́зеро | lake |
| па́русный спорт | sailing |
| похо́д | trip, hike |
| ры́бная ло́вля | fishing |
| се́верный | northern |
| теплохо́д | ship |
| тре́кинг по сиби́рской тайге́ | tracking in the Siberian taiga |
| тур | tour |
| фестива́ль (m.) иску́сств | arts festival |
| фло́ра и фа́уна | flora and fauna |
| Эсто́ния | Estonia |

## Insight

**Тре́кинг по сиби́рской тайге́: по** (and the dative case) is a useful preposition when talking about travel, and it can be translated in a number of ways into English:

| | |
|---|---|
| по пути́ домо́й | on the way home |
| по Во́лге | down the Volga |
| по всей стране́ | all over the country |

## Key phrases

🔊 **CD 2, TR 7, 04:29**

Can you remember how to say the following in Russian? Listen to the recording and practise saying each phrase.

 **a** What sort of resort is it?
 **b** Where are you going on holiday?
 **c** It's the best hotel.
 **d** There is nothing to drink.
 **e** I want to book a room with a shower.

## Test yourself

**1** In the following sentence, would you insert **какóй** or **котóрый** in the blank to complete the question *Which resort have you chosen?* —— курóрт вы вы́брали?

**2** In the following sentence, would you insert **нигдé** or **нéгде** to complete the statement *I can't see Irina anywhere!* – Я —— не ви́жу Ири́ну .

**3** Your hotel room doesn't have a towel. How would you ask the dezhurnaya for one?

**4** If you ask someone where they are going on holiday, would you use **где** or **кудá** for *where*?

**5** You are told that your hotel room is **на четвёртом этажé**. Which floor will you go to?

**6** Complete the following phrase which means *in the most beautiful resort*: **на** —— **краси́вом курóрте**.

**7** If someone says **Не беспокойтесь!** to you, what instruction are you being given?

**8** **Обéд начинáется в час** (*Lunch starts at one*). Why is the verb reflexive in this phrase?

**9** Complete this phrase with the prepositional plural adjective endings: **В наш — нóв — гостúницах** (*in our new hotels*).

**10** How would you say *I'd like to book a room, please?*

# 18

## Что случилось?
What happened?

In this unit you will learn
- *How to ask what has happened*
- *How to report on what has happened and what has been said*
- *How to ask what is wrong*
- *How to express concern and purpose*

### Dialogue

Anna is at Ira's flat; they are waiting for Volodya, who arrives late, looking pale and shaken.

| | |
|---|---|
| **Йра** | Уже́ семь часо́в! Где же Воло́дя?! |
| **А́нна** | Наде́юсь, что всё в поря́дке. |
| **Йра** | (*Ring at the door.*) Наконе́ц! |
| **Воло́дя** | А́нна, Йра, здра́вствуйте. Извини́те, что я по́здно пришёл. |
| **Йра** | Воло́дя! Что с тобо́й? Ты ужа́сно вы́глядишь! Сади́сь! |
| **Воло́дя** | Спаси́бо. |
| **А́нна** | Чайку́ хо́чешь? Да? Я сейча́с принесу́. |
| **Йра** | Ну, Воло́дя, расскажи́, что случи́лось? |
| **Воло́дя** | На у́лице произошла́ ава́рия. Я всё ви́дел. |
| **Йра** | Бо́же мой! Ты не ра́нен, наде́юсь? |

◆ CD 2, TR 8, 00:06

| | |
|---|---|
| **Воло́дя** | Нет, нет. |
| **А́нна** | Вот тебе́ чай, Воло́дя. |
| **Воло́дя** | Спаси́ бо, А́нна ... Вот ... Я шёл по у́лице к ста́нции метро́. Вдруг уви́дел ста́рую же́нщину, кото́рая переходи́ла че́рез у́лицу. Она́ не ви́дела грузовика́, кото́рый подъезжа́л к перекрёстку ... |
| **Йра** | Ой. Воло́дя ... |
| **Воло́дя** | Я подбежа́л к ней, закрича́л, что́бы останови́ть её, но она́ не услы́шала меня́. Грузови́к не смог останови́ться и уда́рил её ... Подбежа́ли лю́ди. Пото́м ско́рая по́ мощь увезла́ её в больни́цу .... |
| **Йра** | Ужа́сно! |
| **Воло́дя** | Пото́м, понима́ете, я до́лжен был рассказа́ть милиционе́ру обо всём, что ви́дел ... Он хоте́л увезти́ меня́ в медпу́нкт, сказа́л, что я в состоя́нии шо́ка. Я не захоте́л и сказа́л, что позвоню́ в поликли́нику, е́сли на́до бу́дет. |

QUICK VOCAB

| | |
|---|---|
| **где же** | *where on earth* |
| **что с тобо́й?** | *what's the matter with you?* |
| **ужа́сно (ужа́сный)** | *terrible, dreadful* |
| **чайку́** (diminutive) **хо́чешь?** | *would you like some tea?* |
| **приноси́ть/принести́** | *to bring* |
| **расскажи́! (расска́зывать/ рассказа́ть)** | *tell (to tell, relate)* |
| **что случи́лось? (случа́ться/ случи́ться)** | *what happened? (to happen)* |
| **произошла́ (происходи́ть/ произойти́)** | *happened (to happen)* |
| **ава́рия** | *accident, crash* |
| **ра́нен (ра́неный)** | *hurt, injured* |
| **грузови́к** | *lorry* |
| **падьезжать/подъе́хать** | *to drive up to* |
| **перекрёсток** (fleeting **o**) | *crossroads* |

| | |
|---|---|
| подбега́ть/подбежа́ть | to run to |
| закрича́л (крича́ть/ закрича́ть) (2nd conj.) | I/he shouted (to shout) |
| что́бы (+infinitive) | in order to |
| остана́вливать(ся)/ останови́ть(ся) | to stop |
| ударя́ть/уда́рить | to strike, hit |
| ско́рая по́мощь | ambulance |
| милиционе́р | policeman |
| увози́ть/увезти́ | to take away (by transport) |
| состоя́ние шо́ка | state of shock |

## Insight

Verbs of motion have three forms of the past tense:

- **Он ходи́л** – *he used to go/walk; he has been going* (**ходить** – habits; return journeys)
- **Он шёл** – *he was going* (**идти́** – one occasion, one direction)
- **Он пошёл** – *he has gone/set off* (**пойти** – single action in the past).

The traffic police deal with accidents and with infringements of traffic regulations (for which they might impose a fine, **штраф**). A traffic accident is known as a **ДТП** (**доро́жно-тра́нспортное происше́ствие** – lit. *a road traffic incident*).

Here are some more important words for the car driver.

| | |
|---|---|
| бензи́н | petrol |
| запа́сные ча́сти | spare parts |
| запра́вочная ста́нция | petrol station |
| ремо́нт | repairs |
| ста́нция техни́ческого обслу́живания | service station |

## Questions

### 1 *True or false?*

**a** Ира не понимает, где Володя.
**b** Ира говорит, что Володя хорошо выглядит.
**c** Володя шёл домой, когда увидел аварию.
**d** Грузовик подъезжал к мосту (*bridge*).
**e** Милиционер спросил Володю обо всём, что случилось.

### 2 *Answer the questions!*

**a** Как Володя выглядит?
**b** Что Анна предлагает ему выпить?
**c** Что делала старая женщина, когда Володя увидел её?
**d** Куда увезли старую женщину?
**e** Володя в каком состоянии?

## How do you say it?

How to:
**1** *Ask what has happened*

Что случилось?

**2** *Report what has happened*

Произошла авария.
Рассказать обо всём, что видел/видела/видели.

**3** *Ask what is wrong/express concern*

Что с тобой?
Что с вами?
Ты не ранен/ранена?
Вы не ранены?

**4** *Ask what has happened*

Он сказа́л, что я в состоя́нии шо́ка.
Я сказа́л, что позвоню́ в поликли́нику.

**5** *Express purpose*

Что́бы останови́ть её.

---

## Grammar

### 1 *Emphatic particle* же

This is an emphatic particle – it gives an extra emphasis to a word in the sentence; in English this might be rendered just by the tone of voice or by adding some extra phrase such as *on earth*:

| | |
|---|---|
| **Где же вы бы́ли?** | *Where (on earth) have you been?* |
| **Когда́ же он пришёл?** | *When (on earth) did he arrive?* |
| **Кто же сказа́л э́то?** | *Who (on earth) said that?* |
| **Мы пое́дем сего́дня же!** | *We'll go today (this very day)!* |

Note also Я же вам говори́л[а]!, *I told you so!*

### 2 *Indirect statement*

This is the term used in English to describe reported statements (i.e. reports of what people have said).

Direct speech:
    The policeman said, 'You are in a state of shock.'
    I said, 'I will ring the clinic.'

Indirect speech:
    The policeman said I was in a state of shock.
    I said I would ring the clinic.

As you can see, in English there is a change of tense between direct and indirect statement (you are → I was; I will → I would). In Russian the tense in the indirect statement remains the same as it was in the direct statement (although, as in English, there may be some change of pronouns, e.g. *you are → I was*).

Direct speech:
> Милиционе́р сказа́л: «Вы в состоя́нии шо́ка.»
> Я сказа́л: Я позвоню́ в поликли́нику.

Indirect speech:
> Милиционе́р сказа́л, что я в состоя́нии шо́ка.
> Я сказа́л, что я позвоню́ в поликли́нику.

Note that in Russian the word **что** (*that*) always appears in indirect statements, preceded by a comma.

## Insight

In the Russian examples above, the same tense is used in the direct and indirect statements, but the English tense changes. Below is an example of what happens when the direct statement involves the past tense – i.e. there is no change to the Russian verb, but the English verb changes from *didn't* to *hadn't*:

Direct: **Я ничего́ не ви́дел!** *I didn't see anything!*
Indirect: **Он сказа́л, что ничего́ не ви́дел.** *He said he hadn't seen anything.*

### 3 *Purpose*

To say *in order to do something*, use **что́бы** + infinitive:

**А́лла позвони́ла Ва́ле,**     *Alla rang Valya to find out*
**что́бы узна́ть об ава́рии.**     *about the accident.*

Notice that **что́бы** is always preceded by a comma (unless it is the first word in the sentence).

English quite often says simply *to*, rather than *in order to*, but in Russian the only occasion when **чтобы** can be omitted is after a verb of motion:

**Милиционе́р пришёл**    *The policeman arrived to*
**помо́чь же́нщине.**          *help the woman.*

### 4 Prefixed verbs of motion

In Unit 15 we met a series of prefixes used with the suffixes **-ходи́ть/-йти́**; the same prefixes (followed by the same prepositions) can be used with other verbs of motion and have the same meanings as with **-ходи́ть/йти́**.

| Suffix | Meaning | Example of prefixed form | |
|---|---|---|---|
| -бега́ть/-бежа́ть | *run* | подбега́ть/подбежа́ть | *to run up to* |
| -води́ть/-вести́ | *lead* | вводи́ть/ввести́ | *to lead in* |
| -вози́ть/-везти́ | *transport* | увози́ть/увезти́ | *to take away by transport* |
| -лета́ть/-лете́ть | *to fly* | прилета́ть/прилете́ть | *to arrive by plane* |
| -носи́ть/-нести́ | *carry* | приноси́ть/принести́ | *to bring* |
| -плыва́ть/-плы́ть | *swim, sail* | отплыва́ть/отплы́ть | *to swim/ sail away* |

Note especially the prefixed forms of **-езжа́ть/-е́хать** (in each case the imperfective is first conjugation and the perfective works just like **-е́хать**):

| | | | |
|---|---|---|---|
| *to approach* | (by transport) | подъезжа́ть/ подъе́хать | (к + dat.) |
| *to arrive* | (by transport) | приезжа́ть/ прие́хать | (в+ acc.) |
| *to cross; move house* | (by transport) | переезжа́ть/ перее́хать | (че́рез + acc.) |

| to exit | (by transport) | выезжа́ть/ вы́ехать | (из + gen.) |
|---|---|---|---|
| to leave | (by transport) | уезжа́ть/уе́хать | (из + gen.) |
| to pass | (by transport) | проезжа́ть/ прое́хать | (ми́мо + gen.) |

## Insight

You have now met eight verbs of motion and nine prefixes, so you have the building blocks for many new verbs. E.g. for *to bring* in Russian, use the 'arrive' prefix (**при-**) and the 'carry' suffix (-**носи́ть**/-**нести́**): **Я принесу́ чай** (*I'll bring the tea*). See Unit 15 for all nine prefixes.

### 5 Всё, что ... *All that ...*

In order to say *everything which/that*, **что** preceded by a comma must be used:

**обо всём, что случи́лось**  *about everything that happened*

### 6 *Object of a negative verb*

The genitive case may be used instead of the accusative for the object of a negative verb; the genitive is preferred if the negative verb is to do with perception:

| **Он не ви́дел грузовика́.** | *He didn't see the lorry.* |
|---|---|
| **Он не обраща́л внима́ния на неё.** | *He didn't pay any attention to her.* |

Note: this rule is not always observed, especially with concrete masculine and neuter nouns, so that, for example, you might hear:

**Она́ не ви́дела грузови́к.**  *She didn't see the lorry.*

If the object of a negative verb is a feminine noun which refers to a person, then the accusative should be used:

**Мне ка́жется, что он не зна́ет Та́ню.** (lit. *It seems to me he doesn't know Tanya*).

---

## Practice

### *18.1 Read, look and answer!*

Match the sentences on the left with the traffic signs on the right:

**1** Ремо́нтные рабо́ты      a

**2** Поворо́т напра́во запрещён      b

**3** Ке́мпинг      c

**4** Пункт медици́нской по́мощи      d

**5** Ме́сто стоя́нки      e

**6** Перекрёсток      f

| | |
|---|---|
| **ремо́нт** | *repairs* |
| **поворо́т** | *bend, turn* |
| **запрещён** | *forbidden* |
| **стоя́нка** | *parking* |

### 18.2 Read and write!

Read the extract from the policeman's notebook and then write a sentence for each one, reporting what the witness said:

| | **Милиционе́р** | **Свиде́тель** (*witness*) |
|---|---|---|
| **a** | Куда́ вы шли? | К ста́нции метро́ |
| **b** | Во ско́лько э́то бы́ло? | Э́то бы́ло часа́ в четы́ре |
| **c** | Что вы ви́дели? | Грузови́к и ста́рую же́нщину |
| **d** | Что вы сде́лали? | Я подбежа́л к ней |
| **e** | Как вы себя́ чу́вствуете сейча́с? | Не о́чень хорошо́ |
| **f** | Вы хоти́те пое́хать в медпу́нкт? | Нет, не хочу́ |

**a** Свиде́тель сказа́л, что он шёл к ста́нции метро́.

---

### Insight

In 18.2 the approximate time is given (*at about 4 o'clock*) by putting the unit of time first – **часа́ в четы́ре**. You can use this sort of inversion with other units of time, e.g.: **Мы жи́ли в Ита́лии го́да три** (*We lived in Italy for about three years*).

---

### 18.3 Read and answer!

Read the police report below and answer the questions:

**a** Where was Amelia Green staying?
**b** What items were stolen?
**c** Where were they stolen from?
**d** When did the theft occur?

# МВД
Управление внутренних дел
гор. Москва
20 отделение милиции
от 29 марта 2009г

Начальник 20 отделения милиции г. Москвы

/ Ка____ В.Н.

# СПРАВКА
Дана гр. Великобритании Грин Амелия, прож.
в гостинице Можайская – 410 о том, что 28
марта 2009 года она обратилась в 20 отделение
милиции г. Москвы с заявлением по поводу
кражи из её номера следующих вещей»
1. Фотоаппарат «Миранда»
2. 30 фунтов стерлингов
3. 5,000 рублей

| | |
|---|---|
| **Великобрита́ния** | *Great Britain* |
| **кра́жа** | *theft* |
| **фотоаппара́т** | *camera* |
| **фунт** | *pound* |

### 18.4  Read, answer and listen!

You are having a chat with Ivan. Complete your part of the
conversation, then listen to the complete conversation on the
recording.

| **Вы** | **(a)** Tell Ivan he looks dreadful. |
|---|---|
| **Ива́н** | Да, я пло́хо себя́ чу́вствую. |
| **Вы** | **(b)** Ask what's the matter with him. |
| **Ива́н** | Я то́лько что ви́дел ава́рию. |
| **Вы** | **(c)** Ask what happened. |
| **Ива́н** | Грузови́к уда́рил ста́рую же́нщину. |
| **Вы** | **(d)** Say 'that's terrible'. Tell him to sit down. |

**CD 2, TR 8, 01:55**

| Ива́н | Спаси́бо. |
|---|---|
| **Вы** | **(e)** Ask him if he'd like some tea. |
| **Ива́н** | Да, о́чень хочу́. Вы о́чень добры́. |
| **Вы** | **(f)** Say 'don't mention it (you're welcome)'. |

## Insight

**То́лько что** (*only just*) is easy to use – simply put it before a verb: **мы то́лько что получи́ли письмо́** (*we've only just received the letter*). **Как то́лько** (*as soon as*) often involves the future tense: **я позвоню́, как то́лько прие́ду** (*I'll ring as soon as I arrive*).

### 18.5  Read and write!

Complete the following description of Tamara's journey, using the prefixed forms of **-езжать/-ехать**:

На про́шлой неде́ле Тама́ра _____ (*arrived*) в Псков на по́езде. Она́ _____ (*cross*) че́рез го́род на такси́. Они́ _____ (*drove out of*) из це́нтра го́рода и _____ (*drove past*) ми́мо ста́рых заво́дов. Наконе́ц такси́ _____ (*drove up to*) к гости́нице.

### 18.6  Read and answer!

Match the questions with the answers:

| | | | |
|---|---|---|---|
| **1** | Почему́ вы звони́те ей? | **a** | Пло́хо |
| **2** | Где произошла́ ава́рия? | **b** | Что́бы узна́ть, как дела́ |
| **3** | Как вы себя́ чу́вствуете? | **c** | Милиционе́ру |
| **4** | Что вы хоти́те купи́ть в апте́ке? | **d** | Недалеко́ от ста́нции метро́ |
| **5** | Кому́ вы рассказа́ли обо всём э́том? | **e** | Табле́тки |

## 18.7 Read and answer!

Read the passage about what happened to Petya yesterday, then answer the questions:

Вчера́ по доро́ге на рабо́ту Пе́тя зашёл в универса́м. Поэ́тому (*therefore*) он по́здно пришёл на рабо́ту, часо́в в де́сять. Он пообе́дал в два часа́ в буфе́те и верну́лся на рабо́ту часа́ в три. В четы́ре часа́ Ле́на позвони́ла ему́ и сказа́ла, что у неё два биле́та в кино́, ита́к (*and so*) вчера́ ве́чером они́ ходи́ли в кинотеа́тр. По́сле фи́льма они́ поу́жинали в рестора́не и Пе́тя о́чень по́здно верну́лся (*to return*) домо́й ... В результа́те он сего́дня ещё раз по́здно пришёл на рабо́ту ... полоди́ннадцатого.

**a**  Во ско́лько Пе́тя пришёл на рабо́ту вчера́?
**b**  Во ско́лько он пообе́дал вчера́?
**c**  Что он де́лал вчера́ ве́чером?
**d**  Во ско́лько он пришёл на рабо́ту сего́дня?

---

## Comprehension

### 1 *Conversation*

**Read, listen and answer!**

Marina has left her umbrella and bag at the cinema and is ringing the lost property office (**бюро́ нахо́док**) to try and trace them.

| | |
|---|---|
| **Мари́на** | Алло́? Бюро́ нахо́док? |
| **Де́вушка** | Да, слу́шаю. |
| **Мари́на** | Я забы́ла в кинотеа́тре «Ко́смос» зо́нтик и су́мку. |
| **Де́вушка** | Когда́? |
| **Мари́на** | Вчера́ ве́чером. |
| **Де́вушка** | Опиши́те, пожа́луйста, зо́ нтик. |
| **Мари́на** | Но́вый, кра́сный. |

| | |
|---|---|
| **Де́вушка** | А су́мка како́го цве́та? |
| **Мари́на** | Чёрная. |
| **Де́вушка** | Что бы́ло в су́мке? |
| **Мари́на** | Кошелёк, па́спорт, косме́тика, ро́зовый носово́и плато́к, чёрная ру́чка. |
| **Де́вушка** | Как ва́ша фами́лия? |
| **Мари́на** | Белоу́сова. |
| **Де́вушка** | Подожди́те. Я пойду́ посмотрю́ ... |
| **Мари́на** | Спаси́бо вам большо́е. |
| **Де́вушка** | ... Вам везёт. Ва́ши ве́щи у нас. Приезжа́йте! |
| **Мари́на** | Я так ра́да! Когда́ лу́чше прие́хать? |
| **Де́вушка** | Сейча́с же, е́сли мо́жно. Ведь бюро́ закрыва́ется в 5 часо́в. |
| **Мари́на** | Спаси́бо большо́е. До свида́ния. |
| **Де́вушка** | Пожа́луйста. До свида́ния. |

**QUICK VOCAB**

| | |
|---|---|
| **забыва́ть/забы́ть** | *to forget* (here: *leave*) |
| **зо́нтик** | *umbrella* |
| **опи́сывать/описа́ть** | *to describe* |
| **кошелёк** | *purse* |
| **косме́тика** | *make-up* |
| **носово́ й плато́к** | *handkerchief* |
| **вам везёт** | *you are lucky/in luck* |

## Insight

**Ведь бюро́ закрыва́ется**: like **же**, **ведь** is an 'emphatic particle', and is used to express a gentle warning, or to emphasize something the speaker finds surprising or very obvious. In English **ведь** might be expressed as, e.g., *you realize/know*, *after all*, *indeed* (or sometimes just by the tone of voice).

**a** Мари́на забы́ла зо́нтик и су́мку в _____.

**b** Она́ звони́т в _____.

**c** Бюро́ закрыва́ется в _____.

**d** У неё _____ су́мка.


## 2 Reading

**Read the text and answer the questions in English.**

**a** What different roles did Peter the Great fulfil?

**b** Where did he spend his childhood?

**c** What happened at the Battle of Poltava?

**d** Why did Peter the Great build Petersburg?

**e** Why would people interested in Peter the Great want to visit the Hermitage?

**f** What happened in 1824?


Пётр I – удиви́тельный челове́к: ру́сский импера́тор, полково́дец, диплома́т и кораблестрои́тель, роди́лся в 1672 году́. Его́ де́тские го́ды прошли́ в Москве́.

В 1709 году́ под Полта́вой произошло́ гла́вное сраже́ние Се́верной войны́ (1700–1721), в кото́ром ру́сская а́рмия под кома́ндованием Петра́ I победи́ла войск шве́дского короля́ Ка́рла XII. Санкт-Петербу́рг был осно́ван Петро́м I в 1703 году́ как но́вая столи́ца Росси́и, как «окно́ в Евро́пу». Деревя́нный до́мик Петра́, па́мятник пе́рвых лет Санкт-Петербу́рга, мо́жно ви́деть и сего́дня. Мо́жно посети́ть и ле́тний дворе́ц Петра́, Эрмита́ж (среди́ экспона́тов кото́рого – ли́чные ве́щи Петра́), Петропа́вловскую кре́пость, го́род фонта́нов – Петродворе́ц.

Пётр I у́мер в 1725 году́. Са́мый изве́стный па́мятник Петру́ «Ме́дный вса́дник»; так называ́л Пу́шкин э́тот па́мятник, кото́рый счита́ется эмбле́мой го́рода. Пу́шкин, кото́рый после́дние го́ды про́жил и у́мер в Санкт-Петербу́рге, написа́л поэ́му «Ме́дный вса́дник». Э́то поэ́ма о наводне́нии, кото́рое случи́лось в Санкт-Петербу́рге в ноябре́ 1824 го́да. До сих пор э́то наводне́ние счита́ется са́мым ху́дшим наводне́нием в исто́рии го́рода.

| | |
|---|---|
| война́ | *war* |
| войска́ (n. pl.) | *troops, forces* |
| дворе́ц | *palace* |
| деревя́нный | *wooden* |
| гла́вный | *main* |
| Евро́па | *Europe* |
| импера́тор | *emperor* |
| кораблестрои́тель | *shipbuilder* |
| кре́пость (f.) | *fortress* |
| ли́чный | *personal* |
| Ме́дный вса́дник | *Bronze Horseman* |
| наводне́ние | *flood* |
| называ́ть/назва́ть | *to call, name* |
| окно́ | *window* |
| осно́ван | *founded* |
| побежда́ть/победи́ть | *to conquer, vanquish* |
| полково́дец | *general* |
| сраже́ние | *battle* |
| среди́ (+ genitive) | *among* |
| удиви́тельный | *amazing, surprising* |
| фонта́н | *fountain* |
| шве́дский коро́ль | *Swedish king* |
| экспона́т | *exhibit* |

### Санкт-Петербу́рг – Ме́дный вса́дник
St Petersburg – the Bronze Horseman

## Key phrases

◆) **CD 2, TR 8, 03:41**

Can you remember how to say the following in Russian? Listen to the recording and practise saying each phrase.

    **a** What has happened?
    **b** What's the matter with you?
    **c** Where on earth have you been?
    **d** How are you feeling now?
    **e** You are very kind.

## Test yourself

**1** What form of the verb *pay* would you use after **чтобы** if you wanted to say *in order to pay*?

**2** If you wanted to ask someone what was wrong with them, would you say **Что с вáми?** or **Что случи́лось?**

**3** *He said he would ring me!* What tense would you have to use in Russian for *he would ring*?

**4** If you wanted to explain that you were walking along the street when you bumped into a friend, which form of the past tense would you choose: **мы ходи́ли, мы шли** or **мы пошли́**?

**5** How would you explain that you've just bought the tickets?

**6** **Мы ___ éхали чéрез мост.** Which prefix would you add to make this mean *we drove across the bridge*?

**7** *Where on earth are you going?* **Кудá ___ ты идёшь?** Add the missing word.

**8** *It would be better if ...* **Бы́ло ____ лу́чше, е́сли ____ он пришёл в 8 часо́в.** Add the two missing words.

**9** **Я забы́ла в такси́ очки́!** What have you done with your spectacles?

**10** You plan to arrive at about 10 o'clock. How will you say *at about 10 o'clock*?

# 19

# Спасибо за письмо
## Thank you for the letter

In this unit you will learn
- *How to present formal and informal letters in Russian*
- *How to report what people have asked*
- *How to further express feelings and opinions*

## Dialogue

Ira has just received a letter from her sister, Nina, and is telling her mother about it.

CD 2, TR 9, 00:06

| | |
|---|---|
| **Йра** | Мама, я сегодня получила письмо от Нины. |
| **Мама** | Я надеюсь, что у неё всё в порядке. Она долго не писала. |
| **Йра** | Не беспокойся, мама. Вот что она пишет: «Милая Йрочка! Спасибо за письмо. Прости, что так долго не писала. Последние три недели были довольно напряжёнными ...» |
| **Мама** | Боже мой! Я надеюсь, что она не заболела! |
| **Йра** | Не волнуйся, мамочка ... «... потому, что на работе мы готовили договор с французской компанией ...» |
| **Мама** | Я же говорила ей, что было бы лучше работать учительницей ... |

| | |
|---|---|
| **Йра** | Ма́ма, прошу́ тебя́, не перебива́й меня́! |
| | «... и, коне́чно, мне на́до бы́ло рабо́тать над перево́дами ра́зных докуме́нтов. Но тепе́рь мы ко́нчили всю э́ту рабо́ту и дире́ктор сказа́л, что он о́чень дово́лен мое́й рабо́той ...» |
| **Ма́ма** | Ну, коне́чно, ведь Ни́ночка така́я у́мная, спосо́бная де́вушка! |
| **Йра** | Ма́ма! |
| | «и вчера́ он спроси́л меня́, хочу́ ли я пое́хать с ним в Пари́ж ...» |
| **Ма́ма** | Что за безобра́зие! Она́, коне́чно, отказа́лась от тако́го приглаше́ния? |
| **Йра** | Ма́мочка, прошу́ тебя́, слу́шай! |
| | «в ка́честве перево́дчицы. Бу́дет о́чень ве́село и интере́сно, потому́ что Мари́я Никола́евна, жена́ дире́ктора, то́же е́дет (ты по́мнишь, она́ рабо́тает в Эрмита́же здесь в Санкт-Петербу́рге). Она́ уже́ была́ в Пари́же и пока́жет нам са́мые интере́сные места́. Мы пое́дем че́рез де́сять дней, то есть пятна́дцатого числа́. Всем приве́т! Пиши́! Целу́ю, Ни́на.» |
| **Ма́ма** | Чуде́сно! ... По́чта по-мо́ему откры́та до девяти́. |
| **Йра** | Не понима́ю. |
| **Ма́ма** | Ну, я где́-то ви́дела ру́чку ... вот она́ ... Напиши́ письмо́ как мо́жно скоре́е, скажи́ Ни́ночке, что в Пари́же на́до купи́ть и духи́, и ... |

| | |
|---|---|
| **дово́льно** | *quite* |
| **напряжённый** | *pressurized, tense, strained* |
| **Бо́же мой!** | *good gracious! (lit. My God)* |
| **волнова́ться/взволнова́ться** | *to be agitated, upset, worried* |
| **догово́р** | *agreement, contract* |
| **компа́ния** | *company* |

| | |
|---|---|
| **перебива́ть/переби́ть** <br> **(перебью́, перебьёшь)** | *to interrupt* |
| **рабо́тать над** <br> (+ instrumental) | *to work on* |
| **перево́д** | *translation* |
| **у́мный** | *clever* |
| **спосо́бный** | *able, efficient* |
| **что за безобра́зие!** | *it's disgraceful!* |
| **отка́зываться/отказа́ться от** | (+ genitive) *to refuse* |
| **в ка́честве** (+ genitive) | *as, in the capacity of* |
| **перево́дчица** (m. **перево́дчик**) | *translator, interpreter* |
| **то есть (т.е.)** | *that is (i.e.)* |
| **всем приве́т** | *greetings to everyone* |
| **целу́ю** | *love from (lit. I kiss)* |
| **чуде́сно (чуде́сный)** | *wonderful* |
| **до девяти́** | *until nine o'clock* |
| **где-то** | *somewhere* |
| **как мо́жно скоре́е** | *as soon/quickly as possible* |

........................................................................

## Insight

Negative commands tend to be formed from the imperfective, (as when Ira says to her mother: *don't get upset!, don't interrupt me!*), and also when urging someone (*do listen!*) Nina uses a perfective command (**Прости́** – *forgive me*), because she is referring to one thing (*that she hasn't written for ages*).

........................................................................

### Letters

Headings and endings vary depending on whether the letter you are writing is formal or informal. Here are some examples of formal and informal approaches.

## Formal

*Headings*

**Уважа́емый господи́н дире́ктор!**
lit. *respected director* – rather than just **Уважа́емый господи́н** *Dear Sir*, use the title of the person's job

**Уважа́емая Мари́я Никола́евна!**
For someone you don't know well enough to call just by their first name – equivalent to the English *Dear Mrs Jones*

**Глубокоуважа́емый профе́ссор Бы́ков!**
lit. *Deeply respected Professor Bykov*

*Endings*

**С уваже́нием**
lit. *with respect* – the equivalent of both *yours sincerely* and *yours faithfully*

**И́скренне Ваш (Ва́ша)**
*Yours sincerely*

**С глубо́ким уваже́нием**
lit. *with deep respect – yours most sincerely*

## Informal

*Headings*

**Дорого́й Бори́с**
*Dear Boris!*
**Дорога́я Та́ня**
*Dear Tanya!*
**Ми́лый Пе́тя!**
*Dear Petya!* – use **ми́лый** for your nearest and dearest (but not between men)

## Endings

| | |
|---|---|
| Целу́ю | lit. *I kiss* – equivalent to *love from* |
| Всего́ хоро́шего/до́брого | *All the best* |
| Всего́ вам са́мого наилу́чшего | *All the very best* |
| До ско́рого свида́ния | *See you soon* |
| Твой Пе́тя | *Your Petya* |
| Ва́ша Га́ля | *Your Galya* |

Russian addresses used to be in reverse order to Western European practice (i.e. they used to start with the country and end with the name of the addressee); it is now the norm to write an address as follows:

| | |
|---|---|
| Яблокову, В.Н. | *(surname in dative, initials of first name and patronymic)* |
| улица Одоевского, д. 42, кв. 73 | *(street, house no., flat no.)* |
| Пермь 36 | *(town and district number)* |
| Россия | *(country)* |

Tourists addressing cards and letters to Great Britain should write the address in the normal way, but write **АНГЛИЯ** next to the word **КУДА** (*where to*). Letters, postcards and parcels *walk* by post (**Из Росси́и в А́нглию письмо́ идёт дней во́семь**, *a letter takes about eight days from Russia to England*).

## Insight

E-mails can begin with the informal **Приве́т!** (*Hi!*) and end with **Пиши́!** (*Write!*) An e-mail address is either **электро́нный а́дрес** or **име́йл.** The word for an inbox (**входя́щие**) comes from the prefixed verb of motion for to enter, and the word for the *at* sign (@) is **соба́ка** (lit. *dog*).

One of the ways of saying *snail mail* in Russian is *tortoise mail* (**черепа́шья по́чта**), which fits in with the following cartoon indicating that some Russians think their postal service is rather slow off the mark (**сро́чный,** *urgent*).

## Questions

**1** *True or false?*

a Мáма получи́ла письмó от Ни́ны.
b Ни́на мнóго рабóтала за послéдние три недéли.
c Мáма всё врéмя перебивáет Йру.
d Дирéктор приглаои́л Йру в Пари́ж.
e Пóчта закрывáется в дéвять часóв.

**2** *Answer the questions!*

a Когдá Йра получи́ла письмó?
b Кем рабóтает Ни́на?
c Где онá рабóтает?
d Кудá онá поéдет чéрез дéсять дней?
e Что онá должнá бýдет купи́ть в Пари́же для мáмы?

## How do you say it?

How to:
**1** *Open and close informal letters*

Ми́лая Йро́чка!
Дорого́й Бори́с!
Целу́ю
Всего́ хоро́шего

**2** *Open and close formal letters*

Уважа́емая Мари́я Никола́евна!
Уважа́емый господи́н дире́ктор!
С уваже́нием

**3** *Report what people have asked*

Он спроси́л меня́, хочу́ ли я пое́хать с ним в Пари́ж.

**4** *Express feelings and opinions*

Я наде́юсь, что ...
Бо́же мой!
Что за безобра́зие!
Чуде́сно!

## Grammar

### 1 *Instrumental case*

In the phrase **после́дние три неде́ди бы́ли дово́льно
напряжёнными** the adjective **напряжённый** is in the instrumental
case. This is because the complement of the verb *to be* (that which

completes our knowledge of the subject of the verb *to be* – i.e. the word which tells us more about the subject) in the past, future or imperative (command) form – *but not in the present!* – must usually be in the instrumental case:

Де́сять лет наза́д (*ago*) он был студе́нтом, а тепе́рь он перево́дчик.
*Ten years ago he was a student, but now he is a translator.*

### 2 Indirect questions

In English we introduce an indirect question by either *if* or *whether*:

**Direct question:**   He asked 'Do you want to go to Paris?'
**Indirect question:**   He asked if/whether I wanted to go to Paris.

In Unit 18 we saw that Russian indirect statements retain the tense of the original statement, and this also applies to indirect questions. In Russian there is only one way to introduce an indirect question – with the particle **ли** (never use **е́сли** in an indirect question). Word order is important in indirect questions:

**a** *He asked (they wondered etc).*
**b** *comma*
**c** *verb*
**d** *ли*
**e** *subject*

}   Он спроси́л меня́, хочу́ ли я пое́хать в Пари́ж.

**Ма́ма хоте́ла знать, отказа́лась ли Ни́на. Ни́на не зна́ла, пое́дут ли они́.**

*Mother wanted to know if/ whether Nina had refused. Nina didn't know if they would go.*

## Insight

In English we can use the word *if* for conditions (see Unit 16) and for indirect questions. If you can replace *if* with *whether*, you know you're dealing with an indirect question. Never try to use **éсли** in an indirect question in Russian – use **ли** instead!

### 3 Как мóжно ... *As ... as possible*

The formula **как мóжно** + comparative adverb can be used in a number of useful expressions, for example:

| как мóжно бóльше | *as much as possible* |
| как мóжно лýчше | *as well as possible* |
| как мóжно тúше | *as quietly as possible* |

### 4 *Cardinal numerals in time phrases*

In the phrase **до девятú** the cardinal numeral **дéвять** (*nine*) is in the genitive case (**до** + genitive = *until, as far as, before*). All cardinal numerals decline (i.e. have case endings) – it is particularly useful to know these when you are dealing with time phrases, e.g.: *from* (**с** + gen.) *9 a.m. until* (**до** + gen.) *5 p.m., by/at about* (**к** + dat.) *3 p.m.* Cardinal numerals like **дéвять** which end in a soft sign decline like a feminine soft sign noun (e.g. **дверь**; note that **вóсемь** has a fleeting **e** which is replaced by a soft sign in all cases except the instrumental); **одúн** declines like **э́тот**. The declensions of 2, 3, 4 resemble one another and have very distinctive sounds which make them easy to remember:

| Nom. | два/две | три | четы́ре |
| Acc. | два/две | три | четы́ре |
| Gen. and Prep. | двух | трёх | четырёх |

| | Dat. | **двум** | **трём** | **четырём** |
| | Instr. | **двумя** | **тремя** | **четырьмя** |

| | |
|---|---|
| **Он рабо́тал с восьми́ до** | *He worked from 8* |
| **оди́ннадцати.** | *until 11.* |
| **Приезжа́йте, пожа́луйста,** | *Please be here by 3.* |
| **к трём часа́м.** | |

---

### Insight

Good news: most cardinal numerals end in a soft sign and their endings are the same as those of feminine soft sign nouns! See Appendix 1 for more detail on cardinal numerals.

---

### 5 Где-то *Somewhere*

This is an example of an indefinite adverb and means *somewhere*. The particle **-то** can be used in a similar way with other interrogative adverbs (*when? how?*) and interrogative pronouns (*who? what?*):

| | |
|---|---|
| **когда́-то** | *sometime* (with some specific time in mind) |
| **кто́-то** | *someone* (with some specific person in mind) |
| **что́-то** | *something* (with some specific thing in mind) |

| | |
|---|---|
| **Кто-то позвони́л тебе́** | *Someone rang you at about eight.* |
| **часо́в в во́семь.** | |

If the meaning is vaguer than this, the particle **-нибудь** is used:

| | |
|---|---|
| **когда́-нибудь** | *sometime* (with the sense of *any time at all, whenever it may be*) |
| **кто́-нибудь** | *someone* (with the sense of *anyone at all, whoever it may be*) |

| что́-нибудь | *something* (with the sense of *anything at all, whatever it may be*) |
| Мне ску́чно. Дава́йте пое́дем куда́-нибудь. | *I'm bored. Let's go somewhere.* |

## 6 Declension of surnames

The surname of the addressee on an envelope must be in the dative case. Russian surnames hold a few surprises; for example, masculine surnames ending in **-ов, -ев** or **-ин** decline exactly like a regular masculine noun ending in a consonant, except for the instrumental which ends in **-ым**; feminine surnames which end in **-ова, -ева** or **-ина** decline like a regular feminine noun ending in an **-а**, except for the genitive, dative and instrumental which all end in **-ой**. Surnames which end in **-ский** decline exactly like adjectives. So in addresses, **И.П. Петро́вич, В.М. Петрова** and **Н.Б. Петро́вский** would appear as:

Петровичу, И.П. Петровой, В.М. Петровскому, Н.Б.

---

# Practice

### 19.1 Read and answer!

Look at the details of the following people and then write out the address of each one as you would on an envelope.

**a** Бори́с Никола́евич Шмелёв живёт в Санкт-Петербу́рге (109262); а́дрес: у́лица Заце́па, дом 20, кварти́ра 57

**b** Мари́я Алекса́ндровна Пло́тникова живёт в Воро́неже (394001); а́дрес: Ряби́новая у́лица, дом 21, кварти́ра 76

**c** Фёдор Ива́нович Соколо́вский живёт в Москве́ (117552); а́дрес: Ми́нская у́лица, дом 62, кварти́ра 15

## 19.2 Read, look and answer!

Look at the following advertisement for a competition and answer the questions.

**a** *How often is the prize offered?*
**b** *What is it awarded for?*
**c** *Who may take part in the competition?*
**d** *What may competitors write about?*

**ЕЖЕГОДНЫЙ ПРИЗ
ЖУРНАЛА «ПУТЕШЕСТВИЕ»
В РОССИИ ЗА ЛУЧШУЮ
ПУБЛИКАЦИЮ О ТУРИЗМЕ
В РОССИИ**

Приз «Добрый путь»
присуждается иностранным
писателям за опубликование
материалов о туристской поездке
в России:
о достопримечательностях,
природе, памятниках истории и
культуры России, встречах с
русскими людьми, о турах,
экскурсиях, национальной кухне
и современной жизни в России.

QUICK VOCAB

### 19.3 Read and write!

Natasha is feeling very uncertain today! Give her answers to Petya's questions.

| **Пе́тя** | **Ната́ша** |
|---|---|
| **a** Ма́ма уже́ получи́ла моё письмо́? | Я не зна́ю, получи́ла ли она́ письмо́. |
| **b** Ни́на сказа́ла, что она́ пое́дет в Пари́ж? | |
| **c** Бори́с прие́дет сего́дня? | |
| **d** Вади́м лю́бит смотре́ть телеви́зор? | |
| **e** Ва́ля прочита́ла всю кни́гу? | |
| **f** Дире́ктор подписа́л (*sign*) догово́р? | |

### 19.4 Read and answer!

Read the following information about Lyuda.

Лю́да живёт в Новосиби́рске. У неё оди́н брат, Са́ша, кото́рый живёт с ма́мой в Москве́. Са́ша не жена́т. Лю́да за́мужем. Му́жа зову́т Никола́й. Лю́да стара́ется писа́ть ма́ме раз в неде́лю, но иногда́ она́ так занята́, что у неё про́сто нет вре́мени. Тогда́ она́ звони́т ма́ме по телефо́ну, хотя́ иногда́ э́то то́же тру́дно. Она́ предпочита́ет писа́ть пи́сьма, е́сли есть вре́мя.

| **жена́т** | *married (of a man)* |
|---|---|
| **за́мужем** | *married (of a woman)* |

Now answer these questions

| about Lyuda: | And about yourself: |
|---|---|
| **a** Где Лю́да живёт? | **i** Где вы живёте? |
| **b** У неё есть сестра́? | **ii** У вас есть бра́тья и |
| **c** Как зову́т её му́жа? | сёстры? |
| **d** Она́ ча́сто пи́шет ма́ме? | **iii** Вы жена́ты/ |
| **e** Почему́ иногда́ она́ не | за́мужем? |
| мо́жет писа́ть? | **iv** Вы предпочита́ете |
| | писа́ть пи́сьма и́ли |
| | говори́ть по |
| | телефо́ну? |

### 19.5 Read and answer!

Read the letter and answer the questions.

**a** Кем рабо́тает профе́ссор Смит?
**b** Когда́ он узна́ет, где мо́жно получи́ть авиабиле́т?
**c** Когда́ он до́лжен подтверди́ть, что прие́дет на Конгре́сс?

г. Москва́
20 апре́ля 2010 го́да

Уважа́емый профе́ссор Смит!
    Организацио́нный комите́т XII конгре́сса психо́логов информи́рует, что Вы включены́ в число́ уча́стников Конгре́сса.
    В конце́ ию́ня – нача́ле ию́ля мы сообщи́м Вам, где мо́жно получи́ть авиабиле́т.
    Про́сим подтверди́ть Ва́ше уча́стие в Конгре́ссе, сообщи́в да́ту, но́мер ре́йса не поздне́е 1 а́вгуста 2010г.
    С уваже́нием,

Секрета́рь
И.С. Хмеле́вский

## Comprehension

**1** *Conversation*

**Read, listen and answer!**

A journalist is interviewing Marina Vladimirovna, a television producer.

CD 2, TR 9, 02:39

| **Журнал**и**ст** | Мар**и**на Влад**и**мировна, кем вы раб**о**таете? |
| **Мар**и**на** | Я режисс**ё**р. |
| **Журнал**и**ст** | В чём **и**менно состо**и**т в**а**ша раб**о**та? |
| **Мар**и**на** | Я режисс**ё**р документ**а**льных ф**и**льмов. |
| **Журнал**и**ст** | Как**и**х, напр=им**е**р? |
| **Мар**и**на** | Ну, ... ф**и**льмов по литерат**у**ре, по ист**о**рии ... |
| **Журнал**и**ст** | Ск**о**лько лет вы раб**о**таете режисс**ё**ром? |
| **Мар**и**на** | Лет д**е**сять. До **э**того я раб**о**тала перев**о**дчицей. |
| **Журнал**и**ст** | И как**у**ю раб**о**ту вы предпочит**а**ете? |
| **Мар**и**на** | Кон**е**чно, интер**е**сно б**ы**ло раб**о**тать перев**о**дчицей, но я б**о**льше люблю раб**о**тать режисс**ё**ром. |
| **Журнал**и**ст** | Почем**у**? |
| **Мар**и**на** | Ну ... раб**о**та так**а**я интер**е**сная, тв**о**рческая. |

| Журнали́ст | Мари́на Влади́мировна, над чем вы сейча́с рабо́таете? |
|---|---|
| Мари́на | Сейча́с мы снима́ем фильм о жи́зни в Санкт-Петербу́рге в нача́ле э́того ве́ка. |
| Журнали́ст | Ско́лько часо́в в день вы рабо́таете? |
| Мари́на | Тру́дно сказа́ть, но теорети́чески я рабо́таю с девяти́ до шести́. |
| Журнали́ст | А на пра́ктике? |
| Мари́на | На пра́ктике я ещё в телесту́дии в де́сять, да́же в оди́ннадцать часо́в ве́чера. |

| | |
|---|---|
| **режиссёр** | *producer* |
| **в чём и́менно состои́т рабо́та?** | *what exactly does the job involve?* |
| **тво́рческий** | *creative* |
| **снима́ть/снять фильм** | *to shoot a film* |
| **теорети́чески** | *in theory* |
| **на пра́ктике** | *in practice* |
| **телесту́дия** | *television studio* |

## Insight

Note the use of the instrumental in the Conversation with relation to people's jobs:

- **Кем вы рабо́таете?** (lit. *as whom do you work*)
- **Я рабо́тала перево́дчицей** (*I worked as a translator*)

See Unit 8 to revise the uses of the instrumental case.

**1** Марина режиссёр

   **a** романти́ческих фи́льмов
   **b** музыка́льных переда́ч
   **c** спорти́вных програ́мм
   **d** документа́льных фи́льмов

**2** Де́сять лет наза́д она́ рабо́тала
   **a** режиссёром
   **b** перево́дчицей
   **c** учи́тельницей
   **d** врачо́м

**3** Сейча́с она́ снима́ет фильм
   **a** о Москве́
   **b** о Санкт-Петербу́рге
   **c** о журнали́стах
   **d** о писа́телях

**4** Теорети́чески она́ рабо́тает
   **a** с восьми́ у́тра до девяти́ ве́чера
   **b** с девяти́ у́тра до десяти́
   **c** с девяти́ у́тра до шести́ ве́чера
   **d** с десяти́ у́тра до шести́ ве́чера

## 2 *Reading*

◀》 **CD 2, TR 9, 04:03**

**Read and listen to the letter and answer the questions in English.**

   **a** What was Galina pleased to learn from John's letter?
   **b** How much holiday do teachers get every year in Russia?
   **c** What does Galina like to do most of all in her holidays?
   **d** How did she feel towards the end of June?
   **e** Where did she go as soon as her holiday began?
   **f** What was the temperature at the beginning of July?
   **g** What was her opinion of the Black Sea resort?

г. Пермь
7 сентября 2010г.

Дорого́й Джон!

Мне бы́ло о́чень прия́тно получи́ть Ва́ше письмо́ и узна́ть, что о́тпуск Ваш прошёл хорошо́.

Я то́же дово́льна свои́м о́тдыхом. О́тпуск преподава́телей ву́зов и шко́льных учителе́й составля́ет в на́шей стране́ 48 рабо́чих дней (то есть 8 неде́ль), так что у меня́ была́ возмо́жность занима́ться дома́шними дела́ми и путеше́ствовать – после́днее мне о́чень нра́вится. К концу́ уче́бного го́да (то есть к концу́ ию́ня) я почу́вствовала, что о́чень уста́ла. Поэ́тому в нача́ле ию́ля, как то́лько я вы́шла в о́тпуск, я уе́хала за́ город к ро́дственникам (на ле́тнюю кварти́ру, и́ли, как мы говори́м, на «да́чу»). Там я пла́вала, гуля́ла (температу́ра днём до + 35 гра́дусов) и помога́ла мои́м ро́дственникам в саду́, где ле́том всегда́ мно́го рабо́ты. Пото́м я уе́хала на куро́рт на Черномо́рское побере́жье – чуде́сно! – мя́гкий кли́мат, тёплое мо́ре и хоро́шие усло́вия для о́тдыха.

Сейча́с мой о́тпуск уже́ позади́; впереди́ мно́го рабо́ты – в э́том году́ мы перехо́дим на но́вые уче́бные пла́ны. И до́ма есть рабо́та – пора́ сде́лать ремо́нт в кварти́ре.

Вот пока́ и все мои́ но́вости. Переда́йте, пожа́луйста, приве́т Ва́шим колле́гам, с кото́рыми я познако́милась, когда́ я была́ в Ва́шей стране́ в про́шлом году́. Пиши́те! Мне бу́дет интере́сно узна́ть о Ва́шем ле́тнем путеше́ствии (где, в каки́х места́х бы́ли, что ви́дели интере́сного). Жду Ва́шего отве́та!

Ва́ша Гали́на.

| **возмо́жность** (f.) | *opportunity* |
| **впереди́** | *ahead, in front* |
| **да́ча** | *holiday home; house in the country* |
| **колле́га** | *colleague* |
| **но́вости** (f. pl.) | *news* |
| **позади́** | *behind* |
| **поэ́тому** | *therefore* |
| **путеше́ствовать** | *to travel* |
| **ро́дственник** | *relative, relation* |
| **составля́ть/соста́вить** | *to make up, put together, compose* |
| **уче́бный год** | *academic year* |

## Insight

Galina's letter includes lots of useful time phrases. E.g.:

- **в нача́ле ию́ля** — *at the beginning of June*
- **в э́том году́** — *this year*
- **днём** — *during the day*
- **к концу́ ию́ня** — *towards the end of June*
- **как то́лько** — *as soon as*
- **ле́том** — *in the summer*

---

## Key phrases

◀» **CD 2, TR 9, 06:12**

Can you remember how to say the following in Russian? Listen to the recording and practise saying each phrase.

- **a** *Dear Boris ...*
- **b** *Yours sincerely ...*
- **c** *As soon as possible.*

**d** *I hope everything is all right.*

**e** *Good gracious!*

---

## Ten things to remember

**1** You can form a command from either the imperfective or the perfective – see Unit 3 for formation of commands (the imperative).

**2** If you are addressing a letter in Russian, remember to use the dative of the person's surname.

**3** If you want to ask if it's OK to send something by e-mail, you can say **Мóжно послáть по имáйлу**

**4** The usual word order in an indirect question is verb + **ли** + subject of the verb: **Я не знáю, лю́бят ли онú кóфе** (I don't know whether they like coffee).

**5** You can make some really useful phrases based on **как мóжно** + comparative adjective, e.g. **как мóжно скорéе** (as quickly as possible). See Unit 14 for comparative adverbs.

**6** If you add **-нибудь** to words like *who, what, where, when, why* it gives a very broad, unspecific sense of *anyone at all* (**ктó-нибудь**), whereas **-то** is more specific, e.g. **ктó- то** (*someone* – i.e. a specific person, but unknown to the speaker).

**7** **Такóй** (*such* a, *so*) must agree with the noun it describes: **Он такóй хорóший актёр!** (*He is such a good actor*). Note its resemblance to **какóй** (*which, what a, what sort of*).

**8** If you want to express the idea after a certain length of time has elapsed – e.g. *I'm going to Paris in ten days' time* – use **чéрез** + accusative: **Чéрез дéсять дней я поéду в Парúж.**

**9** To say *at the beginning of* use **в нача́ле** + genitive and
**к концу́** + genitive *for towards the end of*.

**10 Му́жа зову́т Никола́й** (lit. *husband they call Nikolai*).
Remember that you need to use the accusative of the person
whose name is given (and **му́жа** is animate accusative,
see Unit 5).

# 20

## Приезжайте к нам опять!
## Come and see us again!

In this unit you will learn
- *Further expressions involving possession and self*
- *How to use numerals in a more detailed way*
- *How to use other ways of expressing appreciation and thanks*

## Dialogue

Anna is spending her last evening in Moscow at Ira's flat. Sasha and Volodya are there too.

CD 2, TR 10, 00:07

| | |
|---|---|
| **Ира** | А вот и Са́ша. Ты принёс с собо́й буты́лку шампа́нского, да? |
| **Са́ша** | Да, вот она́. (Pours out champagne.) Воло́дя сейча́с придёт. Он сказа́л, что принесёт свой фотоаппара́т ... А вот и он. |
| **Ира** | Приве́т ... Ну, чей э́то бока́л? Мой, да? ... Хорошо́, я предлага́ю тост за А́нну! |
| **Все** | За А́нну! |
| **А́нна** | Спаси́бо. Я то́же хочу́ предложи́ть тост ... за свои́х ру́сских друзе́й! |
| **Ира** | Спаси́бо, А́нна ... Ну, скажи́, как тебе́ понра́вилось твоё пребыва́ние в Москве́? |
| **А́нна** | О́чень. Всё удиви́тельно интере́сно. |

| | |
|---|---|
| **Воло́дя** | Да́же на ле́кциях о жи́вописи? |
| **Йра** | Что ты, Воло́дя! Ведь таки́е ле́кции о́чень интере́сны для тех, кто лю́бит иску́сство. |
| **А́нна** | Да ... но для меня́ интере́снее всего́ бы́ло познако́миться с И́рой и с её друзья́ми. |
| **Йра** | Спаси́бо, А́нна! |
| **А́нна** | Я действи́тельно о́чень благода́рна вам всем за всё – за биле́ты в теа́тр, и за пое́здку за́ город ... Спаси́бо. |
| **Йра** | Ещё шампа́нского! |
| **Са́ша** | Во ско́лько самолёт вылета́ет за́втра, А́нна? |
| **А́нна** | Полдеся́того. |
| **Воло́дя** | Ты уже́ купи́ла все свои́ сувени́ры? |
| **А́нна** | Да, я купи́ла два краси́вых платка́ (э́то ма́ме и тёте), кассе́ты для бра́та, матрёшку для племя́нницы, пять–шесть интере́сных книг для друзе́й ... |
| **Йра** | Мно́го! А что ты купи́ла для себя́? |
| **А́нна** | (*Sighs.*) Пока́ ничего́. Вре́мени не́ было. |
| **Йра** | Я так и ду́мала! ... Ну вот. А́нна, э́то пода́рок от нас всех ... ру́сская балала́йка. |
| **А́нна** | Спаси́бо. Вы о́чень добры́. |
| **Йра** | Пожа́луйста ... приезжа́йте к нам опя́ть! Мы бу́дем о́чень ра́ды. |

| | |
|---|---|
| **ты принёс с собо́й** | *you have brought with you* |
| **чей э́то бока́л?** | *whose champagne glass is this?* |
| **за свои́х ру́сских друзе́й** | *to my Russian friends* |
| **пребыва́ние** | *stay* |
| **для тех, кто** | *for those who* |
| **интере́снее всего́** | *most interesting of all* |
| **благода́рный** | *grateful* |
| **все свои́ сувени́ры** | *all your souvenirs* |
| **плато́к** (fleeting **о**) | *shawl* |
| **матрёшка** | *matryoshka doll* |
| **племя́нница** (m. **племя́нник**) | *niece* |
| **для себя́** | *for yourself* |
| **пока́ ничего́** | *nothing yet* |

QUICK VOCAB

| я так и ду́мала | I thought as much |
| балала́йка | balalaika |
| приезжа́йте к нам опя́ть | come and see us again |

---

### Insight

To say *I am grateful for*, use the short form of the adjective **благода́рный за** + accusative: **я благода́рен** (m.)/ **я благода́рна** (f.)/**мы благода́рны за всё** (*I/we are grateful for everything*). See Unit 6 for **спаси́бо за** + accusative and Unit 15 for **предлага́ть тост за** + accusative.

---

#### Сувени́ры *Souvenirs*

A balalaika is a stringed musical instrument (usually 2–4 strings) with a triangular body – the Russian version of a guitar. It is commonly used in a **фолькло́рный анса́мбль** to accompany national folk songs and dances. Balalaikas come in different sizes and there are balalaika orchestras (with instruments ranging in size from that of a violin to a double bass).

Traditional matryoshka dolls are wooden and painted as if in peasant dress with successively smaller identical dolls fitted one inside the other. Other popular souvenirs are the fur hat (**мехова́я ша́пка**) and the samovar (**самова́р**) – a sort of decorative urn for boiling water to make tea; these used to be heated by charcoal, but are now fitted with connections like an electric kettle.

---

## Questions

**1** *True or false?*

**a** Воло́дя принёс с собо́й буты́лку шампа́нского.
**b** И́ра предлага́ет тост за Са́шу.
**c** А́нна благодари́т свои́х ру́сских друзе́й.

344

**d** Самолёт вылета́ет в 9 ч. 30 мин.
**e** А́нна купи́ла матрёшку для бра́та.

## 2 Answer the questions!

**a** Како́й тост А́нна предлага́ет?
**b** Как А́нне понра́вилось пребыва́ние в Москве́?
**c** За что́ она́ благодари́т И́ру, Са́шу и Воло́дю?
**d** Что А́нна купи́ла ма́ме?
**e** Како́й пода́рок А́нна получа́ет от И́ры, Воло́ди и Са́ши?

---

# How do you say it?

How to:
**1** *Ask about possession*

Чей э́то бока́л?

**2** *Indicate possession (one's own)*

Са́ша принесёт свой фотоаппара́т.
А́нна предлага́ет тост за свои́х ру́сских друзе́й.

**3** *Talk about oneself*

Ты принёс с собо́й буты́лку шампа́нского?
А что ты купи́ла для себя́?

**4** *Express appreciation*

Я о́чень благода́рна вам за всё.

**5** *Say how many and of what kind*

два краси́вых платка́
пять–шесть интере́сных книг

## Grammar

### 1 *Indicating possession with* свой

This word indicates possession by the subject of the nearest verb and can mean *my own*, *your own*, *his/her own*, *our own*, *their own*. As far as **я, ты, мы, вы** are concerned, **свой** is an alternative to **мой, твой, наш, ваш** (although you are more likely to find **свой** in conversational Russian, especially as an alternative to **твой**):

| | |
|---|---|
| **Я чита́ю мою́/свою́ кни́гу.** | *I am reading my book.* |
| **Ты забы́л свой фотоаппара́т?** | *Have you forgotten your camera?* |

However, it is *not* an alternative to **его́, её, их**; when you are dealing with *his*, *her*, *their* you must work out whether you mean *his own, her own, their own* or not:

| | |
|---|---|
| **Бори́с чита́ет свою́ кни́гу.** | *Boris is reading his (own) book.* |
| **Бори́с чита́ет его́ кни́гу.** | *Boris is reading his book* (i.e. a book belonging to someone else). |

Remember: **свой** indicates possession by the subject of the verb, it cannot describe the subject of the verb; if you want to describe the subject of a verb you must use **мой, твой, его́, наш, ваш, их**:

| | |
|---|---|
| **Моя́ сестра́ преподаёт италья́нский язы́к.** | *My sister teaches Italian.* |
| **Он сказа́л, что его́ сестра́ уже́ купи́ла балала́йку.** | *He said that his sister had already bought a balalaika.* |

### 2 Себя́ *Oneself*

**Себя́** means *oneself*; it is used in all cases except the nominative:

| | | | | | |
|---|---|---|---|---|---|
| Accusative: | себя́ | Dative: | себе́ | Instrumental: | собо́й |
| Genitive: | себя́ | Prepositional: | себе́ | | |

It can refer to any person of the verb (i.e. **я**, **ты**, **он**, etc). and it must be used when *self*, referring back to the subject of the verb, is stated or can be understood:

**А что ты купи́ла для себя́?** *And what have you bought for yourself?*

**Са́ша принёс с собо́й шампа́нское.** *Sasha has brought the champagne with him(self).*

## Insight

*Boris and Viktor said good-bye and Boris shut the door behind him* – note how precise Russian is about the identity of *him*: **Бори́с закры́л за собо́й дверь** (i.e. behind himself – **себя́** can only refer to the subject of the verb:); **Бори́с закры́л за ним дверь** (i.e. behind Viktor).

### 3 Чей *Whose*

This means *whose* (it is an interrogative pronoun); in the singular its masculine, feminine and neuter forms are:

чей: **Чей э́то бока́л?** *Whose is this (champagne) glass?*
чья: **Чья э́то матрёшка?** *Whose is this matryoshka doll?*
чьё: **Чьё э́то письмо́?** *Whose is this letter?*

The plural form (irrespective of gender) is **чьи**:

чьи: **Чьи э́то сувени́ры?** *Whose are these souvenirs?*

## Insight

The answer to the question *whose* will involve the use of either the genitive case (see Units 5 and 7) or a possessive adjective (Units 1 and 20), e.g.:

**Чей э́то па́спорт? Э́то па́спорт Мари́и.** (*Whose is this passport? It's Maria's.*)
**Чьи э́то пода́рки? Мой.** (*Whose are these presents? Mine.*)

## 4 Numerals

When numerals are used with adjectives as well as nouns, use the genitive plural of both the adjective and the noun if you are dealing with numbers 5 and above: **пять интере́сных кни́г.**

Note that this does not apply to 2, 3, 4 and their compounds (32, 44, etc.). With these numbers use the genitive plural of the adjective and the genitive singular of masculine and neuter nouns:

| | |
|---|---|
| **три́дцать два англи́йских тури́ста** | *32 English tourists* |
| **три интере́сных письма́** | *3 interesting letters* |

Use the nominative (or the genitive) plural of the adjective and genitive singular of feminine nouns:

| | |
|---|---|
| **три ру́сские [ру́сских] балала́йки** | *3 Russian balalaikas* |

**Оди́н, одна́, одно́** (and their compounds) behave like adjectives (and it doesn't matter how large the number – if the last digit is *one*, then the following adjective and noun agree with *one*!):

| | |
|---|---|
| **одна́ но́вая кни́га** | *1 new book* |
| **ты́сяча пятьсо́т два́дцать одна́ но́вая кни́га** | *1,521 new books* |

Note that **оди́н** has a plural form, **одни́**, which like **оди́н** and **одна́** can be used if you want to say *alone*:

| | |
|---|---|
| **Бори́с и Ири́на пое́хали в Со́чи одни́.** | *Boris and Irina went on their own/alone to Sochi.* |

(For further notes on the use of numerals, see Appendix 1.)

The use of numerals in Russian is a bit complicated! Try learning a few phrases to help you memorize the rules:

**Моему́ сы́ну 21 год** (*My son is 21*).
**У меня́ два ста́рых кота́ и две молоды́е соба́ки**
(*I have two old cats and two young dogs*).

## 5 Тот *That*

**Тот** is a demonstrative pronoun meaning *that*. The construction **тот, кто** means *the one who*, *he who*. Note that the verb after **те, кто** (*those who*) is usually in the singular:

**для тех, кто лю́бит иску́сство**   *for those who love art*

Note that **тот же** means *the same* and **тот же са́мый** *the very same* – both **тот** and **са́мый** must agree with the noun they describe:

**Он чи́тал ту же (са́мую)**     *He read the (very) same*
**газе́ту ка́ждый день.**       *paper every day.*

(A full declension of **тот** is given in Appendix 1.)

---

## Practice

### 20.1 *Read and answer!*

Match the questions with the answers:

**1** Во ско́лько самолёт вылета́ет?    **a** Свою́ балала́йку
**2** Что ты принёс с собо́й?         **b** О́чень. Всё так
                                       интере́сно!
**3** Чья э́то кни́га?                   **c** За пое́здку за́ город

**4** Как вам нра́вится э́тот     **d** К трём часа́м
город?                          **e** Моя́
**5** За что вы благодари́те их?

## 20.2 Look, read and answer!

Look at the advertisement below and answer the questions:

**a** Apart from footwear and jewellery, what can be bought at the shop?
**b** Where exactly is the shop situated?
**c** Which season's collection is on show?

| | |
|---|---|
| **бижуте́рия** | *jewellery* |
| **вы́лет** | *departure* |
| **о́бувь** | *footwear* |
| **проду́кты** | *food* |
| **това́ры** | *goods* |

QUICK VOCAB

## 20.3 Read and write!

You have just returned from a holiday in Moscow and decide to write and thank your friend. Read the extracts below from your diary and address book and thank your friend for each point mentioned. Address the card appropriately.

| Суббо́та: | 2 биле́та в теа́тр на бале́т «Снегу́рочка» |
| Воскресе́нье: | Пое́здка за́ город (собира́ли грибы́ два часа́!) |
| Понеде́льник: | Экску́рсия в дом-музе́й П.И.Чайко́вского |
| Вто́рник: | Обе́д в рестора́не «Колобо́к» |

Губа́нов, А.П. (Анато́лий)
Первома́йская ул., д. 45, кв. 29
105554 Москва́

### 20.4 Read and answer!

Look at the form below and answer the questions:

#### БЛАНК-ЗАКА́З НА СТИ́РКУ/ХИМЧИ́СТКУ

| Но́мер ко́мнаты: | _____ |
| Фами́лия: | _____ |
| Да́та отъе́зда: | _____ |
| Наименова́ние веще́й: | _____ |
| По́дпись: | _____ |
| Да́та: | _____ |
| Примеча́ние: | 1. Прие́м зака́за ежедне́вно до 11.00 утра́. |
| | 2. Запо́лните бланк и оста́вьте на столе́. |

**a** What information must you provide if you want washing/dry cleaning done?

**b** How often are orders taken for this service?

**c** What must you do with the form when you have completed it?

| | |
|---|---|
| **QUICK VOCAB** | |
| сти́рка | washing |
| химчи́стка | dry cleaning |
| отъе́зд | departure |
| наименова́ние | name/naming |
| по́дпись (f.) | signature |
| ежедне́вно | daily |
| оставля́ть/оста́вить | to leave |

### 20.5 Read and answer!

Read the following information about **Ли́дия Па́вловна Ка́рпова** and answer the questions.

Ли́дия Па́вловна живёт в Хабаро́вске, в Сиби́ри. Хабаро́вск нахо́дится на восто́ке страны́. Она́ на пе́нсии и живёт одна́ потому́, что её муж у́мер де́сять лет наза́д. У неё в семье́ сын, неве́стка и два вну́ка. К сча́стью её сын, Ко́ля, живёт недалеко́ от неё и он ча́сто помога́ет ей: наприме́р, е́сли она́ больна́, он де́лает поку́пки. У Ли́дии два вну́ка, Пётр и Андре́й. Вот что Ли́дия расска́зывает о свои́х вну́ках: «Пе́тя студе́нт, хо́чет стать врачо́м. Он о́чень интересу́ется му́зыкой, прекра́сно игра́ет на скри́пке – серьёзный тако́й ма́льчик. Андрю́ша всё ещё у́чится в шко́ле. Он увлека́ется футбо́лом и на́до сказа́ть, что он не о́чень лю́бит занима́ться кни́гами! Они́ ча́сто захо́дят ко мне, помога́ют мне.»

| | |
|---|---|
| **QUICK VOCAB** | |
| страна́ | country |
| на пе́нсии | retired (lit. on a pension) |
| семья́ | family |
| неве́стка | daughter-in-law |
| внук | grandson |
| расска́зывать/рассказа́ть | to tell, relate |

| | |
|---|---|
| скри́пка | *violin* |
| учи́ться | *to study* |
| увлека́ться/увле́чься (+ instr.) | *to be enthusiastic about* |

QV

## Insight

If you are talking about your hobbies, you are likely to use **занима́ться** (*to be busy/occupied with*), **интересова́ться** (*to be interested in*) and **увлека́ться** (*to be enthusiastic about*): remember that they are all followed by the instrumental case, as you can see in the passage above (and see Unit 8).

| О Ли́дии | О себе́ |
|---|---|
| **a** Где нахо́дится Хабаро́вск? | **i** Где нахо́дится ваш го́род?/ва́ша дере́вня? |
| **b** Почему́ Ли́дия живёт одна́? | **ii** Кто есть в ва́шей семье́? |
| **c** Кто есть в её семье́? | **iii** Как их зову́т? |
| **d** Как зову́т её вну́ков? | **iv** Что они́ де́лают в свобо́дное вре́мя? |
| **e** Что они́ де́лают в свобо́дное вре́мя? | **v** Расскажи́те, чем вы интересу́етесь, что вы де́лаете в свобо́дное вре́мя. |

### 20.6  Read, answer and listen!

Complete your part of the dialogue:

| | |
|---|---|
| **Воло́дя** | Чем вы интересу́етесь? |
| **Вы** | **(a)** Say you're interested in Russian music. |
| **Воло́дя** | Вы лю́бите спорт? |
| **Вы** | **(b)** Say 'yes', you sometimes play tennis in the summer. |
| **Воло́дя** | Что вы обы́чно де́лаете по суббо́там? |
| **Вы** | **(c)** Say you do the shopping, work in the garden and sometimes go to the cinema. |
| **Воло́дя** | Когда́ вы уезжа́ете? |
| **Вы** | **(d)** Say 'tomorrow'. Your plane leaves at 10 a.m. |

◆ CD 2, TR 10, 02:25

# Comprehension

## 1 *Conversation*

**Read, listen and answer!**

Alla is leaving for a new job and has come to say goodbye to the director.

| | |
|---|---|
| **Дире́ктор** | Ита́к, вы за́втра уезжа́ете, да? |
| **А́лла** | Да. Самолёт вылета́ет в шесть часо́в утра́. |
| **Дире́ктор** | Наде́юсь, что вы не волну́етесь! |
| **А́лла** | Насчёт ре́йса, нет ... но, коне́чно, я немно́жко беспоко́юсь о свое́й но́вой рабо́те. |
| **Дире́ктор** | Не на́до. Я уве́рен, что вам понра́вится э́та но́вая рабо́та. И я зна́ю, что ва́ши бу́дущие колле́ги с больши́м нетерпе́нием ждут ва́шего прие́зда. |
| **А́лла** | Почему́ вы так ду́маете? |
| **Дире́ктор** | Я то́лько что говори́л по телефо́ну с дире́ктором фа́брики «Медве́дково» и объясни́л ему́, како́й вы спосо́бный лабора́нт. |
| **А́лла** | Спаси́бо вам, Никола́й Петро́вич. |
| **Дире́ктор** | Не́ за что ... Я хочу́ поблагодари́ть вас, А́лла Константи́новна, за всю ва́шу рабо́ту здесь у нас. Е́сли я не ошиба́юсь, вы уже́ де́сять лет рабо́таете в на́шей лаборато́рии, да? |
| **А́лла** | Пра́вильно. |
| **Дире́ктор** | Я зна́ю, что ва́ши колле́ги бу́дут скуча́ть по вас! Прими́те, пожа́луйста, э́ту ру́чку от и́мени всего́ коллекти́ва. |
| **А́лла** | Золота́я ру́чка! Спаси́бо большо́е! |
| **Дире́ктор** | Мы жела́ем вам всего́ са́мого наилу́чшего – успе́ха, здоро́вья и сча́стья. |

| | |
|---|---|
| **Áлла** | Спаси́бо Никола́й Петро́вич, я о́чень благода́рна вам за всё. |
| **Дире́ктор** | Éсли вы бу́дете в Свердло́вске, приезжа́йте к нам, Áлла Константи́новна. Мы бу́дем о́чень ра́ды. |

| | |
|---|---|
| **колле́га** | *colleague* |
| **нетерпе́ние** | *impatience* |
| **ждать с нетерпе́нием** | *to look forward to* |
| **прие́зд** | *arrival* |
| **лабора́нт** | *laboratory assistant* |
| **скуча́ть** | *to miss* (**по** + dative of nouns, **по** + prepositional of pronouns) |
| **от и́мени всего́ коллекти́ва** | *on behalf of all the staff* |

### True or false?

**a** Áлла уезжа́ет послеза́втра.
**b** Она́ беспоко́ится о но́вой рабо́те.
**c** Она́ рабо́тает перево́дчицей.
**d** Она́ де́сять лет рабо́тает в лаборато́рии.
**e** Она́ получа́ет золоты́е часы́ (*watch, clock*) от колле́г.

◀) **CD 2, TR 10, 04:38**

### 2 Reading

Read and listen to the text and answer the questions in English.

**a** Where is the Dostoevsky Museum situated?
**b** How many children did Dostoevsky have?
**c** How did his wife describe the flat?
**d** What used Dostoevsky to do in the sitting room?
**e** What did he like to have around him in his study?
**f** In what way did he want to change the world?

Éсли вы бу́дете в Санкт-Петербу́рге, посети́те музе́й-кварти́ру вели́кого ру́сского писа́теля Фёдора Достое́вского (1821–1881). А́дрес музе́я: Кузне́чный переу́лок, дом 5. Здесь Достое́вский прожи́л с семьёй – жено́й А́нной Григо́рьевной и двумя́ детьми́, Фе́дей и Лю́бой – после́дние го́ды свое́й жи́зни. «Кварти́ру на́няли: на углу́ Я́мской и Кузне́чного переу́лка ...» сообщи́л Фёдор Миха́йлович бра́ту Никола́ю в октябре́ 1878 го́да. А́нна Григо́рьевна вспомина́ла «Кварти́ра на́ша состоя́ла из шести́ ко́мнат и находи́лась на второ́м этаже́».

Век спустя́ со́здали в до́ме на Кузне́чном литерату́рно-мемориа́льный музе́й. Из о́кон гости́ной, где Достоевский чита́л де́тям «Капита́нскую до́чку» Пу́шкина, «Тара́са Бу́льбу» Го́голя, «Бородино́» Ле́рмонтова (но никогда́ не чита́л им своего́), тепе́рь открыва́ется тот же вид, что и мно́го лет наза́д. Тот же са́мый поря́док в кабине́те, где роди́лся рома́н «Бра́тья Карама́зовы» – «Газе́ты, коро́бки с папиро́сами, пи́сьма, кни́ги ... всё должно́ бы́ло лежа́ть на своём ме́сте...» вспомина́ла дочь Достое́вского, Любо́вь Фёдоровна.

Достое́вский ду́мал о переустро́йстве ми́ра по зако́нам приро́ды и пра́вды, добра́ и красоты́; он писа́л об э́том в «Идио́те», в «Преступле́нии и наказа́нии». Достое́вского называ́ли и называ́ют психо́логом. «Непра́вда, – говори́л Достое́вский, – я реали́ст. Моя́ цель – найти́ в челове́ке челове́ка.»

| | |
|---|---|
| **вспомина́ть/вспо́мнить** | *to recall, remember, reminisce* |
| **добро́** | *good* |
| **зако́н** | *law* |
| **«Идио́т»** | *'The Idiot'* |
| **коро́бка** | *box* |
| **красота́** | *beauty* |
| **нанима́ть/наня́ть** | *to rent, hire* |
| **папиро́са** | *cigarette* |
| **переу́лок** | *lane, alleyway* |
| **переустро́йство** | *reorganization* |
| **«Преступле́ние и наказа́ние»** | *'Crime and Punishment'* |
| **создава́ть/созда́ть** | *to create* |

| состоя́ть | to consist of |
| спустя́ | later, after |
| цель (f.) | goal, aim |

## Key phrases

🔊 **CD 2, TR 10, 06:33**

Can you remember how to say the following in Russian? Listen to the recording and practise saying each phrase.

   **a** Whose is this camera?
   **b** I propose a toast to you
   **c** More champagne!
   **d** Come and see us again!
   **e** What time does the plane leave?

## Ten things to remember

**1** To express how long someone has been doing something, use the present tense: **Она́ де́сять лет рабо́тает в лаборато́рии** (and see Unit 2).

**2** The different ways of asking *at what time*: **В кото́ром часу́? Во ско́лько?**

**3** **Оди́н, одна́, одно́** (and their compounds) behave like adjectives: **оди́н день** (*1 day*), **два́дцать одна́ неде́ля** (*21 weeks*), **со́рок одно́ окно́** (*41 windows* – **окно́** can also mean *window* in the sense of a space in your schedule).

**4** To ask someone how they like something use the verb **нра́виться/понра́виться** (*to be pleasing*); remember that the construction is a) dative of person b) verb in the right tense, and agreeing with what is pleasing: **Вам/тебе́ понра́вилась Москва?** (*Did you like Moscow?* Literally: *to you pleased Moscow?*).

**5** **Послеза́втра** means *the day after tomorrow* (literally: *after tomorrow*). **Позавчера́** (*the day before yesterday*) is a little more complicated, but it is based on the word **вчера́** (*yesterday*). Be careful not to confuse **вчера́** with **ве́чер** (*evening*).

**6** Very often it is possible to work out what a word means if you can recognize a 'root'; for example, **краси́вый** is the adjective meaning *beautiful* and the noun for *beauty* is **красота́**; you can see the same root in the word *splendid* – **прекра́сный**.

**7** **Мы жела́ем вам всего́ са́мого наилу́чшего** (*we wish you all the best*): remember to use the genitive case of the thing(s) wished for after the verb **жела́ть**.

**8** **Са́мый** is used to make the superlative (see Unit 17); when used with **тот же**, it means the very *same*. Remember that both **mom** and **же** must agree with the word they are describing: **Я говори́ла с той же самой де́вушкой.**

**9** When *if* refers to the future, use the future tense (even though the present tense would be used in English): **Éсли вы бу́дете в Москве́, приезжа́йте к нам!** (literally: *If you will be in Moscow, come to us*).

**10** To express the hope that you will see someone again soon, say: **До ско́рого! Ско́рый** means *fast* (of a train, e.g.) or *soon*, and the phrase **до ско́рого** is short for **до ско́рого свида́ния** (literally *to a soon meeting*).

# Appendix 1: Grammar

---

## Spelling rules

**1** *Never* write **ы, ю, я** after **г, к, х, ж, ч, щ, ш**; instead write **и, у, а** (except for some nouns of foreign origin, e.g. **парашю́т, жюри́**).

**2** *Never* write unstressed **о** after **ж, ч, ш, щ, ц**; instead write **е**.

---

## Nouns

**NB** The **animate accusative** is formed in exactly the same way as the genitive case – as explained in **Units 5** and **7**, it affects **masculine singular** animate objects and all **plural** animate objects.

### *Masculine nouns – declension*

*Singular*

| | | | |
|---|---|---|---|
| Nom: | журна́л | трамва́й | автомоби́ль |
| Acc: | журна́л | трамва́й | автомоби́ль |
| Gen: | журна́ла | трамва́я | автомоби́ля |
| Dat: | журна́лу | трамва́ю | автомоби́лю |
| Instr: | журна́лом | трамва́ем | автомоби́лем |
| Prep: | о журна́ле | о трамва́е | об автомоби́ле |

Some masculine nouns take **-ý** or **-ю́** in the prepositional singular:

| | | |
|---|---|---|
| аэропо́рт | *(airport)* | в аэропорту́ |
| бе́рег | *(shore, bank)* | на берегу́ |
| бой | *(battle)* | в бою́ |

| быт | (everyday life) | в быту́ |
|---|---|---|
| глаз | (eye) | в глазу́ |
| год | (year) | в году́ |
| гроб | (grave) | в гробу́ |
| Дон | (River Don) | на Дону́ |
| край | (edge) | на краю́ |
| Крым | (Crimea) | в Крыму́ |
| лёд | (ice) | на льду́ |
| лес | (forest) | в лесу́ |
| лоб | (forehead) | на лбу́ |
| луг | (meadow) | в лугу́ |
| мост | (bridge) | на мосту́ |
| порт | (port) | в порту́ |
| пруд | (pond) | в пруду́ |
| рот | (mouth) | во рту́ |
| сад | (garden) | в саду́ |
| снег | (snow) | в снегу́ |
| таз | (bowl) | в тазу́ |
| у́гол | (corner) | в углу́ |

Some masculine nouns ending in -a, -я (e.g. дéдушка, *grandfather*, дя́дя, *uncle*) decline like feminine nouns.

*Plural*

| Nom: | журна́лы | трамва́и | автомоби́ли |
|---|---|---|---|
| Acc: | журна́лы | трамва́и | автомоби́ли |
| Gen: | журна́лов | трамва́ев | автомоби́лей |
| Dat: | журна́лам | трамва́ям | автомоби́лям |
| Instr: | журна́лами | трамва́ями | автомоби́лями |
| Prep: | о журна́лах | о трамва́ях | об автомоби́лях |

Some masculine nouns have the nominative plural ending -á or -я́:

| áдрес | (address) | адреса́ |
|---|---|---|
| бéрег | (shore, bank) | берега́ |
| вéчер | (evening, party) | вечера́ |
| глаз | (eye) | глаза́ |
| гóлос | (voice) | голоса́ |

| | | |
|---|---|---|
| го́род | (town) | города́ |
| дом | (house) | дома́ |
| до́ктор | (doctor) | доктора́ |
| лес | (forest) | леса́ |
| луг | (meadow) | луга́ |
| мех | (fur) | меха́ |
| но́мер | (number, room) | номера́ |
| о́стров | (island) | острова́ |
| па́спорт | (passport) | паспорта́ |
| по́езд | (train) | поезда́ |
| учи́тель | (teacher) | учителя́ |
| цвет | (colour) | цвета́ |

Some masculine and neuter nouns take the nominative plural ending -**ья**:

| | | Nom. | Acc. | Gen. | Dat. | Instr. | Prep. |
|---|---|---|---|---|---|---|---|
| брат | (brother) | ья | ьев | ьев | ьям | ьями | ьях |
| де́рево | (tree) | ья | ья | ьев | ьям | ьями | ьях |
| лист | (leaf) | ья | ья | ьев | ьям | ьями | ьях |
| стул | (chair) | ья | ья | ьев | ьям | ьями | ьях |

Note especially **друг** (*friend*) and **сын** (*son*):

| | | |
|---|---|---|
| Nom: | друзья́ | сыновья́ |
| Acc: | друзе́й | сынове́й |
| Gen: | друзе́й | сынове́й |
| Dat: | друзья́м | сыновья́м |
| Instr: | друзья́ми | сыновья́ми |
| Prep: | о друзья́х | о сыновья́х |

Nouns ending in -**анин** or -**янин** in the plural:

**англича́нин**    (*Englishman*):

| | |
|---|---|
| Nom: | англича́не |
| Acc: | англича́н |

| Gen:   | англича́н          |
|--------|-------------------|
| Dat:   | англича́нам        |
| Instr: | англича́нами       |
| Prep:  | об англича́нах     |

Irregular plurals: **де́ти** (*children*), **лю́ди** (*people*):

| Nom:   | де́ти     | лю́ди     |
|--------|-----------|-----------|
| Acc:   | дете́й    | люде́й    |
| Gen:   | дете́й    | люде́й    |
| Dat:   | де́тям    | лю́дям    |
| Instr: | детьми́   | людьми́   |
| Prep:  | о де́тях  | о лю́дях  |

Nouns ending in **ж, ч, ш, щ** have the genitive plural
ending **-ей**.

### *Feminine nouns – declension*

#### *Singular*

| Nom:   | ко́мната    | неде́ля   | ста́нция   | дверь    |
|--------|-------------|-----------|-----------|----------|
| Acc:   | ко́мнату    | неде́лю   | ста́нцию   | дверь    |
| Gen:   | ко́мнаты    | неде́ли   | ста́нции   | две́ри   |
| Dat:   | ко́мнате    | неде́ле   | ста́нции   | две́ри   |
| Instr: | ко́мнатой   | неде́лей  | ста́нцией  | две́рью  |
| Prep:  | о ко́мнате  | о неде́ле | о ста́нции | о две́ри |

#### *Plural*

| Nom:   | ко́мнаты     | неде́ли    | ста́нции    | две́ри     |
|--------|--------------|------------|-------------|------------|
| Acc:   | ко́мнаты     | неде́ли    | ста́нции    | две́ри     |
| Gen:   | ко́мнат      | неде́ль    | ста́нций    | двере́й    |
| Dat:   | ко́мнатам    | неде́лям   | ста́нциям   | дверя́м    |
| Instr: | ко́мнатами   | неде́лями  | ста́нциями  | дверя́ми   |
| Prep:  | о ко́мнатах  | о неде́лях | о ста́нциях | о дверя́х  |

Note the irregular feminine nouns **дочь** (*daughter*) and **мать** (*mother*):

|  | Singular | Plural | Singular | Plural |
|---|---|---|---|---|
| Nom: | дочь | до́чери | мать | ма́тери |
| Acc: | дочь | дочере́й | мать | матере́й |
| Gen: | до́чери | дочере́й | ма́тери | матере́й |
| Dat: | до́чери | дочеря́м | ма́тери | матеря́м |
| Instr: | до́черью | дочерьми́ | ма́терью | матеря́ми |
| Prep: | о до́чери | о дочеря́х | о ма́тери | о матеря́х |

### Neuter nouns – declension

Singular

|  |  |  |  |
|---|---|---|---|
| Nom: | ме́сто | мо́ре | зда́ние |
| Acc: | ме́сто | мо́ре | зда́ние |
| Gen: | ме́ста | мо́ря | зда́ния |
| Dat: | ме́сту | мо́рю | зда́нию |
| Instr: | ме́стом | мо́рем | зда́нием |
| Prep: | о ме́сте | о мо́ре | зда́нии |

Plural

|  |  |  |  |
|---|---|---|---|
| Nom: | места́ | моря́ | зда́ния |
| Acc: | места́ | моря́ | зда́ния |
| Gen: | мест | море́й | зда́ний |
| Dat: | места́м | моря́м | зда́ниям |
| Instr: | места́ми | моря́ми | зда́ниями |
| Prep: | о места́х | о моря́х | о зда́ниях |

Note the declension of neuter nouns ending in **-мя**:

|  | Singular | Plural |
|---|---|---|
| Nom: | вре́мя | времена́ |
| Acc: | вре́мя | времена́ |

| Gen:   | вре́мени    | времён       |
|--------|------------|--------------|
| Dat:   | вре́мени    | времена́м     |
| Instr: | вре́менем   | времена́ми    |
| Prep:  | о вре́мени  | о времена́х   |

### Stress patterns in nouns

In many Russian nouns the stress remains constant throughout the declension of the noun, but in some nouns the pattern changes. The most effective approach is to learn the most common examples of where stress changes in a noun's declension:

**a** We have already seen, for example, that some masculine nouns take stressed endings in the plural (e.g. **дом, го́род** etc.).

**b** Some common feminine nouns which are stressed on the ending throughout the singular are stressed on the stem throughout the plural, e.g.:

| гроза́   | *thunderstorm*            |
|---------|---------------------------|
| игра́    | *game*                    |
| сестра́  | *sister* (pl. сёстры)     |
| страна́  | *country*                 |

**c** Some common feminine nouns are stressed on the ending except in the accusative singular and nominative and accusative plural, e.g.:

| вода́     | *water*           |
|----------|-------------------|
| голова́   | *head*            |
| нога́     | *leg, foot*       |
| рука́     | *arm, hand*       |
| сторона́  | *side, direction* |

**d** Some common feminine nouns are stressed on the stem except in the plural oblique (gen., dat., instr., prep.) cases, e.g.:

| вещь | thing |
| дверь | door |
| лóшадь | horse |
| нóвость | news |
| часть | part |
| чéтверть | quarter |

**e** Some common neuter nouns are stressed on the endings throughout the singular and on the stem throughout the plural, e.g.:

| винó | wine |
| кольцó | ring |
| окнó | window |
| письмó | letter |
| числó | number, date |

**f** Some common neuter nouns are stressed on the stem through the singular and on the endings throughout the plural, e.g.:

| дéло | matter, affair |
| мéсто | place |
| мóре | sea |
| пóле | field |
| прáво | right |
| сéрдце | heart |
| слóво | word |

---

## Adjectives – declension

### Unstressed

|  | Masculine | Feminine | Neuter | Plural |
|---|---|---|---|---|
| Nom (new): | нóвый | нóвая | нóвое | нóвые |
| Acc: | нóвый | нóвую | нóвое | нóвые |
| Gen: | нóвого | нóвой | нóвого | нóвых |

| Dat: | нóвому | нóвой | нóвому | нóвым |
|------|--------|-------|--------|-------|
| Instr: | нóвым | нóвой | нóвым | нóвыми |
| Prep: | о нóвом | о нóвой | о нóвом | о нóвых |

### *Stressed*

| Nom (*young*): | молодóй | молодáя | молодóе | молодые |
|------|--------|-------|--------|-------|
| Acc: | молодóй | молодýю | молодóе | молодые |
| Gen: | молодóго | молодóй | молодóго | молодых |
| Dat: | молодóму | молодóй | молодóму | молодым |
| Instr: | молодым | молодóй | молодым | молодыми |
| Prep: | о молодóм | о молодóй | о молодóм | о молодых |

### *Soft*

| Nom (*early*): | рáнний | рáнняя | рáннее | рáнние |
|------|--------|-------|--------|-------|
| Acc: | рáнний | рáннюю | рáннее | рáнние |
| Gen: | рáннего | рáнней | рáннего | рáнних |
| Dat: | рáннему | рáнней | рáннему | рáнним |
| Instr: | рáнним | рáнней | рáнним | рáнними |
| Prep: | о рáннем | о рáнней | о рáннем | о рáнних |

Note the following carefully:

## 1 трéтий (*third*)

| Nom: | трéтий | трéтья | трéтье | трéтьи |
|------|--------|-------|--------|-------|
| Acc: | трéтий | трéтью | трéтье | трéтьи |
| Gen: | трéтьего | трéтьей | трéтьего | трéтьих |
| Dat: | трéтьему | трéтьей | трéтьему | трéтьим |
| Instr: | трéтьим | трéтьей | трéтьим | трéтьими |
| Prep: | о трéтьем | о трéтьей | о трéтьем | о трéтьих |

## 2 мой (твой, свой) *and* наш (ваш)

| Nom: | мой/наш | моя́/нáша | моё/нáше | мои/нáши |
|------|--------|-------|--------|-------|
| Acc: | мой/наш | мою́/нáшу | моё/нáше | мои/нáши |
| Gen: | моегó/нáшего | моéй/нáшей | моегó/нáшего | мои́х/нáших |
| Dat: | моемý/нáшему | моéй/нáшей | моемý/нáшему | мои́м/нáшим |

| Instr: | мои́м/на́шим | мое́й/на́шей | мои́м/на́шим | мои́ми/ |
|--------|-------------|-------------|-------------|--------|
|        |             |             |             | на́шими |
| Prep:  | о моём/на́шем | о мое́й/на́шей | о моём/на́шем | о мои́х/на́ших |

## 3 *Irregular short comparative adjectives*

| | | |
|---|---|---|
| бли́зкий | near | бли́же |
| бога́тый | rich | бога́че |
| большо́й | big | бо́льше |
| высо́кий | high, tall | вы́ше |
| глубо́кий | deep | глу́бже |
| гро́мкий | loud | гро́мче |
| далёкий | distant | да́льше |
| дешёвый | cheap | дешё́вле |
| до́лгий | long (time) | до́льше |
| дорого́й | dear, expensive | доро́же |
| жа́ркий | hot | жа́рче |
| коро́ткий | short | коро́че |
| кре́пкий | strong | кре́пче |
| лёгкий | light, easy | ле́гче |
| ма́ленький | little | ме́ньше |
| молодо́й | young | моло́же |
| ни́зкий | low | ни́же |
| плохо́й | bad | ху́же |
| по́здний | late | по́зже |
| ра́нний | early | ра́ньше |
| сла́дкий | sweet | сла́ще |
| ти́хий | quiet | ти́ше |
| у́зкий | narrow | у́же |
| хоро́ший | good | лу́чше |
| ча́стый | frequent | ча́ще |
| чи́стый | clean | чи́ще |
| широ́кий | wide | ши́ре |

## 4 Suffix -айший or -ейший

This is sometimes added to adjectives to form the superlative; this form of the superlative is most frequently met in written Russian, thus you might read about Pushkin, for example:

**Пу́шкин – велича́йший ру́сский поэ́т** *Pushkin is the greatest Russian poet* (from the adjective **вели́кий**, *great*)

---

## Pronouns – declension

### Personal pronouns

| Nom: | я | ты | он/оно́ | она́ | мы | вы | они́ |
|---|---|---|---|---|---|---|---|
| Acc: | меня́ | тебя́ | его́ | её | нас | вас | их |
| Gen: | меня́ | тебя́ | его́ | её | нас | вас | их |
| Dat: | мне | тебе́ | ему́ | ей | нам | вам | им |
| Instr: | мной | тобо́й | им | ей | на́ми | ва́ми | и́ми |
| Prep: | обо мне | о тебе́ | о нём | о ней | о нас | о вас | о них |

**NB** Always add **н** to the beginning of **его́/ему́/им/её/ей/их/и́ми** if they are preceded by a preposition.

### Reflexive pronouns

| Acc: | себя́ |
|---|---|
| Gen: | себя́ |
| Dat: | себе́ |
| Instr: | собо́й |
| Prep: | о себе́ |

### Interrogative pronouns

| Nom: | кто | что |
|---|---|---|
| Acc: | кого́ | что |
| Gen: | кого́ | чего́ |
| Dat: | кому́ | чему́ |
| Instr: | кем | чем |
| Prep: | о ком | о чём |

## Demonstrative pronouns

|  | Masculine | Feminine | Neuter | Plural |
|---|---|---|---|---|
| Nom: | этот/тот | эта/та | это/то | эти/те |
| Acc: | этот/тот | эту/ту | это/то | эти/те |
| Gen: | этого/того | этой/той | этого/того | этих/тех |
| Dat: | этому/тому | этой/той | этому/тому | этим/тем |
| Instr: | этим/тем | этой/той | этим/тем | этими/теми |
| Prep: | об этом/о том | об этой/о той | об этом/о том | об этих/о тех |

## Determinative pronouns

|  | Masculine | Feminine | Neuter | Plural |
|---|---|---|---|---|
| Nom: | весь | вся | всё | все |
| Acc: | весь | всю | всё | все |
| Gen: | всего | всей | всего | всех |
| Dat: | всему | всей | всему | всем |
| Instr: | всем | всей | всем | всеми |
| Prep: | обо всём | о всей | обо всём | о всех |
| Nom: | сам | сама | само | сами |
| Acc: | сам | саму | само | сами |
| Gen: | самого | самой | самого | самих |
| Dat: | самому | самой | самому | самим |
| Instr: | самим | самой | самим | самими |
| Prep: | о самом | о самой | о самом | о самих |

---

# Prepositions

| Preposition | Case | Meaning |
|---|---|---|
| без | + genitive | without |
| в | + accusative | into, to |
| в | + prepositional | in, at |

| | | |
|---|---|---|
| вме́сто | + genitive | *instead of* |
| для | + genitive | *for* |
| до | + genitive | *until, as far as, before* |
| за | + accusative | *for, on behalf of* |
| за | + instrumental | *behind, beyond* |
| из | + genitive | *from* |
| к | + dative | *towards, to the house of* |
| кро́ме | + genitive | *except, apart from* |
| ме́жду | + instrumental | *between* |
| ми́мо | + genitive | *past* |
| на | + accusative | *onto, to; (intended) for* |
| на | + prepositional | *on, at* |
| над | + instrumental | *over* |
| о/об | + prepositional | *about* |
| о́коло | + genitive | *near, approximately* |
| от | + genitive | *from* |
| пе́ред | + instrumental | *in front of; before* |
| по | + dative | *along, according to* |
| под | + instrumental | *under* |
| по́сле | + genitive | *after* |
| при | + prepositional | *at the time of, in the reign of, in the presence of* |
| про́тив | + genitive | *against, opposite* |
| ра́ди | + genitive | *for the sake of* |
| с | + genitive | *from, since* |
| с | + instrumental | *with* |
| среди́ | + genitive | *among, in the middle of* |
| у | + genitive | *by, at the house of* |
| че́рез | + accusative | *across, through* |

Note the following nouns, which cannot be used with **в** + prepositional to mean in or at, and must be used with **на** + prepositional to mean in or at:

| | | | |
|---|---|---|---|
| вокза́л | *station* | се́вер | *north* |
| восто́к | *east* | спекта́кль | *performance* |
| вы́ставка | *exhibition* | стадио́н | *stadium* |
| заво́д | *factory* | ста́нция | *station* |

| | | | |
|---|---|---|---|
| за́пад | west | у́лица | street |
| конце́рт | concert | Ура́л | Urals |
| куро́рт | seaside resort | уро́к | lesson |
| ле́кция | lecture | фа́брика | factory |
| пло́щадь | square | факульте́т | faculty |
| по́чта | post office | экза́мен | exam |
| рабо́та | work | юг | south |
| ры́нок | market | | |
| *(fleeting о)* | | | |

---

## Numerals

All numerals decline (see Unit 19) and we have seen in the units how to use numerals in the nominative case and in expressions of time.

### *Further notes on numerals*

**1** 40 (**со́рок**), 90 (**девяно́сто**), 100 (**сто**) have only two forms: **со́рок, девяно́сто, сто** (nom., acc). and **сорока́, девяно́ста, ста** (all other cases). With 50 (**пятьдеся́т**), 60 (**шестьдеся́т**), 70 (**се́мьдесят**), 80 (**во́семьдесят**) both halves of the numeral decline:

| Nom/Acc: | пятьдеся́т |
|---|---|
| Gen: | пяти́десяти |
| Dat: | пяти́десяти |
| Instr: | пятью́десятью |
| Prep: | о пяти́десяти |

Both halves of the hundreds of numbers decline too:

| Nom/Acc: | две́сти | пятьсо́т |
|---|---|---|
| Gen: | двухсо́т | пятисо́т |

| | | |
|---|---|---|
| Dat: | двумста́м | пятиста́м |
| Instr: | двумяста́ми | пятьюста́ми |
| Prep: | о двухста́х | о пятиста́х |

**2** Use of numerals with:

**a** animate accusative nouns:

2, 3, 4 have an animate form:

Он ви́дит двух ма́льчиков.     *He sees two boys.*

5 and above (including compounds of 2, 3, 4) behave as they would in the nominative:

Она зна́ет три́дцать три     *She knows thirty-three*
студе́нта.                  *students.*

**b** numbers in all other cases except nominative/accusative:

The numeral and the noun must be in the same case, and the noun will take plural endings (except after *one*):

Он идёт в те́атр с одно́й     *He is going to the theatre*
де́вушкой.                *with one girl.*
Он идёт в те́атр с тремя́     *... with three girls.*
де́вушками.
Он идёт в те́атр с         *... with twenty-five girls.*
двадцатью́ пятью́ де́вушками.

**c** numerals with distance (**в** + prepositional of the numeral and of the measurement):

Заво́д нахо́дится в трёх     *The factory is three*
киломе́трах от го́рода.     *kilometres from town.*

## Verbs

### Regular verbs

| First conjugation | Second conjugation |
|---|---|
| я рабóтаю | я говорю́ |
| ты рабóтаешь | ты говори́шь |
| он рабóтает | он говори́т |
| мы рабóтаем | мы говори́м |
| вы рабóтаете | вы говори́те |
| они рабóтают | они говоря́т |

### Irregularities

**1** In second conjugation verbs the first-person singular of the present and future perfective has a consonantal change if the stem of the verb ends in:

| | | | |
|---|---|---|---|
| **б → бл** | люби́ть | *to like, love* | я люблю́, ты лю́бишь |
| **в → вл** | готóвить | *to prepare* | я готóвлю, ты готóвишь |
| **д → ж** | ви́деть | *to see* | я ви́жу, ты ви́дишь |
| **з → ж** | возúть | *to transport* | я вожу́, ты вóзишь |
| **п → пл** | спать | *to sleep* | я сплю, ты спишь |
| **с → ш** | носи́ть | *to carry* | я ношу́, ты нóсишь |
| **т → ч** | лете́ть | *to fly* | я лечу́, ты лети́шь |
| **ст → щ** | посети́ть | *to visit* | я посещу́, ты посети́шь |

**2** Verbs in **-овать** and **-евать** in the present and future perfective tense lose the **-ов/-ев** of the infinitive, e.g. **совéтовать** (*to advise*):

| -ую | совéтую |
|---|---|
| -уешь | совéтуешь |
| -ует | совéтует |
| -уем | совéтуем |
| -уете | совéтуете |
| -уют | совéтуют |

**3** Verbs in **-авать (except пла́вать** to *swim*) lose the syllable **-ав** throughout the present tense:

**дава́ть** *to give*

| | |
|---|---|
| даю́ | даём |
| даёшь | даёте |
| даёт | даю́т |

**4** Some common irregular verbs

| | |
|---|---|
| **брать** (*to take*) (imperfective) | беру́, берёшь, берёт, берём, берёте, беру́т |
| **взять** (*to take*) (perfective) | возьму́, возьмёшь, возьмёт, возьмём, возьмёте, возьму́т |
| **есть** (*to eat*) | ем, ешь, ест, еди́м, еди́те, едя́т |
| **ждать** (*to wait*) | жду, ждёшь, ждёт, ждём, ждёте, ждут |
| **жить** (*to live*) | живу́, живёшь, живёт, живём, живёте, живу́т |
| **е́хать** (*to travel*) | е́ду, е́дешь, е́дет, е́дем, е́дете, е́дут |
| **идти́** (*to walk*) | иду́, идёшь, идёт, идём, идёте, иду́т |
| **класть** (*to put*) | кладу́, кладёшь, кладёт, кладём, кладёте, кладу́т |
| **мочь** (*to be able*) | могу́, мо́жешь, мо́жет, мо́жем, мо́жете, мо́гут |
| **писа́ть** (*to write*) | пишу́, пи́шешь, пи́шет, пи́шем, пи́шете, пи́шут |
| **хоте́ть** (*to want*) | хочу́, хо́чешь, хо́чет, хоти́м, хоти́те, хотя́т |

**5** Imperative (see Unit 3). Note that if the first person singular of the verb has an unstressed ending preceded by a single consonant, the imperative ends in **-ь (ты), -ьте (вы):**

| | |
|---|---|
| **отве́тить** (perfective, *to answer*) | я отве́чу → отве́ть! отве́тьте! |

Note that imperatives formed from the imperfective infinitive are generally more polite/friendly, while those formed from the perfective infinitive are more of a brusque order:

| | |
|---|---|
| Сади́тесь, пожа́луйста! | *Please (do) sit down!* |
| Ся́дьте! | *Sit down!* |

# Appendix 2: Pronunciation

**1** **т, н, д:** these are 'dental' consonants in Russian, pronounced with the tip of the tongue against the top teeth (in English they are pronounced with the tip of the tongue against the alveolar ridge behind the top teeth).

**2** **р** is rolled (with the tip of the tongue vibrating against the alveolar ridge).

**3** **ж, ш:** try to extend your bottom jaw when pronouncing these.

**4** **й** is used with vowels to make diphthongs, in the same way as *y* and sometimes *i* are used in English:

| | | |
|---|---|---|
| e.g.: | **а + й → ай** | (sounds like *ai* in Th*ai*land) |
| | **о + й → ой** | (sounds like *oy* in *boy*) |

**5** **л:** keep the back of your tongue low, away from the roof of your mouth; the tip of your tongue should push against your upper teeth.

**6** **ы:** there is no real equivalent in English – the nearest is the *y* in 'physics' or the *i* in '*i*ll'; keep your mouth as still as you can (try saying it while holding a pencil between your teeth) and draw your tongue as far back in your mouth as you can.

**7** **ъ** and **ь:** before we can deal with the hard sign and the soft sign, the ideas of 'hard' and 'soft' sounds need to be looked at.

Russian has ten letters denoting vowels and these fall into two groups:

| Hard | а | э | ы | о | у |
|------|---|---|---|---|---|
| Soft | я | е | и | ё | ю |

'Soft' vowels 'soften' or 'palatalize' the consonants which precede them – 'softened' or 'palatalized' consonants are produced by arching your tongue against the roof of your mouth (the soft palate). This is not something restricted to Russian; consider the following English words and notice how a 'y' sound is introduced in the 'soft' version – say the words aloud and listen to the difference:

| Hard | Soft |
|------|------|
| *moon* | *music* |
| *pool* | *pew* |
| *stool* | *stew* |

The fact that Russian has a set of soft consonants is helpful, since it tells us when to 'palatalize'. Consider these Russian words and try saying them out loud:

| Hard | | Soft | |
|------|------|------|------|
| **да** | *(yes)* | **дя́дя** | *(uncle)* |
| **экра́н** | *(screen)* | **éсли** | *(if)* |
| **лы́жи** | *(skis)* | **ли́дер** | *(leader)* |
| **тост** | *(a toast)* | **тётя** | *(aunt)* |
| **душ** | *(shower)* | **дю́жина** | *(dozen)* |

The soft sign (**ь**) usually softens (palatalizes) the preceding consonant. This is especially important after the letters **л** and **т**:

**ль** is pronounced with the back of your tongue arched against the palate (instead of being low in your mouth): **то́лько**, *only*.

**ть** is palatalized (think of how you pronounced the *t* in 'stew' above): **мать**, *mother*.

When the soft sign occurs between a consonant and a soft vowel it separates the two, so that they are pronounced separately: e.g. **семья́**, *family*.

The hard sign (ъ) also has a separating function and it keeps the preceding consonant hard: e.g. **отъéзд**, *departure*. (**NB** The hard sign is far less common than the soft sign.)

There are three letters that resist the temptation to be softened: **ж**, **ш** and **ц** are *always* hard, so that, for example:

| **Written** | | | **Pronounced** |
|---|---|---|---|
| **ужé** | *(already)* | is pronounced | **ужэ́** |
| **цирк** | *(circus)* | is pronounced | **цырк** |
| **шёлк** | *(silk)* | is pronounced | **шолк** |

And there are two letters which are *always soft*: **ч** and **щ**, so that, for example:

| **чáсто** | *(often)* | is pronounced | **ча́сто** |
|---|---|---|---|

## 8  To summarize the effect of stress on vowels

- **а** when stressed: slightly shorter than **a** in father (sometimes described as **u** in hut)
  in syllable before stress: like **o** in another (спаси́бо)
  otherwise: **a** in around (кни́га)

- **е** when stressed: like **ye** in yet
  when unstressed: like **i** or **yi** (дела́; ещё)

- **о** when stressed: like **aw** in law
  in syllable before stress: like **o** in another (соба́ка)
  otherwise: like **a** in around (хорошо́)

- **я** stressed: like **ya** in yak
  in syllable before stress: like **yi** (яи́чница)
  otherwise: like short **ya** (но́вая)

Two final points about Russian pronunciation:

**9** It is more 'reliable' than English, i.e. the sound of the whole word is, by and large, produced by joining together the sound of individual letters (unlike English words such as *drought* and *draught*; *I have read* and *I read after supper*; *I excuse you* and *What an excuse*). The hard/soft distinction isn't really difficult – if you pronounce the soft vowel correctly, you'll find you automatically soften the preceding consonant.

**10** In Russian, as in other languages, many consonants can be grouped into pairs, one of which is 'voiced' (i.e. the vocal chords vibrate) and one 'unvoiced' (i.e. the vocal chords are not used) – consider the English sounds *g* (voiced) and *k* (unvoiced): both are produced in the same way, but one uses the vocal chords and one does not. In English, for example, we have the following pairs:

| Voiced | Unvoiced |
|--------|----------|
| *bay* | *pay* |
| *dug* | *tug* |

In Russian we have the following pairs:

| Voiced | Unvoiced |
|--------|----------|
| б | п |
| в | ф |
| г | к |
| д | т |
| ж | ш |
| з | с |

This is important because the voiced consonants are usually pronounced as their unvoiced partner when they occur at the end of words:

| Written | | Pronounced |
|---------|---|-----------|
| бага́ж | (*luggage*) | бага́ш |
| хлеб | (*bread*) | хлеп |

| друг | (*friend*) | друк |
|------|-----------|------|
| сад  | (*garden*) | сат  |

In groups of consonants, all are voiced if the last consonant in the group (e.g. **б** in **футбо́л**) is voiced: **футбо́л** (*football*) is pronounced **фудбо́л** (because the last consonant in the group is voiced). All the consonants in a group are unvoiced if the last consonant in the group is unvoiced: e.g. **во́дка** (*vodka*) is pronounced **во́тка**.

........................................................................

# Key to the exercises

Please note that *t = true* and *f = false*.

## Introduction

**1** **a** London **b** Lancaster **c** Madrid **d** Cornwall **e** Amsterdam
**f** Aberdeen **g** Huntingdon **h** Birmingham **i** Epsom **j** Melbourne
**2** **a** Stephanie Brown 208 **b** Jane Clark 202 **c** Margaret Davies
209 **d** Richard Harrison 207 **e** Simon Mackenzie 205 **f** Hugh
Riley 206 **g** John Smith 201 **h** Nicholas Taylor 210 **i** Veronica
Thomson 203 **j** Lilian West 204

## Unit 1

**Questions 1** **a** *f* **b** *f* **c** *t* **2** **a** Да, Áнна англичáнка **b** Её
фамúлия – Принс **Practice 1.1** **a** Russian **b** Vorobyova
**c** pianist **1.2** **a** Джим америкáнец. Он журналúст **b** Марúя
итальянка. Она актрúса **c** Борúс рýсский. Он инженéр **d** Пáтрик
ирлáндец. Он студéнт **1.3** St Petersburg **1.4** **1** d **2** c **3** a
**4** b **1.5** **a** Вот моя декларáция **b** Вот моё письмó **c** Вот мой
багáж **d** Вот мой журнáл **e** Вот моя вúза **Comprehension**
**1** **a** *f* **b** *t* **c** *t* **2** **a** Moscow **b** journalist **c** Bolshoi Theatre,
Moscow University and Kremlin

## Test Yourself (Unit 1)

**1** It will end in either **o**, **e** or **ие**. If you weren't sure of the answer,
it would be a good idea to check the section on groups of nouns
in the Grammar section, point 4 of Unit 1, and make sure you
know the endings for each of the three genders (masculine,
feminine and neuter).

**2** There is no word for *the* or *a* in Russian, so, for example,
**журналúст** means both *a journalist* and *the journalist*.

**3** If you want to turn a written statement into a question, just put a question mark at the end. If you are speaking, just raise your voice on the last stressed syllable of the final word.

**4** Because the words for *my, your, our* must 'agree' with the noun they are describing – so, if a noun is feminine (like **ви́за**) then you must use the feminine form of *my, your, our*. If you weren't sure of the answer, look again at the 'My, our, your' in Grammar section 6 in Unit 1.

**5** It's the middle name which is based on the father's first name and which is used in formal situations. So, if a man called Viktor had a father called Ivan, the polite, formal way to refer to him would be **Ви́ктор Ива́нович**; if Viktor had a sister called Nina, she would be **Ни́на Ива́новна.**

**6** In reply to **спаси́бо** (*thank you*) you should say **пожа́луйста** – *don't mention it, you're welcome* (literally *please*).

**7** **Где** (**как** means *how*).

**8** **До свида́ния** (remember to pronounce it as though it were one word).

**9** Look at Unit 1, Grammar section, point 8, to check.

**10** **Вы** is the polite way to talk to a person when you meet them for the first time.

## Unit 2

**Questions 1** **a** *f* **b** *t* **c** *f* **2** **a** Хорошо́ **b** В Бри́столе **c** жи́вопись **Practice 2.1** **a** рабо́таем **b** преподаёт **c** живёте **d** зна́ют **e** говорю́ **2.2** **a** 4 **b** 1 **c** 2 **d** 3 **2.3** **a** Bolshoi Theatre **b** 292-00-50 **2.4** **b** Са́ша рабо́тает в саду́ **c** Ты рабо́таешь в шко́ле **d** Гали́на рабо́тает в лаборато́рии **e** Вы рабо́таете в бюро́ **f** Я рабо́таю в гости́нице **g** Бори́с рабо́тает в Москве́ **2.5** **a** J.S. Bach **b** Mozart **c** Schumann **2.6** **b** Я живу́ в Би́рмингаме. Я говорю́ по-англи́йски **c** Пьер живёт в Пари́же. Он говори́т по-францу́зски **d** Хосе́ живёт в Испа́нии. Он говори́т по-испа́нски. **e** Вы живёте в Москве́. Вы говори́те по-ру́сски **Comprehension 1** **a** *f* **b** *t* **c** *t* **d** *f* **e** *f* **2** **a** large cultural and administrative centre **b** about 5 million **c** in the centre in a flat **d** beautiful – e.g. Winter Palace, Hermitage **e** university

## Test Yourself (Unit 2)

**1** *I work* (**я рабо́таю**); *I speak* (**я говорю́**); *you work* (**вы рабо́таете**); *you speak* (**вы говори́те**).

**2** The stem, and the endings for **ты** and **вы** (have another look at Unit 2, Grammar section, point 1b on irregular verbs to remind yourself of this).

**3** **Меня́ зову́т** … and your name!

**4** **В университе́те; в шко́ле; в письме́.** If you got stuck with any of those, take another look at the explanations in Unit 2, Grammar section, point 3.

**5** **Вы говори́те по-ру́сски?**

**6** **Здесь** = *here*; **там** = *there*; **о́чень** = *very*; **а** = *and* or *but*; **да** = *yes*; **нет** = *no*.

**7** When you meet someone for the first time – the phrase **о́чень прия́тно** means *pleased to meet you* (it means *very pleasant too,* so you might use it when you're being complimentary about something).

**8** When you're saying *excuse me, please.* This is a really useful phrase, which also can also be used when you're apologizing: *sorry.*

**9** **Я живу́ в ..... и я рабо́таю в ....** – complete by adding the names of the places where you live and work, e.g.: **Я живу́ в Ли́дсе и я рабо́таю в о́фисе в Брэдфо́рде** (*I live in Leeds and work in an office in Bradford*).

**10** **Мой па́спорт** = *my passport*; **ва́ша ви́за** = *your visa*; **на́ша гости́ница** = *our hotel*.

## Unit 3

**Questions 1** a *f* b *f* c *t* **2** a Нет, он не зна́ет b Дом 120, ко́рпус 3, кварти́ра 5 c напра́во **Practice 3.1** a куда́ b в Óмске c в университе́те d в апте́ку e в рестора́не f Я́лту g деклара́ция h Óльгу **3.2** a ballet b Don Quixote **3.3** b Ви́ктор живёт в Ки́еве c Я живу́ в А́нглии d Ты живёшь в Оде́ссе e Мари́я и Антóнио живу́т в Ита́лии **3.4** a Как пройти́ в апте́ку? b Э́то далеко́? c Спаси́бо большо́е **3.5** a Как вас зову́т? b Где вы

живёте? **c** Где вы рабо́таете? **d** Куда́ вы идёте? **e** У вас есть
план? **Comprehension 1** 1 c 2 b 3 a 4 a **2 a** Mashatin
**b** works in chemist's shop **c** 3 years **d** in a flat on the outskirts
of Moscow **e** not big; kitchen, bathroom, bedroom and sitting
room **f** supermarket, chemist's, cinema, school, metro station

## Unit 4

**Questions 1** **a** *t* **b** *t* **c** *f* **2 a** В ка́ссе **b** Ка́рту и деревя́нный
стул **c** Фотографи́ровать **Practice 4.1** 1 c 2 a 3 d 4 b
**4.2 a** Извини́те, пожа́луйста **b** Как пройти́ в це́рковь?
**c** Спаси́бо. Где музе́й? **d** Где мо́жно купи́ть биле́ты? **e** Спаси́бо.
До свида́ния **4.3 a** Don't smoke in the lift **b** Don't smoke in
bed **c** Chocolate **4.4 b** Кака́я э́то це́рковь? **c** Како́й э́то музе́й?
**d** Како́е э́то зда́ние? **e** Кака́я э́то кни́га? **f** Како́й э́то дом?
**4.5** Пря́мо, напра́во, пря́мо, напра́во, пря́мо, напра́во
**4.6 a** Меня́ зову́т ... **b** Я живу́ в ... **c** Я рабо́таю в ... **d** Я живу́ в ...
**e** У меня́ (e.g.) ма́ленькая кварти́ра **Comprehension 1** **a** *f*
**b** *t* **c** *f* **d** *f* **e** *t* **f** *f* **2 a** Golden ring **b** old, beautiful, historic,
Russian **c** churches, cathedrals, museums, monuments **d** tractors,
computers, beautiful crystal **e** because it has museums, monuments,
ancient architecture **f** beautiful gardens and kitchen gardens with
cucumbers and tomatoes

## Test Yourself (Unit 4)

1 **Мо́жно** (usually followed by an infinitive – the 'to do' part of
   the verb).
2 Although it is second conjugation, so works like **говори́ть** in
   the present tense, the **я** form has an additional **л**: **люблю́**
3 **-ы** and **-и**. You can check everything about nominative plural
   nouns in part 1 of the Grammar section.
4 It will end in **-ое**, and this is logical, if you remember that
   neuter nouns end in **-о** or **-е**.
5 Either that one may not or it is not possible to do something,
   e.g.: **Здесь нельзя́ кури́ть!** *No smoking here!* (literally: *Here
   one may not smoke!*)

**6** In Russian you say *I like to watch television* – **Я люблю́ смотре́ть телеви́зор** … in other words for the thing you like to do, use the infinitive (the 'to do' part of the verb).

**7** **Города́.** It is worth spending some time to master the common irregular plurals (see Unit 4, Grammar section, point 1 on plural nouns).

**8** **Вы хоти́те** means *Do you want? Would you like?* Possible replies would be **Я хочу́** or **Я не хочу́**.

**9** You would use **на́до** (literally: *it is necessary*).

**10** After **г, к, х, ж, ч, ш, щ**; remember to learn this rule, as it will keep cropping up!

## Unit 5

**Questions 1** a *f* b *f* c *t* **2** a Биле́ты в цирк b На у́лице, нале́во от апте́ки, недалеко́ от ста́нции метро́ c Восемьдеся́т рубле́й **Practice 5.1** 4: А́нны, биле́та, Че́хова, сестры́ **5.2** a У вас есть па́спорт? b Где нахо́дится кио́ск? c Ско́лько сто́ит план го́рода? d Где он рабо́тает? e Вы лю́бите Че́хова? **5.3** b **5.4** b У Вади́ма есть автомоби́ль и телефо́н, но у него́ нет соба́ки c У Ни́ны есть соба́ка и автомоби́ль, но у неё нет телефо́на d У Алексе́я есть автомоби́ль и телефо́н, но у него́ нет соба́ки **5.5** a Ви́ктора b пье́са c о́перу d пье́су e Влади́мир **Comprehension 1** 1 c 2 c 3 b 4 a **2** a Ukraine b very old city c 2 million d It's very beautiful; parks, forests, gardens, campsites, hotels, monuments e planes, televisions, motorcycles

## Unit 6

**Questions 1** a *t* b *t* c *f* d *f* e *f* **2** a Нет, не о́чень b О́чень краси́вые карти́ны c Потому́, что она́ худо́жник d Чай **Practice 6.1** a зна́ете b Да, вот он c рабо́тает d Да, мо́жно e багажа́ f Бори́су **6.2** a В го́роде есть музе́и? b Э́ти музе́и недалеко́ от гости́ницы? c Что есть в музе́е? d Ско́лько сто́ит биле́т в музе́й? e Спаси́бо большо́е и до свида́ния **6.3** a молока́ b Бори́су c нам d гости́ницы e мне **6.4** b Воло́дя предпочита́ет игра́ть на гита́ре c Вади́м предпочита́ет игра́ть на кларне́те d Ле́на предпочита́ет игра́ть в хокке́й e Све́та предпочита́ет игра́ть в ша́хматы **Comprehension 1** **1** b **2** d **3** d **2** a beautiful, typically Russian **b** centre of Moscow, near metro station Tretyakovskaya **c** Sergei Mikhailovich Tretyakov, rich Muscovite merchant **d** 19th-century painters, who depict life and problems of 19th-century Russia

## Test Yourself (Unit 6)

**1** The accusative, because Boris would be the subject and opera and ballet the objects: **Бори́с предпочита́ет о́перу и́ли бале́т?** (See Unit 3.)

**2** Prepositional because you would be explaining *where at*: **Я рабо́таю в о́фисе** (see Units 2 and 5).

**3** The genitive, because you will be using the preposition **от**: **мой дом нахо́дится далеко́ от вокза́ла** (Unit 5).

**4** Genitive, because you will be saying *the book of Olga*: **кни́га О́льги** (Unit 5).

**5** Accusative, because you are asking *where to*: **Вы идёте в гости́ницу?** (Unit 3).

**6** Dative, because the word **на́до** is used to express *need*: **Сего́дня Влади́миру на́до рабо́тать** (*Today it is necessary for Vladimir to work*) (see Unit 6).

**7** The genitive case (Unit 5).

**8** The accusative, e.g.: **Спаси́бо за вино́** (*Thank you for the wine*).

**9** The accusative (*to play at*): **Я люблю́ игра́ть в те́ннис.**

**10** The dative, because you will need to use the preposition **к** (which means *towards, to the house of* and which is used with the dative): **Ты идёшь к А́нне сего́дня ве́чером?** (Unit 6).

## Unit 7

**Questions 1** a *f* b *t* c *f* **2** a Краси́вые b Пять c Нет. А́нна хо́чет посла́ть име́йл домо́й **Practice 7.1** Извини́те, сего́дня у нас нет: **b** театра́льных биле́тов **c** интере́сных книг **d** ру́сских газе́т **e** свобо́дных мест **f** англи́йских журна́лов **7.2** **a** Извини́те, пожа́луйста **b** Ско́лько сто́ит посла́ть откры́тку в А́нглию? **c** Да́йте, пожа́луйста пять ма́рок по пятна́дцать рубле́й **d** Да, спаси́бо, э́то всё

**7.3** Professional business **7.4 b** Па́трик хо́чет посла́ть шесть откры́ток в Аме́рику. Зна́чит ему́ на́до купи́ть шесть ма́рок по шестна́дцать рубле́й **c** Ты хо́чешь посла́ть три откры́тки в И́ндию. Зна́чит тебе́ на́до купи́ть три ма́рки по шестна́дцать рубле́й пятьдеся́т копе́ек **d** Мы хоти́м посла́ть семь откры́ток во Фра́нцию. Зна́чит нам на́до купи́ть семь ма́рок по пятна́дцать рубле́й **e** Са́ша хо́чет посла́ть две откры́тки в Петербу́рг. Зна́чит ему́ на́до купи́ть две ма́рки по двена́дцать рубле́й **f** Я хочу́ посла́ть де́сять откры́ток в Кана́ду. Зна́чит мне на́до купи́ть де́сять ма́рок по шестна́дцать рубле́й пятьдеся́т копе́ек **7.5 1** c **2** a **3** b **4** e **5** d **7.6 a** как **b** ско́лько **c** куда́ **d** где **e** как **f** каки́е **Comprehension 1 1** c **2** c **3** b **2 a** father of Russian cities **b** 9th **c** Moscow to St Petersburg **d** many beautiful old churches and interesting monuments **e** religious picture of saint(s) **f** restoring frescoes of the 14th century **g** Many years

## Unit 8

**Questions 1** **a** *t* **b** *f* **c** *f* **d** *t* **e** *t* **2 a** в углу́ **b** молодо́й челове́к **c** Нет, они́ не о́чень голодны́ **d** моро́женое **e** чай с лимо́ном **Practice 8.1 a** [Да́йте] мне, пожа́луйста, сала́т с помидо́рами **b** Спаси́бо, нет. Я не о́чень го́лоден/голодна́ **c** Ско́лько сто́ит бефстро́ганов? **d** [Да́йте] мне, пожа́луйста, бефстро́ганов **e** [Да́йте] мне, пожа́луйста, моро́женое **f** [Да́йте] мне, пожа́луйста, сок и чай с лимо́ном **8.2 b** Са́ша предпочита́ет суп с помидо́рами и́ли с гриба́ми? Он предпочита́ет суп с гриба́ми **c** Са́ша предпочита́ет котле́ты с ри́сом и́ли с карто́шкой? Са́ша предпочита́ет котле́ты с ри́сом **d** Са́ша предпочита́ет ры́бу с гарни́ром и́ли с жа́реной карто́шкой? Са́ша предпочита́ет ры́бу с жа́реной карто́шкой **e** Са́ша предпочита́ет бифште́кс с ри́сом и́ли с гарни́ром? Са́ша предпочита́ет бифште́кс с гарни́ром **8.3 1** c **2** a **3** e **4** b **5** f **6** d **8.4 a** закры́т **b** свобо́дно **c** рад **d** за́няты **e** дово́льны, вку́сны **f** согла́сна **8.5 a** сала́т с помидо́рами **b** суп с гриба́ми **c** омле́т с сы́ром **d** фру́кты **e** сок и чай **Comprehension 1 1** a **2** d **3** c **4** d **2 a** cold, hot, fish, meat, vegetable **b** cabbage **c** with sour cream and with garlic **d** fish **e** flour, butter, egg, salt

## Test Yourself (Unit 8)

1 **Извини́те за пробле́му** (see Unit 3 for the accusative case).
2 **Спаси́бо за обе́д** (see Unit 3 for the accusative case).
3 At the end of the meal, because **счёт** means *bill*.
4 At the beginning of the meal, because **заку́ски** are *starters*.
5 C: **бутербро́д с сы́ром** (*cheese sandwich*); **суп с гриба́ми** (*mushroom soup*).
6 He will need to use the genitive after **нет** because *not any* is a quantity: **Сего́дня нет ры́бы** (see Unit 5 to revise uses of the genitive).
7 She will prefer **о́вощи** (*vegetables*), because **мя́со** is *meat*.
8 You would use the word **како́й** (*which, what sort of, what a*): **Каки́е у вас бутербро́ды?** (See Unit 4 to revise **како́й**.)
9 **Рестора́н закры́т.**
10 No, you can only use short form adjectives in simple statements where the word order is *X is Y*. So, if you're saying *the restaurant is new,* you could say **рестора́н нов,** but if you want to say *I prefer the new restaurant*, you'll need to use the long form: **Я предпочита́ю но́вый рестора́н.**

## Unit 9

**Questions 1** a *f* b *t* c *f* d *f* e *t* **2** a В по́лночь b В семь часо́в c Она́ говори́т, что э́то краси́вый го́род d Потому́, что тепло́ и прия́тно e У неё биле́т в оди́н коне́ц и обра́тный биле́т
**Practice 9.1** a Шесть часо́в b Два часа́ c Полшесто́го d Без двадцати́ де́вять e Де́сять мину́т оди́ннадцатого f Че́тверть девя́того **9.2** b В шесть часо́в ве́чера c В полови́не девя́того/полдевя́того утра́ d в полови́не двена́дцатого/полдвена́дцатого ве́чера **9.3** a Ско́лько сто́ит биле́т в Я́лту? b Да́йте пожа́луйста, два биле́та в Я́лту c Вот пятьсо́т рубле́й d Извини́те, у меня́ нет ме́лочи e Во ско́лько идёт/отхо́дит по́езд? f От како́й платфо́рмы отхо́дит по́езд? **9.4** a Business, tourism, transit b Sleepers c Europe and Asia d Have a pleasant journey **Comprehension**
**1 1** c **2** c **3** b **4** b **2** a A large red letter 'M' b Because it is well organized, quick, convenient, trains run quickly and frequently. c Between 90 seconds and 10 minutes (average time 2.5 minutes).

## Test Yourself (Unit 9)

**1** Genitive: **всего́ хоро́шего,** because the verb **жела́ть** must be followed by the genitive case, and even though you don't actually say *I wish* (**я жела́ю**), the rule still applies.

**2** The stem is **бу́д-** and the first and second persons are **я бу́ду, ты бу́дешь.** If you know these three points, then it's easy to remember the rest of the future of the verb *to be*.

**3** **Остано́вка** means *stop* and **переса́дка** means *change*. Did you notice the genitive plural of these words in the Conversation section? **Че́рез шесть остано́вок** (*after six stops*) and **без переса́док** (*without changes*). (To revise the way the genitive plural is formed, see Unit 7.)

**4** Accusative, because when you ask for a ticket to a place, you are dealing with direction, not position (i.e. you're not already in Novosibirsk, but you want to get there).

**5** You would need to add the word **у́тра** (literally *of the morning*) – i.e. the genitive case of **у́тро** (*morning*).

**6** **Снача́ла** means *at first, first* and **пото́м** means *then, next*.

**7** You would be asking: *What time is it?*

**8** We need to form the present tense from the first infinitive, because we are dealing with a habit (and not one occasion, one direction).

**9** Tomorrow evening; remember that lots of time phrases involve the use of the instrumental case (see part 2 of the Grammar section).

**10** **Потому́ что** – *because* (**почему́?** means *why?* – see Unit 7).

## Unit 10

**Questions 1** **a** *f* **b** *t* **c** *f* **d** *f* **e** *t* **2 a** сцена́ристом **b** рабо́тает до́ма, пи́шет сцена́рии **c** на маши́не **d** ра́но у́тром **e** сиди́т до́ма, слу́шает ра́дио, смо́трит телеви́зор, чита́ет интере́сную кни́гу **Practice 10.1** **b** чёрную ю́бку **c** деревя́нный стул **d** интере́сную кни́гу **e** ру́сский журна́л **f** но́вую ка́рту **10.2 a** Italian **b** Russian, Maths, English **10.3** живёт/рабо́тает/говори́т/хо́дит/мо́жет/ лю́бит/игра́ет/пи́шет/пла́вает/гуля́ет **10.4 a** Я встаю́ в семь часо́в

у́тра  **b** На трамва́е  **c** Я начина́ю рабо́тать в де́вять часо́в у́тра
**d** Часо́в де́вять  **Comprehension 1**  **1** c  **2** d  **3** b  **4** d  **2** **a** radio
and television programmes, cinema, theatre, reading, sport,
tourism  **b** a multitude of different ones  **c** they have sections
entitled 'crosswords, humour, chess'  **d** everywhere – home, park,
school  **e** CIS, Germany, Canada, Mexico, France, USA

## Unit 11

**Questions 1**  **a** *f*  **b** *f*  **c** *t*  **d** *f*  **2** **a** Потому́, что там бу́дут грибы́
**b** На авто́бусе  **c** В метро́  **d** В семь часо́в  **Practice 11.1**
**a** бу́дет игра́ть  **b** напишу́  **c** бу́ду де́лать  **d** позвоню́  **e** бу́дут
обе́дать  **11.2** **a** Хо́лодно, идёт снег  **b** Тепло́/жа́рко, све́тит
со́лнце  **c** Идёт дождь  **d** Ве́тер ду́ет  **11.3** **b** Серёжа живёт в
Арха́нгельске, о́чень далеко́ от Москвы́. Сего́дня идёт снег, о́чень
хо́лодно́  **c** Еле́на живёт в Ки́еве, далеко́ от Москвы́. Сего́дня тума́н,
тепло́  **d** Ю́рий живёт в Ташке́нте, о́чень далеко́ от Москвы́.
Сего́дня све́тит со́лнце, ду́шно  **e** Га́ля живёт в Екатерпнбу́ріе,
далеко́ от Москвы́. Сего́дня ду́ет ве́тер, па́смурно  **11.4**
**a** Спаси́бо, я не могу́, потому́ что сего́дня ве́чером мне на́до
(бу́дет) рабо́тать  **b** Извини́те, за́втра я пое́ду/пойду́ к О́льге
**c** Спаси́бо, а сего́дня о́чень хо́лодно. Е́сли в четве́рг бу́дет хо́лодно,
я не о́чень хочу́ смотре́ть хокке́йный матч  **d** Ла́дно, я позвоню́
вам в сре́ду часо́в в во́семь  **e** Не зна́ю, э́то зави́сит от пого́ды
**11.5** **a** News  **b** Documentary film 'Suzdal'  **c** Tennis at 18.30
on Tuesday and hockey at 19.15 on Thursday  **d** 'Hello, music',
'Musical kiosk' and 'Musical telephone'  **e** Monday, 20.15,
Spanish, and Tuesday, 19.30, Italian  **Comprehension 1**
**1** c  **2** b  **3** d  **4** c  **2** **a** no rain at the beginning of the week, then
showers and thunderstorms  **b** water will be at 16–18 degrees
**c** St Petersburg  **d** Central Asia  **e** in forests of Central Asia
**f** Northern Urals  **g** St Petersburg

## Test yourself (Unit 11)

**1** Definitely your fur hat, because **моро́з** means *frost* and so
**три́дцать гра́дусов моро́за** means −30°.

**2** The dative case is needed for the person you will ring and **в** + accusative when you ring a place (to remind yourself of the dative case for *you* and other personal pronouns, see Unit 6).

**3** You would say **Вы хоти́те/ты хо́чешь пойти́ со мной?** See exercise 11.4.

**4** **Кака́я сего́дня пого́да?** See Unit 4 if you're not sure about **како́й** (meaning *which, what sort of, what a*).

**5** **Каки́е у вас/тебя́ пла́ны на вто́рник?** (See Unit 10 for days of the week.)

**6** Because it means *I will always do my shopping here* and indicates a repeated action in the future.

**7** **Э́то зави́сит от А́нны** – i.e. the genitive case after **от** (see Unit 5, Grammar section 3).

**8** Use **за́втра** instead of **сего́дня** and insert the word **бу́дет**: **За́втра мо́жно бу́дет смотре́ть телеви́зор.**

**9** When you want to say *let's* (and remember it is always followed by a verb in the simple future).

**10** Going for a stroll, because **за́ го́родом** means *in the country* (literally *beyond the town*).

## Unit 12

**Questions 1** a *t* b *f* c *f* d *t*  **2** a Нет, она́ хо́чет позвони́ть И́ре
b А́нне/Ей о́чень понра́вилась пое́здка c Послеза́втра d У вхо́да
в Большо́й теа́тр  **Practice 12.1**  **1** d **2** a **3** e **4** c **5** b
**12.2** a игра́л b написа́ла c де́лала d смотре́ли, позвони́л
e прочита́ла, пообе́дала  **12.3** marketing/management
**12.4** b Вчера́ я позвони́л(а) И́ре. Мы говори́ли о пое́здке в Се́ргиев
Поса́д c Вчера́ я позвони́л(а) Макси́му. Мы говори́ли о францу́зском
фи́льме d Вчера́ я позвони́л(а) А́лле. Мы говори́ли о но́вом уче́бнике
e Вчера́ я позвони́л(а) Воло́де. Мы говори́ли о плохо́й пого́де
**12.5** a В 7 часо́в b На ку́хне c Она́ рабо́тала в библиоте́ке 2 часа́
d В буфе́те e Она́ пригото́вила у́жин, написа́ла письмо́ и смотре́ла
телеви́зор f Вчера́ Вади́м был о́чень за́нят. Он встал полшесто́го
у́тра и поза́втракал на ку́хне. У́тром он рабо́тал на заво́де пять

часóв, потóм он пообéдал в рестора́не. Пóсле обéда он рабóтал на заводе три часа́. Вéчером он игра́л в футбóл, смотрéл телеви́зор и чита́л газéту  **Comprehension 1**  **1** b **2** c **3** c  **2** **a** Live without their mobile phones **b** life without mobile phones **c** their personal and social life **d** about three hours **f** mobile shopping and texting

## Unit 13

**Questions 1**  **a** t **b** f **c** f **d** t  **2** **a** нева́жно **b** Гóрло и голова́ **c** чéрез дежу́рную **d** Сéргиев Поса́д  **Practice 13.1**  **b** Óле хóлодно **c** Серёже плóхо **d** Ви́ктору ску́чно  **13.2** **a** У меня́ боли́т голова́ **b** У меня́ боли́т гóрло **c** У меня́ боля́т ру́ки **d** У меня́ боли́т живóт **e** У меня́ боли́т спина́  **13.3** **a** Здра́вствуйте, дóктор. У меня́ боли́т гóрло **b** Я ду́маю/мне ка́жется, что у меня́ высóкая температу́ра **c** Что мне дéлать? **d** Когда́ мне принима́ть табле́тки?  **13.4** **b** Врач рекоменду́ет мне лежа́ть в посте́ли **c** Врач рекоменду́ет мне не пить вóдку **d** Врач рекоменду́ет мне пить чай с лимóном  **13.5** **1** c **2** b **3** c **4** b  **13.6** **b** У Та́ни/нога́ боли́т/она́ должна́/ей нельзя́ **c** У вас/боли́т спина́/вы должны́/вам нельзя́ **d** У А́ллы/боли́т гóрло/она́ должна́/ей нельзя́ **e** У негó/боли́т глаз/он дóлжен/ему́ нельзя́  **Comprehension 1**  **a** f **b** f **c** t **d** t **e** f **f** t  **2** **a** health **b** children **c** diabetes **d** not all are free **e** looking for fruit and vegetables **f** eat

## Test Yourself (Unit 13)

1 Мне хóлодно.

2 Нé за что.

3 У меня́ боли́т голова́.

4 Я интересу́юсь ру́сской литерату́рой.

5 Я жа́луюсь на ску́чную экску́рсию.

6 It is in the plural to agree with *tablets*.

7 нельзя́ (see Unit 6).

8 Мне чай с лимóном, пожа́луйста.

9 *Don't worry.*

10 Мне лу́чше.

## Unit 14

**Questions 1** a *f* b *f* c *t* d *t* e *f* **2** a Недалеко́ от ста́нции метро́ Академи́ческая **b** Потому́ что я́рко-кра́сный сви́тер мал **c** Потому́ что чёрный сви́тер ей о́чень идёт **d** Я́ркие, весёлые цвета́ **e** Чёрный **Practice 14.1** a ничего́ не **b** никого́ не **c** нигде́ не **d** никогда́ не **e** никуда́ не **14.2** a Извини́те, пожа́луйста, у вас есть мехов́ые ша́пки? **b** Покажи́те, пожа́луйста, э́ту ша́пку … вон там, нале́во **c** Мо́жно её приме́рить? **d** Я ду́маю/мне ка́жется, что она́ мне велика́ **e** Пожа́луйста, да **f** Да, вы пра́вы. Я возьму́ э́ту ша́пку **14.3** a two **b** two – men's and children's **c** Kievskaya **d** three **14.4** 1 c 2 a 3 e 4 d 5 b **14.5** b чёрную ю́бку/краси́вее/кра́сной ю́бки **c** зелёный сви́тер/деше́вле/чёрного сви́тера **d** кра́сное пла́тье/я́рче/се́рого пла́тья **e** но́вый га́лстук/веселе́е/ста́рого га́лстука **14.6** a Чита́ть рома́ны **b** романти́ческие **c** биогра́фию **d** в кни́жном магази́не **Comprehension 1** 1 d 2 c 3 b 4 c **2** a father and son **b** Moscow Textiles Institute **c** Japan, Australia, India **d** classical (English) suit **e** music and painting **f** teacher and constant example

## Test Yourself (Unit 14)

1 **Мо́жно её приме́рить?**
2 **Се́рый костю́м.** Russian has different words for *brown* and *grey*, depending on what is being described: **седо́й** for grey hair (otherwise use **се́рый**); **ка́рий** for brown eyes (otherwise **кори́чневый**).
3 **не.**
4 **бо́лее.**
5 The dative case (see Unit 13): **Тебе́ лу́чше, А́нна?**
6 **Кра́сная руба́шка мне идёт?**
7 To take the green shirt.
8 **Я возьму́ её** (notice **её** – the accusative of **она** and referring to the shirt).
9 **Я уве́рен, что ты прав.**
10 **Я никогда́ ничего́ не понима́ю** (literally: *I never nothing don't understand*).

## Unit 15

**Questions 1**  a *t*  b *f*  c *f*  d *t*  e *t*   **2** а потому́ что он лю́бит спорт  **b** за Воло́дю  **c** три́дцать семь лет  **d** в Ки́еве, на Украи́не  **e** э́то междунаро́дный же́нский день   **Practice 15.1**   **1** e  **2** d  **3** g  **4** f  **5** b  **6** a  **7** c   **15.2** а New Year  **b** Birthday   **15.3** Оле́г Петро́вич Быко́в ру́сский, роди́лся в Я́лте 12-ого апре́ля 1972-ого го́да. Оле́г живёт в Краснода́ре, где он рабо́тает учи́телем.  **15.4** а больши́х рестора́нах  **b** кни́га о спортсме́нах  **c** иностра́нным тури́стам  **d** ру́сских музе́ях  **e** све́жего молока́  **f** но́вых кварти́рах   **15.5** а Моя́ фами́лия Бра́ун  **b** Я англича́нин/ англича́нка  **c** Я роди́лся/родила́сь двена́дцатого апре́ля ты́сяча девятьсо́т шестьдеся́т восьмо́го го́да  **d** Я роди́лся/ родила́сь в Ли́дсе, на се́вере А́нглии  **e** Я рабо́таю журнали́стом/ журнали́сткой   **15.6** прихо́дит/выхо́дит/подхо́дит/схо́дит/ перехо́дит/ вхо́дит/прохо́дит/вхо́дит   **Comprehension 1**  **1** седьмо́го а́вгуста  **2** Оле́г  **3** ду́хи и́ли кассе́ты  **4** он хорошо́ игра́ет на гита́ре   **2** а tree  **b** kind old man with white beard, in white fur coat, with sack of presents  **c** granddaughter, the Snow Maiden  **d** to the old year (year that has just finished)  **e** happiness, health, success

## Test Yourself (Unit 15)

**1** Remember that in Russian **что** must be used – i.e. you must say *I hope* ***that*** *you are feeling better.*

**2** Masculine.

**3** The stress moves to the end of the word: **в октябре́**.

**4** **Како́го числа́?** Note that this is in the genitive case.

**5** **из.**

**6** **в.**

**7** **Впя́тницу** (в + accusative singular) means *on Friday* (a specific day) and **по пя́тницам** (по + dative plural) is a generalization (*on Fridays*) – see Unit 10.

**8** **Кем вы рабо́таете?** (Literally *as whom do you work?*) See exercise 15.5 and Unit 8).

**9** **Я предлага́ю тост за Ви́ктора** (note that **Ви́ктора** is in the animate accusative – see Unit 5).

**10** **в лу́чших рестора́нах** (prepositional plural).

## Unit 16

**Questions 1** a *f* b *t* c *f* d *t* e *f* f *t*  **2** a В четвёрг b Óпера «Отéлло» c В Центрáльном теáтре кýкал d Он дýмает, что бы́ло бы скýчно e Когдá он достáнет билéты  **Practice 16.1** a котóрый b котóрой c котóром d котóрого e котóрыми f котóрую  **16.2** a November b 13th c Dostoevsky d 19.00  **16.3** b [e.g.] Éсли бы у меня́ бы́ло мнóго дéнег, я купи́ла бы нóвую маши́ну c [e.g.] Éсли бы я плóхо себя́ чýвствовал(а), я пошёл (пошлá) бы в поликли́нику d [e.g.] Éсли бы я потеря́л(а) собáку, я позвони́л(а) бы в полицéйский учáсток  **16.4** a – Что вы лю́бите бóльше, спорт, мýзыку и́ли живопи́сь? – Бóльше всегó я люблю́ мýзыку b – Что вы лю́бите бóльше, теáтр, кинó и́ли цирк? – Бóльше всегó я люблю́ кинó c – Что вы лю́бите бóльше, óперу, балéт и́ли футбóл? – Бóльше всегó я люблю́ óперу  **16.5** b Ви́ктор не óчень энерги́чный человéк. Он гимнáст. Бы́ло бы лýчше, éсли бы он рабóтал администрáтором c Вади́м твóрческий человéк. Он шофёр. Бы́ло бы лýчше, éсли бы он рабóтал журнали́стом d Натáша дóбрый, энерги́чный человéк. Онá телефони́стка. Былó бы лýчше, éсли бы онá рабóтала медсестрóй e Ми́ша óчень серьёзный человéк. Он футболи́ст. Бы́ло бы лýчше, éсли бы он рабóтал адвокáтом  **16.6** 1 d 2 c 3 a 4 e 5 b  **Comprehension 1** 1 d 2 b 3 a  **2** a P.I. Tchaikovsky born b 53 c 9 years d 100,000 e first entry in visitors' book dates from then f everything just as it was in his lifetime g on Tchaikovsky's birthday and anniversary of his death

## Unit 17

**Questions 1** a *t* b *f* c *f* d *t* e *f*  **2** a Немнóжко лýчше b Ей нýжно отдохнýть c И́ра d Сóчи – лýчший курóрт, éсли хóчешь и отдохнýть, и вы́лечиться e Зáвтра ýтром  **Practice 17.1** 1 b 2 d 3 e 4 a 5 c  **17.2** a Hotels b in the mountains c Egypt, Thailand, Turkey, Israel, Scandinavia  **17.3** b Э́то оди́н из сáмых прия́тных курóртов в странé c Э́то óди́н из сáмых бы́стрых пóездов в странé d Э́то оди́н из сáмых мя́гких кли́матов в странé e Э́то однá из сáмых интерéсных прогрáмм в странé f Э́то одио из сáмых краси́вых зданиn в странé  **17.4** a Здрáвствуйте. Есть свобóдные номерá? b Я хочý заказáть нóмер, пожáлуйста c Нóмер

на одного с ду́шем, с телефо́ном и с телеви́зором, пожа́луйста
**d** На пять дней, до пя́тницы  **e** Спаси́бо. Где мо́жно взять
ключ?   **17.5 b** На́де не́когда смотре́ть телеви́зор  **c** Ва́ле не́чем
писа́ть письмо́  **d** Бори́су не́куда идти́ сего́дня ве́чером  **e** Мари́не
не́где рабо́тать  **f** И́горю не́ на что жа́ловаться  **g** Со́не не́кому
подари́ть кассе́ту  **Comprehension 1**  **1** c  **2** c  **3** b   **2 a** plane/
ship/train/bus/car  **b** to arts festivals/rest and treatment/
business trips/river and sea cruises  **c** Moscow  **d** Estonian  **e** 5–7
days  **f** tennis/windsurfing/sailing/fishing/volleyball/basketball/table
tennis/mountain hikes

## Test Yourself (Unit 17)

1 **Како́й,** because it is a word used for asking questions; **кото́рый**
   is a word which makes a link in a sentence, giving further
   information (see Unit 16).
2 **Нигде́,** because you are using it with a verb in the present tense
   (see Grammar section 3, Unit 17).
3 **Да́йте, пожа́луйста, полоте́нце (у меня́ в но́мере нет полоте́нца).**
4 You would use **куда́,** because your question is about direction,
   not position (see Unit 3).
5 The third floor. Literally, **на четвёртом этаже́** means *on the
   fourth floor,* but remember that in Russian the first floor
   (**пе́рвый эта́ж**) is the ground floor.
6 **На са́мом краси́вом куро́рте.** See Grammar section 1 above for
   the superlative, and Unit 12 for prepositional singular adjective
   endings.
7 *Don't worry!* (from the verb **беспоко́иться/по-**).
8 Because lunch is starting itself (it doesn't have an object – see
   Grammar section 2 above).
9 **В на́ших но́вых гости́ницах.** See Unit 15 for prepositional
   plural endings.
10 **Я хоте́л/хоте́ла бы заказа́ть но́мер, пожа́луйста.**

## Unit 18

**Questions 1**  **a** *t*  **b** *f*  **c** *f*  **d** *f*  **e** *t*   **2 a** Ужа́сно  **b** Чай (чайку́)
**c** Она́ переходи́ла че́рез у́лицу  **d** В больни́цу  **e** Он в состоя́нии
шо́ка   **Practice 18.1**  **1** d  **2** a  **3** f  **4** e  **5** b  **6** c   **18.2 b** Свиде́тель

сказа́л, что э́то бы́ло часа́ в четы́ре  **c** Свиде́тель сказа́л, что он ви́дел
грузови́к и ста́рую же́нщину  **d** Свиде́тель сказа́л, что он подбежа́л
к ней  **e** Свиде́тель сказа́л, что он не о́чень хорошо́ себя́ чу́вствует
**f** Свиде́тель сказа́л, что он не хо́чет пое́хать в медпу́нкт  **18.3**
**a** Hotel Mozhaiskaya  **b** Camera, £30 sterling and 5,000 roubles
**c** Her room  **d** 28 March 2009  **18.4 a** Вы ужа́сно вы́глядите!
**b** Что с ва́ми?  **c** Что случи́лось?  **d** Э́то ужа́сно. Сади́тесь  **e** Хоти́те
чай/ча́йку?  **f** Не́ за что/Пожа́луйста  **18.5** прие́хала/перее́хала/
вы́ехали/прое́хали/подъе́хало  **18.6 1** b  **2** d  **3** a  **4** e  **5** c  **18.7**
**a** Часо́в в де́сять  **b** В два часа́  **c** Он ходи́л в кинотеа́тр с Ле́ной
**d** Полоди́ннадцатого  **Comprehension 1  a** кинотеа́тре  **b** бюро́
нахо́док  **c** 5 часо́в  **d** чёрная  **2  a** Emperor, general, diplomat
and shipbuilder  **b** Moscow  **c** Peter conquered the troops of the
Swedish king  **d** As the new capital of Russia and a 'window on
Europe'  **e** Exhibits include his personal things  **f** Worst flood in
Petersburg's history

## Test Yourself (Unit 18)

**1** You would use the infinitive: **что́бы заплати́ть**

**2** **Что с ва́ми?** (**Что случи́лось?** means *What has happened?*)

**3** The future, because what the person said at the time was *I will
ring you.*

**4** **Мы шли по у́лице,** because the sentence is describing the action
in progress on a specific occasion and in a specific direction
(see Unit 12).

**5** **Я то́лько что купи́л(а)биле́ты.**

**6** **пере** (**Мы перее́хали че́рез мост**).

**7** **же.**

**8** See Unit 16 to revise the conditional – the missing word for
both blanks is **бы.**

**9** You've left (forgotten) them in the taxi (**забыва́ть/забы́ть**).

**10** **Часо́в в де́сять.**

## Unit 19

**Questions 1**  **a** *f*  **b** *t*  **c** *t*  **d** *f*  **e** *t*  **2 a** Сего́дня  **b** Перево́дчицей
**c** В Санкт-Петербу́рге  **d** В Пари́ж  **e** Духи́

**Practice**

**19.1 a** Шмелёву, Б.Н.
Улица Зацепа, д.20, кв.57,
Санкт-Петербург 109262
Россия

**b** Плотниковой, М.А.
Воронеж 394001
Рябиновая улица, д.21, кв.76
Россия

**c** Соколовскому, Ф.И.
Минская улица, д.62, кв.15,
Москва 117552
Россия

**19.2 a** Every year **b** Best publication about tourism in Russia
**c** Foreign writers **d** Tourist journey, sights, nature, historical
and cultural monuments of Russia, meetings with Russian
people, tours, excursions, national cuisine and modern life of
Russia **19.3 b** Я не знаю, сказала ли Нина, что она поедет в
Париж **c** Я не знаю, приедет ли Борис сегодня **d** Я не знаю,
любит ли Вадим смотреть телевизор **e** Я не знаю, прочитала
ли Валя всю книгу **f** Я не знаю, подписал ли директор
договор **19.4 a** В Новосибирске **b** Нет, у неё нет сестры. У
неё брат **c** Её мужа зовут Николай **d** Она старается писать раз
в неделю **e** Потому что она так занята **19.5 a** Он работает
психологом **b** В конце июня – начале июля **c** Не позднее 1 августа/
до 1 августа **Comprehension 1** **1** d **2** b **3** b **4** c **2 a** That his
holiday went well **b** 48 working days/8 weeks **c** Travel **d** Very
tired **e** To her relations' 'dacha'/summer flat/holiday home
**f** During the day it was up to 35 degrees **g** Wonderful! – mild
climate, warm sea, good conditions for a holiday

# Unit 20

**Questions 1** **a** *f* **b** *f* **c** *t* **d** *t* **e** *f* **2 a** Тост за своих русских
друзей **b** Очень, всё удивительно интересно **c** За всё. За билеты
в театр, за поездку за город **d** Красивый платок **e** Она получает
русскую балалайку **Practice 20.1** **1** d **2** a **3** e **4** b **5** c

**20.2 a** Clothes, souvenirs, children's goods, food **b** Sheremetevo airport departure lounge **c** Winter **20.3** e.g.:

---

*Дорогой Анатолий!*
*Спасибо вам большое за*
*билеты в театр: мне очень*
*понравился балет*
*«Снегурочка». Сласибо за*
*поездку за город. Спасибо*
*тоже за экскурсию в дом*
*музей Чайковского и обед в*
*ресторане «Колобок». Всё*
*было очень интересно.*
*Всего хорошего*

Губанову, А.П.
Первомайская ул., д.45, кв.29
105554 Москва
Россия

---

**20.4 a** Room number, surname, date of departure, name of things, signature, date **b** Every day before 11 a.m. **c** Leave it on the table **20.5 a** В Сиби́ри, на восто́ке страны́ **b** Потому́ что её муж у́мер де́сять лет наза́д **c** Сын, неве́стка и два вну́ка **d** Пётр (Пе́тя) и Андре́й (Андрю́ша) **e** Пе́тя игра́ет на скри́пке, а Андрю́ша игра́ет в футбо́л **20.6 a** Я интересу́юсь ру́сской му́зыкой **b** Да, иногда́ я игра́ю в те́ннис ле́том **c** Я де́лаю поку́пки, рабо́таю в саду́, иногда́ хожу́ в кинотеа́тр **d** За́втра. Самолёт вылета́ет в 10 часо́в утра́ **Comprehension 1 a** *f* **b** *t* **c** *f* **d** *t* **e** *f* **2 a** In St Petersburg on Kuznechnyi Lane **b** 2 – Fedya and Lyuba (son and daughter) **c** As having 6 rooms and situated on second (i.e. first) floor **d** Read to his children **e** Newspapers, boxes of cigarettes, letters, books **f** To reorganize it according to the laws of nature, truth, good and beauty

# Russian–English vocabulary

а  *and, but*
ава́рия  *accident*
а́вгуст  *August*
авто́бус  *bus, coach*
автомоби́ль (m.)  *car*
адвока́т  *solicitor*
англи́йский  *English*
англича́нин (pl. англича́не)
  *Englishman*
англича́нка  *Englishwoman*
А́нглия  *England*
антра́кт  *interval*
апре́ль (m.)  *April*
апте́ка  *chemist's shop*

бага́ж  *luggage*
бассе́йн  *swimming pool*
бе́гать/бежа́ть (бегу́, бежи́шь,
  бегу́т)/побежа́ть  *to run*
бе́дный  *poor*
без (+ gen.)  *without*
бе́лый  *white*
бензи́н  *petrol*
бе́рег (pl. берега́)  *bank, shore*
беспла́тный  *free, at no*
  *charge*
беспоко́иться/
  побеспоко́иться  *to worry, be*
  *anxious*
биле́т  *ticket*
благодари́ть/поблагодари́ть
  (за + acc.)  *to thank (for)*
благода́рный  *grateful*
бланк  *form*

ближа́йший  *closest*
бли́зкий  *near*
блины́  *pancakes*
бога́тый  *rich*
боль (f.)  *pain*
больни́ца  *hospital*
больно́й  *ill*
бо́льше всего́  *most of all*
большо́й  *big*
борода́  *beard*
брат (pl. бра́тья)  *brother*
брать (беру́, берёшь)/взять
  (возьму́, возьмёшь)  *to take*
брю́ки (f.)  *trousers*
бу́дущий (adj.)  *future*
буты́лка  *bottle*
бы́стрый  *quick*
бюро́ (indeclinable)  *office*
бюро́ нахо́док  *lost property*
  *office*

в (+ acc.)  *to, into*
в (+ prep.)  *in, at*
ва́жный  *important*
ва́нная  *bathroom*
ваш  *your*
вдруг  *suddenly*
ведь  *you realize/know, after*
  *all, indeed*
везде́  *everywhere*
век  *century*
вели́кий  *great*
велосипе́д  *bicycle*
вертолёт  *helicopter*

весёлый *cheerful*
весна *spring*
весь, вся, всё, все *all*
ве́тер (fleeting e) *wind*
ве́чер (pl. вечера́) *evening, party*
вещь (f.) *thing*
взро́слый *adult*
вид *view, type*
ви́деть/уви́деть *to see*
вино́ *wine*
вку́сный *tasty, delicious*
вме́сте *together*
вме́сто (+ gen.) *instead of*
внизу́ *downstairs/below, down below*
внима́тельный *careful, attentive*
внук/вну́чка *grandson/daughter*
во́время *on time*
вода́ *water*
води́ть/вести́ (веду́, ведёшь)/ повести́ *to lead, take (on foot)*
возвраща́ться)/верну́ться (верну́сь, вернёшься *to return*
во́здух *air*
вози́ть/везти́ (везу́, везёшь)/ повезти́ *to transport, take (by transport)*
возмо́жность (f.) *opportunity, possibility*
война́ *war*
вокза́л *(railway) station*
волнова́ться/взволнова́ться *to be agitated, upset, worried*
во́лосы (gen. pl. воло́с) *hair*
воскресе́нье *Sunday*

восто́к *east*
вот *here/there is/are*
врач *doctor*
вре́мя (n., pl. времена́) *time*
всегда́ *always*
всего́ *in all, only*
всё *everything*
вспомина́ть/вспо́мнить *to recollect, reminisce, remember*
встава́ть/встать (вста́ну, вста́нешь) *to get up*
встре́ча *meeting*
встреча́ть/встре́тить *to meet*
встреча́ться/встре́титься *to meet one another*
вто́рник *Tuesday*
вход *entrance*
входи́ть/войти́ *to enter*
вчера́ *yesterday*
вы *you* (pl. or polite form sing.)
вы́глядеть (+ instr). *to look (e.g. smart)*
высо́кий *tall, high*
выходи́ть/вы́йти *to go out*
выходно́й день *day off*

га́лстук *tie*
где *where*
гла́вный *main*
глаз (pl. глаза́) *eye*
глу́пый *stupid*
говори́ть/сказа́ть *to speak, talk, say*
год *year*
голова́ *head*
голубо́й *light blue*
гора́ *mountain*

го́рло  *throat*
го́род (pl. города́)  *town*
горя́чий  *hot (to the touch)*
гости́ная  *sitting room*
гости́ница  *hotel*
гость (m.)/го́стья  *guest/female guest*
гото́вить/пригото́вить  *to prepare*
гра́дус  *degree* (of temperature)
грипп  *flu*
гроза́  *(thunder)storm*
гру́ппа  *group*
гуля́ть/погуля́ть  *to stroll*

да  *yes*
дава́й[те]  *let's*
дава́ть/дать (дам, дашь, даст, дади́м, дади́те, даду́т)  *to give*
да́же  *even*
далеко́  *far, a long way*
дари́ть/подари́ть  *to give as a present*
дверь (f.)  *door*
дворе́ц  *palace*
де́вушка  *girl*
действи́тельный  *real, actual*
дека́брь (m.)  *December*
деклара́ция  *currency declaration*
де́лать/сде́лать  *to do, make*
де́ло  *matter, affair*
делово́й  *business* (adj.), *businesslike*
день (m.; fleeting e)  *day*
день рожде́ния  *birthday*
де́ньги (pl., gen. де́нег)  *money*
дере́вня  *village, countryside*

де́ти  *children*
дешёвый  *cheap*
дли́нный  *long*
дли́тельный  *long, lengthy*
для (+ gen.)  *for*
до (+ gen.)  *before, as far as, until*
до свида́ния  *goodbye*
до́брый  *good, kind*
дово́льно  *enough, quite*
дово́льный  *content, satisfied*
догово́р  *agreement, contract*
договори́лись  *agreed*
доезжа́ть/дое́хать  *to reach, travel as far as*
дождь (m.)  *rain*
до́лго  *for a long time*
до́лжен, должна́, etc.  *must, have to, duty-bound*
дом (pl. дома́)  *house, home*
дома́шний  *domestic*
доро́га  *road, way, journey*
дорого́й  *dear, expensive*
достава́ть/доста́ть (доста́ну, доста́нешь)  *to get, obtain*
достопримеча́тельность (f.)  *sight (e.g. tourist sights)*
дочь (f., pl. до́чери)  *daughter*
друг (pl. друзья́)  *friend*
ду́мать/поду́мать  *to think*
дуть/поду́ть  *to blow*
духи́ (m. pl.)  *perfume*
душ  *shower*
ду́шный  *suffocatingly hot*
дя́дя  *uncle*

еди́ный (биле́т)  *all in one (ticket)*

ежего́дный  *annual*

ежедне́вный  *daily*

е́здить/е́хать (е́ду, е́дешь)/
  пое́хать  *to go (by transport),
  to travel*

ёлка  *fir/Christmas tree*

е́сли  *if*

есть  *there is/are*

есть (ем, ешь, ест, еди́м, еди́те,
  едя́т)/съесть  *to eat*

ещё  *still, again, more*

жа́ловаться/пожа́ловаться (на +
  acc.)  *to complain (about)*

жа́ркий  *hot*

ждать (жду, ждёшь, ждут)/
  подожда́ть  *to wait for*

жела́ть/пожела́ть
  (+ genitive)  *to wish*

жёлтый  *yellow*

жена́  *wife*

же́нщина  *woman*

жи́вопись (f.)  *painting*

живо́т  *stomach*

жизнь (f.)  *life*

жить  *to live*

журна́л  *magazine*

за (+ instr.)  *behind, beyond*

заболева́ть/заболе́ть  *to be/
  fall ill*

забыва́ть/забы́ть  *to forget, to
  leave*

зави́сеть от (+ gen.)  *to depend
  on*

заво́д  *factory*

за́втра  *tomorrow*

за́втракать/поза́втракать  *to
  have breakfast*

загля́дывать/загляну́ть  *to
  glance, to drop in*

зака́зывать/заказа́ть  *to order,
  book, reserve*

закрыва́ть(ся)/закры́ть (ся)
  (закро́ю [сь], закро́ешь [ся])
  *to close*

замеча́тельный  *splendid*

занима́ть(ся)/заня́ть (ся)
  (займу́ [сь], займёшьъ [ся])
  *to occupy (be occupied)*

заня́тие  *occupation, activity*

за́нятый  *busy, occupied,
  engaged*

за́пад  *west*

заполня́ть/запо́лнить  *to fill in*

запреща́ть/запрети́ть  *to
  forbid*

зато́  *on the other hand*

заходи́ть/зайти́  *to pop in*

звать/позъа́ть, назъа́ть
  *to call*

звони́ть/позвони́ть  *to ring,
  telephone*

зда́ние  *building*

здесь  *here*

здоро́вье  *health*

здоро́вый  *healthy* (short
  form – *well*)

здра́вствуйте  *hello*

зелёный  *green*

зима́  *winter*

знако́миться/
  познако́миться  *to meet*

знать  *to know*

значит *that means, so*
зонтик *umbrella*
зуб *tooth*
зубной врач *dentist*

играть/сыграть *to play*
игрушка *toy*
из (+ gen.) *from (out of)*
известный *famous*
извинять/извинить *to excuse*
изучать/изучить *to study, learn*
или *or*
именно *namely, precisely*
имя (n., pl. имена) *(first) name*
иногда *sometimes*
иностранный *foreign*
интересный *interesting*
интересоваться/
  заинтересоваться (за +
  instr.) *to be interested (in)*
искать (ищу, ищешь) *to look
  for*
испанский *Spanish*
итак *and so, so well*
итальянский *Italian*
июль (m.) *July*
июнь (m.) *June*

к (+ dat.) *towards, to the
  house of*
к сожалению *unfortunately*
к счастью *fortunately*
кабинет *office, study*
казаться/показатся
  (мне кажется) *to seem (it
  seems to me)*
как *how, as*

как будто *as if*
как жаль *what a shame/pity*
как только *as soon as*
какой *which, what sort of*
каникулы (f. pl.) *(school)
  holidays*
карий (soft adjective) *hazel,
  brown (eyes)*
картина *picture*
касса *cash desk, ticket office*
кататься на лыжах *to ski, go
  skiing*
кафе (indeclinable) *café*
каша *porridge*
кашель (m.; fleeting e) *cough*
кашлять *to (have a) cough*
квартира *flat*
кинотеатр *cinema*
коллега *colleague*
командировка *business trip*
команата *room*
конец *end, direction,
  destination*
конечно *of course*
конкурс *competition*
конфета *sweet*
кончать(ся)/кончить(ся) *to
  finish, end*
коричневый *brown*
коробка *box*
короткий *short*
костюм *suit*
кошелёк *purse*
кража *theft*
красивый *beautiful*
красный *red*
Кремль (m.) *Kremlin*

кричать/закричать (кричу,
  кричишь) *to shout*
кроме (+ gen.) *apart from,
  except*
крупный *major, large*
кто *who*
куда *(to) where*
курить/закурить *to smoke*
кухня *kitchen*

ладно OK
лёгкий *light, easy*
лежать (2nd conjugation) *to
  lie, be lying down*
лекция *lecture*
летать/лететь/полететь *to fly*
лето *summer*
личный *personal*
лошадь (f.) *horse*
лучший *better, best*
лыжи (f. pl.) *skis*
любить *to love, like*
любой *any*
люди *people*

май *May*
маленький *small*
мало (+ gen.) *little*
марка *stamp*
март *March*
маршрут *route, itinerary*
масло *butter; oil*
мать (f., pl. матери) *mother*
машина *car*
мебель (f.) *furniture*
медсестра *nurse*
между (+ instr.) *between, among*
международный *international*

мелочь (f.) *change*
место *place*
месяц *month*
метель (f.) *snowstorm*
милиционер *policeman*
милый *dear, sweet*
мимо (+ gen.) *past*
мир *world, peace*
много (+ gen.) *a lot, many*
мода *fashion*
может быть *perhaps*
можно *it is possible, one may*
молодой *young*
молоко *milk*
море *sea*
мороженое *ice cream*
мороз *frost*
морской *sea* (adj.), *marine*
москвич[ка] *Muscovite*
мост *bridge*
мочь (могу, можешь, могут;
  past tense: мог, могла)/
  смочь *to be able*
музей *museum*
мы *we*
мягкий *soft, gentle*
мясо *meat*

на (+ acc.) *to, onto, (intended)
  for*
на (+ prep.) *on, at*
набирать/набрать *to dial*
над (+ instr.) *over, on top of*
надевать/надеть (надену,
  наденешь) *to put on*
надеяться (надеюсь, надеешься
  надеются) *to hope*
надо *it is necessary*

наза́д  *ago*
назва́ние  *name*
называ́ть/назва́ть (назову́, назовёшь)  *to name, call*
наконе́ц  *finally*
напи́ток  *drink*
наприме́р  *for example*
наро́д  *people, nation*
насчёт (+ gen.)  *as regards to, concerning*
находи́ть/найти́  *to find*
находи́ться  *to be situated*
нача́ло  *beginning*
начина́ть(ся)/нача́ть(ся) (начну́, начнёшь)  *to begin*
не  *not*
неде́ля  *week*
не́который  *some, certain*
нельзя́  *it is forbidden, not possible*
нет  *no*
нетерпе́ние  *impatience*
нигде́  *nowhere* (position)
никогда́  *never*
никто́  *no one*
никуда́  *nowhere* (motion)
ничего́  *nothing, never mind*
но́вый  *new*
но́вости (f. pl.)  *news*
нога́  *leg, foot*
носи́ть  *to wear*
носи́ть/нести́ (несу́, несёшь; past tense: нёс, несла́)/ понести́  *to carry*
носо́к (fleeting o; pl. носки́)  *sock*
ночь (f.)  *night*

ноя́брь (m.)  *November*
нра́виться/понра́виться  *to please, be pleasing*

о/об (+ prep.)  *about*
обе́дать/пообе́дать  *to have lunch*
о́бувь (f.)  *footwear*
объясня́ть/объясни́ть  *to explain*
обы́чный  *usual*
обяза́тельно  *without fail, certainly*
о́вощи (m. pl.)  *vegetables*
оде́жда (sing. only)  *clothes*
одея́ло  *blanket*
одна́ко  *however*
о́зеро  *lake*
окно́ (pl. о́кна)  *window*
о́коло (+ gen.)  *near, approximately*
октя́брь (m.)  *October*
он  *he, it*
она́  *she, it*
оно́  *it*
они́  *they*
опи́сывать/описа́ть  *to describe*
опуска́ть/опусти́ть  *to drop, lower*
опя́ть  *again*
ора́нжевый (adj.)  *orange*
о́сень (f.)  *autumn*
осо́бенно  *especially*
оставля́ть/оста́вить  *to leave*
остана́вливать(ся)/ останови́ть(ся)  *to stop*
остано́вка  *(bus) stop*
от (+ gen.)  *(away) from*

от и́мени (+ gen.) *on behalf of, in the name of*

отвеча́ть/отве́тить *to answer*

о́тдых *rest, holiday*

отдыха́ть/отдохну́ть *to rest, have a holiday*

оте́ц (fleeting e) *father*

отка́зываться/отказа́ться от (+ gen.) *to refuse*

открыва́ть(ся)/откры́ть (откро́ю, откро́ешь) (ся) *to open*

откры́тка (gen. pl. откры́ток) *postcard*

отли́чный *excellent*

о́тпуск *leave*

отсю́да *from here*

отту́да *from there*

отходи́ть/отойти́ *to leave, move away from*

о́тчество *patronymic*

о́чень *very*

о́чередь (f.) *queue*

очки́ (m. pl.) *spectacles, glasses*

ошиба́ться/ошиби́ться *to be mistaken*

оши́бка *mistake*

пала́тка *tent*

па́мятник *monument*

па́мять (f.) *memory, remembrance*

па́смурный *overcast*

перево́дчик/перево́дчица *translator, interpreter*

переса́дка *change (e.g. of train)*

пе́рвый *first*

пе́ред (+ instr.) *in front of*

переда́ча *programme*

передава́ть/переда́ть *to pass, pass on*

переу́лок (fleeting o) *lane, alleyway*

переходи́ть/перейти́ *to cross*

пи́во *beer*

пиро́г *pie*

писа́ть (пишу́, пи́шешь)/написа́ть *to write*

письмо́ (pl. пи́сьма) *letter*

пить (пью, пьёшь)/вы́пить *to drink*

пла́вать/плыть (плыву́, плывёшь)/поплы́ть *to swim, sail*

пласти́нка *record*

пла́тье (gen. pl. пла́тьев) *dress*

племя́нник/племя́нница *nephew/niece*

плохо́й *bad*

по (+ dat.) *along, according to*

пого́да *weather*

под (+ instr.) *under*

пода́рок *present*

подпи́сывать/подписа́ть *to sign*

по́дпись (f.) *signature*

подтвержда́ть/подтверди́ть *to confirm*

по́езд (pl. поезда́) *train*

пое́здка *journey*

пожа́луйста *please*

по́здний *late*

пока́зывать/показа́ть *to show*

покупа́ть/купи́ть  *to buy*
пол  *floor*
по́лдень (m.)  *midday*
по́лночь (f.)  *midnight*
полови́на  *half*
полоте́нце  *towel*
получа́ть/получи́ть  *to receive*
помидо́р  *tomato*
по́мнить/вспо́мнить  *to remember*
помога́ть/помо́чь (+ dat.)  *to help*
по-мо́ему  *in my opinion*
по́мощь (f.)  *help*
понеде́льник  *Monday*
понима́ть/поня́ть (пойму́, поймёшь)  *to understand*
поня́тно  *clear, understood*
пора́ (+ infin.)  *it is time to*
поря́док (fleeting o)  *order*
поса́дка  *boarding (of train, plane, etc.)*
посети́тель (m.)  *visitor*
посеща́ть/посети́ть  *to visit*
по́сле (+ gen.)  *after*
после́дний  *last, latest*
послеза́втра  *the day after tomorrow*
посте́ль (f.)  *bed*
постоя́нный  *constant*
посыла́ть/посла́ть (пошлю́, пошлёшь)  *to send*
посы́лка  *parcel*
пото́м  *then, next, after*
потому́ что  *because*
почему́  *why*
почему́-то  *for some reason or other*

по́чта  *post office, post*
поэ́тому  *therefore*
пра́вда  *truth*
пра́вило  *rule*
пра́вильный  *correct*
пра́здник  *holiday, celebration, festive occasion*
предлага́ть/предложи́ть  *to suggest, propose*
предпочита́ть/предпоче́сть (past tense: предпочёл, предпочла́)  *to prefer*
преподава́тель (m.)  *teacher*
преподава́ть/препода́ть  *to teach*
при (+ prep.)  *at the time of, in the reign of, in the presence of*
привози́ть/привезти́  *to bring (by transport)*
приглаша́ть/пригласи́ть  *to invite*
приём  *reception*
приме́р  *example*
приме́ривать/приме́рить  *to try on*
принима́ть/приня́ть (приму́, при́мешь)  *to receive, take, accept*
приноси́ть/принести́  *to bring*
приро́да  *nature*
прихо́д  *arrival*
приходи́ть/прийти́  *to arrive, come*
прия́тный  *pleasant*
пробле́ма  *problem*
проводи́ть/провести́  *to spend (of time)*
прогно́з  *forecast*

продава́ть/прода́ть  *to sell*
продаве́ц (fleeting e)  *shop assistant (male)*
продавщи́ца  *shop assistant (female)*
производи́ть/произвести́  *to produce*
происходи́ть/произойти́  *to happen*
проси́ть/попроси́ть (+ acc.)  *to ask, request*
просто́й  *simple*
про́сьба  *request*
про́тив (+ gen.)  *against*
прохла́дный  *cool, chilly*
проходи́ть/пройти́  *to go through, past*
про́шлый  *last, past*
проща́ть/прости́ть  *to forgive, excuse*
путеше́ствие  *travel, journey*
путеше́ствовать  *to travel*
путь (m.)  *journey, way*
пя́тница  *Friday*

рабо́та  *work*
рабо́тать  *to work*
рад  *glad*
ра́ди (+ gen.)  *for the sake of*
разгово́р  *conversation*
разме́р  *size*
ра́зный  *different, various*
ра́неный  *hurt, wounded, injured*
ра́нний  *early*
ра́ньше  *earlier, formerly*
расска́зывать/рассказа́ть  *to tell, relate*

ребёнок (pl. де́ти)  *child*
результа́т  *result*
река́  *river*
рекомендова́ть/порекомендова́ть  *to recommend*
ремо́нт  *repair*
реша́ть/реши́ть  *to decide*
роди́ться  *to be born*
ро́дственник  *relative, relation*
ро́зовый  *pink*
роль (f.)  *role*
рот  *mouth*
руба́шка  *shirt*
рубль (m.)  *rouble*
рука́  *hand, arm*
ру́сский  *Russian*
ру́чка  *pen*
ры́ба  *fish*
ряд  *row, series, rank*
ря́дом с (+ instr.)  *next to*

с (+gen.)  *from, since*
с (+ instr.)  *with*
сад  *garden*
сади́ться/сесть  *to sit down, to catch* (e.g. *bus*)
самолёт  *aeroplane*
све́жий  *fresh*
свети́ть  *to shine*
све́тлый  *light*
свобо́дный  *free, vacant*
се́вер  *north*
сего́дня  *today*
седо́й  *grey (hair)*
семья́  *family*
сентя́брь (m.)  *September*

сердце *heart*
серый *grey*
сестра (pl. сёстры) *sister*
сидеть *to sit, be seated, to stay (at home)*
сильный *strong*
синий *dark blue*
скрипка *violin*
скучный *boring*
слишком *too, too much*
сложный *complicated*
случаться/случиться *to happen*
слушать/послушать *to listen to*
слышать (слышу, слышишь)/услышать *to hear*
смешной *funny, amusing*
смотреть/посмотреть *to watch, look at*
сначала *at first*
СНГ *CIS (Commonwealth of Independent States)*
снова *again*
собака *dog*
собирать/собрать *to collect, gather*
собираться/собраться *to prepare oneself, intend, assemble*
совет *advice, council*
советовать/посоветовать (+ dat.) *to advise*
совещание *meeting, conference*
современный *modern, contemporary*
совсем *quite, entirely, at all*
согласный *in agreement*

сок *(fruit) juice*
сообщать/сообщить *to communicate, announce*
состояние *condition*
спальня *bedroom*
спасибо *thank you*
спина *back*
способный *talented*
спрашивать/спросить (+ acc.) *to ask, enquire*
спустя *later, after*
среда (pl. среды) *Wednesday*
среди (+ gen.) *among*
средний *average*
срочный *urgent*
становиться/стать (стану, станешь; + instr.) *to become*
станция *station (bus or underground)*
старый *old*
стараться/постараться *to try*
столица *capital*
стоить *to cost*
стоянка *parking*
стоять *to stand*
страшный *terrible (dreadful)*
стул (pl. стулья) *chair*
суббота *Saturday*
сухой *dry*
сходить/сойти *to get off*
счёт *bill*
считать(ся) *to consider (to be considered)*
сын (pl. сыновья) *son*
сыр *cheese*

так *so*
также *also*

такой   *such a, so*
такси (n.)   *taxi*
там   *there*
телевизор   *television*
тёмный   *dark*
теплоход   *ship*
тёплый   *warm*
терять (теряю, теряешь)/
 потерять   *to lose*
тётя   *aunt*
тихий   *quiet*
то есть (т.е.)   *that is (i.e.)*
товары (m.)   *goods, wares*
тогда   *then, in that case*
тоже   *also*
только   *only*
точка   *point, full stop*
трамвай   *tram*
трудный   *difficult*
туда   *to there*
туман   *fog, mist*
турист   *tourist*
ты   *you (informal singular)*

у (+ gen.)   *by, at the house of*
уважаемый   *respected*
уважение   *respect*
уверенный   *certain, sure*
увлекаться/увлечься (+ instr.)
  *to be enthusiastic about*
угол (fleeting o)   *corner*
ударять/ударить   *to hit,
 strike*
удивительный   *surprising,
 amazing*
удобный   *comfortable,
 convenient*

удовольствие   *pleasure*
уже   *already*
ужин   *supper*
узкий   *narrow*
узнавать/узнать   *to find out,
 to recognize*
улица   *street*
улучшать/улучшить   *to
 improve*
умирать/умереть (past tense:
 умер, умерла)   *to die*
умный   *clever (intelligent)*
универмаг   *department store*
универсам   *supermarket*
уникальный   *unique*
условие   *condition*
успех   *success*
уставать/устать (устану,
 устанешь)   *to get tired*
я устал[а]   *I'm tired*
утро   *morning*
уходить/уйти   *to leave; be
 spent (of time)*
учитель (m.)   *teacher*
учительница   *teacher*

фамилия   *surname*
февраль (m.)   *February*
фотоаппарат   *camera*

хлеб   *bread*
ходить/идти (иду, идёшь; past
 tense: шёл, шла)/пойти   *to go
 (on foot), to walk*
ходьба   *walk, walking*
холодный   *cold*
хороший   *good*

хоте́ть (хочу́, хо́чешь, хо́ чет, хоти́м, хоти́те, хотя́т)/ захоте́ть  *to want*
хотя́  *although*

цвет (pl. цвета́)  *colour*
цвето́к (pl. цветы́)  *flower*
цель (f.)  *goal, aim*
це́рковь (f.; fleeting o) *church*
цирк  *circus*

час  *hour*
ча́сто  *often*
часы́ (pl.)  *watch, clock*
чей, чья, чьё, чьи  *whose*
челове́к (pl. лю́ди)  *person*
че́рез (+ acc.)  *across*
чёрный  *black*
чесно́к  *garlic*
четве́рг  *Thursday*
че́тверть (f.)  *quarter*
число́  *date, number*

чита́ть/прочита́ть  *to read*
что  *what*
чу́вствовать/почу́вствовать себя́  *to feel*
чуде́сный  *wonderful*

широ́кий  *wide, broad*
шкаф  *cupboard*
шко́ла  *school*
шу́ба  *fur coat*
шу́мный  *noisy*
шу́тка  *joke*
щи  *cabbage soup*

эта́ж  *floor, storey*

ю́бка  *skirt*
юг  *south*

я  *I*
язы́к  *language, tongue*
янва́рь (m.)  *January*
я́ркий  *bright*

# English–Russian vocabulary

*able (to be, can)*  мочь (я могу́, ты мо́жешь)/смочь

*accident*  ава́рия

*activity*  заня́тие

*adult*  взро́слый

*advise (to)*  сове́товать (я сове́тую, ты сове́туешь)/ посове́товать (+ dat.)

*aeroplane*  самолёт

*after*  по́сле

*again*  опя́ть

*ago*  наза́д

*agreed!*  договори́лись,

*air*  во́здух

*all*  весь (вся, всё, все)

*already*  уже́

*also*  та́кже, то́же

*always*  всегда́

*and*  и, а

*and so*  ита́к

*annual*  ежего́дный

*answer (to)*  отвеча́ть/отве́тить

*any*  любо́й

*April*  апре́ль (m.)

*arm*  рука́

*arrival*  прихо́д (on foot); прие́зд (by transport)

*arrive (to)*  приходи́ть/прийти́ (on foot), приезжа́ть/ прие́хать (by transport)

*as*  как

*as far as*  до (+ gen.)

*as if*  как бу́дто

*as soon as*  как то́лько

*ask (to)*  проси́ть/попроси́ть (+ acc.)

*August*  а́вгуст

*aunt*  тётя

*autumn*  о́сень (f.)

*back*  спина́

*bad*  плохо́й

*bank (money)*  банк

*bank (shore)*  бе́рег

*be (to)*  быть

*beard*  борода́

*beautiful*  краси́вый

*because*  потому́ что

*because of (+ noun)*  из-за (+ gen.)

*bed*  крова́ть (f.); посте́ль (f.)

*bedroom*  спа́льня

*beer*  пи́во

*before*  до (+ gen.)

*begin (to)*  начина́ть/нача́ть

*beginning*  нача́ло

*behind*  за (+ instr.)

*best*  лу́чший

*better*  лу́чший

*bicycle*  велосипе́д

*big*  большо́й

*bill*  счёт

*birthday*  день (m.) рожде́ния

*black*  чёрный

*blanket*  одея́ло

*blow (to)*  дуть/поду́ть

*blue (dark)* си́ний
*blue (light)* голубо́й
*boarding (of train, plane)*
  поса́дка
*book* кни́га
*book (to)* зака́зывать/заказа́ть
  (я закажу́, ты зака́жешь)
*boring* ску́чный
*bottle* буты́лка
*box* коро́бка
*bread* хлеб
*breakfast* за́втрак
*bridge* мост
*bright* я́ркий
*brother* брат
*brown* кори́чневый
*brown* (eyes; hazel) ка́рий
*building* зда́ние
*bus* авто́бус
*bus stop* остано́вка авто́буса
*business* би́знес
*businessman* бизнесме́н
*but* а, но
*buy (to)* покупа́ть/купи́ть

*cabbage* капу́ста
*cabbage soup* щи
*cafe* кафе́
*camera* фотоаппара́т
*car* автомоби́ль (m.); маши́на
*careful* внима́тельный
*carry (to)* носи́ть/нести́/
  понести́
*cash desk* ка́сса
*century* век
*chair* стул
*change (e.g. of a train)* переса́дка
*change (money)* ме́лочь (f.)

*cheap* дешёвый
*cheerful* весёлый
*cheese* сыр
*chemist's shop* апте́ка
*child* ребёнок (pl. де́ти)
*cinema* кино́
*colour* цвет (pl. цвета́)
*condition* состоя́ние
*Christmas* Рождество́
*Christmas tree* ёлка
*church* це́рковь (f.)
*clever* у́мный
*clock* часы́
*close (to)* закрыва́ть(ся)/
  закры́ть(ся)
*closed* закры́т (закры́та,
  закры́то, закры́ты)
*closest* ближа́йший
*clothes* оде́жда
*coffee* ко́фе
*cold* холо́дный
*comfortable* удо́бный
*competition* ко́нкурс
*complain (to)* жа́ловаться/
  пожа́ловаться (на + асс.)
*computer* компью́тер
*concert* конце́рт
*convenient* удо́бный
*cool (chilly)* прохла́дный
*cost (to)* сто́ить
*countryside* дере́вня
*cross (to)* переходи́ть/перейти́
  (on foot); переезжа́ть/
  перее́хать (on transport)
*cupboard* шкаф
*currency (foreign)* валю́та
*currency declaration form*
  деклара́ция

*daughter* дочь (f.)
*day* день (m.)
*day off* выходной день (m.)
*dear (expensive)* дорогой
*dear (sweet)* милый
*December* декабрь (m.)
*delicious* вкусный
*department store* универмаг
*depend on (to)* зависеть от
  (+ gen.)
*describe (to)* описывать/
  описать
*die (to)* умирать/умереть
*dining room* столовая
*do (to)* делать/сделать
*doctor* врач
*don't mention it* не за что
*door* дверь (f.)
*dress* платье
*drink* напиток
*drink (to)* пить/напить
*dry* сухой

*ear* ухо (pl. уши)
*earlier* раньше
*early* ранний
*east* восток
*easy* простой
*eat (to)* есть/съесть
*even* даже
*evening* вечер
*every* каждый
*everything* всё
*example* пример
*excellent* отличный
*except* кроме (+ gen.)
*excuse me, please* извините,
  пожалуйста

*exit* выход
*eye* глаз (pl. глаза)

*factory* завод, фабрика
*far (a long way off)* далеко
*father* отец; папа
*February* февраль (m.)
*feel (to)* чувствовать/
  почувствовать себя
*fill in (to; e.g. a form)*
  заполнять/ заполнить
*finally* наконец
*finish (to)* кончать(ся)/
  кончить(ся)
*first* первый
*fish* рыба
*flat* квартира
*floor* пол
*floor (storey)* этаж
*flower* цвет (pl. цветы)
*fly (to)* летать/лететь/полететь
*fog* туман
*foot* нога
*footwear* обувь (f.)
*forbid (to)* запрещать/
  запретить
*forget (to)* забывать/забыть
*form* бланк
*fortunately* к счастью
*free* свободный
*fresh* свежий
*Friday* пятница
*friend* друг (m.)/подруга (f.)
*from (away from)* от (+ gen.)
*from (out of)* из (+ gen.)
*from here* отсюда
*from there* оттуда
*frost* мороз

*fur coat* шу́ба
*fur hat* мехова́я ша́пка
*future* бу́дущее

*garden* сад
*garlic* чесно́к
*get up (to)* встава́ть (я встаю́,
ты встаёшь)/встать (я вста́ну,
ты вста́нешь)
*girl* де́вушка
*give (to)* дава́ть (я даю́, ты
даёшь)/дать (я дам, ты дашь)
*go (to)* ходи́ть/идти́/пойти́
(on foot) е́здить/е́хать/
пое́хать (by transport)
*go out (to)* выходи́ть/вы́йти
*good* хоро́ший
*good (kind)* до́брый
*goodbye* до свида́ния
*granddaughter* вну́чка
*grandfather* де́душка
*grandmother* ба́бушка
*grandson* внук
*grateful* благода́рный
*green* зелёный
*guest* гость (m.)/го́стья (f.)

*hair* во́лосы
*half* сюлови́на
*hand* рука́
*happen (to)* происходи́ть/
произойти́
*head* голова́
*health* здоро́вье
*healthy* здоро́вый
*hear (to)* слы́шать (я слы́шу,
ты слы́шишь)/услы́шать
*heavy* тяжёлый

*hello* здра́вствуйте
*help (to)* помога́ть/помо́чь
(я помогу́, ты помо́жешь)
(+ dat.)
*her* её; свой (своя́, своё, свой)
*here* здесь
*here is/here are* вот
*his* его́; свой (своя́, своё, свой)
*home* дом (до́ма, *at home*;
домо́й, *homewards*)
*hospital* больни́ца
*hot* жа́ркий (weather);
горя́чий (to the touch)
*hotel* гости́ница оте́ль (m.)
*hour* час
*house* дом
*how* как
*how many/how much* ско́лько
*husband* муж

*ice cream* моро́женое
*if* е́сли
*ill* больно́й
*impatience* нетерпе́ние
*impossible* невозмо́жный
*in* в (+ prep.); на (+ prep.)
*interesting* интере́сный
*interpreter* перево́дчик/
перево́дчица
*into* в (+ acc.); на (+ prep.)
*invitation* приглаше́ние
*invite (to)* приглаша́ть/
пригласи́ть

*January* янва́рь (m.)
*jeans* джи́нсы
*joke* шу́тка
*juice* сок

*July* июль (m.)
*June* июнь (m.)

*kitchen* кухня
*know (to)* знать

*lake* озеро
*last, latest* последний
*late* поздний
*left (on the, to the)* налево
*leg* нога
*letter* письмо
*like (to)* любить (я люблю, ты любишь)
*listen (to)* слушать/послушать
*live (to)* жить
*lose (to)* терять/потерять
*luggage* багаж
*lunch* обед

*magazine* журнал
*make (to)* делать/сделать
*many/much* много (+ gen.)
*March* март
*May* май
*meat* мясо
*midday* полдень (m.)
*midnight* полночь (f.)
*milk* молоко
*minute* минута
*mist* туман
*mistake* ошибка
*Monday* понедельник
*money* деньги (m. pl.; gen. pl. денег)
*month* месяц
*monument* памятник
*more* больше (+ gen.)

*morning* утро
*mother* мать (f.)
*mouth* рот
*museum* музей
*must (to have to)* должен, должна etc.
*my* мой (моя, моё, мой)

*near* близкий
*necessary (it is ...)* надо (+ infinitive)
*nephew* племянник
*never* никогда
*never mind* ничего
*new* новый
*newspaper* газета
*next* следующий
*niece* племянница
*night* ночь (f.)
*no* нет
*no one* никто
*noisy* шумный
*north* север
*nothing* ничто, ничезо
*November* ноябрь (m.)
*nowhere* нигде (position); никуда (motion towards)
*nurse* медсестра

*obtain (to)* доставать/достать (я достану, ты достанешь)
*occupied* занятый (занят, занята, занято, заняты)
*occupy* (to; to be occupied) занимать(ся)/занять(ся)
*October* октябрь (m.)
*of course* конечно
*often* часто

*OK* ла́дно
*old* ста́ый
*open* откры́тый (откры́т, откры́та, откры́то, откры́ты)
*open (to)* открыва́ть/откры́ть
*opinion* мне́ние
*opinion (in my)* по-мо́ему (по моему́ мне́нию)
*order (to)* зака́зывать/заказа́ть
*our* наш (на́ша, на́ше, на́ши)
*over there* вон там

*palace* дворе́ц
*pancakes* блины́
*parking* стоя́нка
*party* ве́чер
*pay (to)* плати́ть/заплати́ть
*perfume* духи́ (m. pl.)
*person* челове́к (pl. лю́ди)
*petrol* бензи́н
*piece* кусо́к
*place* ме́сто
*play (to)* игра́ть/сыгра́ть
*please* пожа́луйста
*policeman* милиционе́р
*poor* бе́дный
*possible* возмо́жно
*post office* по́чта
*postcard* откры́тка
*prefer (to)* предпочита́ть/предпоче́сть
*prepare (to)* гото́вить/пригото́вить
*present (gift)* пода́рок
*problem* пробле́ма
*purse* кошелёк

*rain* дождь (m.)
*read (to)* чита́ть/прочита́ть
*receive (to)* получа́ть/получи́ть
*reception* приём
*red* кра́сный
*rest (to)* отдыха́ть/отдохну́ть
*restaurant* рестора́н
*return (to)* возвраща́ться/верну́ться
*rich* бога́тый
*right (on the, to the)* напра́во
*ring (to)* звони́ть/позвони́ть (+ dat.)
*river* река́
*room (hotel)* но́мер (pl. номера́)

*Saturday* суббо́та
*school* шко́ла
*sea* мо́ре
*see (to)* ви́деть/уви́деть
*sell (to)* продава́ть (я продаю́, ты продаёшь)/прода́ть (я прода́м, ты прода́шь)
*September* сентя́брь (m.)
*shirt* руба́шка
*shout (to)* крича́ть (я кричу́, ты кричи́шь)
*show (to)* пока́зывать/показа́ть (я покажу́, ты пока́жешь)
*sister* сестра́
*sit (to, to be seated)* сиде́ть (я сижу́, ты сиди́шь)
*sit down (to)* сади́ться/сесть (я ся́ду, ты ся́дешь)
*skirt* ю́бка
*smoke (to)* кури́ть/закури́ть
*snow* снег

snowstorm метель (f.)
sometimes иногда
sock носок (pl. носки)
south юг
speak (to) говорить
  (e.g. по-русски)
spring весна
stand (to) стоять
station вокзал; станция
still ещё
straight on прямо
street улица
suddenly вдруг
sugar сахар
suit костюм
summer лето
sun солнце
Sunday воскресенье
supper ужин
surname фамилия
sweater (pullover) свитер
swim (to) плавать/плыть (я
  плыву, ты плывёшь)/поплыть

take (to) брать (я беру,
  ты берёшь)/взять (я возьму, ты
  возьмёшь)
tea чай
television телевизор
tell (to) сказать (скажите,
  пожалуйста, tell me, please)
terrible ужасный
thank you спасибо
then потом (next); тогда
  (at that time)
there там
there is/are вот
think (to) думать/
  подумать

this этот (эта, это, эти)
this is/these are это
throat горло
Thursday четверг
ticket билет
tie галстук
time время
today сегодня
tomorrow завтра
tooth зуб
towel полотенце
town город
trousers брюки
try (to) стараться/
  постараться
Tuesday вторник

understand (to) понимать/
  понять (я пойму, ты поймёшь)
unfortunately к сожалению
usually обычно

very очень

waiter/waitress официант/
  официантка
want (to) хотеть (я хочу,
  ты хочешь)/захотеть
warm тёплый
water вода
weather погода
week неделя
west запад
when когда
where где (position);
  куда (motion towards)
which какой
who кто
whose чей (чья, чьё, чьи)

*why*  почему́
*wide*  широ́кий
*wife*  жена́
*wind*  ве́тер
*window*  окно́
*wine*  вино́
*winter*  зима́
*with*  с (+ instr.)
*wonderful*  чуде́сный
*work (to)*  рабо́тать

*worry (to)*  беспоко́иться/
побеспоко́иться
*write (to)*  писа́ть (я пишу́, ты
пи́шешь)/написа́ть

*yes*  да
*yesterday*  вчера́
*young*  молодо́й
*your*  ваш (ва́ша, ва́ше, ва́ши);
твой (твоя́, твоё, твой)

# Index to grammar points

|  | Unit |
|---|---|
| accusative case | 3, 5, 6, 7, 10 |
| adjectives | 4, 8, 13, 14, 16 |
| adverbs | 8, 14, 19 |
| comparative | 14, 19 |
| conditional | 16 |
| dates | 15 |
| dative case | 6, 10, 13, 14 |
| declension of surnames | 19 |
| demonstrative pronouns (*this*, *that*) | 6, 20 |
| determinative pronouns (*all*, *self*) | 9, 16 |
| future tense | 9, 11 |
| genitive case | 5, 7 |
| imperative (command form) | 3 |
| indirect question | 19 |
| indirect statement | 18 |
| instrumental case | 8, 9, 19 |
| interrogative pronouns (*who*, *what*, *whose*) | 8, 20 |
| irregular verbs | 2, 4, 10, 13, 14 |
| negative expressions | 3, 14, 17, 18 |
| nominative plural nouns | 4 |
| numerals | 5, 7, 9, 20 |
| past tense | 12 |
| personal pronouns | 1 |
| possessive adjectives | 1, 20 |
| prepositional case | 2, 5, 12, 15 |

| | |
|---|---|
| present tense verbs | **2** |
| purpose | **18** |
| | |
| reflexive pronoun | **20** |
| reflexive verbs | **8, 17** |
| relative pronoun (*who, which*) | **16** |
| | |
| superlative | **17** |
| | |
| time constructions | **9, 10, 15, 19** |
| | |
| verbs of motion | **9, 15, 18** |

..........................................................................

# Credits

**Front cover:** © Comstock Images/Getty Images

**Back cover and pack:** © Jakub Semeniuk/iStockphoto.com,
© Royalty-Free/Corbis, © agencyby/iStockphoto.com,
© Andy Cook/iStockphoto.com, © Christopher Ewing/
iStockphoto.com, © zebicho – Fotolia.com, © Geoffrey Holman/
iStockphoto.com, © Photodisc/Getty Images, © James C.
PruittliStockphoto.com, © Mohamed Saber – Fotolia.com

**Pack:** © Stockbyte/Getty Images